With Best Wishes,

Graham V. Ledgerwood

KEYS TO
HIGHER
CONSCIOUSNESS

KEYS TO
HIGHER
CONSCIOUSNESS

Graham V. Ledgerwood

EVEREST

PUBLISHING COMPANY

*This book is dedicated
to your inner self.*

HIGHER CONSCIOUSNESS

Higher Consciousness is the universal awareness and power which sustains life. This consciousness not only maintains you physically, but at every level— spiritually, mentally, emotionally, and materially. When you realize your innate higher consciousness you will discover your amazing faculties for a better, more fascinating life.

ACKNOWLEDGEMENTS

Ambika Hanan Hanna has lovingly typed the manuscript of this book and shepherded these pages through several edits. Thank you always, Ambika.

Who knows how many hours out of a busy life Dr. Pat Kubis has devoted to helping me edit this book? Your advice has been kindly, forthright and invaluable, Dr. Kubis. And, thank you for your comment which is on the cover.

Thank you, Chris Rodriguez, for your part in researching a number of the anecdotes and illustrative facts and figures in this book. Thank you also, Chris, for arranging and assisting in the interviews contained in this book—and for your photograph of me.

I wish to thank the great, humble yoga master, Baba Hari Dass, for reading and commenting on my first draft.

For adding significantly to the richness of this book, I wish to express my gratitude to the religious leaders and teachers who very kindly and generously shared their time and insights. I thank you, gentlemen, for being so loving, open, and helpful:

Archbishop Tomas Clavel
Rabbi David Eliezrie
Reverend William Hornaday
Reverend Elwin Pelletier
Reverend Mahathera Piyadassi
Professor Satya Pal Sharma
Reverend Muzammil Siddiqi
Bishop John T. Steinbock
Rabbi Frank Stern
Swami Swahananda

My thanks to you, Don Clark, in Akron, Ohio, for your professional recommendations.

Thank you, Bob Cobb, publisher's representative in New York City, for your advice over the years and your help with the preparation of *Keys to Higher Consciousness*.

I thank all who encouraged me to write *Keys*, who reviewed this manuscript, and who prepared the index.

I would also like to extend my gratitude to the library staffs of University of California at Irvine, the Claremont School of Theology, the Huntington Beach Public Library, and the Huntington Library in San Marino.

FOREWORD

Welcome to the field of higher consciousness. You can use this book to survey supernormal awareness and speculate about your own talents. You can glimpse a world in which a new faculty of awareness will be as common as thinking and feeling, and even more useful.

You can also practice the numerous enjoyable techniques in this book—one by one—and enrich your life. After a general "read through," spend a week or a month with each chapter. Practice each technique thoroughly and marvel at the changes in your awareness. Enjoy frequent reflections and open the doors of your great inner self.

Likely, you will find your higher consciousness is by far your greatest treasure.

Recognizing no book can replace a capable teacher of higher consciousness but that there are so few such teachers in the world today, I offer this labor to your common sense, and your drive to know the truth you intuit about yourself: You do have superconscious abilities within you which are able to benefit you immensely.

To live without contacting and utilizing your higher consciousness is a tragedy! Most of the potential for fulfillment is ignored. Why not acknowledge your gifts?

I wish you restlessness for a better life and world. May you have courage, too; courage to begin a magnificent journey. Also, may you be steady, with patient good will for yourself and your endeavors—then you cannot fail.

May you discover what is right now within you. Higher consciousness awaits you.

— Graham Ledgerwood

ABOUT THE AUTHOR

Graham Ledgerwood is internationally known as one of the finest teachers and experts in the field of higher consciousness. Living in California since the mid-60's, he is an honored Master and Guru of Yoga, Meditation, Mysticism, and Metaphysics. He is the Founder and Director of the Spiritual World Society, which comprises members of many faiths. Also, he is Director of the Yoga Center of California in Costa Mesa and on Palomar Mountain, California.

Born in Alberta, Canada, Mr. Ledgerwood studied honors English at Arizona State University (1960-62). He was a private playwriting student of the eminent John Gassner at Yale University in 1963. Noted for his speaking voice, he was a newscaster and radio announcer in Canada and San Jose, California. He was also a reporter and copy editor for the Arizona Weekly Gazette in Phoenix, Arizona for two years.

Mr. Ledgerwood began practicing meditation in 1958 and started studying mysticism in 1963. In San Francisco in 1967, he entered intensive practice of yoga under the guidance of Swami Kriyananda, a direct disciple of the yoga Master, Paramahansa Yogananda.

In the summer of 1969 Mr. Ledgerwood spent five months in silence and solitude at Ananda Meditation Retreat near Grass Valley, California. Here he experienced a major spiritual breakthrough. In 1971, the yoga Master, Baba Hari Dass, was the first to declare the author a Guru. Baba Hari Dass encouraged him to teach and write about Truth—and higher consciousness.

In the practice of mysticism, the author attained the level of *Illuminati* (spiritually awakened), and experienced the enlightenment called cosmic consciousness.

Mr. Ledgerwood twice journeyed through central India in 1974-75. He received many initiations and advanced training while there. Sri Surath Chakravarti and Sri Paramananda Nath gave him further training as a Guru of numerous spiritual paths and disciplines. In 1976 the author received *Avadhut* status (literally, one who lives in Spirit)—meaning he had become a Master of yoga and higher consciousness.

The great woman saint and spiritual leader, Ananda Moyi Ma, sent the author a gift and honors in 1976. Numerous other spiritual leaders, teachers, and officials have visited Mr. Ledgerwood in the U.S.A.—Chandra Swami, Swami Dharmananda, the First Minister (Governor) of Gujarat, Panditji Sadasiva Shastri, Dr. Vasant Merchant, Sister Margarita, Paramahansa Muktananda, and the

Honorable Lakhan Mehrotra, Consul General of India. Several of them lovingly gave Mr. Ledgerwood the titles: *Maharishi* (man of wisdom); *Maharaj* (enlightened man, or "great king"); *Swamiji* (knower of the True Self); *Babaji* (revered father); and Sri Paramananda Nath declared the author a *Paramahansa* (supremely enlightened) in 1978.

Mr. Ledgerwood has also received the spiritual name Ramakrishna Ananda which he uses in his Guru and yoga Master capacities.

Mr. Ledgerwood has shared the wonders of higher consciousness with many thousands of interested people. A popular lecturer, he has spoken in universities, schools, churches, and a convent. He has been interviewed on radio and television a number of times.

Also, he's written several plays about great religious or historical men and women: Teresa of Avila, St. Vincent de Paul, William Tyndale, Sri Ramakrishna, Augustus Caesar, Frederick the Great, Abelard and Heloise, and Benjamin Franklin.

Graham Ledgerwood feels that in the exciting times to come, world conditions will improve rapidly as more and more people discover their higher consciousness. This book is a treasure guide for those inspired adventurers.

CONTENTS

PART III
PERSONAL RELATIONSHIPS AND TECHNIQUES
FOR HIGHER CONSCIOUSNESS

PART IV
AGONIES AND ECSTASIES

PART V
MASTER AND INITIATE

PART VI
AWAKENING AND ENLIGHTENMENT

PART VII
DIFFERENT PATHS

KEYS TO
HIGHER
CONSCIOUSNESS

I

HIGHER CONSCIOUSNESS
AWAITS YOU

1

ARE YOU AWARE OF YOUR HIGHER CONSCIOUSNESS?

What do you really want from life?

Are you aware of the amazing faculties and skills locked within you? Do you have instant access to your marvelous inner wisdom? Have you discovered the power to make yourself significantly more successful? Are you aware you have a *higher consciousness* capable of helping you overcome your worries and problems while improving your health and making you a more prosperous, happier person?

What is higher consciousness?

Simply said, higher consciousness is the universal power which sustains life. This consciousness not only maintains you physically but at every level—spiritually, mentally, emotionally, and materially.

Moreover, you have *direct access* to higher consciousness at all times. With patience and application you can discover dozens of life-enriching abilities in this protective and nurturing consciousness. With relatively little effort you can attract numerous opportunities for a finer life. You can establish an ongoing sense of well being and self-esteem that is endlessly satisfying.

THE IMPORTANCE OF SELF-KNOWLEDGE

Suppose someone deposited three million dollars into your bank account this morning but did not tell you about it. Despite having three million dollars, you would spend your whole day normally, unaware of your great wealth. Unless you found out about that three million dollars, you would live your life as if your millions didn't exist. You wouldn't have the benefit of using your treasure or the security of knowing it's there. Unless you were already by some other means a millionaire, you would live your life spending each day with no concept of yourself as a wealthy person, nor of your nearby opportunities. You might even live as an extremely poor person, worried about the next meal or the utility bills, while at the same time being, in fact, extremely wealthy. Feeling poor, you would undoubtedly live a life of frustration and anxiety, sensing failure, believing yourself unable to meet your needs or the needs of loved ones.

Not knowing about your great treasure is an immense barrier to the fulfillment of your life. Ignorance of your treasure is, in effect, as powerful a limitation as not having any treasure at all. For unless you are aware of your phenomenal resources, you don't use them. Unless you have access to your great wealth, it may as well not be there. Days and years might go by without your life or outlook having the benefit of this wealth. You would likely call this ignorance of your true economic stature a tragedy, wouldn't you? A costly tragedy.

Yet, great wealth has, *in fact*, been placed within you and every person—such wealth that three million dollars looks like a petty or incomplete treasure when compared to what is within you already. This treasure is called higher consciousness. It also has other names like superconsciousness, cosmic consciousness, or spiritual awareness, but most commonly it is called higher consciousness. Yes, it is a reality to thousands upon thousands of dynamic, creative people who draw upon it every day. But have *you* experienced it? Can you turn to your higher consciousness at will and find, with delight and ease, an especially wonderful energy and insight flowing through you and your world? Look far and wide, you will find there is no greater treasure available to you for happiness and fulfillment than your already existing and *available* higher consciousness. Also, with the aid of this consciousness you can solve your problems, know love, and be of great benefit to your fellow man and woman.

Though it would be a tragedy to die of poverty while actually and unknowingly being a millionaire, a greater tragedy—and the strangest paradox of all—is that most people have astonishing resources for happy lives and a better world; but, instead, they ignore these great capacities of their higher consciousness. People let their hopes remain fantasies rather than discover the means to make dreams real. What a strange situation! Yet people tend to chase all over the world, often behaving like beggars in search of small benefits which will tide them over until the next crisis in their lives. Imagine having the capability for great satisfaction already within reach and yet not turning toward it. Imagine not being able to raise your awareness to numerous—yes, *infinite*—possibilities that can make your life richer and more satisfying.

Another case in point—what would you think of someone who had millions but died of a heart attack when the cost of living rose five percent? Twenty percent? Such things have happened. Have you heard about immensely wealthy people who were so frightened of poverty that they lived in incredible misery? Remember the woman in New York who slept in most meager rooms, starving herself, hiding from the cold in an old fur coat? When she died, stocks and bonds totaling tens of millions of dollars were found inside her coat and ancient mattress.

Similarly, an old farmer in North Dakota felt he could not afford to heat his cabin, even in the middle of Dakota winters! Every evening he would visit a friend who could afford heat. Then, late at night, he would take some coals from his friend's stove, carrying them to his own cabin in a bucket. The warmth of these coals enabled him to survive until morning. When he died it was discovered "the man of miserable winters" was, in fact, a wealthy man. One part of his fortune, fifty thousand dollars, was found under his floor boards, an entertaining nest for the mice!

You may laugh or weep at that farmer but what are *your* priorities? Where are you searching for your fulfillment? Where have you traveled in your hopes? Higher consciousness awaits your attention. Infinite possibilities for fulfillment already exist within your higher consciousness. Most people search everywhere and often their memoirs reflect they did not achieve what they'd hoped for in life. Their years didn't build into permanent well being.

The possibilities of higher consciousness ride *within you* wherever you roam the earth's surface in search of satisfaction. Without sensing your higher consciousness you may feel you have to force your will on others or outsmart them so you can get what you want. But your inner wealth already exists and the wisdom of your higher consciousness can show you how to fulfill bigger dreams than you ever dared dream.

Ignorance of your higher consciousness is very costly. Not only are you robbed of its tremendous ability to help you with your life, but you live cut off from the source of your strength and insight. Without the help of your inner power and wisdom, you feel cut off from others. Relationships are difficult to sustain, or even begin. Loneliness and a sense of separation from others is commonplace because it is your higher consciousness which provides the sense of harmony and interrelationship in life. Without awareness of your higher consciousness, your life will often seem without meaning and, indeed, without purpose. In ignoring your higher consciousness, the stress of life will wear away at you and significantly shrink your number of years. Without the underlying sense of interrelationship which higher consciousness reveals, life becomes mainly conflict. With conflict come the effects of victory—which usually assures that there will be more conflict and battle, or defeat—and the defeated often feel worthless and give up or turn to the consolation of their private fantasies. The cost of ignoring your higher consciousness is so extreme that no one who understands the cost would ever want to pay such a price.

NINE-TENTHS!

Suppose, due to some accident, a tenth of your mind was lost. Suppose, too, that some highly-skilled surgeon could restore to you the missing one-tenth of your mind. This would be very exciting, wouldn't it? Reclaiming that lost part of your mind would be worth any price, don't you agree? Imagine the terror of living with one-tenth of your mental capacity missing. What a joyous reunion if such realignment might occur. You would be inclined to do anything, pay any fee, that this one-tenth might be returned to its rightful owner, wouldn't you? Now, are you ready to hear this?

When we are talking about higher consciousness, we are not talking about discovering a missing tenth of our mind and our overall capacity for life. We are talking about *nine-tenths*. Nine-tenths! When you do not have access to your own marvelous and magnificent higher consciousness, most of the qualities and aptitudes for success, in any degree, are missing. Without your higher consciousness, life is filled with disappointments. There is no lasting contentment. The consequences of poor judgment keep burdening you and adding to your problems each day. Of course, contacting your higher consciousness does not mean an end to your problems but a re-freshing intelligence and power is unleashed which enables you to solve your problems and accomplish your goals much, much more effectively.

The claim that when you are not in contact with your higher consciousness you are missing a whole nine-tenths of yourself, and of your capacity for a fine life, is not yet provable in a laboratory. However, those who have left their limited consciousness and dis-covered superconsciousness find so much benefit and enrichment that they commonly agree nine-tenths is a fair estimate of how much aptitude for fulfillment was missing. Many feel they were as if dead —dead!—before finding their higher consciousness. Now, immea-surably uplifted, they feel they have left that dead, limited, mechan-ical way of life. Some say living in attunement with their higher consciousness is like living in a heaven on earth.

Great life-enhancement awaits you, too, if you will stop ignor-ing your higher consciousness—the other nine-tenths of your facul-ties for a finer life.

AN EXPERIMENT

Perhaps you can experience a little of your higher consciousness sooner, rather than later.

Try this experiment if you are of sound mind and physical health, and not given to an overly vivid imagination: Think of some-one you love who is in a distant city or town. Sit calmly and feel in your heart—actually, in the center and front of your chest—how much you love him (or her). Sense the emotion of love.

Now feel that from the center of your chest the light of your love, the energy of your love, is reaching out and touching that beloved one. Have no desire to intrude. Be perfectly willing, if you feel a blockage, to abandon the practice until another time. Usually, however, people love to feel your love. They welcome it. So, very likely you'll find you can extend, from the center of your chest, the feeling of your love and appreciation. You can contact a far-off per-son—even though you are separated by thousands of miles.

You will notice, as your love subtly touches that person's life, that you will receive—with practice—a sense of what that person is feeling and, even, mentally preoccupied about. Notice, as your love flows, whether you feel he or she is emotionally "up" or sad and at a loss. You may even find that on the mental screen of your forehead you will sense some images or concepts from your loved one's mind.

After a period of attunement, write down your experiences and impressions. Then, if you can, phone the beloved one whom you have contacted with your heart and learn whether your love has revealed a faculty of knowing, which is far beyond the normal. You may find that even in doing this practice for the very first time you have sensed at a superconscious level many emotional and mental activities of a dear person thousands of miles distant. You may conclude that in this manner you can know someone more compassionately and fully than ever before.

While it takes years for most students in this field of knowledge to become adepts, you can likely prove to yourself within a few weeks that you have the consciousness which reveals the condition of another person a great distance away.

Often people who live in the same house do not use their resources for truly knowing how a dear one is thinking and feeling. This "love contact" experiment can enrich your relationships immediately, in addition to establishing—when you find yourself successful—that there are higher levels of awareness that become readily available to you if you simply love.

These supernormal, or "sixth sense," experiences are only a small part of the whole field of higher consciousness which awaits you!

2

WHAT IS YOUR GREATEST TREASURE?

What do you have a right to expect from your higher consciousness?

If you make the effort and refuse to fool yourself with fantasies, you will begin to find *four priceless faculties* within yourself. As these faculties become more instantly available to your attuned mind and heart, they will prove themselves to be your finest assets.

Not only do these four initial capacities of your higher consciousness have great value in themselves, they will be *extremely useful* in helping you create the life you yearn for. Many of the old goals which you failed to achieve can, if you find this consciousness inside you, be realized pleasantly. Still, higher consciousness is itself so thrilling and presents such a satisfying dimension to life that several old goals will no longer seem important to you. Rather, you will begin to perceive greater possibilities within yourself.

Let's consider the four delightful capacities of *your* higher consciousness. Keep in mind, as you read, the importance not only of having these faculties within your easy reach every day, reflect also what these four wondrous capacities can bring into manifestation for you as you allow yourself a *superconscious way* of doing things.

1   INSIGHT — CREATIVE INTELLIGENCE

Have you noticed you're generally at your worst, as is most everyone else, when the big decisions of life have to be made? Too frequently, the events of life press us, push us, knock us around until we react and make a change. Decisions of immense signifi-cance to the rest of our lives are often made in moments of emo-tional chaos when we're merely *reacting* to inner or outer pressures. How many people think clearly when choosing a mate, deciding on a career, or making a big purchase? These decisions will be a major factor in our lives for decades! The decision about a lifetime partner, a suitable profession, or a new residence, for example, will be a major reason for your daily and long-term happiness or sorrow. Yet it is not even popular to think clearly at the time of choosing one's mate for life. People often stumble into their careers, victims of blind circumstance. And, purchases involving years of debt are of-ten made emotionally: "Well, I don't know, but I *feel* this is the right one."

Very often the pressure of a deadline determines what you think and do about a particular problem. With more time to think, along with more information, wouldn't you choose differently at times? Much of the time?*

The good news is: in becoming aware of your higher conscious-ness, you discover a tremendous talent which helps you meet the challenges of your life. This faculty of your higher self is called crea-tive intelligence, or superconscious insight. Through your creative intelligence you will be at your very best when making a decision. You will be able to see your problems clearly, in all their aspects. You will distinguish between true opportunity and much suffering disguising itself as opportunity. Insights from your higher conscious-ness will develop your mind, emotions, and will into a constructive team, improving not only your decisions but the advice you give to professional colleagues and loved ones.

Again and again people with worried, turbulent minds make snap decisions—shortsighted decisions which bring hurt and even ruin into their lives. Sometimes a person without creative intelli-

---

* Possibly you are one of the rare "clear-minded" and you enjoy much peace and success because of your excellent decisions. Good for you!

gence puts all his energy into getting the goal of his dreams, only to find that goal was not worth the effort. His or her dream falls to the pavement and smashes to bits. The hope for happiness and love becomes pain and criticism. Pleasure deteriorates into torture. The hope of being close to someone often makes you blind about what that "special person" is really like. Your distorted mind confuses the relationship and the "yearned for" intimacy becomes instead a sense of revulsion, or even self-hatred.

Insight, creative intelligence from deep within you, helps you avoid many losses, many tears. Insight keeps you from being stuck in a horrible problem for years, stuck in futility and lack of self-expression.

Insight from your higher consciousness is creative. It helps generate not only solutions for your problems but new opportunities and options for you. Consider the American immigrant who found he didn't have to spend his life being a busboy while anxiously hoping for a waiter's position. Instead, he discovered within himself the abilities to become a millionaire in real estate. He more than solved his problems—he creatively found a new life.

Consider another example. Years ago doctors routinely threw out moldy blood samples by the thousands. However, Alexander Fleming, the Scottish bacteriologist, followed an intuitive insight to *study the mold* on a blood sample which had gone bad. Fleming's insight was the beginning of the discovery of penicillin and antibiotics. In many ways Fleming's creative intelligence—and that of a small group of colleagues at Oxford University—changed the world.

Your life pretty much reflects the decisions you've already made. Your present lot in life is the best indicator of how good your decisions are. It's easy to see the choices you made when confronted with challenges and opportunities. Are you happy with your choices? Good for you if you are. If you're happy with your choices, you likely have a degree of this marvelous insight from your higher consciousness already available to you.

However, if you look back at your life with frustration and wonder "What happened?," you do not have access to your best assets, including superconscious insight. Do you wonder why some friends became so successful and happy while you, who had equal opportunity and perhaps even superior talents, have to poke through the ashes of your years searching for the few remaining embers of happiness? What happened?

Chances are *you made bad decisions*, selected the wrong alternatives. You probably ignored your best opportunities. Perhaps you responded to people in a way that made your life less successful and progressively narrow. Perhaps, due to the turbulence of your mind, you didn't notice people who could have been your good friends for life. Did you instead choose projects and colleagues who crippled your talents? Perhaps your numberless opportunities for happiness were not perceived clearly and you chose instead numbness, boredom, or a cynic's attitude. In any case, how very sad it is that day in, day out, for years you did not seek or heed your creative intelligence—nor the other wonders within your higher consciousness.

Life has so many turning points. Each turning point involves a choice, a decision to be made. Why not be at your best? You can be at your best, not only meeting these turning points with excellent, beneficial decisions, but also your superconscious insight will reveal the turning point to you *before* it occurs. Your faculty of creative intelligence prepares you again and again to make the best, the very best, of your decades on planet earth. With this special insight you can see the finest direction and course for the furtherance of your life. But without superconscious insight there is a blindness of your whole being much more profound than that of not having eyes. It is a blindness of mind and soul. We are, in this state, not capable of *seeing* the way to fulfillment or lasting happiness.

What wouldn't you give to be able to make excellent decisions? What would it be worth to choose wisely, to know how best to meet your challenges, to know when to act and when to be quiet, to know when to move and when to wait? You can have superconscious insight. You can experience this creative intelligence every day if you learn how to contact your higher consciousness.

2   SECURITY

To many people, the growing sense of security and comfort is the most wonderful aspect of higher consciousness. Even sophisticated and seemingly powerful people with numbered Swiss bank accounts, weighty diamonds, and $140,000 cars yearn for a sense of security. A seemingly omnipotent boss confided on the way to his third coronary, "I spent half my life to get this management desk. I have to spend the rest of my life fighting to keep it."

We all need to feel there are safe and untroubled places in our lives where we can relax and confidently refresh our energies. At times we need a spot free of disturbance or any unwanted infringement. Without daily periods in which we feel definitely secure, we can become progressively neurotic and spend all our time in considerable discomfort. Without a profound sense of security, worry and fear become our way of life and we cannot feel—deep within us— that it is good to be alive, or that it is good to be a distinct individual.

Your life is precious, you are precious. When you still the hub-bub of your thoughts and emotions for awhile, you can sense the strong comfort of your higher consciousness. You sense the immensity of your inner strength. When you discover your mighty inner security, a renewed sense of purpose fills your mind. In the security of your higher consciousness, you also gain a sense of self-esteem. You are more able to discern superconscious insight and learn how to accomplish your projects. This enriching security calms your heart and nerves; it helps your blood pressure. Security prepares you to enjoy your life and achieve your goals at will.

Again and again the challenges and demands of life may try to frazzle you or make you feel limited or incapable of dealing with your problems. Even when you're harried or feeling inadequate, you can turn to your higher consciousness. Then security and comfort will spring into your mind, into your body cells—and even into the atmosphere around you.

It's interesting to note the derivation of the word *comfort*, which is such an important attribute of profound security. Comfort comes from two Latin words: *com* (*cum*) means with; *fort* comes from the Latin *fortis*, meaning bravery. The initial concept of the word comfort is that one who is *comforted* is instilled with bravery. When you are comforted in the true sense, you have the ability to look honestly at reality and use your capabilities to bring about improvement. In your higher self you will discover a security you can find nowhere else, a sense of security that is complete. No other *place* in the world can provide so definite a sense of security. To live without this vital part of your potential is to live in worry and fear. If you choose, your higher consciousness will grant you a deep and abiding sense of security.

3 PEACE AND JOY

An important point to understand is that your thoughts and feelings are wearing you out. Literally, your mental/emotional activity is probably shortening your life. Would you drive your car twenty-four hours a day? If you did, how long would it last? Any machine kept going without rest and maintenance starts to malfunction in short time. Quite similarly, those who allow their thoughts and feelings to churn continually, every day, as most people do, suffer in many ways.

Is thinking and feeling, then, bad for you? Certainly not. In a world starving for love and great ideas, genuine good will and inspiration are vitally important. What is meant by "churning mind" is the undirected, random drift of thoughts. Most people allow their thoughts to come and go as they please—memories, sensations, fantasies, and other ideas continually moving in haphazard, generally chaotic, fashion.

Similarly, the emotions wildly move within us—a warfare of hope, fear, desire, resentment, love, and hatred. Also, thoughts and feelings often clash in their separate pursuits. For example, you may have a feeling of grief which dominates and limits your mental range of thought; or your repeated thoughts about a negative situation will likely make a good mood vanish. Usually there are several *layers* of mental/emotional turbulence going on within, even during sleep.

This turbulence wastes your energy and is destructive in several ways. Principally, mental/emotional turbulence destroys your sense of well being. Very importantly, too, constant mental/emotional turbulence costs a great deal: the activity of nerves and glands is at a more intense and regularly debilitating level. So, not only does your mental/emotional happiness start to break down; but the body, too, in time, simply cannot bear the constant strain. The weakest parts begin to malfunction and disease occurs.

According to a number of stress researchers, stress diseases are the major killers in North America and Europe today. The pressure of mental/emotional turbulence causes countless headaches, including numerous migraine headaches. Many allergies, too, are caused directly or indirectly by stress, and asthma is generally brought about through stress. Much heart disease, arterial disease, colitis, and ulcers are attributed to stress. Also, stress is considered to be a precondition which enables many forms of cancer to gain a foothold in the body. Stress also breaks down our immunities to common diseases such as colds and influenza. The body is not designed to withstand continual mental/emotional activity—especially when it expresses as worry and fear, or the predisposition to flee from reality which most mental turbulence mirrors.

Unfortunately, the chaos does not end when we fall asleep. Those who have continually random thoughts and feelings simply go into many dream and anxiety levels while they sleep. Due to a sleep which isn't deep, their attitude about life is bedraggled. The physical deterioration continues in bed. The body continues to wear out.

Do you know the average person can only keep his mind on one thing for *six to eleven seconds* at a time? The average used to be eleven seconds about ten years ago, but psychologists think that—due to social pressures, chronic television-viewing, and drug damage—the average concentration span is now only six seconds; and it's getting worse. So, even when you're thinking about something you choose to think about, something you *like* to think about, your mind will tend to wander every six seconds if you're average. You will have to consciously make an effort to bring it back. This inner chaos goes on and on. A sense of well being and the ability to think clearly is destroyed whenever thoughts or feelings are turbulent.

Millions of people have indicated in various surveys that they seek peace of mind above all. Great historical figures from the past have indicated they would give anything for peace of mind. Marcus Aurelius spoke of the great difficulty which he, the emperor of the whole Roman Empire, found in establishing *peace of mind*. Peace of mind is a greater treasure than most emperors can win.

You will gain peace of mind greater than emperors have been able to find when you experience your higher consciousness. As you develop you will be able to establish periods of peace whenever you choose. Later, as you develop even more, you will be able to sense *peace filling your being* in the midst of your activity. You will be able to become actively calm and calmly active. Scarcely any people living in the world today have found a state of deep peace in the midst of their activities. Actively calm and calmly active, you will discover a most blissful and heavenly quality in your daily activity.

Peace feels so good. As peace begins to occur to your mind and spreads through your head and face down into your chest, it ultimately feels like a quiet, cooling river flowing beneath your skin from head to toe, making your entire body feel very pleasant. The mind enjoys the refreshment of not having to churn out more and more thoughts. The heart is able to put aside envy, fear, anger, and feel good about life. At last, abiding in the peace of your higher consciousness, you have found a most delightful place to be.

Not only is peace a wonderful place to experience regularly, and ultimately to live in, peace is extremely valuable in another way. Peace gives you freedom of choice. Prior to having peace, your thoughts and feelings, even your decisions, will tend to be forced on you by your previous attitudes and experiences. These old attitudes will mechanically dominate your not-so-free will.

Old attitudes, believe it or not, almost always dictate what you're going to do about new problems and possibilities. That is, the momentum of past experiences, old thoughts and feelings, will *persuade* you to simply continue going in the direction you've been going. You will not be able to stop and look at the problem fully, think clearly, and consider new options until you have peace.

Peace is like the neutral gear on a car. Without a neutral gear you cannot switch from a forward movement to a backward movement—at least not easily. If you try switching from a fast forward to a reverse you will ruin your gears and other parts of your engine as well. Similarly, we need peace in order to switch gears. We need peace in order to stop the momentum of the past, to stop its dominance. Through peace you think creatively and determine the best decision.

So, not only is peace a most beautiful aspect of being alive, it's also extremely helpful—perhaps essential—in freeing us to choose the best alternatives at each and every turning point in our lives.

AND THEN THERE'S JOY

Believe it or not, peace of mind is not the goal or the main quality of the higher consciousness. How far can you drive your car in neutral gear? Nowhere, unless you put your car in neutral and let someone drag you. In that case, some force outside yourself has to provide the impetus. However pleasant, peace is a *neutral* state. Peace will generally not get you where you want to go. It will give you relief, it will give you breathing space, it will give you a chance to change your life. Peace enables you to be a more conscious person; it frees you of many errors that you would tend to make without peace. All of this is wonderful. However, once again, peace is not a positive, dynamic state. It is a neutral state.

Numerous wise men of past and present seem to deplore the peaceful state. They emphasize again and again that one should not linger (or seek to linger) in the neutral, unproductive, and unexpressive state of peace. Perhaps they speak emphatically because some people who have had hectic lives are so desirous of peace of mind that they want to bury themselves in peace, even wishing to disappear from the face of the earth. That is, they would become addicted to nonactivity and doing nothing if the needs of life did not demand that they earn their bread and toothpicks.

Fortunately, the wonderful problem that peace presents is solved when you choose to move forward and go more deeply into your own higher consciousness. By changing the direction of your activities or your life in general, peace next enables you to experience a thrilling level of higher consciousness: JOY.

Joy is vast. Words are inadequate. Joy is not an occasional bubble of cheerfulness. Joy is ongoing, self-renewing happiness. It is a positive state of well being which, as it develops, permeates your entire life. It floods your mind with happiness and great ideas. It fills your spinal cord and other nerves with an ecstatic sense. Your heart, lungs, and chest area feel light, clear, and expansive in a profound delight. Ultimately, your eyeballs, ears, and other senses, along with your bones, ligaments, muscles, skin, and other tissues feel like they are vibrating or dancing with exquisite and ever-pleasing joy. This joy is beyond description and must be experienced.

This level of joy isn't easy to discover. Much aspiration and deliberate focus are required in order to know the higher consciousness this intimately. Most people who find joy never dreamed that they would be able to experience something so lofty. However, this capacity of the higher consciousness which we are calling by a short, little word—joy—is already locked within each and every human being, awaiting discovery. As a consequence of not only *visiting* but ultimately *living* in a state of joy, you will find joy and ecstasy continually playing within your being.

There are many practical applications of joy. For those who must seek a benefit before they make an endeavor, consider this. Most people live in the hope that their work, their sporting activities, their marriages, their children, their inventions, their plans, their hard work, will bring them happiness. They look at money as something which will, if accumulated appropriately, also bring happiness. What if *you* could find happiness far beyond your expectation? What if you could find it directly? What if you could find it delightedly blazing inside you, ever-new, and never boring? What if it could so pour out of you that it would help your health, make your mind sharper and clearer, make your emotions more balanced, and enable you to be a much more mature, alive, and able person? What if this happiness increased your coordination? Your respect of other people? Your capacity to accomplish projects and solve problems? What if this joy sloughed off old hurts and pains, making your life feel fresh and clean? What if this joy made you a winner, a more successful person, full of enthusiasm and the capacity to lead and inspire other people?

These are some of the benefits to be found in yourself as you develop awareness of your higher consciousness. Your joy will not only directly satisfy innumerable emotional needs but will also spread like a positive disease, perhaps becoming an epidemic of good will in your part of the country.

4   INNER POWER

We feel very puny in this part of the twentieth century. Small and impotent, we feel the burden of a potential nuclear holocaust, a holocaust which might occur intentionally or, then again, perhaps by accident. The ground beneath our feet shakes. Hurricanes blow towns out of existence. There are cracks in our nuclear power plants. Our life-sustaining atmosphere is turning brown from poisons; its ozone layer has holes the size of continents. We now fear the possibilities of global droughts, for several reasons.

Additionally, there is the threat that our credit system—perhaps even the international banking system—might collapse and create a world where fleshless fingers clutch at ground fish patties and powdered milk.

Nor is any job secure. Careers are being wiped out. Manufacturing jobs are declining from 19,367,000 in 1970 to a projected 18,160,000 in the year 2000. More than 1.2 million jobs! Durable goods jobs will likely decline from 11,210,000 to 10,731,000. Nearly another half million.

Young people today may have to change their careers three to five times in order to have jobs. Service producing jobs are expected to skyrocket from 47,147,000 in 1970 to 94,478,000 by the turn of the century.* But, these years multitudes of crestfallen, talented workers watch their companies die or their jobs move away to the Orient.

And then there's crime. So many people are not safe in their homes, nor are they safe to go to the store or take a night class at the local college. Across the nation, one woman in every ten will be raped during her lifetime!† And in Los Angeles, for example, statistics say one woman in three will likely be raped in her lifetime. Half of Los Angeles' murders go unsolved each year. Also, even those tried and found guilty of murder are often returned to society in five to ten years.

---

* *Statistical Abstract of the United States*, 1988, page 380. (Incidentally, the Service Producing Jobs are: transportation and public utilities; wholesale and retail trade; finance; insurance; real estate; communications; and services in: hotel, business, amusement, health, education, legal, and social fields.)

† According to *CBS News Nightwatch*, May 18, 1989.

According to FBI nationwide statistics,* a crime is committed every two seconds. A violent crime occurs every 21 seconds! Every three seconds we have a property crime. Forcible rape happens every six minutes. Every minute, night and day, on average, there's a robbery in our land. We have aggravated assaults every 37 seconds, a burglary every 10 seconds, larceny-theft every four seconds, and a motor vehicle theft every 24 seconds. And, every 26 minutes someone is murdered!

Worse, the President's Task Force on Victims of Crime, 1982, estimates that fifty percent of violent crimes go unreported!

Further, it's hard to be a child today. Across the land, in 1985, there were 1,928,000 reported cases of child maltreatment; and sexual maltreatment constituted 11.7 percent of the reported cases, according to the American Humane Association study.† Another study by D'Agostino and colleagues in 1985 says, "at least 652,000 children are demonstrably harmed by child maltreatment annually."‡

One can feel very small, unimportant, *and frightened*, today.

Yet the fourth marvelous faculty of your higher consciousness is *inner power*. Though you may at times feel very weak and incapable of changing oppressive conditions in your world and personal life, you actually *do* possess an inner power to change things! It's always there within you. You can unleash it as soon as you discover it and work with it. Why ignore it?

When you feel weak, confronted by a multitude of obstacles, when fears amass and offensively charge you, *seek your higher consciousness*. Often superconscious insight guides you and you will *know* what to do. Or perhaps you may be given a deeply secure and comforting awareness which helps you to deal with your dread. You may find a sweet peace or a sense of the underlying beauty and joy of life. Also, perhaps early in your experience of higher consciousness, you will discover that mindfully taking your thoughts,

---

* *Crime in the U.S.*, United States Federal Bureau of Investigation Crime Reports, Crime Clock 1987, page 6. (The study emphasizes the figures represent "the annual rates of crime to fixed time intervals," and "should not be taken to imply a regularity in the commission of . . . offenses.")

† "National Study on Child Neglect and Abuse Reporting," American Humane Association, Denver, *Statistical Abstract of the United States*, 1988, page 164.

‡ "Investigation of Sex Crimes Against Children," in *Rape and Sexual Assault*, D'Agostino, et. al., Ann Wolbert Burgess, editor, New York; Garland Publishing, 1985, page 110.

feelings, attitudes, and your present understanding of your difficult situation into your higher consciousness enables you to find *that subtle power* which changes your situation.

When you find higher consciousness you find a marvelous power which moves into the chaos or the menace. The inner power may turn your problem into a benefit or dissolve the problem. The power might even delay your menaces until your situation is completely improved. You will find yourself growing from the sense of being puny and inadequate into a state of faith and certainty that knows good will inevitably express, right will be done, truth will prevail. *You have this inner power.* It is available in your distress and in the good times, too. Never forget you have this wonderful inner power to improve your life, and yourself.

NEW POSSIBILITIES

Here we are, sharing the modern world. We have so many advantages over previous times in history. We live in a world of new possibilities—computers, space travel, instant communication with the world via satellite. One agricultural representative in the United States says we could, in this country alone, produce enough food to feed eleven billion people!

Thousands of Americans become "new millionaires" every year because of their hard work, and the way they maximize opportunities which are often unseen by others. Approximately 100 people become millionaires every day in the U.S. By far, owners of small businesses "make up the largest number of millionaires."* *Ebony* Magazine finds "one million American families are worth $1,000,000 or more!"† Who knows how many millionaires there will be in ten years?

Just as key people throughout history have sensed new possibilities and have given birth to great inventions, inspiring works of literature and art, gorgeous symphonies, so too you may reach out to your higher consciousness and further the entire human race in its progression.

It has always been the case that some people refused to merely accept the menaces and problems which afflicted their society. They refused to be destroyed by challenges to their health or their very

---

* *Nation's Business*, November, 1988.

† *Ebony* Magazine, October, 1988.

existence. They sought solutions—sometimes very desperately. In their quest they again and again reported enlightening experiences which sparked their greatest creativity. They clearly indicated that they, by design or accident, entered into the higher consciousness. Consider Newton's observations about falling objects; the pre-war discoveries of radar by Watson-Watt and others; Frederick the Great's observations that countries should rule themselves, not be dominated by an empire; Ben Franklin's observations that people should be free to rule themselves, not dominated by a foreign power or tyrannical government; and on and on. Mozart, Beethoven, Madame Curie, da Vinci, Dante, Shakespeare, Gandhi, Michelangelo, Einstein, people who contacted their higher consciousness, not only rose above the collective problems of their age but became its genius.

And today, despite a few hopeful signs, we continue to face the possibilities of global war and planet-wide annihilation, the possibilities of poisoned water, air and soil, the breakdown of the family, crime most everywhere, revolution, terrorism, agonizing poverty. All of these things have placed us, very likely, at the most delicate moment in history. Yet this world is a product of the way we have thought, felt, and acted over many centuries. In its triumphs and in its shuddering inadequacies, it represents what we as a human race have been thinking about life and ourselves so far. Our regular way of doing things has resulted in the present worldwide condition— good and bad.

Considering humanity as a unit—which it most assuredly is, is it not?—might it not be that standing on the precipice of nuclear war, standing together as one humanity, we might observe that however numerous and wondrous our advances as human beings are, there is very obviously some woeful shortcoming in our way of thinking and doing things? Have we not, in a most awesome manner, missed the point somewhere? Must we not in some way be blocking or frustrating the aptitudes and skills necessary for survival and uninterrupted well being here on earth? At this most significant time in humanity's struggle to be, could we not agree that our present state of awareness is not adequate to our needs? Could we not agree that increased awareness and concern is absolutely necessary?

All around us we see partial solutions which cause problems that haunt us later. For example, getting rid of a few insects with poisons may be a good temporary solution, but what happens to those poisons later on has to be part of the thought process even when shortsighted solutions are considered. Changing the face of nature can bring floods, and death. Holding back bright kids can have a devastating effect on the well being of the nation later on. Political motivation can often do great harm, as well as great good.

The point is, here at a major crossroad in human history, *you are alive*. Our world today is a product of what we've thought and felt and done in the past. Surely it is clear that a new way of dealing with life's challenges is imperative.

REFLECTION

Is life a prison to be escaped—
A mystery to be solved?
Or, is life a gift to be *Received*,
Opened, Treasured, Realized?

3

DO YOU LIKE YOUR LIFE TODAY?
The Secret of Consciousness

More pertinently, do you like yourself? Happy with what you've become? Do you think you have developed some very important qualities? On the other hand, are there some extremely self-destructive attitudes or behaviors which you wish you didn't have—which you would very much like to change this minute?

Your reading this book is a private experience. No one is watching your thoughts. You can be as honest with yourself as you want to be. There will be no test scores—the *quality* of your life is the only true test, after all. In this private and personal study you can create a better life, becoming the person you yearn to be through practice of the techniques in this book.

However, *a kind and unpretentious honesty is a necessary foundation*. In many ways, it's fun to be honest. Abraham Lincoln, and other sages, said it's better to speak the truth because then you won't have to keep all your lies straight. Sincerity with yourself is the beginning of sincerity with other people! It is the bedrock of good will and mutual respect. If you can't be honest with yourself, you will find it very difficult to improve your life in any lasting way. All movement toward higher consciousness involves facing problems, shortcomings, and then being willing to make changes.

Of course it's difficult to be honest with ourselves. It's so easy to be self-deluded into thinking we are always in the right, we are always the offended party or hero from the "good side."

Nevertheless, being as honest as you can be, in a calm state of good will for yourself and others, you can start a process that more and more clearly reveals how wonderfully you have been created and how pleasantly old, self-limiting ways can be tossed into the garbage. Level with yourself. Accept yourself as you are and be willing to grow. Your kind honesty will assure an end to the inner conflicts and subtle self-hate which always sabotage your heartfelt desires from becoming realities. Ending the campaign of self-deception, which so many people wage on their world, makes it possible for you to discover tremendous inner knowledge and power—great aids to your future achievements.

Again, are you happy with your life? Are you happy with yourself? What would you like to change? What would make your world and personal esteem significantly greater? Take the time now. Think about these questions until you have created two lists:

1) In My Life And In Myself I Am Happy With:
2) In My Life And In Myself I Deeply Want To Change:

Then, when you've thoughtfully completed both lists, read them out loud, if you're alone. Be sure you feel happy with both lists, that they are more than satisfactory. Check to see that your lists reflect your most sincere try. Likely, writing these two lists has unburdened your heart and you feel calm, with an attitude that important change has already begun.

How many exiles live in our world today? An exile is one who lives away from his home for a long time, often wandering aimlessly. Do you feel far away from a sense of home?

Even if you've lived in the same neighborhood for thirty years, do your activities there seem meaningless—like an *aimless wandering* of your mind and heart?

According to sociologists, vast numbers of people living in cities feel they're exiles. The shrill bustle of life, the distances involved in commuting, absorption in the job and desire for anonymity, while living in such close quarters with other apartment and condominium dwellers, create a sense of being alien to others. It's common now to live without a sense of community, separate from the acceptance and the understanding of other people. Rats in laboratories, placed in quarters modeled after human city life, became neurotic and strange. They displayed anger and frustration. They hurt one another and showed little sense of community.

An estimated twenty-five percent of the population of the United States is afraid to go out after dark. This shocking statistic, psychologists and television hosts say, is mainly due to fear of becoming the victim of crime. But it also reflects an attitude about being unsafe in the presence of strangers. Or, even more, that of being an exile far from "home," far from the world we want and need.

Modern Americans look the other way when they pass on the streets. Oftentimes, less than half the registered voters take the trouble to exercise a privilege which was fought for at the cost of many lives throughout history. People rush through yellow lights, not being concerned how those turning left are ever expected to make their turn. Not getting involved, not wanting to be responsible, not lending a helping hand has become the philosophy for millions. Many are afraid to report a crime lest they be hurt by the same viciousness that they are witnessing.

Certainly these characteristics are not true of everyone. However, these behaviors are commonplace in our cities and in increasing numbers in small communities throughout the land. Simply paging through newspapers or watching television yields fresh statistics about the high cost of these antisocial attitudes. These are the attitudes of exiles—those who feel they do not belong, who are not at home here, who feel they cannot make a difference.

The seeker of higher consciousness *begins a new life by ending his or her exile and becoming much more conscious.* He becomes more conscious of the vital components of his life. He also becomes very much more aware of other people. Higher consciousness *requires an expansion of awareness,* requires the joy of "coming home" to a sense of relationship, to a *sharing* of life with other people. Higher consciousness bestows a universal perspective through which it is not only thrilling to look at the world, but this expanded vision also grants optimism and personal strength.

Let's first look at the word *consciousness.* It would be good to share the same definitions. These are not specialized definitions but come from a number of modern dictionaries. Consciousness, according to *Webster's New World Dictionary,* is:

1) the state of being conscious; awareness of one's own feelings, what is happening around one, etc.
2) the totality of one's thoughts, feelings, and impressions; conscious mind.

Let's also look at the word *conscious*:

1) having a feeling or knowledge (of one's own sensations, feelings, etc., or of external things); aware; cognizant.
2) able to feel and think; in the normal waking state.
3) aware of oneself as a thinking being; knowing what one is doing and why.
4) same as self-consciousness.
5) accompanied by an awareness of what one is thinking, feeling, and doing; intentional (e.g., conscious humor).
6) known to or felt by oneself (e.g., conscious guilt).

When the word conscious is used in this book, it means being able to feel and think in the normal waking state. It means being aware of ourselves as thinking beings, knowing what we are doing and why. Certainly in being conscious we are aware of what we are thinking, feeling, and doing. Mental illness generally occurs when one enters a *habit* of not being aware of what one is thinking, feeling, or doing; or when one is not aware of *why* he or she is doing that particular thing. When you enter a rage you lose most of your control and mental capacity. Your knowledge of what you are doing, and why, is temporarily suspended due to the intensity of your emotional outpouring.

Also, when—from any cause—you are not fully conscious, you become *dangerous* to yourself and others. History is full of cases where people of diminished consciousness have made tremendous errors. According to network newscasts, accidents caused by those who were taking drugs or drinking on the job cost their industries eighty-two *billion* dollars in 1987.

Regarding drugs alone: in the workplace an estimated "37 percent of people in business and industry use an illegal drug on a daily basis." This costs "$47 billion per year (!) in lost efficiency, lost productivity, accidents on the job, claims for worker's compensation, medical expenses, absenteeism, and crime costs." Further, "the drug user is three and one-half times as likely to be involved in a plant accident; five times as likely to file a worker's compensation claim; receives three times the average level of sickness benefits; and functions at 67 percent of work potential."*

How important it is to be conscious. Workers in the United States suffer a work-related accident every 16 seconds. And someone dies in a work-related accident every 45 minutes.† Of course, not all accidents are caused by neglect, but how many might be avoided if people were simply mentally *present?*

Who can estimate the colossal damage caused when an oil tanker is driven into a reef near Port Valdez in Alaska—or any port?

As to driving fatalities, "alcohol was a factor in nearly 55 percent of fatal automobile accidents."‡ Over 20,000 people are killed every year by drinking drivers who are not fully conscious as they aim their cars down the road.§

THE CONSCIOUS

On the other hand, the heroes of our world are usually *especially conscious.* Whether it's a halfback rescuing a touchdown pass while surrounded by opponents, or a surgeon deftly removing a cancer, humanity applauds intensely conscious people. Isn't it true that whenever a matter is truly important, you shy away from those who seem to be less conscious? Instead, you hire or prefer to work only with people who are able to be particularly aware.

A surgeon at work is a particularly vivid example of near superhuman conscious activity. So, too, is the splendid focus of a symphony conductor or jet pilot. Or, a fine editor facing a deadline, a lawyer in research, a craftsman at his bench. Where would we be without conscious people—those who are clearly, energetically aware of their thoughts, feelings, actions, and the world around them? Could civilization exist without conscious activity? Intense conscious activity is so prized that many people leave their homes and travel to large halls which they have dedicatedly built with their

* "The Government Strategy to Combat Drug Use Will Work," Opposing Viewpoints, 1986 annual, *Criminal Justice*, John C. Laun (Administrator of the Drug Enforcement Administration), page 295.

† *1988 Information Please Almanac*, page 793.

‡ National Institute on Alcohol Abuse and Alcoholism, 1984 data, reported in *Chemical Dependency* by David Bender and Bruno Leone (editors), Greenhaven Press, St. Paul, 1985, page 13. (They add that alcohol was a factor in nearly 60 percent of violent crimes.)

§ *Statistical Abstract of the United States*, 1988. There were 20,659 fatal accidents in 1986.

taxes in order to hear a hundred musicians express their consciousness of tone and tempo so precisely that it seems all hundred are one great instrument. Also, a hundred thousand football devotees dress up warm and trek out in the winter winds so they can watch thousands of acts of intense consciousness in the course of one game.

In fact, audiences themselves must be keenly aware of what they are experiencing or the whole endeavor is ruined. Imagine a symphony or play or ballet being performed where members of the audience felt free to talk, laugh, and detract from the special purpose of those gathered together. And, isn't it agonizing to attend a sporting event where audience members disturb the game or pay no attention?

Have you noticed also that when people gather together to enjoy a concert, play, ballgame, or other special event of intensified consciousness that many barriers of hostility and prejudice melt away in the enjoyment of musicians, actors, and athletes intensely exploring their human potential?

Further, in sports there are extraordinarily precious times when rivalries are put aside. Often the crowd exclaims in enchanted delight at the amazing skill and courage of some opponent from a distant city. Such events are remembered for years. They are often played back on television programs around the world.

Whether on the gridiron or the keyboard, these moments show all people more of what a person can be. We gain a glimpse of something new within us which inspires our own efforts and standards. We try harder, reach farther. In all fields, acts of superb awareness join men and women, black and white, young and old, together in the pageant of life. We unite in marveling at human consciousness.

So, by the words *conscious person* we mean someone who is aware of his thoughts, feelings, and actions. He knows, reasonably well, what he is doing and why he is doing it—even if his knowledge of what and why is short-term and merely expedient.

Then what on earth do we mean by *higher consciousness?* Are we simply referring to regular consciousness applied with great vigor? No. By higher consciousness we are implying a realm of awareness *beyond* regular consciousness. Higher consciousness is awareness *at the source* of our thinking, feeling, and acting. Higher consciousness is that dynamic awareness which *enables* ordinary consciousness. Higher consciousness *enables* you to think, *enables* your feeling nature to work. It enables you to act wisely and well. Higher consciousness

is the essential intelligence, energy, and power that enables breathing and brain function, that enables sensations to enter us through
our sense organs.

This incredible consciousness can do far more for you than
merely maintain your blood flow. However astonishingly profound
its abilities in maintaining your faculties and existence, your higher
consciousness will enable you to have greater ability in all areas of
your life—mentally, emotionally, spiritually, as well as materially.

Higher consciousness is *not* lofty thought. Thoughts are *too slow*
to enter into this incomparable realm. Similarly, ordinary emotions
are not subtle enough to contact or comprehend it. Your higher consciousness is the creative power of your existence itself, that which
enables you to be. Is this clear?

Perhaps some analogies will help.

An electric motor may have ingenious coils within itself and
extremely fine engineering, but it will not be able to do anything at
all unless it is plugged into some source of energy. In this case, a
wall socket gives the motor a contact with the energy which allows it
to function.

Another example, our body is made up of various chemicals
and lots of water—we are approximately eighty percent water.
(Water, of course, is chemical in nature too—combined hydrogen
and oxygen.) These chemicals of our being could be put in various
envelopes and little boxes. We could take a medium-sized barrel and
empty all the envelopes and cartons into that barrel, add water, and
we would still not have a person. We would not have a thinking,
feeling, and acting being, would we? Of course not. The higher
consciousness is that which can take the various chemicals of the
earth, along with the watery constituents and, because of its presence, because of its potency and ability, enable you to think, feel,
and act as no barrel of chemicals can.

It cannot be overemphasized that you can experience and become a delighted partner of your own higher consciousness, that you
can intimately know the awareness which *enables life* and *sustains
regular consciousness*. This higher consciousness is the *source,* and *sus-
tainer,* of your ability to think, feel, act, and to be sensitive to your
outer world.

Because higher consciousness is the *source* of your normal
awareness, you will feel invigorated and revitalized whenever you
succeed in turning your thoughts, feelings, and actions inward. In
directing your attention toward the sustaining consciousness you
will, with patient practice, discover how to unleash your inner

potentials for fulfillment. Simply, seek to know the source of your regular consciousness. Ask:

"What enables me to think these thoughts? What empowers my heart to beat? What enables me to feel happiness or surprise?"

When your body is calm and your thoughts and feelings successfully turn toward the awareness which sustains them, beautiful, heavenly experiences will occur. It does take practice. At first it is difficult to turn the direction of your thoughts, feelings, and actions from the outer world to this higher world, but beautiful experiences do begin to occur as soon as your attention is truly redirected. As mentioned in Chapter One, the redirection of your thoughts, feelings, and actions toward the higher consciousness creates a transcendental awareness. This heightened awareness is so profound and pleasant that you will relish it a great deal.

In your rediscovered *home* beyond normal thought or feeling, you will find priceless insight, sublime security, peace, and joy, along with a marvelous inner power. All of these are beyond the reach of normal consciousness and they immeasurably enrich each day. As the experiencer of higher consciousness, such depth and extended dimensions are added to your life that you will know, in a universal or cosmic view, who you really are, what you are doing and why.

REFLECTION

My higher consciousness is sustaining my life, including every breath and each heartbeat. My higher consciousness awaits my interest and attention that it may even more fully enrich the activities of my mind and emotions. It will make my words and actions sure and more successful. My higher consciousness will move through my life, uplifting my loved ones and my world, too. My higher consciousness abides within me now.

4

THE CHOICE

How do you choose to look at your life? So much of your future delight or sorrow is a matter of choice. *Choice.*

Consider the elderly man who sat red-faced and fuming in his car. He shook as he tucked the nitroglycerine tablets into his mouth, hopeful they would forestall another coronary.

"You have no idea how to drive that van, young man," he shouted. "Did you call the police?" he asked the sneering fellow. "You ruined it, my new car.

"Worked all my life for a car like this," the old man muttered to the air as he closed his window. "What if the police believe that young fool? What if they say it's my fault? Why, he was going too fast, never even looked around. I've been driving on this street thirty years.

"I *need* to drive. I know I don't see so well, but I need to drive. I'm an important man. And my wife needs me to drive her, especially now that she's sick," he decided, rationalizing, trying to calm his racing heart. "There's no way we can get around by taxi. Not here. How would we ever go to our cabin? What if the police believe that young idiot? He's acting like it's my fault. Snickering at me. When I was his age I thought I owned the road, too. If I can't drive, how will I see my grandchildren?"

A young policeman arrived shortly. The van driver went to him and waved his arms. He laughed and threw both hands in the air in apparent exasperation.

The policeman, who looked like a high-school kid, approached the old man. "Have you ever had a course on how to drive a car, sir?"

The old man lost his breath and collapsed in another heart attack.

Sure that he had been found guilty, the elderly gentleman chose to think he had lost almost everything. Fortunately, he lived to learn that the policeman was new at his job and was required, because of a survey, to ask *all* drivers in all car accidents whether they had been to driving school!

The poor man had *chosen* to see matters in a tragic way.

The way we choose to see life most of the time is based on the flow of our thoughts and feelings. And, usually, the way we speak or act is, again, *based* on our thoughts and feelings. Our mental/emotional habits often distort our perceptions of what is happening in the outer world. Not too many people have elected to be conscious enough to notice what is going on in reality. There's too much chaos inside people for them to be able to see life's events clearly. Riots have occurred over two cents. People have been shot because of what somebody wrongly thought or blindly felt. The famous medieval scholar, Peter Abelard, was castrated because Canon Fulbert *thought* Peter was forcing Fulbert's niece, Heloise, to become a nun. Peter was, in fact, scholars report, helping Heloise to hide in a convent far from the grasp of Canon Fulbert.

Your consciousness—that is, your thoughts, feelings, actions, and awareness of the outer world—is the main force toward life-enrichment.

AWARENESS EXERCISES

Your thoughts and feelings, for good or ill, usually *dominate* your perceptions of the outer world and so many of your actions. So, to stop the self-destructive tyranny of chaotic, incorrect thoughts and feelings, start now to do exercises of simply watching your thoughts or feelings come and go. Become familiar with the content of your mind and the myriad flows of your emotions. Also, strive to be truly aware of what your senses are conveying from the outer world.

One more extremely valuable practice: rather than simply reacting to important events by habit, strive to allow your actions to express your well-considered thoughts. In this way you will give your creative intelligence a chance to make your acquaintance.

5

WHAT WILL PREVAIL?

You may find you have to struggle in order to be more conscious. Despite wonderful benefits close at hand, you will nevertheless find yourself fighting what seems at times a tedious, uphill battle. Why? Old tendencies are very powerful. *Your habits will almost always win.* It's not a question of sincerity, either. Of course you'd like to be a more loving, creative person. Who wouldn't? Certainly it would be wonderful to contact your higher consciousness with its thrilling insight and inner power. No question it's a worthwhile endeavor. No question it's worth persistence and quantities of attention. Nevertheless, your old tendencies, the way you *habitually* think and feel—your most regular attitudes about life from yesterday and yesteryear—will not easily yield to a happier you.

Very often we sincerely make commitments to ourselves. We may even tell others about the new person we are striving to be. Yet a few weeks down the road we are all too often the same. Endeavoring to shape a new life, in one way or another, can be gallingly frustrating. We usually fail. The old way of doing things, the old habit patterns, are so familiar and apparently powerful. Too frequently we resign and give in to the idea that while other people may succeed in their transformation projects, we are somehow less qualified as human beings. Others must have tremendous will power, whereas ours must indeed be very puny. Or, then again, were we truly sincere? Maybe we didn't mean it. Obviously we must not have valued our commitment to our new dreams and goals because we gave up so easily. We failed with such total surrender. It only took a few weeks and here we are, unsuccessful once again. We feel either weak-willed or are convinced that our sincerity is most ingenuine.

Next time, when a good idea comes our way we decide not to be fooled into believing we're sincere. That's that. So it goes. We joyously jump into failure.

But the fact is you're not alone. You're normal. Most everyone, despite helpful inspiration and a deep sincerity, will fail or give up ("giving up" is a nicer word for failure) before accomplishing vitally important goals. Many people will *generally* fail.

Then, with failure, the guilt feelings come along. Unhappy with yourself, you often lash out at others, or you refuse to have good will, not only for other people but for yourself as well. The guilt feelings last a long time and regularly tell you you're not a very good person—you're not worthy or capable of a better life. Certainly, you feel you're not worthy of higher consciousness. You develop a secret. Despite the right clothes or the right words, you know down deep you're inferior to other people. You know your failures. You know your limitations. Other people don't know. They can't see how badly you've fallen short of your dearest hopes. They don't know, or do they?

"Is my inadequacy visible?" you wonder.

When you know you're an inferior person, what's the point of trying? So, when you've failed several times you do the obvious: find fitting compromises, find a niche for your inadequate self and muddle along as best you can. Of course it's helpful to be quite critical of other people so you can be mindful of their inferiorities as well as your own aching ego. Compromise is the rule of the day and, after all, isn't that what everybody does? Isn't everyone, in fact, something of a joke? A blunderer? Yes, why does anyone ever try to be more than he or she was yesterday?

The road to hell is paved with good intentions. This is widely stated. Good intentions are pleasant in their own way but how do you, *how can you,* take good intentions and make them into realities? How can you in truth become more conscious and accomplish, in fact, not in fantasy, what you so powerfully yearn for?

HOW TO SUCCEED

It is so important to understand something of the process of success. In whatever area you seek success, you must understand that *your tendencies, your habits, will prevail.* Most often, old tendencies and habits frustrate and generally smother the new life you are striving to create. Your old tendencies took years of development. Each of us is deeply entrenched in old ways. How can we expect a new rivulet created in three minutes or three days of aspiration to possibly stand against the mighty, deep rivers we have built over ten, fifteen, twenty-five years?

Yet the fact that you are reading this book indicates you have already begun breaking free of old, destructive tendencies. You are searching for a new vision. You are raising your consciousness to new possibilities. You are thinking of higher and alternate ways of doing things. You are contemplating the possibility that higher consciousness does exist, and is available to you. You even suspect that higher consciousness is this very minute locked within you, ready to be unleashed. Further, you appreciate that some higher consciousness is already at work throughout your life in order for you to be able to breathe, walk, talk, think, feel. This attitude allows your attention and emotions to overflow the banks of old riverbeds of habits to seek new directions.

Old tendencies will never—repeat, *never*—be able to stop you if you thoroughly understand the following process. The main thing that must be understood at every step along the way to a more conscious and even superconscious life is this: *The seeker of higher consciousness and fulfillment must create new tendencies!* Your greater success in life is based on your willingness to not only think about new possibilities but to *redirect the flow* of your thoughts and feelings, *the flow of your life force,* into new tendencies and habits of living. New tendencies must be formed, habits and attitudes which will be truly constructive and which at no point will block or inhibit your heartfelt purposes. Almost all failure, especially regarding the achievement of higher consciousness, is caused by our not forming new tendencies.

But be careful. Somehow people think that merely having a new idea or an enthusiastic, heart-pumping time at some lecture will bring about the new fulfillment or extraordinary capacities. If this were the case, our planet would be instantly out of trouble. The world today is filled with people who get excited about a new idea or way of life almost every month. As soon as they begin to lose their inspiration, and old habits start to sweep them away from the goal once glimpsed so brightly, they move onto something else and proceed through life, jag after jag. Later they look back at their lives and notice they haven't accomplished much of anything. They notice friends they met along the way, friends who seem to have gained the fruits of success—friends who were more constant in their focus on goals. The *jaggers* find they themselves have traveled far but arrived nowhere.

To accomplish your fulfillment and know your higher consciousness, vigorous, constant, new tendencies have to be formed. These tendencies will become so strong that no old habits will be able to overcome them. Also, when these new tendencies are consciously and lovingly created, shocks and deceptions of the outer world will not be able to knock you off course or out of stride.

It's important also to value those constructive tendencies you have already developed. Not all old tendencies are bad. Take time to evaluate which habits of thought, feeling, and action have always been constructive and valuable in your life. Appreciate them anew, give them a chance to grow and expand, becoming more serviceful aids in your life's new directions. The habits of being kind, or of being able to concentrate easily and well, for example, are extremely helpful tendencies which all too many seekers of higher consciousness have to reestablish or perhaps build from scratch.

Please keep in mind as you progress that many wonderful ideas will come your way. Many partial skills will be revealed to you, too. But none of these significant gifts along your path will be truly yours until you have fully established new tendencies. New habits of thought, feeling, and self-esteem must become an integrated part of you. When you find it particularly easy and natural to behave in the new way that you have chosen, you will succeed. You will succeed for you have formed the tendencies that will get you there.

To repeat, *intellectual* understanding of higher consciousness *in no way assures* that you will ever experience higher consciousness. Myriad intellectuals lie in heaps along the roadside. They have the ideas but have not used those ideas to create new tendencies.

Even if your heart palpitates in sympathy with some great mission, your thoughts and emotions in no way assure that you will be able to accomplish that mission or even stay true to it for two days.

Another thing must be understood about these all-important tendencies. A true tendency is a product of your whole being. Since every part of your life must work in harmony with the other parts, a tendency cannot be created without the *cooperation of your thoughts and your feelings.* While more is actually required, it is essential that you first understand that mind and emotions must come to an agreement in the endeavor to create a new tendency. If the thought nature is saying, "How silly. How superstitious!" or "How worthless!" while the emotional nature is striving to move toward a clearly important fulfillment, no new tendency will be formed and there will be inner conflict. Indeed, a personal civil war can only result. Yet there will be times when the mind wants to enter activities or accomplish goals which are in direct conflict with the desires of the heart. These cross-purposes lead to deep problems—even mental illness—if the civil war is particularly severe.

Sometimes, your mind may wish to engross itself in a project—perhaps a design or invention. However, if your emotions have another agenda, if they "prefer" to indulge in grief, jealousy, or some form of numbness, no successful tendency will be formed. The civil war will resume on a new front and the mind will not generally have enough thrust, enough power, to develop the new project. And, your health may be affected as well. Weakness, nerve, or digestive problems, for example, may occur.

So, for a new tendency and a victory over the past, you must consider your new goal mentally and emotionally. You have to be sure that the two can work together on each important goal. When your mind is convinced that "The New Tendency Project" is worthwhile, it will not sabotage the project but will pitch in and help, bringing to the forefront its resources of ideas and concepts. Your mind will help create new images which will be extremely beneficial —indeed, essential—for the new tendency and its fulfillment. Your emotions will contribute inspiration, excitement, comfort, encouragement, and a dogged endurance.

Whenever you seek to be more successful in any way, stop and have a huddle within yourself. Dialogue. Introspect. Marshal your reason. Examine your feelings, clarify them. Then mentally and emotionally conceive the ideal thoughts and feelings for your new endeavor. Whenever the two powerful forces of thoughts and feelings work together as a unity, you will form an extremely strong, new tendency. When they work together they will not be denied. You will succeed through the help of your cooperative allies.

But, thoughts and feelings aren't the whole story. As your thoughts and feelings combine, they must also have the cooperation and assistance of your life force and your physical body. By *life force* we mean the energy within you that enables your heart to beat, your breath to move in and out, peristalsis to occur in your abdomen, the energy that makes your blood circulate. No, we're not implying that this energy has a mind of its own, but without question it has a *momentum* of its own. After all (are we agreed?), life force is sustained by a most brilliant higher consciousness. Your life force regularly carries out exploits of life support which baffle the understanding of your regular mind, doesn't it? When you are changing your life, especially when you are creating a new tendency, you want your life force to move in this new direction, too. You want it to move cooperatively along the lines that your mind and emotions have agreed upon. It's important to spend quiet time with your mind and emotions interplaying with the new tendency while encouraging your life force, your physical energy, to move in this new way also. Your life force readily responds to the direction of your thoughts and feelings.

Metaphysicians and mystics have often demonstrated that what you think and feel can affect your vitality level or improve the functioning of your breathing or your heartbeat. While the relationship of thoughts and feelings with vital energy is a vague field of science at this point, or perhaps is considered scarcely scientific at all, you can, through conceiving mentally/emotionally of the new goal, enable your life force to become more readily supportive of the new tendency. Simply, make slow, long exhalations as you mentally picture your goal and emotionally direct your feelings toward the goal as well.

While direction of life force may seem a difficult area to understand, you will know that your life force is cooperating in the formation of a new tendency when you experience extra energy—in fact, vitality to spare—as you work toward the new reality that you have determined to bring about.

As you can see, it's very important to be sure you wish to create the new tendency before you marshal your thought processes, your emotional nature, and even your life force toward the new tendency and goal!

Lastly, the physical body itself has to cooperate. If it's prone to laziness or inactivity, or if by habit it has behaved in a most contrary fashion to the assistance you now wish, then your physical habits have to be turned around too. If your physical body doesn't cooperate, you will suffer the frustrations of civil war once again. It's extremely helpful to train your body to serve you in each new tendency you choose. When you have mentally and emotionally focused on formation of a new tendency, conceive also the ideal behavior you expect of your body. Then, patiently develop the physical skills and habits. Too often the body's role in success is not considered.

Suppose you want to accomplish something which greatly involves your mental nature. If your body won't sit still or is continually resisting the intensity of mental work, it can easily keep you from success. On the other hand, if you have chosen to accomplish something through vigorous activity, your body can't have a habit of being lethargic. In this case your body may have to be toned up and strengthened through exercise in order not to let you down.

Frankly, there is one more factor in forming a new tendency but you'll have to work on it in subsequent chapters. You have to be nearly superconscious in order to deal with this one remaining potential ally (or potential foe). It is the ego, or sense of self. If your ego is determined to grow and change and sacrifice itself to a new way of living, it will be a great ally. However, many people have an ego sense which is very self-destructive and balky. Their sense of self ignores enriching possibilities while sabotaging worthwhile projects presented to it by the mental and emotional nature.

So, at present, your ego can most significantly help you if you maintain an attitude of willingness to grow—a readiness to become a finer person. With this initial cooperation of your sense of self, you will enable a tremendous force to help establish each new tendency. Believe it or not, large numbers of people have an ego which seeks failure and suffering rather than prosperity and well being.

Summing up, life-enriching new tendencies—*as they are forged consciously and with your whole being*—can be established fairly quickly. True tendencies win! They have momentum. They carry you through. Well-formed tendencies enable you to succeed when the going gets tough. They enable you to prevail despite outward circumstances. In many ways, your greatest treasures are your constructive tendencies. They are more powerful than thoughts, feelings, and negative habits of doing things. If you will take the time and patiently combine all your energies in the formation of tendencies that you would really like to have, you will be one of those few people who ultimately succeeds whenever you set out toward a new and important goal. You will be among the less than ten percent who understand the process of success. In forming powerful, constructive tendencies, you will also be accomplishing the consolidation you need in order to know your higher consciousness.

A LIFE-ENRICHING AFFIRMATION

You may wish to say this affirmation with deep, clear thought each morning. It will help you develop new tendencies.

My constructive tendencies enable me to prevail despite outward circumstances. I recognize my positive tendencies and attitudes are among my most precious assets. They enable me to establish greater personal health, prosperity, emotional well being and mental efficiency today and every day. With intensity and repetition I have created the habits which bring success and higher consciousness.

6

WITH THEM YOU SUCCEED — WITHOUT THEM YOU FAIL

Would you like to know one more extremely important principle in the formation of new tendencies?

The principle is this: *Intensity and Repetition*. Keep "intensity and repetition" in mind as you gather thoughts, emotions, vital force, and body together.

Memory experts say you can best remember information you seek to memorize by first *paying attention with intensity* and, then, *repeatedly thinking* about the information. Similarly, *you can more easily create a new tendency with intensity and repetition.*

INTENSITY

To give birth to a new tendency, focus intensely on it. Think vividly of your new success habit. Picture it as clearly as you can and get your positive emotions involved. Hold your thoughts and feelings on the ideal tendency as intensely as you can for a minute or two several times a day. Keep in mind, however, intensity does not mean *strain*. Your intensity needs to be comfortable—both before, during, and after focus periods—and invigorating.

Whether your new tendency is mainly a physical, emotional, or mental one, it is necessary that body, mind, and emotions join in focusing together—each one contributing its intensity. This does not mean the body muscles are to be tensed but, rather, *raptly attuned* with the new tendency. While you may have to spend weeks or months developing the knack of focusing your body, thoughts, and feelings intensely for short periods each day, you will enjoy the delights of feeling progressively *more alive* as you make progress. You will gain many benefits in addition to expertise in forming new tendencies. Of course the physical/mental/emotional intensity rouses your vital life force too and focuses its support on the new tendency as well. For example, you will find it much easier to think clearly and to harmonize your emotions.

REPETITION

These periods of intensity must be *repeated* once or twice a day, each and every day, *until the new tendency is established*. Even when the new tendency seems established, continue your intensity and repetition from time to time. Refocus on established tendencies once a week, preferably. Alertly maintain the new tendency until it is strongly and undeniably a part of your life.

Remember, the same principles of unified intensity and repetition apply if you are striving to develop a new physical habit—a better backhand, for example. Use intense concentration, emotional agreement, and enthusiasm. Be sure your life force doesn't stray—keep gathering it into the new backhand habit. Also, intensely repeat the physical movement of your hand and racket, coordinating them with your feet and whole body. Unified intensity must be repeated again and again and again for the new backhand to become a part of your life.

For new mental tendencies—learning a language or the multiplication tables, for example—relax your body and sit calmly in a state of well being for a minute or two. Then direct your feelings of happiness toward the new knowledge you seek; be happy, enthusiastic, or pleasantly calm in focusing your feelings on your subject. A focused enthusiasm will greatly increase your ability to learn and will substantially diminish the too-common sabotage from emotions which wander while you are trying to concentrate your mind.

Then, with your physical and emotional support, focus your thoughts on your new knowledge. Let your thoughts energetically pour into the subject. Leaving other thoughts and subjects aside for awhile, let your thoughts penetrate deeply into what you seek to know. Become absorbed in your concentration. You will likely gain your new mental abilities more quickly, more lastingly, than ever before. And you will find the experience exhilarating!

Also, for new emotional tendencies, the same harmony and co-operation are extremely helpful. Suppose you want to be a more supportive—less cynical and grumpy—person. Take ten minutes each day and sit quietly. Relax your body thoroughly. A tense or fidgeting body will thwart your intensity. Now, let your mind co-operate. Too often, the turbulent mind prevents emotional focus and transformation; so, encourage your mind to realize the new behavior appreciatively. Let your mind understand the absurdly high cost of cynicism and negativity—in hampering your personal happiness and your relationships.

Think of the new behavior, the new tendency, in its many aspects; analyze and let go of the old tendency which prompted the old behavior. When your mind is free to focus on the new ideal tendency, bring your new feelings fully into your attention. Patiently generate the emotions which you wish to become your new way of feeling and being. Let go of old feelings, old emotional habits, as you direct your emotions to move intensely, joyously, toward your new way of living.

Of course, these ten-minute periods of intensity will prove an excellent *beginning* of change but you will need to practice your new skills in the real world *often*. Practice redirecting your feelings and thoughts away from old tendencies whenever they try to return. Guide your feelings and mind back toward your ideal, kindly and patiently, but with *persistence*.

As your new feelings gain strength, a powerful momentum will establish both the new tendency and a new life. Intensity and Repetition will win!

DON'T IGNORE THE PRINCIPLE OF TRANSFORMATION

Whatever your area of focus, when you are speaking of success, and especially when you are seeking to know your higher consciousness, you are striving to transform old physical habits into new physical habits; old movements of the life force into a new movement of life force; old emotional tendencies into new ones; and old mental tendencies into new ones. People who ignore this important principle of transformation do not succeed. They certainly never find their higher consciousness. Each person who finds higher consciousness capitalizes on his or her good tendencies. Each aspirant patiently, perhaps even relentlessly, day by day, through attention and repetition, gathers mind and heart together and establishes undeniable, powerful, and exhilarating successful tendencies.

When all your tendencies are constructive, an ongoing sense of well being and a freedom from inner conflict occurs. You feel more a master of your life and less the victim of circumstance. You have established yourself as a likely candidate for higher consciousness. You become capable of maintaining the rights and privileges which are bestowed on one who knows the higher consciousness. With the right tendencies you succeed; without them you fail.

Hopefully this entire book will be of great help to you in choosing and creating those tendencies which will greatly reward you.

REFLECTION

My tendencies are mighty rivers
Flowing toward my future.

7

THE YEARNING

Late one night you may find yourself saying:

"But I don't care about the alleged benefits of higher consciousness. And, I'm not interested in forming new tendencies or discovering greater talents. I need help for the agony in my heart! I seem to be suffering from life itself, from the limitations of mortality. I'm not interested in being more conscious or less conscious. My problem is this gnawing in my gut, my deep sense of incompleteness. Even when I achieve what others call meaningful, I feel empty. Even when I'm a hero it seems meaningless. All the activities of life seem merely expedient—only a shadow play without substance. I am suffering within my skin, within the hollows of my skull. I yearn to live with purpose, yet my eyes are too coated to perceive worthwhile purposes in the 'get up/go to work/come home/eat/watch television/go to bed humdrum.' I ask others why they are doing what they are doing. After they say they are making a living or starting their kids through the same ultimate process, I ask them again. Then *they say they don't know!*

"I feel like Paul who said, 'Things I want to do, I don't do; things I don't want to do, I do.' I look at all of us pushing through life and ask why. Is the main purpose of existence only to maintain existence? Birth, copulation, death—is that it? Really?

"Sometimes I can preoccupy myself and drown out the yearning for a few days. Then it comes back. What's wrong with me that I can't be happy with the humdrum until I'm sixty-five? Why can't I look forward to retirement and the doctors escorting me to my hopefully penultimate tomb? Above all, either satisfy my yearning, pacify this aching heart and perplexed mind or take away, please take away, this yearning. I yearn to be better than I am. I crave that life have more value."

Do you have these feelings? Have you ever felt this way? If this yearning were to continue unabated, without being satisfied, it could be dangerous. Without finding satisfaction you will likely develop impaired functioning and diminished ability to relate to other people. In your neurosis, reality can become obscured—and who knows what illnesses might develop after that.

Yet this perplexity is a common experience to most people who ultimately realize the higher consciousness. These people are not merely intrigued by the benefits of higher consciousness. They are desperate people, driven to a quest for meaning. They are haunted by the hope of deep and total satisfaction in the realization of their underlying humanity and spirituality. These seekers crave sight of the polestar that will guide them to values they can wholeheartedly live for and enthusiastically accomplish.

Being desperate, they're somewhat menacing to the happiness of others. Their lack of satisfying fulfillment in the regular things of life hurts loved ones and friends who are quite content with the way life is going. These driven ones seem to sneer at society.

"They must be snobs the way they're unable to share in the common joys of life," parents and old friends say. "Their discontent can make them *pessimists* for life! They're ignoring excellent career opportunities! These strange ones say so emotionally that they're not alive merely to exist. Well, who is? They must be missing crucial brain circuits! And being nice to them doesn't help. Being nasty merely adds to their apparent martyrdom for the ridiculous. Worse, they might turn to dope or alcohol. They seem to be life's fugitives." Beneath these remarks is the judgment that the discontented are too self-indulgent in their dissatisfactions; they are apparently too lazy or too weak to get on with their lives and fulfill their roles in family and society.

Former friends wonder, "They talk about their yearnings and their need to understand life. This *yearning* looks more like an excuse for eccentricity and a rationale for putting other people down. Yearnings? We all have yearnings. Why do *they* act so exclusive?"

Yet, in life we all have a choice. The path of higher consciousness is much like a freeway. People turn onto this royal road from the most adjacent community of thought. They also turn off this road when some activity or community beside the road looks more appealing and interesting than the pleasure of continuing toward an as yet unknown reality.

Many people turn onto the road of higher consciousness when they reach a personal state of deep yearning. They do not much care about the benefits enumerated and exclaimed over in earlier chapters. They do not have to make an effort to be more conscious. They already crave greater consciousness. They enter the freeway at this point exclusively because of their yearning. They need—they deeply need—to find higher consciousness. Nothing they know, nothing they have found out so far, either from respected teachers or from their own musings, has soothed their pain. They have been ejected from routine satisfactions, as well as from the community of thoughts in their own minds. They have to find a love that lasts and satisfies. They have cried quietly for many a night to know the how and why of life. They want to find a place where they will fit in. Somewhere.

So it is that the freeway, which was once traveled mainly by those seeking fuller awareness of their potential, is today newly populated by the sincerely confused. If you are one who seeks fuller awareness of your potential, the newly arrived "sincerely confused" travelers will look at you and wonder what you are doing on the road. They will question your motives, and you, if you are one of the comfortable, unagonized seekers of higher consciousness, may feel: a) superior to these neurotic people, or b) inferior and not worthy to be traveling with them. While you, after all, are planning simply to apply some effort toward a number of specific benefits, these new travelers seem ready to give their all—everything. But at times they act as if the benefits you hope for are merely self-gratifying items on an egoic shopping trip.

The new entrants on the freeway, the sincerely confused, should be appreciated and accepted as fellow human beings. One day you may become similarly motivated, if you're not already. You may, at some stage on your pleasant journey, suddenly convulse in the realization that you are not the person you yearn to be. You may sense there are much more important issues in your life than you have been willing to face before. A sudden, intense dissatisfaction with your character flaws may grip you and not let go. On the other hand, if you, by some special grace, are somehow enabled to value and *appreciate* the goodness and beauty which underlies life, you may never have to know the agony of yearning. You may not need the power of its motivation. You may do extremely well without yearning because of your eagerness to grow, coupled with your honesty and a sense of good will for all, whatever their nature.*

In your eagerness to grow, along with your freedom from "the yearning disease," you will be a bright light, a cheery face, and a harmonious influence in the lives of the dissatisfied. As they move forward, confused about their goals, accepting new possibilities only to reject them, and then sometimes rushing back to seek once again the rejected goal, you will be, in your steadiness, a fine inspiration.

If you find yourself on this freeway toward higher consciousness and you recognize you are a traveler due to your yearning, dissatisfaction, confusion, or perplexity—Welcome! Many have come this way before you and have succeeded. If you yearn to know what's *worth* doing, your question is not regarded as nihilistic by your fellow travelers. Come along. In the meantime, don't stop taking an active part in life, whether or not it makes sense to you. Do! Be about. Be active and perform the work that comes most easily to your hand. Retain your ability to do. Retain your skill in action. Your present abilities will become very, very useful when you find your higher consciousness.

If you view the world and your peers as being very confused, surely you can feel deep compassion for them. Surely you would not condemn them but lend a helping hand, would you not? There is always something you can do. Even if it seems insignificant to your state of mind, there are many ways you can contribute something.

Do you feel you are confused about yourself, that you do not even know who you are? Great philosophers had the same problem —Mahatma Gandhi and Benjamin Franklin, for example. Gandhi studied his life and himself with painstaking honesty for years and years. Franklin, the genius who helped draft the Declaration of Independence, was mainly self-taught. On his own he worked through mathematics manuals, scientific journals, foreign languages, and *daily* exercises in character development. From youth through advanced old age, Franklin's life was a quest for Truth. What made Gandhi,

---

* For all, that is, except bullies who strive to force their will and views on others— and who must at times be regarded with strength as well as compassion.

Franklin, and dozens of others great was *they did everything they could to resolve their yearnings and satisfy their questions.*

THE DESPAIR

Whether you're an eager traveler seeking the benefits of higher consciousness, or a driven traveler desperate for satisfaction and meaning, you're traveling in the same direction. You're sharing the same freeway and most of the events along the way.

While this road to higher consciousness is the road of highest joy, and while a sense of well being and greater wisdom develops quite regularly, you should be warned that there will likely be times of despair. When you travel this road, loved ones and business acquaintances may wonder why. The goal seems so shining and clear to you, yet others who know you cannot sense or perceive your goal at all. They may feel, and express themselves quite emotionally, that you're wasting your time or your resources. They may say you're wasting your time becoming a nothing when you could become someone great. "Superstition, abstraction, unreality," they say.

Friends may accuse you of striving to escape from the facts of life, or from the fun of life if your choices for growth are in conflict with their ways of celebrating life. If they can't see what you're doing and in no way comprehend what you're striving to do, and if they think the deprecatory words they're saying are for your good, you will have to incorporate your despair and their lack of understanding into your quest. Let the obstructions of their unkindness become motivating forces which compel you to succeed. Your compassion and love, along with the strength that you must develop, will be extremely valuable as you enter higher consciousness. If you will be kind, or strong, or strive as best you can to love and serve those who oppose you, you will become successful. Those who are against you today may one day consider you great. They may deem it an honor to have known you way back when you glimpsed the reality of a higher consciousness.

In periods of despair you will primarily sense the painful separation from others, especially those you care about most. You will also feel at times, in your despair, separate from humanity. You will feel the way humanity is going creates much concern in your heart but that you, in seeking higher consciousness, are going in a different direction.

Your most painful despair comes when you feel divided within yourself. You feel that a higher purpose within you is being blocked or cut off due to an inadequate, stubborn, and insensitive nature. You may, in despair, bemoan your inadequacies and lament the seeming wall or chasm between you and where you sense you ought to be.

Multitudes have gone before you. They suffered these moments of despair too. They dried their eyes, got up and went on, as you will. They became more determined in their despair and focused on the great importance of their destination. In their despair their hearts became more universal and they became keenly sensitive to the hearts and minds of other people. Your periods of despair, if not selfishly or slavishly indulged in, can become moments of expanded compassion and of deep concern for the well being of all people. You will find each tear helps to wash away the sense of separateness. Each tear affirms life and your caring heart. Each tear, in this instance, makes your mind clearer and nobler.

The indication that your despair is a genuine aspect of your quest for higher consciousness and not an emotional illness will be: does your despair make your life fresher? As a consequence of your compassionate despair you will find yourself becoming clearer and more loving in daily life. You will begin to develop, even while suffering times of despair at night or during other private times, a more cheerful and accepting attitude for the world and for others. Also, your despair will give you greater insight into your own mind and heart. You will find greater patience with yourself. The quality of your despair, which seems so deep and gloomy, will nevertheless lighten your life noticeably. You will find it a joy to be free of tears stored so long in your heart. It becomes a sweet joy to have a despair borne of a concern for higher values and greater possibilities for everyone.

If your despair does not develop compassionate qualities, then it is destructive and you would be very wise to discuss it with a counselor who can help you work through it, and get back on the road to higher consciousness.

Your periods of despair on your path to higher consciousness affirm life. They also affirm your value and your uniqueness as a precious human being. So, even despair has grand dimensions. The goal, however, is to pass through your periods of despair and go forward as quickly as possible. The journey is much too beautiful to be blotted out by watery eyes and otherwise occupied hearts.

REFLECTION

I don't know where you are.
I don't know if you hear me.
Please, if you are able,
Listen to my heart:
I need you more than air.

8

THE DELIGHTFUL SEARCH

Now the search begins in earnest. It would be wonderful if finding your higher consciousness were as simple as getting on a freeway and staying on the road until the destination is reached. While "road, path, freeway," are excellent ways of describing the quest for fulfillment, we must now go beyond this analogy. It's fair to compare the quest for consciousness to a freeway but, of course, the matter is not that simple.

When you are moved, for one reason or another, to seek higher consciousness, an exciting part of your life begins. New delights are brought before you, vistas you never dreamed of come into your view. One young man found such excitement at this stage of his life that he read into the wee hours of the night. Early each morning he awakened refreshed and with a sense of wonder. His work life became exciting and enchanting. His enthusiasm was charming to his employers. During lunch hour and after work, he rushed to be with teachers and fellow participants in the realms of higher consciousness. He strived to be in tune with everyone and with nature herself. He reported that, despite living in a rather damp climate, he never got rained on during the first six months of his quest! He said he somehow sensed the activity of nature and was able to so attune with it that the rain always occurred while he was indoors or inside his car. Even during a rainy day when he made a short jaunt from his apartment to the store, he would find that for one reason or another the raindrops seemed to await his convenience. Then, after six months, he was rained on in a regular manner—like an ordinary mortal. However, he still enjoys reflecting on the extreme delight and excitement of those beginning days.

When you start to sense the higher consciousness and the vast potentiality available to you—furthermore, when you sense you can definitely experience and *know* the higher consciousness for yourself—you get a tremendous rush of enthusiasm and a feeling of gratitude for life. Life becomes more like a dance. Beauty, unseen before, now reaches out to your appreciative eyes most everywhere you go. The heart and mind glow with eagerness. Aspiration comes easily and dwells for long periods. Inspiring experiences abound.

One day, as a beginner on the path, you will see your first aura, the electromagnetic field of energy surrounding some particularly fine person. At other times your dreams may seem extraordinarily fascinating and profoundly symbolic. Your vitality level seems to double. Well being comes easily.

Now your heart pounds with respect in the presence of those true teachers—and sometimes false ones—who seem to know everything! There's always something new to talk about, something engrossing to think about, some new state of love or concern to dwell in your heart. You feel you're coming up out of the grave, coming into life. You sense a rebirth will definitely occur. Who knows when? Perhaps today. You find it ever so tempting to get gushy and romantic, or to laugh too long and happily at an inane joke. At times you feel a strong desire to close your mouth and savor the sweetness which seems to radiate from roses within.

The early delight in the quest can have a two-fold effect:

1)   People who experience the initial delights sometimes believe the phenomena they've experienced indicate they're enlightened. Yet such "aspirants" will likely be somewhere else, practicing sword fighting or mountain climbing by next year. They often feel they've received in a few months what people generally have to labor years for and, now that they've gained "the illumination" or know what's what, there are other more interesting and exciting fields to move into.

2)   The early and usually joyous beginning of the quest prepares one for the greater joys and challenges ahead. Work and effort will be required. An intensity will be necessary in order to transform old habits into refined tendencies and attributes of character necessary to actually experience the higher consciousness and ultimately *abide* in it. If the beginning of the path is to be more than an adolescent romance, or *crush*, the forward momentum will have to be maintained. Higher consciousness requires those who want more than early thrills, to begin—in however much delight—a very serious undertaking: *You must now determine the best path for your fulfillment in higher consciousness.*

You must earnestly seek the best means, the best way, to go from where you are this very moment toward realization* of your higher consciousness. Just as choosing a career involves a lot of pressure because a bad choice can saddle you with years of misery or frustration, so too the correct selection of your particular path is crucial not only to your success but to your happiness along the way.

Curiously, however, as many ministers have observed, most people take more care investing one hundred dollars than they do investing their lives. People look more deeply into the security and investment of a small sum than in examining the crucial issues of personal security and fulfillment.

The world is full of long-term seekers who are always beginning over again as they drift from one teacher to another. They drift from guru to master, from mystic center to ashram to pagoda, from one sect which claims it alone knows the truth to another sect which makes similar claims. These drifters never succeed. They're always starting. They never finish. They're called "tramps," and are a sad sight on the path. They're so numerous that you will meet many of them. You may probably wonder why they don't persist, why they don't go forward and succeed. Simply, they're refugees from their own private civil war. They have somehow been inwardly restrained from succeeding or fulfilling their quest.

"Tramp seekers" often know more techniques and are personally familiar with more important people than you know, but tramps

---

*   Realization means becoming so fully aware of your higher consciousness that you live in it. At first you *contact* higher consciousness briefly; then, as you develop, you experience it often; with further growth you enter higher consciousness *at will*. Enlightenment, or realization, occurs when you are so transformed that you *live* —continually abide—in higher consciousness.

are very dangerous to follow. If you give these unfortunate people much of your time and attention, they will likely confuse you. They make it difficult for you to choose your particular way and succeed. These tramps often want to pull you away to another teacher, to another school of thought. They continually create a conflict of choice within your mind. To follow them is to become a tramp at an early stage. You will be doing something else next year, feeling that having higher consciousness is not that important. Perhaps next year you will feel it doesn't even exist. Or worse, you may advocate from within the large tramp chorus that *your* fantasies are "true reality," and imagination *is* higher consciousness!

However, with this precaution—"beware of tramps"—clearly in your mind, the time has come for you to actively search for the best means of realizing your higher consciousness. Hardly ever can you achieve it by sitting in your room reading books or meditating in an untutored way. Even this book can at best be only a guide, only a friendly help, along the stages of your quest. Hopefully, *Keys to Higher Consciousness* will enable you to find the means—the right teacher, the right form of study, the right form of discipline—such that you can make rapid progress and fulfill your earnest desire to know your higher consciousness.

A friend of the author's, from India, related that as a young man he searched throughout India in the hope he would find a true Guru who would initiate him and help him realize higher consciousness. Unfortunately, all he found were fakes interested only in his money and, after a few years, he abandoned the search. Later, when he was doing engineering work and other activities in the San Francisco area, he found his Guru, who quickly helped him realize higher consciousness. His Guru was from India and had been living only fifty miles from my friend's home in Bombay!

You will often hear the phrase that "When you are ready, the master will appear." If, as you begin your quest, you do not find a capable and worthy teacher who lives what he teaches and practices what he preaches, then look to your readiness. You are probably not ready. It is a law: *When you are ready, your master will appear.*

If you 1) prepare yourself and 2) are wary of tramps, you are now ready to ask the basic question: "What is the best way or path for my discovery of higher consciousness?"

At this stage in your life a lavish banquet is spread before you. Numerous ways to higher consciousness look delightfully appealing. But you must sample the various offerings with a view to selecting one soon. If you go about the early days of your sublime banqueting with an attitude that you are truly seeking to find the best means for your discovery of the higher consciousness, you will be guided safely through an amazing array of possibilities. You will find some possibilities are genuine and profound but they don't suit your nature; you will also find other possibilities are definitely wacky and not worth much of your time.

Also keep in mind that you are daily seeking to become more conscious. You will find it a safe rule of thumb that during this sampling and tasting phase of your exciting new life you can easily determine whether a particular path or school of thought or teacher is good for you if you truly become *a more conscious, better person as a consequence of your contact.*

You will likely find a number of fake teachers who want to convince you to follow them. Usually they treat you in a manner that satisfies or exalts your ego—your desire to be important. Fake teachers often feel that if they convince you how great you are, you will then—feeling great and important—be willing to do whatever they say or imply. Flattery on this path, as in any other area, is poison. There is a distinct difference between flattery and praise. Flattery will tend to puff up your ego; praise will make you humble and appreciative. Beware of flatterers—especially on the quest of higher consciousness which has so much latitude for fluffy nothings.

A great deal of emperor's clothing is being sold by the yard in little booths alongside the various paths today. But don't be discouraged—be forewarned. Be aware of your joy; resonate with the thrill of your aspirations. Just don't be a naïve, unconscious person. Don't be childish at a time like this. You are seeking the greater values of life. The places you look, the people you meet, should reflect your higher values.

Begin the pilgrimage.

Go out to various truth centers. Explore the main different paths of the world. Find out what they have to share. Compare. Contrast. Ask. Think. Be a humble seeker.

As you seek higher awareness, you will meet a number of the finest people in the world. Those who have experienced higher consciousness in no way wish to limit you or delay you in your quest. They consider themselves your brothers and sisters and will do whatever they can to help you find and stay on your path. They will encourage you. At night they will be praying for you. They will delight in your further growth and in your steadfastness toward your goal. Then, too, when you succeed, they will simply look at you and they will know that you have found the pearl of great price, the treasure of treasures.

As you progress, you will form deeply satisfying relationships. Friendships with people of kindred spirit are most precious. You will very likely begin to form a number of lifelong friendships. You will never forget those who helped you begin your quest. You will never forget their love and good will, their cheerfulness and genuine wisdom. Your new friends will share their experiences with you, inspiring you through troubled times and fair.

Go to bookstores. Buy dozens of books. Read widely. Feel free to disagree with what you read. Feel free to agree also. Notice which books feed your mind and heart most but, above all, maintain your joy and your focus on higher consciousness. It's important to be a discriminating reader, not a foolish one. You have to be alert for substance and inspiration, avoiding sheer fantasy. However, in avoiding fantasy you can also become too skeptical. Strive to experience what you read as a whole person—spiritually and emotionally, as well as mentally. Just remember, nothing can satisfy the unenlightened mind when it's on a doubting spree.

Remember not to spend all your spare time reading. Your body needs exercise. Your emotions need attention. Your spirit needs prayer and meditation. Don't overdevelop your mind while ignoring the rest of you—as many people who become strange do. In maintaining wholeness, inner harmony, as you read, you will enable your higher consciousness to help you sift through and evaluate whatever you read.

Travel. Visit. Attend services. Go to temples, mosques, synagogues. Look into New Thought churches and the marvelous mainstream churches which are often ignored and which have so much to contribute to one who has a humble and genuine yearning. Never visit these places only to take. A taking attitude forestalls any progress whatever on the path. Your path will involve giving in one way or another. When you visit these different places, give of yourself. Be generous in your contribution. Be generous in sharing your voice and your attention. To sit as a skeptic in judgment upon others reflects extraordinary immaturity and most likely presages failure on the path; you are not strong enough yet to make it.

Go forward. Have fun. Keep up your momentum. It's possible that years will be spent readying yourself for your true teacher. But these years are so precious and must be wisely used. Your enthusiasm and joy will tend to wane when the possibilities of higher consciousness are no longer blazingly new to your mind and heart. Pressures of mundane life will tend to take you away from your intensity and your enthusiasm. Keep alive. Stay alive. Sample happily and well. Enjoy to the full the beginning you are making, for a good beginning is perhaps as much as twenty-five percent of the entire quest. A good beginning gives you momentum. With proper study and mature consideration of the views of others you will gain the balance and the insight necessary to be ready to grow most rapidly when your Teacher appears.

There are a number of inspiring correspondence courses available. While they cannot substitute for the presence of a living master, they can certainly enable you to progress a great deal toward higher consciousness and its attributes. Large brotherhoods of men and women have given up many opportunities in the business world to serve for modest salaries in order to help fellow human beings. A number of such brotherhoods and fellowships provide enriching weekly or biweekly lessons and magazines which are precious beyond price. If you are accepted in your application for such a course, try it for at least six months to a year before you consider something else. That is, give yourself a chance in your correspondence courses. Refuse the temptation to be a tramp. Stay with it. Make a personal contribution of your attention and care in order to advance to the next level of your quest.

We've already mentioned the many fakes in the world. They are encamped alongside the numerous spiritual paths, especially. In a world where millions of young people will adore and acclaim rock musicians as sovereigns of their hearts and minds, it isn't surprising that many "spiritual fakes" captivate large audiences too.

Just as musicians, movie actors, and great public personalities strive to find out what people want and then become well-paid experts in fulfilling that great public need (however adolescent it may be), spiritual fakes find the U.S.A. and other technologically developed, but spiritually naïve countries, lands of great opportunity. You must keep your eyes open as you search for true fulfillment.

One young lady wished to know the art of spiritual belly dancing and if belly dancing would improve the flows of energy in her spine, thus enabling her to experience higher consciousness. Her instructor, after teaching the basic moves, required that she dance around the room and then he detoured her into his bedroom. Similarly, another young lady sought initiation from a famous guru—at least that is what he was called. He advised her to come that evening for her initiation. When she arrived he seduced her—as she perplexedly cooperated. She has been undergoing extensive psycho-analysis since then.

Fakes are a part of the way of the world today—in so many fields—so you have the added challenge of maintaining your joy and good will as you sift through occasional fakes to find a true teacher, or genuine devotees. When someone seeks to take advantage of you, move on quickly.

It's pretty much up to you whether you will respond to fakes and challenges in a loving, strong, mature way. If you have what it takes, you will not throw your life away because of the delusions of another person.

SUMMING UP

This is a marvelous time in your life. The beginning of your quest will demonstrate to you how much goodness abides in the world, and how many millions of kind and dedicated people there are. You will begin to find that you feel at home in the presence of devotees of different paths. You'll have more optimism for the future of the world because these fine people are forces for good, are excellent examples of what human life can be. You'll admire them and how they maintain their values and goals while performing their various callings in the world. Carpenters, housewives, executives, students—they occupy most every profession with love and a sweet, kindly distinction. They are generally very good in their particular professions, too, because they're able to bring so much of their higher consciousness into their daily work. Also, their family lives reflect profound idealism.

You will also meet people who are on the spiritual path by default. They're not endeavoring to grow or contribute anything to their paths, nor are they planning to put aside their fantasies and actually experience the higher consciousness. They're on the path to higher consciousness because they find tolerance and acceptance. They find forgiveness and a sense of worth. They often find financial and other help as well. They have temporarily escaped from their responsibilities and from their problems. Love them. Your love is powerful and helps people change.

Do you want to go forward? Keep the aforementioned points in mind. Maintain your joy and your enthusiasm. They're of tremendous benefit. Further, the path you're seeking must suit your nature. It must fit and harmonize with your attributes. You should consider whether you are dominantly a thinking person, an emotional person, or a person who is most comfortable in the development of the will nature. The path you seek must enable you a greater realization of your true nature and show you how to express that nature in your daily life as higher consciousness unfolds.

Also, the path you choose must meet your needs. It must enable you to become more conscious, and to give of yourself in a way that transforms you. You must also be able to receive from your path the inspiration, encouragement, knowledge, and the help you need in order to go forward. Your path must encourage you. It must help you to clarify and improve your sense of values. You must be enabled, through your path, to grow regularly. It must help you to go forward and unfold into new dimensions of awareness, love, and well being. It must be this dynamic. If you're not growing, you're going in the opposite direction. In fact, you're actually dying.

Your path must also encourage your moral sense to become more clarified and mature. It must strengthen your moral nature and not tear it down. Your path must help you overcome character flaws and enable you to become a better person.

Whatever path you choose, it must have the characteristics listed above. If you cannot find these characteristics in your path at present, look more deeply. If you look deeply and still do not find the necessary factors for fulfillment, continue your search—travel on.

KEEP YOUR JOY

As you walk your path, or *run* along it, never let your precious joy slip away. If (shudder) you happen to check yourself for joy some morning and find it missing, spend each day realigning your life with your early joy. The exuberance of your beginning will prevail.

II

ENTER INTO
HIGHER CONSCIOUSNESS

9

STANDING ON THE BRANCH SIDE
OF THE SAW?

Introducing Three Amazing Techniques

Do you find yourself many miles from that special teacher you're searching for? You can, nevertheless, develop greatly and perhaps gain numerous glimpses of higher consciousness if you become adept in the practices of this book. You will become more and more prepared to meet your teacher and will find many benefits occurring in your life from the application of these marvelous principles.

First, you must know that if you're stupid there isn't much hope. Higher consciousness is found through an *increase* in consciousness. If you've developed a habit of being numb in the brain or in general sensitivity, all the tendencies involved in this habit have to be patiently turned around. If you recognize that you're stupid and are willing to patiently do everything you can to activate your consciousness, then perhaps there is hope. Of course, we're all relatively bright and we're all relatively stupid, depending on how comparisons are made. But it's all-important for you to consider whether you've firmly decided to daily become a more conscious person. These principles of higher consciousness have to be applied *with some degree of sensitivity and thoughtfulness in order for them to work. The path here is one of greater consciousness, not magic.* Your ability to be attentive and sensitize yourself to *superconsciousness* is essential in order for you to meet with success.

The legend of Kalidas—India's greatest playwright—always begins with the story that he was extremely stupid. In fact, he may have been the most stupid man in his part of India. Once, some wise men passed by and observed him standing on the limb of a tree and sawing off the limb while standing on the wrong side of the saw! That is, when he had successfully sawed through the branch, he would himself fall down a considerable distance—along with the branch he was removing.

The wise men were seeking a particularly stupid man so they could play a cruel trick on their arrogant princess. They had determined, after receiving considerable abuse from her, to find the stupidest man they could get their hands on and present him to the princess as an extremely wise man, a "fitting" candidate for her royal hand.

They took Kalidas to the palace and presented him as a great sage who was observing a vow of silence, and told the queen he could only communicate through gestures. Previously they'd advised Kalidas to keep his mouth shut under all circumstances and simply move his fingers and fists when questioned. The princess interrogated Kalidas and the responses of his fingers and fists, as interpreted by the wise men, made him seem the wisest man in the kingdom.

Delighted, the princess married him. Shortly after they entered the marriage chamber Kalidas uttered something and the princess, with horror, discovered she was married to a dolt. She kicked him out of the bed chamber and palace. She called him a camel and other such endearing names.

Kalidas was miserable. He determined life was not worth continuing—especially *his* life. He went to the river to drown himself. But once there, he observed that the rocks beside the river had been worn down by the washerwomen who scrubbed and pounded the clothes on the stones of the bank. Kalidas hesitated a moment in his desire for oblivion and studied the hollows worn in the stone banks by the washerwomen.

"If merely washing clothes can wear down something as hard as stone, surely my thick, numb, stupid mind can also be worn through," he said.

Kalidas prayed that this possibility be so. He prayed to the Lord, thinking of the Lord as his divine mother. She appeared to him and bestowed a blessing on his thick head. His stammering tongue was freed, his mind became clear, and his deep heart became unblocked. He became the most eloquent and brilliant poet in Indian history. Kalidas is considered the Shakespeare of India.

Worth thinking about, isn't it? A man who couldn't saw the branch off a tree intelligently became legendary for the subtlety of his mind.

The three techniques that follow in the next chapters are, or can be, of extraordinary value. They awaken consciousness. They release inner potential. They will also brighten your life. From this moment, you need never be bored or have idle time in which you cannot think of anything to do. These three techniques are fascinating to practice. They work in harmony with one another and they can also be practiced separately, as you wish.

There are thousands of specialized techniques which can help a person become more conscious and ultimately discover the higher consciousness within. However, a study of the wide variety of techniques and disciplines will reveal they have much in common with these three excellent practices, which you are about to know. Adherents of most every path practice these techniques in one form or another. Adepts in western mysticism, in metaphysics, and in most all schools of thought in the Western world, as well as masters of Eastern philosophies, including yoga and Zen, focus with particular favor on the three practices in Chapters 10, 11, and 12.

Bear in mind, as you prepare to raise your consciousness with the great techniques ahead, all adepts would urge that no method should become more important to you than your goal. Your method is only your means toward higher consciousness. Methods are not meant to be more than the means. Many Zen advocates, for example, urge that since the mind is ignorant to begin with, the mind must be silenced through paradox or by some other "mind-bypassing" means. The Zen student strives to stop the misperceptions and the distortions which his or her mind regularly creates through its ignorance. Other schools of thought generally say that while the mind is ignorant and generally distorts any particular technique, it would be better that the mind be given some food, some reason or some idea of what it's doing, so that it might cooperate toward a transcendent process which leads to higher consciousness. So, some methods strive to directly calm the mind while others engross and concentrate the mind. Many wondrous levels of awareness become available when either approach is practiced well.

The three techniques in Chapters 10, 11, and 12 comprise what is formally called *kriya yoga* but you will find similar practices under different names throughout the world. Many teachers consider kriya yoga a sublime preparation, clearing the way for an aspirant to enter into a successful relationship with a qualified teacher. On the other hand, some gurus and masters, when they make the acquaintance of their new and beloved student, require him or her to practice these three steps for five or more years. Mastery of these three practices assures a relative ease in the discovery and consolidation of one's life in higher consciousness.

Please note that the term kriya yoga has been used to refer to other practices as well as those which follow. To a few million people, kriya yoga is primarily the series of techniques which involve directing *life force*, or *prana*, up and down specific passages in the spine until body, mind, and emotions are so calm and pure that higher consciousness can be perceived and entered into. Or, more appropriately, that the higher consciousness may descend throughout the individual's faculties without being blocked, distorted, or limited. The term kriya yoga is also popularly used in ways that will seem so bizarre as to make you laugh, or in other ways so strange as to raise eyebrows in perplexity. Since the word *kriya* comes from the Sanskrit root word meaning *action*, many teachers feel free to call any actions they dream up, kriya yoga, or "kriya kriya," or "kriya-robics."

As you practice these three exquisite techniques, please apply them as specifically as possible to your daily life. Use each day to develop in your practice of each one. Please do not allow past destructive habits to dominate these new, life-enriching tendencies. Consider each technique as if you're hearing it for the first time. Apply yourself as never before to the benefits that each chapter yields.

10

SELF-DISCIPLINE

When you say you'll be there at eight a.m., be there at eight a.m.

When you say, "No, thank you, I don't wish dessert," mean it and keep your word.

When you tell someone, "You can count on me, I'll be there," then be there.

When you say the job will be ready at two o'clock, be sure and have it ready at two o'clock.

When you say the project will cost fifty dollars, don't expect to jack the price up to three hundred dollars while maintaining your sense of well being. Mean fifty dollars. If you don't know how much a job is going to cost, or how much time it will take, say so. Don't hurt other people through misinforming them. The world is suffering enough as it is from gross misinformation.

Until we can do what we decide to do, until we can be true to our own word, we're a mess inside. We're stress victims and stress is the number one killer in the United States. It's said to be the principal contributor to heart disease, cancer, and self-destructive behavior. A good part of stress is due to lack of trust—living in fear of the harm that strangers and acquaintances alike may do to you. At the same time you may feel tremendous guilt feelings for behaving badly and taking advantage of acquaintances and strangers. It's vitally important, not only for peace of mind but also for greater success in your life, to *say what you mean and mean what you say.*

"Meaning what you say" doesn't mean you need to become a fanatic, nor that there won't be exceptional times when extreme circumstances may prevent you from fulfilling your resolve. However, these occasional lapses must be very rare and few in your lifetime. Note also, it is possible to be constructive and avoid harming others unnecessarily, even in extraordinary circumstances. Recently, a reservations clerk for a large airline received a phone call. The man said, "I'm very sorry. I won't be able to keep my reservation and fly to New York this morning. You see, my house has just burned down and I have to look after a large number of details. But I just wanted to let you know I won't be able to come today. Please make my seat available to someone else." Something else of great significance interrupted this man but he kept in mind that he had made a commitment and he tried to deal with that commitment as fully and honorably as he could. He had learned the lesson of self-discipline.

Are you ready for the excitement of a challenge? You can meet this challenge at home and in your office. Further, you will gain immense satisfaction every time you successfully meet *the challenge of self-discipline.*

When you determine to go jogging or exercising, do it! When you make up your mind to improve your life in any area, get at it. Self-discipline will enable you to achieve benefit and fulfillment which you cannot realize by any other means.

When you start to practice self-discipline, you determine that you have yielded to willy-nilly circumstances long enough.

SELF-DISCIPLINE TECHNIQUE

Stand before a mirror. Look deeply into your own eyes and then read the thought-transforming passage below out loud to yourself. Look into your eyes with love, concentration, and good will for yourself. Do not strain or try to be fierce. Instead, focus on your own eyes with discipline and your very best wishes. Look into your eyes after you say each sentence and clearly consider the meaning of each of these intentions. Feel free to pause as long as you like between each of these sentences. You may wish to repeat one of them several times before going on. You may also wish to read through the passage from your easy chair or during a break in your office activity. However, it is best to begin the day before your mirror and have a deeply meaningful focus on self-discipline.

"No more! will random events dominate or tyrannize my life! To my utmost I'm going to have the discipline to carry through with all my commitments. I will keep the appointments I make. The ideas which I have chosen to incorporate will actually be incorporated. When I say I'm going to rest, I will rest. I've decided to be a more loving person so I'm going to give of myself. I'm going to pay more attention to my loved ones. When I commit myself financially, my word is good. When I make an error or fall short, I will face what I've done and do my level best to make amends. Furthermore, I will do something extra just to underscore the intensity with which I seek to be in control of my life. As of this moment, in every circumstance, I will be a person who can be counted on. I will not let others down. I will not let myself down.

"Similarly with this physical body. I'm going to train it to be helpful in my life. I'm not going to let its weakness or laziness dominate the important things in my life. My body is an important part of my overall being. I recognize its importance and will keep it well and fit. At the same time I require my body to be still when I want it to be still and vigorous when I choose to be active.

"Furthermore, I'm going to practice these three techniques: a) self-discipline; b) introspection; and c) devotion. I'm going to read them, study them, and, when I choose, I'm going to practice them often, and well. I'm not going to allow outward circumstances, *in any way,* to tyrannize me or keep me from the goals I have chosen, the path I have selected. Enough is enough! I am now and henceforth responsible and in charge of this life, and I appreciate the power within me to develop and richly enjoy self-discipline and its benefits."

In your self-discipline you'll be a most refreshing person to know. You will also find yourself becoming more conscious, with added vitality and magnetic personality. Also, please note, you can practice self-discipline any time—night or day. Please remember also to be good to yourself and not make unfair demands on yourself or your body. Have good will for yourself and all concerned. The clue is to be a constructive person and not a destructive one.

REFLECTION

My thoughts uplift.
My heart is loyal.
My words are true.
You can count on me.

11

INTROSPECTION

[You can learn a great deal about life by studying it. There is a perfect subject for study—you. The more you understand yourself, the more you will be able to understand other people. The more you deal with the variables within yourself, the more you can become a true friend to other people. Self-mastery is based on three principles —self-discipline, introspection, and devotion—and it is very much developed in this second technique called introspection, or self-study.]

By practice of introspection, we mean taking five or ten minutes each day to study yourself. *You will find it very interesting.* You will often be amazed at what is going on inside you.

To practice introspection, use self-discipline! That is, choose ten minutes in the evening before bed, or perhaps in the morning before you go to work. Choose an introspection time and keep it. You will shortly find that you love the experience; and the added efficiency and clarity in your life will convince you how important your introspection time is. Some of the greatest delights of your day will occur during this introspection practice.

THE TECHNIQUE OF INTROSPECTION

Sit comfortably. Relax. For the purpose of describing this technique, let us say you are practicing introspection in the evening. Evening is often the best time but you may have a different preferred time for very good reasons. Take two or three deep breaths which will help to harmonize your life force and enable a greater sense of harmony between your body, life force, emotions, and thoughts.

Now simply recall, as clearly as you can, the day which you have just completed. Recall, think back, to when you awoke. Consider how you got out of bed. Think of your sequence in washing your body and brushing your teeth, in detail. If you were listening to the radio, what songs were played? And in what sequence did they occur? Recall dressing. For instance, what socks did you choose today? Which foot did you dress first? What did the socks feel like—both as you were putting them on and as you continued dressing? What were you thinking while you dressed? What was happening around you as you dressed? Were airplanes overhead? Could you hear the birds? Could you smell the pancakes? (Or were the pancakes your responsibility this morning?) Remember the sizzle of the butter? The sound of clinking glasses?

You get the idea. Recall as vividly as if you were producing a movie. Recall vividly, from awakening this morning, all the events and experiences of your day. Make your day's "film clip" as accurate as you can.

When you have spent ten minutes at this practice, put the film clip aside, even if you were only able to recall a few minutes of your day, or even if you recalled so slowly and thoroughly that your reflection period barely covered five of those waking minutes this morning.

Do the above first phase of the introspection technique for a week.

Do in Class – 3"

SECOND WEEK

Now, as you sit in self-study each evening, strive to move the film clip of your day smoothly and fluently. Strive to see your entire day from early morning to the present time within five to seven minutes! You do have the ability. It is possible. You can recall vividly, and in detail, as you view an eighteen to twenty-four hour period. Mental time is different from physical time. You'll be amazed that you can, through practice, develop the capacity to see a continuous sequence of your day rolling easily from one event to another. You can observe the play of your thoughts as well as the events of your activities in the outer world. Let the continuous sequence of your day pleasantly, and sometimes unpleasantly, roll past your attention. Many insights and much contentment start to occur as you develop this ability to observe yourself in a calm, objective way.

Practice this condensed, daily movie each day for a week, or take longer if you wish.

Some people have difficulty visualizing but it is still possible to practice introspection by recalling the feelings, thoughts, the sounds of your day. Recall your words and conversations. Remember the nonsense sounds, the machinery, all the sounds of bustle and activity in their sequence. Recalling your day in a non-visual way will give you the same benefits as if you were keenly visualizing the picture movie.

THIRD WEEK

Relax and do your deep breathing. Now you are getting into the nitty-gritty. Many of the benefits of introspection will become apparent to you this week. Let your day's movie roll. Be attentive. Now, notice. When you see something you particularly approve of in your film clip, stop the film, suspend it temporarily. Holding the excellent event before your mind, tell yourself something like this: "Yes, I like the way I behaved there. That is the way I wish to speak in the future. That is the way I would like to handle that situation each time it comes up. I like what was done there."

Then, having noted this indication of goodness, and your growth, let the film start again. Stop it each time you see something you have done which makes you happy. Also notice the times that you withheld speaking a word that would hurt another, or withheld a resentful action. Stop the film at each point and notice each part of the movie where you are particularly happy with your conduct.

Proceed in this manner, stopping the film and clearly noticing your good points. Let this practice become automatic. At first it's a little tricky stopping and starting the film clip, but within three or four days you will likely have the hang of it.

FOURTH WEEK

Now you can really make huge gains in creating the kind of life that you want. Now you can much more easily become the person you yearn to be.

At this time, sit comfortably, take your deep breaths, and let the film roll. Enjoy it in vivid detail as it moves effortlessly through your day. Remember to stop the film wherever you particularly like your conduct, where you've said words that proved constructive to other people, when you handled a difficult situation in a manner that was particularly beneficial to all concerned, noting where you stood up for your rights or your values, or where you successfully closed the deal, or happened to be at the right place at the right time. Note each of these as you go through your day.

But, also, stop the film whenever you see yourself performing in a way *that you don't like.* Wherever you're unhappy with what you said or did, wherever you don't like or approve of your underlying feelings or motives, stop the film. Pause and reflect: "I don't like the way I behaved there. I'm not happy with the way I spoke. I certainly wouldn't like to do that again."

With the film pausing but ready to roll on when you say the word, take time to consider for a moment: "What would I rather do? What would have been better for me to say? How could I have handled that better? More importantly, how would I like to handle that next time? What would be a better way to deal with this situation if it comes up again?"

Raise these questions and determine how you'll behave next time, what you will choose to do if given another opportunity. Then you can edit your film. Consciously consider what you will do in the future. What is the ideal conduct? What is the best way to handle this situation if given another chance? Mentally conceive of this, visualize it. Have the feelings now that you would like to have at that time. You can generate a new attitude and a new way of being at the ready for the next chance.

When you have clearly visualized and felt the new ideal behavior that you would prefer to express at the next opportunity, discard the old piece of that movie, the part you don't like. Throw it on your cutting room floor, put it in the trash. If you've learned the lesson of that unpleasant film clip, benefit by it and throw it away. You don't need it anymore. You've been willing to learn from it. You've studied it. You faced the pangs of conscience, or fear or doubt. You have learned. You've done your part.

You may also, at this point, clearly see what you can do to make amends, or to whom you should apologize on the morrow.

Now, go on with your movie. Let the film roll again. As the film rolls, stop it at the good points. Notice them. Clarify them. But also, love yourself enough to stop at the unpleasant points too. You can change them now, here in your easy chair. You *can* create a more ideal you. You can avoid so much suffering and continual rejection if you will study your life.

When you become an expert at this practice you can rapidly accelerate your opportunities for success. Instead of dragging through life, learning only through trial and error, you can easily redirect your consciousness in a short time by becoming more conscious and aware. You can enrich every other area of your life. Furthermore, you'll become a more thoughtful person. You won't forget the good parts of your day, nor the good done you by others so constantly.

The question may occur, "What if I, in the safety of my easy chair, create a new section in my film clip—a new way that I'd ideally wish to behave—but then I go out into that situation again in a few days only to find I fall back on my same old ways, ways I disapprove of, ways I thought I had conquered?"

Don't be discouraged. Keep in mind that as you do this practice you are truly changing your tendencies. Remember how powerful tendencies are? When you find that one period of introspection has not changed an old, deeply ingrained habit, simply determine to keep up the practice one day at a time, until this new state of being becomes your tendency, becomes your habit.

As you view your film clip and recall your most recent failure, you will also gain more insights about the true nature of the problem and more specific information about how to form the new ideal more clearly and effectively. You may also be amazed how quickly new tendencies that you have consciously and lovingly chosen can root out and forever put aside old tendencies, however entrenched. Have good will for yourself and hang in there. You are studying one of the most important subjects in the universe—your life.

We now know two of the three great techniques: self-discipline and introspection. The third great technique follows.

REFLECTION

I witness my life and wonder:
Is my Self the viewer or creator?

12

DEVOTION

This practice is probably the most beautiful, especially if you have a religious nature. But even if you don't, there is something wondrous to be gained. This great technique is called devotion to the spirit in all. It is extremely important to understand the two vital aspects of this term:

a) Devotion itself, and b) Spirit.

DEVOTION

Let's first look at devotion. The first component of devotion is love. Love is primarily self-giving—giving yourself to your beloved, through feelings, thoughts, and deeds. So, devotion involves giving of yourself, loyally and with deep affection.

The second principal component of devotion is humility—humbling yourself before your beloved. Devotion, in the sense of our special technique, is to love and consciously humble yourself before the beloved Spirit.

A person practicing this form of devotion strives daily to let go of pride and arrogance—and give of the self. In pride and arrogance we are unable to give love. We are so engrossed in our own thoughts and attainments that we have no love to spare. Or, we can be so engrossed in our own frustrations and fears that we have no love to give. In either case, our attention is concentrated on our personal feelings.

In using this practice of devotion we can, if we put away our arrogance, learn something from the consciousness, or spirit, dwelling within everyone. We can also, in an attitude of devotion, learn from the events of our lives. We can know our world more deeply, too. We can gaze more clearly into the heavens; we can see more wisely into the atom. There is much a humble person can learn looking out in any direction.

Indeed, most scientific discoveries have occurred when a dedicated human being put aside arrogance or the presumptions of archaic knowledge to behold more accurately than any man or woman before some basic truth of nature. Isaac Newton saw an apple falling and beheld the simple phenomenon with such "devotion" that he discovered the theory of gravity. It's hard to believe he was the first man in thousands of years to see this common act of nature so penetratingly.

Copernicus and Galileo looked at the heavens with fascination —and without bias; they saw what the sun and earth were actually doing to one another. (The sun wasn't going around the earth; the earth and other planets were, in fact, going around the sun—and Mars wasn't really going backwards at times.)

Yoga masters often say, "Why do we try to rape Mother Nature, wresting gold and other valuable things from her, when, if we would just love her, she would readily show us her secrets?"

You will find a common thread moving through the lives of all our great creators, inventors, composers. While they may have various problems and hangups, at the time of creation they are as humble as young children—keenly receptive and extremely appreciative. And they give themselves *devotedly* to their work.

SPIRIT

But devotion is only the first aspect of this great technique. The whole practice is called "devotion to the spirit in every form." By spirit is meant conscious energy, *the life principle*, or *the presence of God*. All things that exist are infused with consciousness—some are greatly infused, some only slightly.

THE PRACTICE

Devotion to the essence or spirit in everything is a marvelous *way of life.* Naturally, this practice is mainly directed toward appreciating the consciousness *within people.* To practice this technique fully, put aside yesterday's thoughts and feelings. *Go about your day striving to see, and perceive in other ways, the essence and spiritual nature of everyone you meet.* Granted, some individuals easily manifest their spiritual natures. It's easy to sense the power of good within them. Others create more of a challenge. The project is to note, despite different levels of essence radiating from each person, nevertheless to note and appreciate—even in a criminal (while not condoning his actions)—that precious essence which all human beings find in common at the core of their beings. This great practice then becomes very exciting.

You are not only striving to have regular, normal relations with people you meet but you are also at the same time seeking out the true nature in back of their eyes, in back of their words and actions. In being humbly appreciative of each person's life and essence, you become a friend of all. Even your enemies will respect you and take your word above that of their colleagues.

This practice tends to drive away loneliness and fear. You walk the earth in an enthusiastic manner, never feeling a stranger anywhere. You have found the key of life and the key to everyone's heart.

Those who practice this technique also strive to value the life essence in animals and all the miraculous creations of nature. We human beings are but one part of nature's great activities.

May you see and feel what you have never known before! And may each day unfold much beauty and fellowship for you in this state of devotion. In addition to the satisfactions of introspection and self-discipline, may you find delight in the renewal of your life through humble devotion to the spirit within others *and yourself.* With these three great techniques faithfully applied, you are well on your way to the satisfaction of your every deep yearning. You are also fulfilling your search for your great potential.

REFLECTION

I am beginning to suspect,
I really know who you are.

13

IF YOU'RE ALWAYS STOPPING AND STARTING, YOU DON'T GO VERY FAR

As you proceed toward higher consciousness you will very likely have periods of doubt. Doubt can be a good sign or it can be very bad, depending on how you deal with the consequences of your doubt. Certainly the road to higher consciousness is no place for the naïve. An observant and discriminating mind is not only helpful, it's essential. Otherwise, you'll believe anything! You will misinterpret your experiences and make so many mistakes that you'll become extremely confused and turn your life off into some trip of fantasy, complete with super-high beings and also a goodly number of hobgoblins.

Some of the definitions of doubt are:

1) an inclination to disbelief;
2) (as a transitive verb) to be uncertain about; to question; to feel distrust of;
3) to have a lack of conviction; a lack of trust or confidence;
4) to be in a condition of uncertainty;
5) (obsolete) apprehension or fear.

The word *doubt* comes from the Latin *dubitare*, "to waver in opinion."

As you proceed toward higher consciousness, you are growing, your life is changing. Set values are being updated and reinforced, while some which prove unworthy of you are being discarded. Thus, it is a normal matter to find yourself at times "wavering in opinion." To be unchanging in your opinion is a sign that you are very likely allowing some deep emotional convictions to dominate you; and your mind is not being given its chance to evaluate, ponder, and develop a new set of concepts which will enable you to better understand the process you are going through.

Many quitters of this great highway to fulfillment refuse to doubt. They are striving to *escape* into a new frontier of life. They refuse to entertain doubt because of their desperation for success and acceptance in a new area. They deny their doubt or drown out their doubt by various means, including a form of unrealistic romanticism. They are too busy having fun to think. Then, several months, or perhaps even years, down the road some shattering doubt which they cannot ignore rises up before them and confronts them in such a powerful manner they fear they cannot escape it. A significant crisis shakes them because all the ignored doubts, all the old apprehensions and mental quibbles, as well as perhaps significant questions unanswered, pour into the awareness of the once-carefree traveler.

In not having prepared for a doubt crisis, in fact, in storing up doubts while at the same time not developing the strength and the sharp mind needed for formulating and understanding new concepts, this poor, unrealistic, and generally immature seeker bites the dust. He leaves in an emotional rage, or his behavior becomes bizarre, totally inappropriate to those who have been sincerely sharing in the journey with him.

Doubts must be faced, not harbored. Of course, they shouldn't be expanded and exaggerated, nor given the freedom to dominate your quest. Nevertheless, any true path, and certainly the field of higher consciousness itself, will not flee in terror from earnest questions, nor will it punish you for being yourself. Certainly it will not withdraw from you simply because you are striving to know and appreciate it more. Sincere doubts are often a sign of growth. Each and every sincere doubt is a potential for greater understanding. While it's true that higher consciousness is a level of awareness far beyond the day-to-day skeptical mind, the integrative wisdom of the higher consciousness nevertheless can reward an inquisitive, interested attitude. Events in your daily life, and also the ideas in the great scriptures of the world, need to be thought about, deeply pondered, in order to be well understood.

The mind can be satisfied in its own territory. There are appealing and powerful reasonings which the mind can achieve, if you are willing to be honest, and if you are not trying to make your mind ignore reality. Be willing to genuinely seek the truth and be genuinely humble in considering your new possibilities and new experiences. Also, deeply study the words of those who have been so wondrously blessed to experience higher consciousness.

Remember the beautiful example of Apostle Thomas?

"Doubting Thomas" said he could not believe Jesus Christ was resurrected and alive unless he, Thomas, could personally see Jesus and touch Jesus' wounds. Jesus did not condemn Thomas or send him away. Rather, Jesus satisfied Thomas' doubts through and through.

However, some people are so foolish that they stop everything whenever they have a doubt. The momentum of their hearts and minds, the tremendous forward movement of their aspiration, is stopped dead while they rummage around with a limited mind, seeking in a generally half-hearted way for some powerful answer. Even if they received a powerful answer, chances are these aspirants would not understand such an answer, being unequipped as yet in terms of concepts and in terms of mental/emotional maturity to appreciate it.

When in doubt, go forward! The answers to your deepest questions will be solved as you're willing to maintain your momentum and *keep going.* The highway to higher consciousness is regularly jammed by those who stop everything when they have a doubt. Those who are always stopping have to start all over again. Frequent doubters, they regularly sputter to a halt. After considering the alternatives of not seeking higher consciousness and noting how empty other attitudes of life seem, they lurch ahead once again.

People who are always stopping and starting do not go very far. There are some who claim to have been seeking higher consciousness for years but, in fact, they have barely started. They stopped so many times, they thoroughly destroyed any aspiration and devotion which they were developing. They have, in fact, scarcely begun. They have not been "at it" for years, they only think they have. In reality, they have been proceeding toward fulfillment for only days —perhaps *minutes*—when you consider the actual amount of their *forward-moving thoughts and attitudes.*

It's possible to be a *stopper* for a lifetime but you won't find success. The road to higher consciousness is dynamic. It involves a continuous forward movement of each aspect of your life.

Just as it would be foolish to try to drive your car sixty-five miles an hour down the road while at the same time holding your foot on the brake, there are perhaps thousands who proceed toward the higher consciousness while insisting on maintaining a dominant attitude of disbelief. In their continual attitude of disbelief, they fail to get anywhere. Indeed, they burn up inside.

If you are not capable of focusing on your ideals while applying self-discipline, introspection, and devotion with hope and an openness, check to be sure some part of you isn't fiercely pushing down on the brake. By brake we mean doubt—the inclination to disbelieve anything and everything that is occurring on your journey.

Let's say it even stronger. Some travel, or at least say they are traveling, while *refusing* to be more conscious. They have developed their doubt into an ongoing state of intentional ignorance. On the road toward higher consciousness you are free to disbelieve or doubt anything you choose but you must make an effort—if you want to succeed—to be *more conscious*. While you might laugh or even be shocked that someone would be fool enough to try to go for a long journey while pressing one foot on the accelerator and the other on the brake, many attempt this absurdity. You will likely meet a number of these people who, by force of habit, fear, or a sense of arrogance, believe they are proceeding toward higher consciousness while totally denying its reality or their own possibilities of experiencing it. Further, these confused doubters seem, additionally, to put on blinders and develop an unwillingness that any of their faculties become more sensitive, more aware.

Keep in mind, however, while there are many self-stopped seekers, generally the most successful people on the paths of enlightenment are those who doubt most sincerely. They are motivated to go forward *in an effort to solve their doubts through verifiable experience.*

Remember also, it is good to doubt *early* on your path. Naïve acceptance doesn't do anyone a favor. Naïveté is a form of ignorance, a form of stupidity, which eliminates a maturing process which is so necessary. Early in your journey develop the habit of paying attention to your doubts, whether they are mental, emotional, or intuitional. Face them. While maintaining your forward momentum, give them a chance to be resolved through your experience and your research. Be honest with them. Your doubts may well be genuine concerns from deep within you.

Your doubts may be your greatest assets—along with your aspiration and sincerity. If you face your doubts and deal with them constructively, you will see the glowing dawn of superconsciousness *soon.*

INSIGHT EXERCISE

At least once a week take fifteen minutes to sit quietly and examine your thoughts and feelings for doubts. Be physically relaxed but mentally alert. Allow your doubts and emotional frustrations to reveal themselves. You may wish to start this insight exercise by first directing your good will outward to your world and then inward to yourself. Then, say aloud, with feeling, something like this:

I will face my doubts. I will learn and grow from them. When I find myself uncertain or wavering in opinion, I will seek greater understanding and attunement. Where appropriate I will seek expert advice and take the help of inspirational scriptures. Whatever my doubt, I will consider it openly and earnestly, directing my mind and heart toward a lasting solution and life-changing insight. I now invite my consciousness to reveal any doubts or emotional resistance I may be harboring. I will examine each doubt thoroughly, thoughtfully, and maturely.

Then, pay *kind* attention to those doubts which float into your sincere, confident view.

14

TURNING POINTS

Another area of doubt is very important—self-doubt, and doubt of life itself.

Since your first day you have turned to others and to your world in general in the confidence they will provide what you want. Your needs were first met by your parents; and as you grew your needs were met by friends, teachers, employers, and, in time, perhaps a marriage partner. Somehow your situation changed from being quite a dependent, "taking" little creature into one who learned, from example, to become a progressively more giving person. Perhaps you are now grown and have little children depending on you; the whole process has started again.

Whatever our age, we tend to count on the world to provide our needs and satisfy us. Not only must it feed us, but it should entertain us as well.

But!—perhaps the economy declines. You lose your job and perhaps the means to pay your rent or keep your car. Or, people who used to make you happy have their own problems now and somehow they're not such fun to be with anymore. Or, perhaps you were playing a sport that gave you a lot of satisfaction and adulation. Suddenly something went wrong. You broke your arm, your hip. Not only do you have lots of pain, but your need for enjoyment of that sport is not capable of being satisfied. Especially is it true that your world changes with the death of a beloved one. You realize how much of your sense of fulfillment depends on the give and take of a love relationship. Now he or she is gone. Grief in its many forms sets in.

When your world changes, a specialized form of doubt usually occurs. When something you were expecting from others or from the world is suddenly denied, you will tend to feel frustration and go through a period of grief. These unfortunate shocks in life create an accompanying major problem as well: *You doubt the ability of the world or anyone to satisfy your deepest needs.*

When your world shocks you into this profound doubt, you find yourself beginning to doubt most everything. You may begin to feel you cannot possibly find happiness or meaningful experience through your present relationships with others. Life is no longer a party. Nor does life seem to promise satisfaction anymore. No matter how good the world looks, it can leave you stranded or cause pain. Life has a vicious stinger. In this way your doubt grows into a gnawing, underlying anxiety that people and things cannot satisfy you in the long run. People may provide some satisfactions, but then again they may go away—through inclination or burial. Having been deeply hurt or disappointed, you look at the world fearfully. You doubt the ability of your world to give you lasting happiness or any comfortable, ongoing fulfillment. You just can't count on the world!

Your doubt can become more deep-seated and even more fearful when it is not caused by someone or something in the outer world that lets you down. Imagine being able to rely on your legs for years, only to find they do not work today—and have to be cut off next week. Imagine having had fine eyes to see with but today all's a blur. What of having great vitality and suddenly you're paralyzed with a stroke? Suddenly illness has a frightening impact on your view of life and of yourself. Similarly, big or frequent shocks in realms of romance and career can push you into this state of deep doubt and anxiety.

In some cases, this form of doubt becomes so pervasive people not only question the ability of others and the world to satisfy them in any lasting or deeply significant way, they even come to *doubt the substantial existence of the outer world.* Of a philosophical and intellectual bent, they sense that the world may be (or is) but an appearance, an inconstant reality which their senses cannot adequately communicate to them and which their minds may be falsely presuming to be as they think it is. To many Buddhists—after years of spiritual exercises—the world is seen as a play of spirit, conscious energy, reaffirming itself every split second, but it is essentially spirit and nothing else. Others say the world may be pure energy expressing itself in combinations of atoms, but the world surely has a *relative reality* since when you move your atomic head against the atomic wall, there will be an atomic pain and perhaps even an atomic bruise.

These "relativists" say whether you want to call the world an atomic/molecular phenomenon or not, *it is real*. Relativists further observe that however involved or non-material your philosophy may be, there are commonly shared views of the world which enable vast possibilities of interrelationships, whether each person's perceptions of reality *are* similar or amazingly divergent. Culture, society, learning, and thousands of other areas establish that there are numerous units of awareness shared *in common* each moment. For example, billions of people travel each day, and most observe traffic laws and courtesies which protect life. At every intersection there is a sharing of reality, even in argumentative societies. Most of the time people agree who should proceed and who should wait for the light to change. Shared perceptions enable people to have standards in cooking, communication, chemistry, medicine, construction, law, and even rock-and-roll. So, relativists maintain the world is real, on its own, independent of human thoughts and feelings, even though each person's mind may register inputs from the world entirely differently.

A consideration of different views of reality is a fascinating pursuit on its own. However, the shocked and overturned doubter wants his pain to stop; he doesn't want to explore philosophies and physics.

As doubt spreads, nothing seems to satisfy. You begin to feel a churning fear that no one and nothing in the world will give you fulfillment. Worse, you doubt your own life. You feel that because of your negative state you are incapable of ever extricating yourself from your miseries. Distrust of the world and of yourself is a most profound doubt. As the doubt becomes interiorized, it extends to your ego—your sense of self. You begin to doubt your capacity ever to be happy. You may doubt the capacity of yourself to know anything. Certainly your self-esteem is shot down. Your self-confidence cracks apart. You feel little joy in being you. You sense your ego is only a makeshift structure which holds you together each flimsy day.

You do not have an intrinsic sense of who you are or that you are a significant and worthwhile person.

This invasion of doubt motivates many suffering people to seek professional counseling. Questions of what makes life worthwhile, and why, result from this shattering of confidence in the outer world, in others, or oneself. Too many people today feel their lives have substantially no value and therefore *life itself* has no substantial value. They run about the planet killing, shooting, and torturing other people in the most insane manner. Doubt of one's worth or capacity for happiness is a highly significant problem, especially in an age which involves considerable disorientation and regular shake-ups of society. Also, at this time young people dread the earth will not survive—that they will not be able to grow old. Even the *existence* of the earth and life itself is in doubt.

What does the seeker of higher consciousness do? If your life has been severely shaken and extreme doubt is invading your mind, don't yield! First study your behavior and attitudes. Seek to be, if you can, more of a giver than a receiver. Seek to be more a satisfier of others' needs than some dependent infant. Stop and think, "Did I ever sign a contract which guaranteed me that other people and the world were designed specifically to satisfy my personal needs?"

The seeker of higher consciousness breaks out of his narcissistic shell. He leaves it behind with glee, realizing that happiness is impossible through total ego-absorption. He sees the world was not built to satisfy him; nor do Mommy and Daddy, or intimate friends, exist solely to satisfy him.

The cure from feeling abandoned or severely unfulfilled is based essentially on a major redirection of understanding. *Life requires that everyone grow.* The pressures of growing will build to a life-changing climax whenever reality is ignored or neglected. And these life-shaking climaxes can bring great doubt into the mind of one who misperceives the nature of the outer world. Dependent attitudes must yield to maturity and independence. These highly significant turning points occur to most everyone. Unfortunately, these changes are too often misunderstood and breed or reinforce deep inner doubts.

When crisis and doubt smash into the seeker of higher consciousness, he does something brilliant. He uses his doubt constructively. He faces his doubts and uses them *for his motivation.*

Move forward. Seek to resolve your doubt. Become progressively determined to find answers and fulfillment whenever doubt surges within you.

"If the world as it appears does not satisfy me, well then, what does? This I must discover."

More vigorously than ever, search for answers and fulfillment. May you become like a warrior, charging into the unknown bravely, ready for whatever befalls, in service of your inner majesty, your Yearning.

PERSONAL DECLARATION

If I do not sense the meaning of my life, then I seek to know who I am and what I am for. If nothing satisfies me for long, then I seek to find and realize what will satisfy me forever. And I will never quit my quest—never! Further, I will be alert for answers and growth. I will also seek the help of others who made the search and found fulfillment. I say this from the flame in my heart!

You are dealing with the unknown. Be like a knight of old. Go forth. Find what you seek. Or, be a scientist, search for reality. Be a philosopher, a *lover of wisdom*, and love wisdom with every sinew. Seek the truth of life. Face your deepest doubts and be on fire to solve the mystery of life!

15

TO HAVE A FRIEND, BE A FRIEND

Companionship is an extremely important part of the quest for higher consciousness. It's nearly impossible to achieve lasting superconsciousness by yourself. You will inevitably need help. It may seem strange that something so subtle which involves going deep within your own being should so keenly require companionship, but it's true. Studying the lives of those men and women who were considered enlightened throughout the ages,* you will find, likely without exception, that each one was significantly helped along the way by one and often several special companions. Most books about higher consciousness† say that it is usually—if not always—bestowed by one who has it upon one who truly seeks it. Further, the seeker must prove to his (or her) enlightened companion that he has enough character always to be constructive while developing immensely increased power and insight.

Often, it appears that the aspirant makes the extreme effort of

---

* By *enlightened* we mean those who have not only contacted higher consciousness but have been transformed by it and live in it. Saints who live continually conscious of God's presence are defined as enlightened.

† For example, *Cosmic Consciousness* by Dr. Maurice Bucke.

being more conscious at every level of his being and then when he is ready, the awakening companion appears. As their special friendship grows and, as the seeker satisfies his mentor with his abilities, the enlightened companion then transmits higher consciousness to the ready student who has pleased him (or her).

Are you a fit companion? To have a friend you must be a friend. As you become more conscious, you will find that your heart aches to be a good companion. Not only do you want to be a good friend to fellow seekers, you're frequently inspired to be a friend to all humanity. Your heart, you see, is getting broader and more universal in its concerns.

It's fairly easy to *imagine* being a good companion. Simply practice the golden rule of many paths: "Do unto others as you would have them do unto you." But, it takes deep thoughtfulness to actually *live* the golden rule. Sympathy and devotion to the spirit in each person is required. All seekers have chosen a delightful but most challenging project—true friendship.

If higher consciousness is particularly important to you, start as soon as you can to be a good friend. One day your goodness and your quality of friendliness will attract an enlightened companion into your life. Your relationship with this special companion will become the most profound relationship in your life. Or, it is possible that your first enlightened companion will reveal to you that he is not the enlightening one in your life but a senior brother or sister who has come to further prepare you, guiding you toward your ultimate companion. In order to sustain your vitally important relationship and realize higher consciousness, you will need to be an especially true friend to this companion. You will need to be caring and concerned about his or her happiness. As a friend, you will want to share his or her concerns and labors. Naturally, you will want to make his, her, life more pleasant. You will have to know life and yourself well enough to become trustworthy, capable of keeping your agreements. To be a friend, your word must be true. A true friend, you will hold good will in your heart even when you misunderstand or distrust your gracious companion. You will refuse to indulge bad moods brought on by your inadequacies. It is not easy to be a true friend.

Consider, however, that the state of higher consciousness involves ultimately becoming a loyal and trusted friend of higher consciousness itself. Are you friendly to the idea of higher consciousness? Do you truly have room for this reality in your active life? Can you put the interests of your quest ahead of your selfish tendencies or bad moods—regularly? Are you willing to share your concerns and your delights with your dawning inner wisdom?

Not only do you become a friend to higher consciousness, fellow students, and the awakening companion, you become a conscious friend of all. You're proceeding, as you seek higher consciousness, toward being an excellent companion, a pleasure to be with. You are getting free of negative moods, sharp words, and cruel thoughts. You are, in becoming more conscious, a clear and living example of what a friend really is.

WHAT IS STRONGER THAN YOUR WILL POWER?

Do you know companionship is stronger than will power? It's true, isn't it? Have you observed how often close friends persuade you to do what their group wants? Even if you have other plans or even if you don't approve of what they're trying to do, they will generally win. If they tend to lose your willing response a few times, they may kick you out of their close fellowship.

People have a deep need to belong. We want to feel the approval and appreciation of other people. Many of our satisfactions come from knowing that other people think well of us. Generally our individual resolve melts before the will of our close friends.

How many young men in jail have been motivated by their friends to commit those crimes for which they now are removed from society? On the other hand, groups of successful people often inspire one another. Due to some exciting synergy a group of business friends can together accomplish far more than the sum of their individual efforts. Successful people tend to influence one another to greater success. Failures spread frustration and discontent liberally. And, often, gangs of young men tempt one another, egg one another on, into violence or drug addiction. For good or ill, companionship is usually stronger than will power.

People are often valued or looked down upon based on the company they keep. Schoolteachers and, later on, policemen find they have to keep an eye on certain groups of youngsters. Most troubles in school halls and city streets come from small groups of people who encourage and reinforce one another in causing trouble.

Very often frustrated writers get together to lament how their genius is being ignored. They tend to form a clique of such sympathetic intensity that they become less creative and ultimately they all find they cannot break out of the "failure gang."

Similarly, sometimes a staff is determined that its job is so difficult, success is impossible. Yet, another group of people may do the job with ease and great success.

The lesson is that *behaviors, attitudes, and abilities of groups of people are crucial to success.* Some men, for example, buy failing radio stations for a pittance. They create a new staff and program format. A few years later the stations are worth millions. There are numerous professionals who specialize in turning failing groups of people (businesses, teams, staffs, organizations) into great successes.

COMPANIONSHIP IN FAMILIES, TOO

Sometimes one family has the attitude that no one can succeed in the world and each child becomes infused with failure, usually succumbing to it—in school, later on in career, and in marriage. Meanwhile, a family next door, in the same apartment house, with a similar total income, is grateful for life in America and so eager to work with gumption and optimism that each child does quite well in school. Very often these children end up with happy marriages and own successful businesses.

Too often children's minds and emotions are soaked through with the world-views of their moms and dads. Where the father has confidence and a friendly view of other people, children look forward to the unfoldment of their own lives. A parent who is angry about his life conveys frustration and fear to his youthful companions. A happy mother is a comforting inspiration to young ones who not only feel loved and "worthwhile" but able to confront their own problems and enjoy happiness too.

In most cases, parents are our primary teachers of "what life is and how to live it." From helpless infancy through unwieldy adolescence, parents are our main companions. From breakfast through dinner, in the evening and through the night, a parent is a principal and extremely influential friend.

Much of what you think about life or feel about yourself is probably based on your experience with your parent companions. Generation after generation is powerfully influenced by the way "mom and dad" think and feel. So much of psychotherapy—perhaps most of it—is based on dealing constructively with life while *unlearning* (or better understanding, as the case may be) what one parent, or both of your parents, taught you by word and example.

The heart and mind of a youth are open containers for the experiences and impressions of others. The quality of companionship directly influences not only what a young person *knows* but what he or she feels about the world and himself or herself. Also, what a youth knows and feels is generally the basis of his actions. Yet the youth acts according to thoughts and feelings which are so often imparted from parents.

The breakdown in the American family unit is generally cited as the main factor in our incredible crime rate. Most juvenile delinquency is linked to family problems—often the physical or emotional absence of the father. And, a recent poll of the prisoners in one penitentiary revealed that *all* inmates said they had been victims of child abuse. Companionships, early or late in life, have a profound impact on what a person does with the gift of life. Under positive influences you can cherish the life in others and, holding all life precious, make the best of your own life, too. But, if you are neglected or influenced by negative views, you will likely have little appreciation for the life of another, or for your own life. You will probably not even see or seek opportunities for a magnificent life.

EXERCISES FOR FULFILLMENT

EXERCISE ONE—*UNDERSTANDINGS*

Most likely, the companionship of parents, other relatives, teachers, and old friends have significantly shaped your thoughts and feelings. Also, the examples and inputs of these key people are probably motivating your way of dealing with life—your drive toward success or failure.

You can benefit from the positive help of your key people and leave the bad behind now. Take five or ten quiet, pleasant minutes regularly and get to know the influences inside you. Simply, review the nature of all the key people in your life—slowly, one at a time. Start with your mother or father, and enjoy clarifying in your mind what good influences you received. For example, appreciate your mother with your whole heart and reflectively consider:

"Dear Mother, I love you. When you were raising me, what were your views of the world? Were you happy, and in love? Were you confident? Did you love Dad? Were you happy in your relationship with him? Did you feel loved?

Did you want to give birth to me? Did you enjoy having me around? As you brought me up, did you love me? Were you generally happy with the way I developed? What were you thinking when you looked at me that way? Or when you said . . . ? Mother, were you often afraid? What were your hurts, fears, disappointments? What were the main influences in your life, Mother? Why did you think the way you did? Why did you speak and act the way you did? (Consider numerous specific examples you find stored inside you.)

"Dear Mother, what did you think about life itself? What were your attitudes about the world? What did you think of other people, other nations, religion, business, sex, money, work, virtue, the soul? Did you have deep feelings about God? What, if anything, really bothered you, Mother? And, what inspired and delighted you most?"

Proceed in this manner while thinking of each key person. Calmly and appreciatively conduct an interview with your past. Add your own questions and vivid examples. Remember to pause for more than a minute after each question to deeply sense the influences inside you, regarding that key person.

If recalling a particular key person is too painful for you, don't do it. Go on; conduct the exercise while thinking of another key person. Likely, in time, you will be calm enough to recall the negative influences in your life without fear or bitterness.

Sometimes, too, you may wish to directly ask your heartfelt questions to your mother, father, and other key persons—if they are alive and willing. If you do conduct a real interview you may be amazed with the fresh insights your key people will spark as they share their points of view. Renewed understanding and compassion occur. Often a child misjudges his parents because he doesn't comprehend what his key people are "going through." However, even if you are unable to talk directly with a key person from your past, Exercise One will immeasurably improve your recognition of many dominant themes in your inner and outer world.

Not only does regular practice of recall reveal your influences, it enables you to choose new and better directions for your life.

NOTE: If you were particularly abused at some point in your past, or, for whatever reason, find yourself confused and unable to cope, seek professional help. Be good to yourself and give yourself a chance—today. Don't wait around and suffer; get moving! Get help today! A more perceptive understanding can help you to create a truly satisfying life.

_____

EXERCISE TWO— *TODAY'S COMPANIONS*

Who are your companions? It's very important to take half an hour, every month or so, and ponder your companions. The days pass and your key people are influencing you constantly. It's essential to take time and understand what's happening to you as a result of your relationships. This exercise will not only tend to free you of harmful influences, but you will, assuredly, become a more thoughtful and appreciative friend.

Sit comfortably and recall your companions, including work associates, one at a time. Feel you are calmly, and with good will, facing a companion. Mentally ask each of these questions and pause after each one to think deeply:

"What are your views of the world? Of life? Of yourself?
"What are you doing with your life? Your resources? Your goals and dreams?
"What do you think of me? Of our relationship? Of our future?
"What are your values? What values do we share? What values don't we share?
"What is your view of the future?
"How is our relationship going?
"How can we make our relationship even better?
"How can I be a better companion to you?"

Do you find yourself in accord with what your companions and associates are doing with their thoughts, feelings, and actions? Remember, everyone has problems. Love and appreciate your companions but you must become aware of the impacts—positive or negative—which they are significantly contributing to *your* thoughts, feelings, actions, and view of the world.

If your companions are destructive, they are also destroying you. You may not be doing them much good either. Work to change your destructive relationships into finer ones through your development of higher consciousness. If you find in a short time that you're not making headway toward more constructive companionships, try again! If you continue to meet great resistance, seek other companions and start a new, exciting life. But be sure your new relationships are genuine—avoid a cult of shared fantasies. Find companions whom you admire and appreciate, and who are truly constructive in the give-and-take of daily life.

EXERCISE THREE— *YOUR MATE*

If you are married, hopefully your mate is the most important influence in your life. Hopefully, your beloved is a true companion and friend to you. Likely, he or she is deeply happy in your times of happiness and deeply touched when you are. Your mate sorrows with you in the sad times and struggles beside you wholeheartedly in times of challenge and difficulty.

Chances are you know much of the time what your companion is thinking and feeling, what would make your mate happier, what your mate is concerned about. Even in a silent moment, you and your partner are communicating. You can tell by a look, or just sensing the atmosphere, what is on your beloved's mind.

You and your mate have truly joined together. You are wedded and blended into one another through the love of your hearts, the sharing of your thoughts, and the weaving of your individual days into a lifetime together. So deeply are you joined that your partner can be the most freeing influence in your life, welcoming you from old thoughts, influences, and habits of conduct, into a new shared heaven. In your partner is a chance for renewal, a chance for self-discovery in the presence of a dear friend.

Your partner is your fellow traveler in your personal life journey. If you two are well met and well married, then you share with one another a truly great life, a life that makes the rest of the world envious, a life that people around you, near and far, would love to experience themselves. From your life and your love will come a happy home. From your love and your sharing will come a sense of security and nurture that makes countries strong.

In your love for one another you will, certainly, sense not only your own souls, but you will see in the deep beauty of your partner's eyes the love of your partner for you, an eternal, unconditional loving that too few mortals have ever known.

On the other hand, perhaps your marriage is not fully happy or, possibly, your marriage is downright unhappy, a wedding of your individual problems compounded by those which have been created by the two of you together. Perhaps you live in held-back tears, crushed dreams. And the world seems empty because of your crushed dreams.

With your heart's great love eclipsed and your mind in shadows, the world and society are deprived of your contribution. All the good that you feel, all the kindnesses you wish to share with others, are probably blocked—held back, in your pain—and the hard lessons of your life are burdensome.

In your sorrows and in your longing, you are very likely not seeing the world, with all its possibilities, as well as you could be seeing it. Likely, you are not fully alive to the opportunities that may be coming your way. Possibly, also, the chances for deeper understanding and reconciliation with your partner are being missed as well in your mutual or personal agonies.

Unless you recognize these negative influences, they will rob you of your life. You will spend your years in a shrouded world and never know how bright and personal the light of love and higher consciousness can be. You will never know your true potential or express it freely and productively.

Whether your marriage is going well or badly, you and your mate continually influence one another. Your companionship is extraordinarily deep. You know and affect one another on all levels. Being wedded, you have, in many ways, not only joined your physical beings but mentally, emotionally, and spiritually you are fused and diffused in one another. You are profound influences on one another.

Here is an exercise that you might wish to try alone, and together, in order to enrich your companionship, or in order to renew and reestablish it.

If you practice this exercise alone, simply feel that you are sitting with your beloved partner, perhaps holding both of your partner's hands in yours and speaking directly to your partner, pausing after each sentence to reflect on each important point—sending your love and insight.

And, of course, at the end of the exercise, feel free to continue with questions and thoughts which are very important for you to consider and find answers for.

If, on the other hand, you and your partner wish to do this practice together, sit facing one another, feel love for one another, and then join hands. When you have joined hands, determine which of you will ask the questions. Remember to let the one who asks the questions continue through the whole set. Pause after each declaration or question to give the answering partner lots of time for a full response. Allow pauses; wait until you both agree it's time to go on to the next question. Don't rush. This is quality time, this is some of the most important time in your life. Remember, companionship is more powerful than most all the other influences in your life.

As best you can, appreciating your partner with your whole being, begin:

"My beloved, I love you. I care about you. I am your friend. Help me to know you and to love you more.

"My beloved companion, are you happy with your life? Do you like the way your life is turning out? Do you like where we are going together? Where do you feel we are coming from? Where do you feel we are going? What are the main things that we share?

"Today, what are your main concerns? What are your worries and fears? How can I help you with these concerns, worries, and fears?

"Looking at your life in the long view, what are your most important goals? How can I help you with them?

"Looking at our life together in the long view, what do you feel our most important goals are? What do you feel is your part in the achievement of our shared goals? What do you feel my part is?

"Looking at our life in a short-range way, what are the main goals that you are working on right now? How can I help you with them?

"In terms of our life these days, are there some things I don't seem to understand that you would like me to understand better?

"Are you happy physically? Are you happy emotionally? Are you happy mentally? Do you have good self-esteem? Are you happy spiritually? Are you happy with our love for one another? Are you happy with the way you love me? Are you happy with the way I love you? I would like to love you more and more. Please help me to love you more. Please be kind and tell me, show me, in what ways I might more fully give you my love and enrich your life.

"How can I be a better friend and companion?

"When I touch you, what does my touch feel like?

"When I speak to you, what do I sound like? Can you hear the love in my voice?

"When I look at you, does my love come through my eyes?

"When I say your name, can you feel that I love you in the way I say your name?

"When you are downtown, or traveling, and suddenly think of me, what happens in your heart? What thoughts fill your mind?

"When we say goodbye and have to be apart for a while, what thoughts and feelings fill your mind and heart?

"In conclusion, my beloved, I open my heart to you. I open it to even more love. I open my mind to you and even more understanding. I open my being to you, for you and I are one. I recognize the love that makes us and holds us as one. You are my companion; you are myself. Love me to love you more."

EXERCISE FOUR— *YOUR SPIRITUAL COMPANION*

Wonderful is the life of a man and woman who not only love one another but also recognize and adore the spiritual nature in their companion! Companionship being stronger than willpower, generally, mates who are conscious of spirit (the essence of life) find tremendous inspiration and comfort from one another. When one partner is weak or blue, spiritual strength flows to him or her from a spirit-filled mate. And, when both are spiritually in touch with the Lord of their heart—and with each other—a synergy beyond comprehension makes their love stronger and ever-new. People who come into the presence of such companions can feel the love and are changed by it.

If your relationship is suffering from psychological problems, don't pretend a spiritual gloss and sweet words will improve your companionship. Just as delicious gravy can't cover the taste of rotten food, so high-sounding words of devotion or the vocabulary of life-essence cannot overcome an unsound relationship. If you and your partner are not having a satisfying time with one another, do yourselves a favor, eliminate much heartache, and select a counselor whom you both trust.

But, if you have a satisfying relationship and sense the life-essence—the spirit—shining in one another, here is an enriching practice. In doing this exercise now, and several times each year, you can profoundly encourage your love to flourish. In making these declarations, you clear the way for new levels of love and wonder.

SPIRITUAL DECLARATIONS

Put an hour aside. Sit facing one another. Get comfortable. Decide who will make the declarations first. You may wish to give your good companion a flower or a symbolic gift before making your declarations.

When you are the listener of these declarations, actively receive the love and intent of your mate. Accept and treasure your friend's declarations. Few people in the world will ever hear such beautiful thoughts spoken with such love.

Whether you are making these declarations or receiving them, strive to speak or listen from your soul—your innermost being. Look into one another's eyes as you do each declaration. Pause in love as long as you like between each one. Perhaps both of you will prefer to close your eyes in brief meditations. Or, after several practices of this exercise, the receiver may wish to make *helpful, non-critical responses* at times. (Of course you will need to talk about your problems on other occasions; but the purpose of these declarations is greater and greater spiritual companionship.) You may wish to join hands. The declarer strives to make these statements with his or her whole heart—as an already experienced actuality, or as a deeply felt ideal:

> "I love you.
> "I love you without limits or conditions.
> "I am your friend.
> "I am your companion throughout life.
> "I'm on your side.
> "I will always strive to make your life more beautiful and pleasing.

"I think of you with good will and appreciation every day.

"Each day I think well of you and speak well of you.

"I pray for your happiness and well being often.

"I am on your side in all the good you are doing.

"I adore your soul and your good qualities.

"I will help you whenever you want help and when life is difficult or challenging.

"I will help you in your devotion to God.

"I will help you find time, freedom, and opportunity to grow spiritually.

"I will always share my soul's love, kindness, and wisdom with you.

"My beloved, may your life be filled with joy.

"May your heart be full.

"May your mind know deep peace and profound faith.

"Before God, I rededicate myself to you. I dedicate myself to your soul and the love and ideals we share.

"I am grateful to God that I am your beloved.

"I pray that I may always take your hand when you reach out to me. May I always be your true spiritual partner."

You may wish to add other declarations which are revealed to your mind and heart in this solemn and especially sweet communion. When you have concluded your declarations, say:

"Beloved, I have shared my soul with you."

Then the receiver of these declarations begins his or her turn and, feeling deep love radiating from the innermost self, extends a flower or symbolic gift and begins the above declarations. The one who made the declarations first must make a point of switching thoughts and feelings into a deeply appreciative and receptive mode in order to be deeply conscious of the declarations which are now being made.

Remember to pause whenever you like and strive to more fully understand and commit yourselves to these profound ideals—these spirit-empowering attunements.

When these declarations, along with additional ones, are shared, embrace.

As you grow toward higher consciousness, and especially as you develop in Exercises One through Four, you will find yourself free! Free to become the person you yearn to be. You will conquer the old, destructive tendencies. In your life, companionship—negative companionship—*will not* be stronger than your will power.

16

THE BIG TEST

Unless you make an effort to be more conscious, your companions will probably dominate your will power and freedom of choice. You will usually be happy or sad, loving or angry, based on the strongly-held sentiments of your family, business colleagues, or closest friends. What a strange way to live! So many people forfeit the opportunities which come their way each day; they don't allow themselves the understanding that brings a greatly enriched life. They merely react to their companions much like puppets, with straw brains, dangling from strings.

Companionship is especially powerful in influencing moods and attitudes. Generally, a few optimists make the others in their group or family more optimistic. The optimists have a subtle influence, so others become keen to accomplish and achieve success. Friends and families gradually grow more willing to create a happy life experience. On the other hand, pessimism commonly shared becomes like a disease and each member of the group goes out into life every morning to seek evidence that his/her pessimism is well-founded and perfectly justified. Other shared moods, from exasperation to ecstasy, pervade the groups of closely involved people.

Hopefully the mood of each new seeker of higher consciousness will be developed into a happy, constructive well being which is strong enough to easily shed destructive moods of others.

Your companions very likely dominate, or at least greatly influence, your attitudes, too. The attitude of prejudice, for example, is still a major factor between neighbors and countries around the world. Some groups form *because* of a shared prejudice. Many times, for no direct reason, a member of a prejudiced group will find himself hating someone he doesn't even know, or trying to block the career of a person he has never met.

The attitude of prejudice works two ways, of course. People in other groups are likely prejudiced against any such group in which you may find yourself. Self-righteous attitudes boomerang almost every time, often resulting in concussions and the letting of blood on the streets. Who knows how much these blind attitudes cost in lost opportunities, economic security, and peace of mind? (Not to mention the harm group prejudice wreaks on world peace and loving practice of the world's religions.)

WHAT TO DO?

Ideally, as you become more conscious, you'll refuse to let the attitudes of others dominate your own thoughts and feelings. As you become more conscious you'll break free of the prejudices and unfounded views of others. Becoming free to think, to find out, and sincerely feel are important qualifications for superconsciousness. You will need to be able to stay calm despite your companions' storms. Sympathize with your friends, of course. Strive to clarify the issues which bother them so intensely. Then help your companions to let go of their frenzy or take positive action toward a change in the trouble. As you develop, influence of your group's destructive attitudes—prejudice, futility, chauvinism, etc.—will progressively diminish.

Not long ago a group of young men and women became friends during the exciting beginnings of their individual quests for higher awareness. They enjoyed fellowship with one another very much and their heads swam delightedly in the new possibilities dawning in their lives.

Months passed. Some of the group began to be critical and unappreciative of their leaders and teachers who seemed to be much too calm and unexcited about the realities the young men and women were learning. The students took the apparent lack of enthusiasm on the part of their teachers and leaders to be a lack of vision. Several students in the group became very sarcastic and skeptical of their leaders' qualifications.

However, a few remained particularly appreciative and delighted with the quest. They also appreciated the maturity and great depth of knowledge they found in their teachers and leaders.

As time passed, the regular gatherings of the students degenerated into negative conversations in which many of the group intensely, or jeeringly, verbalized criticisms against their teachers. A number who had been on "The Path" only for a few months implied their personal enlightenment was already far superior to what they beheld in these "so-called" teachers and adepts.

The meetings of the students began to be unpleasant. Camps of "we" and "they" began to break the once-happy fellowship into pieces.

On the night of the third explosive meeting, a number of students said, "These get-togethers are no longer pleasant or productive. We won't be back next week."

Arguments and denunciations flashed into the stormy atmosphere. Loyalties to the ideals of the Path were questioned. Some students stood accused of ignoring their consciences.

As offense and defense clashed, one aspirant who had been a seeker longer than the others, reached into his chest pocket for a small wallet which contained some pressed rose petals. The rose petals symbolized the vow of love he'd made during his initiation into specific techniques for attaining higher consciousness. He clutched the little wallet with intensity. His fingers turned white from the pressure of his grip. He smiled and gazed at each person in the group with concern and love. Unlike some of the persuasive critics, he was not an extroverted talker. He took a deep breath and spoke up. He had to repeat the name of the main dissenter several times to get his attention. When all the students turned to him in surprise, he smiled at them and said, "Well, we've talked about the faults of others. Now let us talk about *our* faults."

Holding his rose petals he confessed a big inadequacy he found in his own character. Others slowly joined in, sincerely opening their hearts. Eventually, the main denouncer capitulated and was able to think up a few faults that he might have too.

While it would be pleasing to report this young man's devotion to his ideal ultimately saved the group, welding it into a harmonious gathering again, the super-verbal ones actually left the group after several weeks and the more humble ones became strong friends.

Yes, companionship can steal your mind away. It can make you insensitive to love and your potential. But, on the other hand, companionship can flower and blossom into lifelong friendships and much mutual accomplishment.

Enough said about the killer of young devotees: negative companionship which so strongly influences your moods, attitudes, actions, and your future. For the sake of your aspirations and your happiness in life, seek constructive companions. Be alert when associating with negative or self-destructive people; don't let them bowl you over mentally or emotionally.

SUBTLE COMPANIONSHIP

Companions are not always people.

There is subtle companionship too. When you sit alone, there is quite a conversation going on, isn't there? Your thoughts and feelings are your companions too; and they are also, usually, stronger than will power. If your thoughts are happy, uplifting, you will be influenced to a happier, more beneficial life.

Similarly with your emotions. If your feelings are pleasant or joyous, your sense of well being will be exhilarating and resilient. Companionship with fear or anger, however, will often make you feel less capable and sap your motivation for fulfillment. Negative moods like jealousy, fear, or anger can easily dominate your will and your outlook on life, too.

A sad heart can color all your activities with a sense of futility and limitation. Likely your mood of sorrow will pervade your activities and conversations with people until you're known as an unpleasant person to be with. Further, when you're alone, you don't enjoy being with yourself either.

Even if your negative thoughts and feelings have a valid reason to fill your awareness at times (for example, the insult of a loved one or betrayal by a trusted friend), let them pass. Let bad thoughts and feelings stay but a brief time. Then, send them away. Don't let your occasional destructive thoughts and feelings become *your companions*. Ever!

Your thoughts and feelings are your subtle companions. Choose them wisely and you will create a productive, deeply satisfying life.

REFLECTION

Is this a friendship
Or tug-of-war?

17

A THOUGHTFUL PERSON OPENS THE DOOR

In being a true friend you become a thoughtful person. As a thoughtful person you become able to meditate—to center in your true self and realize your ideals. Two splendid states of higher consciousness open before you as a result of thoughtful meditations. Each of these states will render you greater value than can ever be estimated. These two thrilling stages of awareness are *the two major entrances* to higher consciousness. You will find it impossible to achieve these two states without being a thoughtful person or a fit companion. These two states have different names in different disciplines but we will call them: 1) The Good Will Witness, and 2) The Universal Self.

The thoughtful person does not strive to overpower or manipulate other people. He values others and considers their lives as important as his own. He considers the needs and rights of others, too. He looks for opportunities to be of service. He loves to console and uplift. In his personal effort to be more conscious he also strives to help others discover the benefits within them and the possibilities of the days ahead. He becomes *incapable* of thinking only of himself. He always considers the effects of his actions on other people. He goes through life thinking of the welfare and happiness of others as well as his own.

A very important characteristic of the thoughtful person, then, is good will. Good will is delightfully—and frightfully—*essential*. It's great fun to have good will but it's "frightful" not to have good will—because you cannot achieve or maintain higher consciousness without it. The significance of good will cannot be overstressed. *Higher consciousness itself is an ongoing state of good will.*

The main characteristic of good will is: *Wishing others the very best.* The thoughtful man or woman of good will bears no ill will toward other people. He hopes for their happiness and would like to be of help if he can. His emotions are expansive and he does not experience jealousy or an inner resistance as others around him find success or favor. He does not, vocally nor in his mind, insult or look down upon other people who happen to be involved with him in the human race. In becoming a friend to others, he has discovered that his good will must also extend to those who practice different faiths, techniques, and other forms of sincere worship. He wishes them success and fulfillment. He wishes them happiness and dynamic growth. He wishes them whatever they need to be the better.

Do you have good will for others? Do you wish them the very best—even though their paths or goals may be different from yours, or even seemingly in conflict with yours? Can you, in the largeness of your heart, put aside jealousy or condemnation? Do you truly have no ill will for them but instead a fraternal good wish for each and every one?

Do you accept people as they are? Do you notice their needs and struggles? Do you actively and constructively help people close to you and the world at large? Do you also perform these services with a happy attitude, with genuine good will? Helping others from a sense of obligation may still be of value but it *does not* open your life to higher consciousness.

Good will is of extraordinary importance! *You can only achieve in the realm of consciousness that which you hold in good will.* Never forget this. For example, if you are striving to gain higher consciousness, you can only achieve it when you have a very positive and constructive attitude toward it. And higher consciousness can only fill your being when you are a thoughtful person who maintains good will toward others, even when you are in highly exalted awareness. Good will is *vital*.

If you have ill will, fear, or resentment toward higher consciousness you need not worry about whether you will achieve it. It will never become yours. Higher consciousness will never flow into a vessel which is closed.

Furthermore, in your meditations, as you do various practices and techniques to become more conscious, unless you have good will for the focus or techniques of your meditations, you'll not be able to succeed. You must persist and allow your ill will, resentment, or pettiness to be worn through until you develop good will. You must develop a steady flow of good will for yourself, your meditation techniques, and the object of your meditation.

Suppose you're striving to grow through religious observances. A lackadaisical attitude toward your practices, or toward a mantram, or a painting of Christ or Buddha, for example, will result in continual separation from what another part of your mind and heart say they are seeking. Don't you agree, from many observations, that people in an atmosphere of good will draw closer together? Similarly, in good will you and your meditation practices must become closer, more comfortable and intimate.

To succeed in meditation and the higher awareness it will give you, you must become conscious, *appreciative* of what you are doing. To resent your practice as if it is an intruder, to yearn for your time of meditation to be over, or to study your meditation practice with utter boredom is to be in a state of ill will—or certainly an absence of good will. You will not succeed.

Just as ill will makes people separate and grow farther and farther apart, you can become more and more estranged from meditation and the peace of meditation. This division creates a progressively greater distance between yourself and the whole field of higher consciousness and a harmonious life as well.

Are you ready to contact your higher consciousness? Are you patient, thoughtful, and full of good will? In the next two chapters you will learn how to develop The Good Will Witness and The Universal Self.

If you have trouble experiencing either of these two states of superconsciousness within a month of sincere practice, study the previous chapters of this book. Become an expert in the knowledge and application of each chapter. In the field of higher consciousness you must develop at your own rate. And, every effort toward your great fulfillment will add subtle but noticeable benefits in the quality of your daily life.

May you find success and greater fulfillment!

REFLECTION

The soul which dwells within me
Loves and cares about you.

18

THE GOOD WILL WITNESS

Welcome to the doorway of Higher Consciousness!

While higher consciousness is occasionally approached in a way which bypasses the Good Will Witness stage, over ninety percent of seekers first enter higher consciousness through this natural maturation, this exaltation of their good will.

You may wish to study this chapter and its method, pausing in your reading of the rest of this book until you've had several opportunities to practice the Good Will Witness. Please keep in mind as you develop this technique that no book can replace a qualified teacher and that you should only proceed, with any technique in *Keys to Higher Consciousness*, as far as comfort allows. If you ever become uncomfortable, simply sit back, relax, and resume the practice again when you find it comfortable.

Also, if you are doing therapy with a psychologist or psychiatrist, ask his, or her, advice before doing any meditative practice. Many who are suffering mental/emotional illness benefit richly from meditation. But some others become too emotional or are haunted by memories.

Now, if you've striven to be more conscious from morning through night each day, and if you have become a thoughtful person with a heart and mind full of good will, you will find great delight in the following practice. This excellent method, which has helped numerous people, is merely a suggested way. You may have a better way to meditate which will bring about the results you are striving for.

Probably you will have greater success if you first read this whole chapter before doing this method step by pleasant step.

Stand and take a nice stretch.

Then sit comfortably with your spine straight. Do not do this meditation practice until three hours after a meal. It's good to meditate before a meal or in the morning before work, or in the late afternoon after work, or in the evening. Be sure you are awake and aware as you do this. Falling asleep will not precipitate an experience of higher consciousness.

Now choose a meditation object. That is, something to meditate on. The meditation object can be a word, or a physical object that you will look at. It could be a mental picture that you can hold in your mind while your eyes are closed.

Your object could be a specific center in your body. For example, the point half an inch above where your eyebrows meet is an excellent place. It is called the third eye by most people who meditate there. Perhaps a better place for most seekers is called the heart center. Think of a point inside your spine directly back of the heart. As your concentration moves in the area of your forehead or heart center, it will become quite specific and one-pointed. You will soon be able to precisely focus on your chosen center. Try both centers and note which one is most comfortable for you, as well as easiest to focus upon. Then again, you may not choose to make either center your meditation object.

At first, you may wish to try various meditation objects. But remember never to force yourself to focus and remember that the object you select must be *pleasing* to your mind. Your meditation object needs to be relatively easy for you to think about; and you should be able to direct your feelings toward your meditation object, naturally and pleasantly.

Words used as your meditation object could be *Love, Joy, Oneness.* Also, you could choose to think of the *name* of one of the world's great beings: *Jesus Christ, Buddha, Ramakrishna, Moses, Krishna,* or others.

So, first select a meditation object. We are all somewhat differently wired and some people prefer to think about an object in front of them—a picture, a flower, a bowl, a candle flame. Others prefer to visualize in their minds the *form* of Jesus, Buddha, Rama- krishna, Virgin Mary, Sarada Devi, or perhaps one of the great saints or *bodhisattvas* (potential Buddhas who refuse to enter nirvana in order to serve suffering mankind). Some prefer to meditate on a triangle, a cross, or a circle or sphere which they visualize in the front of their minds.

Others prefer to think of formless, infinite expansiveness. How- ever, focusing on the infinite is rather difficult to do. The human mind can hardly ever think beyond names, things, and shapes. But, meditation on the vast sky sometimes helps those who have the abil- ity to think in a formless way. The sky could be considered an ab- stract meditation object.

Choose your meditation object, one that is vivid to you. Make it a color you prefer. Your meditation object needs to be as pleasing and interesting to your mind and emotions as possible.

Having selected your meditation object, put aside your thought of it for a moment. Take three to six deep, slow breaths—if you can comfortably do this. Your exhalation should be calming and pleas- ant. Feel as you bring air into your nostrils that you are imbibing a rare and very subtle wine.

Having done your deep breaths, sit calmly with a relaxed body and an attitude of good will. Now, briefly think of all the people you've made contact with today. Maintain an attitude of good will as you think of each person. Also consider, as you begin meditating, do you have good will for yourself, and for this practice? Or, are your resenting that you are sitting quietly in meditation as other activities come to mind? Are you resenting that you may ultimately achieve higher consciousness and have to change in some ways? (Yes, these are strange questions but some people are against them- selves in most everything they undertake.)

Now, while holding the attitude that you are radiating good will out from yourself—perhaps from your heart center, perhaps from your third eye, perhaps from your chest and face in general— let the energy of your thoughtfulness, of your goodness, move out- ward from you. Enjoy a period of good will.

Encourage the good will to radiate outward in all directions—in front of and behind you, above and below you, right and left. Also, direct your good will to flow through you when you sense it well. Let good will fill your mind and chest, your whole body. Perhaps thoughts of things you don't like about yourself float into your awareness. Let go of them. You can work on your shortcomings with greater insight *after* meditation. For the present, have good will for yourself as well as others.

At this point, the main phase of your meditation begins. Bring your meditation object, now, into your meditation—either the word or words you choose to say, or your heart center, your third eye, the picture before you, or the visualization in front of your mind. All you have to do is simply *hold your meditation object in your awareness and direct your good will to it.* Let your good will *pervade* the meditation object. Let good will saturate it. Fill your meditation object with the light of your love, with the light of your thoughtfulness.

Don't strain, don't try too hard. Maintain your good will even if your concentration or your meditation object flies away at times. Maintain your good will and patiently continue gathering and focusing your good will on your meditation object. Enjoy this. Let your good will develop. It will become progressively stronger with regular practice. Let your applied good will flow easily and naturally into your meditation object, or person.

Now you know how to do it.

THE PORTAL OF HIGHER CONSCIOUSNESS

With patient practice, and several repetitions (sometimes even immediately), the flow of your good will can bring you the following experience:

When your good will becomes steadily concentrated on your meditation object, you will become *keenly aware*. You'll feel extremely wide awake. The feeling of your radiating good will becomes comforting and calming, very sweet. In this state the world out there begins to *feel* like a dream. Your meditation object may remain clear to you or it may diffuse and leave you sitting there perfectly aware, perfectly concentrated. The world has begun to seem like a dream— free of any pressure, pain, or chaos, but you feel very real and more alive than usual. Your mind is clear and free of ideas. You feel no need to think other thoughts or labor your mind with other images. Yet you sense you are more conscious than usual. Thoughts themselves seem too slow, or perhaps too dreamlike in comparison with the quality of higher consciousness you sense so vividly.

This heightened consciousness abides for several minutes. It flows; it becomes continuous good will. You feel heavenly. No other thoughts or emotions intrude. You are in the Good Will Witness state, the portal of higher consciousness.

LIFE-ENRICHING INSIGHTS BECOME POSSIBLE

When you can enter the sublime Good Will Witness state easily, you can enjoy it in periods of reflection as well as meditation—meditation being a means of *centering* in your true nature, while reflection and contemplation focus on ideas, problems, and speculations. This "buddhi state," as it's often called, gives great insight for new inventions, compositions, works of art, solutions to personal and global problems. In most of civilization's advances someone contacted the higher consciousness through the Good Will Witness state.

Depending on your temperament and development, depending on your skills and training, you will sense tremendous inspiration in areas which are important to you. You will perhaps sense musical themes or have direct perceptions—remember, not slow thoughts—*direct perceptions* of beautiful new works of art, or priceless ideas for new career opportunities. You might also gain amazing insights about how to deal with your daily problems, how to love more, how to overcome obstacles, or how to deal with problem people. But on no occasion, if you are able to abide in this *borderland* of higher consciousness, will negative emotions or worrisome thoughts bully you or flood your mind. If unpleasant thoughts or feelings do occur to you, you have been shot down from your high state temporarily, and you must once again patiently direct your good will toward the sublime state.

For your first few weeks, it's best to focus on simply entering the Good Will Witness state. *Try not to reflect upon your problems or seek specific inspirations while you're in it.* Meditate, don't reflect. You won't be able to enter the state if you're preoccupied with your problems or if you think of *the buddhi* only as a place for gathering up bits of information. First become able to enter the Good Will Witness plane of awareness at will. Always be appreciative of your access to this doorway of your higher consciousness. Many new seekers attest that when they take this state for granted or treat it only as a distribution center for personal flashes of wisdom, they soon find great difficulty in entering where they had so easily entered in their more appreciative days.

Consider also, while it's essential to take time each day to think deep thoughts, Witness Consciousness is *beyond* thought. If you think you're in the high Witness state but you're thinking thoughts —even profound ones—you are not in a Witness state, nor in what is called higher consciousness. Beginners often assume they are superconscious when their fantasies or memories are more vivid than before. Remember, thoughts are too slow for higher consciousness. Higher consciousness expresses itself in *direct perceptions*, flashes of wisdom, which are later translated into words by the mind. But, bear in mind, as long as you are thinking *in words* you are in some part of your mind, not in higher consciousness. Your profound-sounding words may be valuable insights or they may be worthless, but you are not in the Good Will Witness State.

Also remember that—in being a beginner—your mind may occasionally translate a direct perception from the Witness state incorrectly. Insights from the Witness must be tested in the light of your day-to-day experiences. You learn through practice how to understand and cooperate with your Witness. You become able to distinguish between your flashes and your wishes.

As you practice directing your good will toward your meditation object, avoid drowsiness. If you get drowsy—rather than extra-aware and relaxed—go lie down, or play tennis. If you try to meditate while feeling sleepy or lazy, and do not maintain your flow of good will, you will allow old memories and subconscious impressions to float into your mind. Your desires will also surface if you're sleepy or if you let your mind go blank. In fact, your desires to be great or important may become highly charged, glorious ego trips in which you think you're having a bona fide *vision* of your greatness and leadership role among mankind.

When thoughts of your great importance or messianic mission float into your meditation they are almost always vivid personal desires from your subconscious—your mental/emotional storage basement.* Inner voices and images which proclaim your greatness are not at all characteristic of the humbling and transforming awe which almost always fills you as you draw near true Witness awareness.

HOW LONG SHOULD YOU MEDITATE AT FIRST?

Abide in your meditation ten or fifteen minutes, preferably fifteen if you're comfortable. Then slowly release the focus on your meditation object. With an attitude of good will (what else?), return your awareness to your body. Tense and relax your legs and arms.

---

* While some systems of thought view the *subconscious* and *higher consciousness* as the same thing, most masters and teachers of higher consciousness define the *subconscious* as that part of your mind where your personal mental and emotional experiences are stored.

Rotate your head clockwise and counterclockwise, if you can do it comfortably.

Calmly sensing your residual good will, gaze around the room. Linger in the pleasantness. This is an excellent time to think about your daily problems in a calm, clear way. In maintaining your good will, you may find insights will spontaneously come from your higher consciousness out into your mental activity.

As mentioned before, your Good Will Witness state is also called *the buddhi*, which means *the first stage of enlightenment*.

May you regularly enter this exalted state of awareness through your thoughtfulness and your good will.

REFLECTION

Without Good Will
I can't know anyone—
I'm even a stranger
To myself.

19

THE UNIVERSAL SELF

That's not all. As your good will matures you're enabled to experience something even more fantastic. This next stage is not for beginners. You need to experience *the buddhi*, the Good Will Witness aspect of higher consciousness regularly first. On the other hand, awareness of the Universal Self is a natural consequence of the development of your good will and thoughtfulness.

If you've practiced daily meditation for several weeks, perhaps you've noticed an extraordinary relationship between your good meditations and the improvement of your life and activities in the outer world. Likely, various inner resources are becoming available to you—greater persistence, concentration, clarity, peace of mind, and understanding.

Further, the good will you are practicing in your daily life makes it easier to relate well with other people and, happily, it's easier to sit down and meditate. Hopefully, you have a *habit* of good will and whenever you sit to meditate you feel a strong surge of good will flowing from you into the meditation object. Keep in mind that if you're not able to sense a definite flow of good will each day, something is definitely amiss. A review of all previous chapters, ideally along with the contact of a qualified and *enlightened teacher*, is

125

most decidedly indicated. (Again, an enlightened teacher is one who can consciously contact higher consciousness at will; or even better, lives in higher consciousness, and/or lives continually conscious of the presence of God.)

Concerning your next stage of development—the Universal Self—have you noticed that your good will makes you more sensitive to others? You become more capable of knowing what other people are thinking and feeling as your good will develops your nature. Your good will holds so much appreciation for others that you become a conscious sharer in life with one and all.

The lives of others are always bombarding you, whether you've been conscious of it or not. Now, as a person developing higher consciousness, you become aware of the profound interrelationships between people. A sure sign of your good will is greater empathy with others. You are capable, at a deeper and deeper level, of understanding others and having compassion for what they are going through. You more readily share their triumphs and sorrows. You are sincerely concerned about what they are concerned about, but you don't allow yourself to become mentally ill through accumulating the worries of others to the point you break apart. You are sympathetic; you are empathetic. But you live from a position of strength, from a deep well of devotion which does not deplete itself but grows as you care about the well being of others.

This increasing sympathy and empathy is crucial to the next development of your awareness.

To discover this next level of your higher consciousness, proceed into meditation as you did in the previous chapter. Stretch. Sit comfortably. Take a few deep breaths. Increase your consciousness of good will. Then direct your good will into your meditation object. As your good will becomes a continual flow, calmly view or hold the thought of your meditation object. Witness the object until the surge of good will overcomes all other thoughts and feelings.

When you enter Good Will Witness awareness, enjoy it. But be open to something greater, a new dimension may be experienced. You can't *force* yourself into the next level of awareness, but you can lovingly *cooperate* with it. Don't let your mind go blank. Stay alert and let your good will swell. Be very conscious of good will, not vacant minded. As best you can, let your good will now expand in all directions. No longer focus on your meditation object, unless, as in some cases, the object begins to expand (in your mind's eye).

As you maintain the Good Will Witness consciousness, you

can, through development, feel *so much good will* that your ego sense gives up its limitations!

Suddenly, in a mellow way, before you notice it and have time to comprehend this great phenomenon, you will no longer feel confined to your body. You will feel that in this vast good will you have dropped off your small sense of self. You will feel—to put it simply —*you are a part of all living things.*

Or, you may suddenly realize there is *one life*, one sustaining life, which not only sustains your individual life but the lives of other people and all living things. In this expanded state of good will you perceive that you are *consciousness.* Further, you are the same consciousness that abides in and sustains the lives of others. You are experiencing the sublime Universal Self in the essence of your stillness. You feel that you are working through all hands, seeing through all eyes. You feel your life is beating in all hearts, you are laughing through all throats, crying through all sorrows, dancing in everyone.

In this rare, expanded view you see the underlying unity of life. You realize that, in good will, your individual life is but a part of this universal life. You have become capable of experiencing not only your individual life but *the universal life.* You can deeply experience the source of life, the empowering consciousness which enables every living thing to breathe and move, which empowers thought and feeling.

In your expanded good will you have temporarily untied the limiting knot of personal ego sense. No longer confined to your body's small dimensions, you have discovered your universal sense of self. This experience is beyond description, so humbling and so moving that you walk the earth forever changed.

After returning to individual consciousness you remember. You remember that the life force and energy expressing in another person's conversation or any activity is something which comes from a source all people share. That energy, that world out there, is an expression of the same living power which is sustaining each pulsation of your heart. Good will has become universal sympathy and universal sympathy has become the unspeakable exaltation of knowing the Universal Self.

After your experience of the Universal Self, your eyes become very calm and you see no strangers. All people are kindred, whether conscious of it or not, whether they behave like it or not. You know, profoundly, their lives are precious to you. Even your enemy is part of you and a friend in disguise.

So, with the development of good will and the faithful practice of some form of meditation—as outlined in Chapter 18—you can know how magnificent it is to be a living being. You can know how utterly worthwhile is your quest for higher consciousness. And even the Universal Self cannot possibly convey to you the beauty and glory of the next states of higher consciousness.

REFLECTION

Your heart beats in mine.
We contain the universe.

20

AND THEN THERE'S FAITH

Faith is not essential to your quest. However, nothing is more helpful. Perhaps you are an inveterate doubter and will have to be shown the attributes of your higher consciousness before you will believe it exists. You will, nevertheless, succeed if you are sincere and open to the possibilities of higher consciousness. If you prejudge or have already decided that there is no such thing, then you will fail. But in being more like a scientist, with sincere curiosity and experiment, you can gain enough experience in the long run to overcome your lack of faith.

A sincere person will define the limits of his intellect within a day or two. He will also acknowledge there must be a phenomenally brilliant and potent consciousness which enables his body to function. There is genius at work in his heartbeat, and in the communication system via the nerves throughout the body. A sincere seeker will readily humble himself before the facts of his own existence: at times he becomes mute or dances for joy as he contemplates the marvels of the external world and its galaxy-filled sky.

Faith is the remarkable human faculty of being able to believe in a reality beyond our comprehension. Even though you have not personally seen or experienced a particular, subtle reality you still can

129

receive great benefit from attuning with it—as best you are able. Of course, faith has to be placed in a *reality*—it must truly exist.

Faith gives tremendous momentum and enthusiasm to those seekers who are willing to restrain their skepticism. True faith—faith that "works"—involves *conviction.* If you have faith you move through daily life *convinced* of the reality of a higher consciousness and you are confident you will experience that higher consciousness as soon as you are prepared. Further, you are confident you are rapidly being prepared through the efficacy of higher consciousness and its assistance in your development. *You are convinced!* Even though you feel you have not yet experienced higher consciousness, you are certain you will.

So, faith means *complete trust, confidence, or reliance.* Faith comes from Middle English and Old French terms as well as the Latin *fides,* which means confidence and belief, or *fidere,* to trust.

Often, beginning seekers assume that all other happy people on the path of higher consciousness are filled with faith while they (the beginners) find very little faith or conviction inside their own hearts and minds.

It's common to assume everyone else has the faith but you are going to have to "tough it" through. At the same time, the other people who are traveling with you on your journey of higher consciousness likely have the opposite opinion. They may feel, looking at your face brimming with joy, that you have extraordinary faith and they should be more like you. They may be trying to emulate your faith!

When you have faith you not only think higher consciousness might be a reality, you are so *convinced* you make every possible effort toward higher consciousness—short of any self-destructive strain or stress. Faith implies action with continuity. Once you have faith you won't stop now and then, feeling everything's in vain—as the more scientific or doubtful seekers tend to do through regular rest stops along the way. You will, because of your hopefully well-placed trust, have *tremendous momentum.* You will be able to deal with your doubts and quibbles while maintaining good speed in your quest toward greater consciousness.

Sympathize with those who do not have faith but don't stop! Keep going. If faith comes more easily to you, accept this great gift and forge onward. When you realize your higher consciousness, then you will be more able to help others. You can speak from definite experience rather than speculations.

You have progressed beyond the stage of a beginner when you

have faith. No longer leading an on-again, off-again life, you don't drag your doubts wherever you go. Now you can order and direct your activities so that each part of your life harmoniously enables you to fulfill your faith in your unfolding experience of higher consciousness.

Faith allows you to concentrate on choosing the best directions toward your goals. You scrupulously guard yourself from a haphazard random life.

Through faith you live in the certainty that higher consciousness is available to you and you go forward confidently. You enthusiastically—enthusiasm now comes easily—put forth effort, clear thoughts, and inspiring feelings. Each of your days is built on a satisfying yesterday.

Faith enables you to be unstoppable. Already *convinced* of the value of what you are doing, you don't have to be "sold" on what you are doing any more. While it may have taken some time for your faith to develop, you can face every setback or worry. You are convinced you will always have whatever you need to overcome any obstacle and continue moving forward. In this trusting state, an inner power and insight routinely and observably come to your aid.

Many problems and worries fall away from you because of your faith. Your life becomes more streamlined. You know what you want to do with your life and you are busy doing it. You're tired of tiddlywinks and superficial investigations into the meaning of life. You've chosen your way and have put an end to shallowness. No longer living as if in a small rowboat, you sense the thrust and undeniability of your convictions. Like a mighty ship you seek your destination with confidence and strength.

HOW DO YOU DEVELOP FAITH?

The key to developing faith is companionship. In your fellowship with those who have discovered their higher consciousness, you will gain faith. Because of their experience, and their goodness, you will often be inspired. Their inspiration and blessings, along with your practice of higher consciousness techniques, will gradually develop your faith.

If you can't find the companionship of enlightened people, strive to be with fellow seekers who are more advanced on the path. Their friendship will not only give you more food for thought, but you'll be encouraged by their inspiration. Your faith will grow stronger. Be aware, though, that these *senior seekers*, not yet being enlightened, may often give you a blurred picture of higher consciousness and downright incorrect advice on how best to proceed.

Also, not yet having experienced higher consciousness in a consolidated and transforming manner, these veterans can—and now and then do—veer off their own path. You will have to be strong enough in your determination to love and help your senior friends get back on course, or when necessary, go on alone.

Many longtime unenlightened seekers are only dabblers resisting transformation. You may have the bittersweet experience of becoming the oldest veteran on your path as all your once-inspiring buddies turn away from the goals you share. You will be grateful to be steady and true to your quest but you'll miss your dear friends, whom you admired so much.

Bearing in mind the precautions about senior devotees, don't lose heart. Look for humble, kind men and women with universal hearts. They will strengthen you when you are weak or on a wild mood swing, give you smiles and helpful words when you feel alone or don't know what to do next. Their faith will give you hope. Their experiences help you to discern true from false, successful development from fantasy.

How do you recognize true companions and fellow seekers? How do you know they will help you develop your faith, rather than smash it in pieces?

By their fruit you will know them. While praying daily to the Lord of your heart for true fellowship, lovingly study the candidates who come your way. Appreciate and consider:

1 Are they filled with good will?
2 Are they free of narrow-mindedness?
3 Do they have a universal attitude—being concerned about all people?
4 Do they regard all the main paths of the world with reverence and appreciation? And at the same time, have they been particularly true to the path which they selected and which they practice?
5 Do they respect your path and goals?
6 Are they clear-minded?
7 Are their emotions pleasant and balanced?
8 Are they devoted?
9 Do they practice what they speak about and what they advocate? Regularly?

10   Do they have sound insight, inner security, concern for the suf-
     fering and difficulties of others?
11   Do they remain humble as they learn about truth, or do they
     become pompous?
12   Do they remain true to the path, despite their failings and oc-
     casional inadequacies?
13   Do your prospective companions express peace and joy? Do
     they seem to be filled with peace and joy? Filled to overflow-
     ing?
14   Is it pleasant for your heart and mind to be near them?
15   Do they, with love, point out errors and misconceptions which
     could cause your downfall?
16   Do they demonstrate, in their prayer life or in their well-chosen
     words, an inner power which alleviates suffering and improves
     circumstances?

Study this list and apply it to yourself as well. For what you
expect in a friend, you should demonstrate as well.

Fellowship with such noble companions is high among the
greatest privileges in the world. In their presence, in the loving,
enthusiastic, and sometimes painfully honest fellowship of these
good people, faith is sparked and blown into flame.

SUBTLE COMPANIONS

Remember, too, that in a subtle sense your thoughts and feelings are highly influential inner companions. In our chaotic world
today it's often difficult to gain fellowship with enlightened people
or advanced seekers. They tend to be hard to find unless you've
done considerable preparation, and can attract or find them. Nevertheless, the companionship you keep is crucial to your success, so it
becomes extremely important to educate your thoughts and your
feelings to be good inner companions.

Study the scriptures which you hold most dear and perhaps
some others you know less well. Don't just read them but take inspiring passages and memorize them. Think about them. Feel them
deeply. And, in the quiet of your mind, have fellowship with them.
These inner companions, based on your love and appreciation of
truth, based on your sincere quest, will comfort your mind and
heart. They will begin to inspire you and, in time, if you are particularly fortunate, they will convince you of the reality of higher
consciousness. In being convinced and living like a convinced

person, you will begin to have faith.

Chances are good that your periods of solitary study will give you the knowledge and insight which will enable you to go out into the world and gain the light of fellow seekers. Likely, in due course, your studies and mental companions will also help you find qualified teachers.

A man and woman of faith lives in faith. Convinced of the reality of the higher consciousness, they behave like it—both when they are conversing with other people and when they are alone, thinking.

AVOID FANTASIES

There is a difference between faith and schizophrenia! When you have faith you seek to know reality itself. Faith gives you actual experiences and you have a more satisfying, integrated, and successful life. In faith you live with progressively more understanding of yourself and your world.

Mental illness involves *splitting* yourself from reality. Perhaps your daily life is too painful, or too boring, or too unappreciative of your individual talents and concerns. In advanced mental trauma you, or your reactions to life (or your chemical/genetic makeup, as some experts say), create a mental/emotional world that is very different—and cut off—from reality.

In the case of sufferers of delusions who seek higher consciousness, elaborate fantasies and deep emotional problems are usually involved. While most everyone releases steam or imagines a better world through some healthy fantasizing, the deeply deluded usually have a need to be extremely important. Sometimes they have made huge mistakes, can't face them, and must be "proven right all along." They may crave the satisfaction of being known to themselves or others as clearly superior—perhaps even a guest from God or space, deigning to serve addled, slow humanity. On the path of higher consciousness where so many subjective feelings and thoughts can masquerade as spiritual, and where the fantasizing seeker can often find much love and respect from fellow seekers who don't know where he or she is coming from, a person can soar far into a near-permanent dream world.

These sufferers often enjoy the recognition and their power over others immensely. They say impressive words and are emotionally unfettered in many areas. One gentleman enjoyed hovering around potential *disciples* in restaurants. He would stare into their eyes and intone: "Do you know who I am? Look at me. Don't you recognize me? I am your spiritual master."

Due to his other activities, police asked him to leave town.

Another sufferer was sure he was the reincarnated Jesus Christ and that people were trying to crucify him before he gave his message. He spent much of his time avoiding his "pursuers."

Unfortunately, mental illness can increase in the lives of those who have deep inner conflicts and who seek to escape reality on the path of higher consciousness rather than *find themselves*. Some people use the abstract vocabulary of higher consciousness to justify their own opinions and validate their inner images as spiritual truths.

What people with extensive inner conflicts think and see can be totally split from reality. In prayer, contemplation, or meditation, an imbalanced sufferer can, with the images of his subconscious mind —and contorted emotional nature—"see" whatever he wishes to see. Such an unfortunate individual may "hear" from within convincing but untrue prophecies or proclamations of his greatness, superiority, or world mission.

Because of the possibilities of self-delusion, it's very important to strive to have companionship with awakened teachers. Study with them. Heed their instructions and cautions attentively. Practice the techniques they suggest, exactly and with the right spirit. Value your teachers. As well, keep good mental/emotional companions inside. Nourish your well being with constructive success-directed thoughts and feelings. Higher consciousness is not a path of "Let's pretend." Faith is rooted in the certainty of a *clearer and more perfect perception of reality.*

In particular, avoid fantasies. When you're daydreaming about your romantic quest of higher consciousness, strive to recognize you are in fact fantasizing and that the thoughts and feelings you are experiencing may or may not be true. You might also ask yourself why you are having recurrent fantasies and, since fantasies are often a reflection of inner pressures, you might ask why your fantasies tend to have a particular quality or theme. Very often, too, a fantasy reveals a need or yearning within you which is not being faced and satisfied in real life.

INSTEAD OF FANTASIZING

Instead of fantasizing, dear seeker, labor to be more conscious and balanced. Strive to have healthy friendships and inner companions of thought and feeling which curb rather than encourage imagination and self-exaltation. This is extremely important. Many of those who enter the spiritual path are actually looking for a license to validate their fantasies; they seek to fulfill, in their own pipe dreams, ambitions which they have done nothing whatever in reality to fulfill.

A genuine seeker cultivates modesty and humility. Mahatma Gandhi's daily prayer was to be lower than the dust on his feet. When you attain higher consciousness you will feel no inclination to exalt your ego. You simply don't have a desire to dominate others or exalt yourself.

However, without desiring it, people in higher consciousness often find they are, in spite of themselves, respected and esteemed by other people. Their lives of faith are beacons to seekers of light.

TURN ON THE POWER

Faith is power. In observing the precaution of avoiding fantasies while striving to more fully apprehend reality, you will find faith becomes a very powerful means for fulfillment. When you live in faith you not only have greater momentum toward your goal, you not only streamline your life and are relieved of many inner conflicts, but some amazing transformations in your daily life or career often happen. This is why faith is so greatly encouraged, even in those who are by nature extremely skeptical.

When you have faith in higher consciousness you will be able to direct it to actively express in your life! Even if you do not know your higher consciousness, even if you have not had much or any experience of higher consciousness, in your faith you become an instrument: a directing point of higher consciousness. Through faith you can attune with whatever you need for your growth and constructive purposes. You can know what you need to know. You can break free of destructive situations and habits.

Of course, your faith can also touch the lives of others you are concerned about—individuals and humanity in general. Wherever they are, whatever they are doing, your faith can help them. Due to your faith, subtle energy and power will move wherever you lovingly ask! Inner power from your higher consciousness will dynamically move out into your life and world as a constructive force. New opportunities will come to you. Through faith you will become much more able to deal with negative conditions in a creative, transforming way. Often what you conceive in your mind can become a real experience for you in the outer world.

What are the dynamics of faith? Hopefully this often-told but wonderful analogy will help increase understanding and effective use of faith: faith is like electricity.

No one fully understands electricity but billions of people use it and enjoy the benefits of this remarkable energy. Indeed, most people have very little idea of what electricity is, yet they light their houses and run myriad machines with it. The tremendous power of electricity waits in attendance to do what people direct.

Now, consider this. When you enter your house in the evening and find your house dark, do you phone the power company and tell them your house is dark, requesting they do something about it? No, of course not. You simply go to a light switch, and whether you understand electricity or not, your room and the whole house can be filled with light. You can even ask your young child, who perhaps cannot even read, to fill the room with light simply by flipping a switch. The little one who has *no knowledge* of the power of electricity will nevertheless experience its benefit by clicking the switch.

When you want to watch the news of the world on a tube in a box, you don't phone the staff of the electric company and ask for images to be sent to your house. Again, perhaps not knowing much at all about television or electricity, you can have the benefit of both of these wonders simply by turning the switch on.

Through electricity you can heat your house in wintertime, cool it down in summer. You can have light to read or work by whenever you want it and most everywhere you want it, provided there is some contact with that power. For the power of electricity to express, you simply flip a switch. When you turn it on, something you may not understand manifests its power and benefits your life.

Similarly with faith and higher consciousness. While you may not understand higher consciousness or how it works, you can experience its benefits any time you find and "flip the switch" of faith. When you need the help of higher consciousness, especially insight or your inner power to change circumstances, here's a simple way to proceed:

1) *Find the "switch of faith"* by focusing your thoughts and feelings on your conviction that higher consciousness exists.

2) *Feel deeply your conviction of the presence* of higher awareness and its *ability* to benefit any and all problems, persons, and conditions. (Deep feeling is not necessary but it's very helpful to have your emotions as allies.) Sometimes a very weak, tentative conviction has been known to work. (Some people have the misconception

that the amount of emotion determines the degree of faith, rather than the level of attunement.)

3) *Flip the switch of faith* by asking it to express. Confidently and humbly ask higher consciousness to move and act in whatever situation or person's life you humbly choose. Certainly your good will and thoughtfulness are needed to determine when to flip the switch of faith. A good rule to consider in your activation of faith is: only be creative and constructive, as best you can; consider always the good of all; "do only unto others"—in your use of faith—"as you would have them do unto you." It is especially helpful to conclude your request adding: "May the higher will be done," or "May God's will be done," so that even if your faith request is unknowingly harmful, it will be amended and perfectly expressed nevertheless.

4) *Let faith work!* Don't try to interfere with the process or tell faith how to accomplish its end. Let it shine. Let it move. Once you have flipped the switch of faith, don't turn it on and off; don't inspect it to see if it's working or not. In using faith, you deal with your doubts or subtle mental/emotional concerns *before* approaching or flipping the switch. When you flip it on, **leave it on.** Know, through your conviction, that higher consciousness and power is moving and working in the area you have requested.

This factor of faith is most exciting. At first you may disbelieve and fiddle around with the "light switch," often saying, "This can't work. This can't be." Thus, you send contrary messages to the higher consciousness. The switch is not actually turned on. As you develop in faith, however, you truly observe the effects of faith. When the switch is really on, power moves and the higher consciousness expresses benefit and transformation in the lives or conditions in your focus. Always keep in mind, though, that faith is not a bully. Faith respects the free will of others and if they are unreceptive to its workings, faith will help as it can without violating the free will of anyone.

You will find it fascinating to watch faith grow. It's even more fascinating to watch faith at work. Perhaps you, a conscious human being, are a key person endowed, through your faith, to help further Creation's purposes! You are furthering life-enriching values and opportunities for others in some sort of partnership with higher consciousness as it emanates outward toward all people. Faith alone is a fascinating study. A lifetime can be well spent in striving to become a person of true faith.

However, sad to say, your beginner's faith usually degenerates. Flashes of success and wondrous manifestations of higher power or intelligence dwindle in number and frequency. As your faith dwindles, you may begin to doubt everything. You may, as many do, doubt the existence of higher consciousness and consider yourself a fool for your enthusiastic conduct on the path. Your path itself may begin to blur and diffuse before your frustrated gaze into nothing. You may even deny its existence. Who knows where you will run or what you will do when your faith dissolves?

In reality, when your faith seems to become ineffective, you are likely making some big mistakes in attitude and understanding. You have probably forgotten vital points in this chapter. The chief error is moving too soon from a humble switch flipper into a "cosmic shooter." As a "beginning beginner" you do not presume to tell higher consciousness how it should work. You acknowledge your ignorance but have a conviction that higher consciousness is real, present, and will express positively and wisely in the areas you request. You lovingly and thoughtfully flip the switch of your faith and leave it on.

But, as you begin to succeed, you may forget the essentials! With each apparently perfect application of your faith, you may begin to get the crazy idea that *you* are the *cause* of tremendous results, that *you are the power!* You may, as many do, begin to get the unsound idea that whenever a problem comes up or a person is sick, you can transform or heal with your "cosmic gun." You feel yourself to be a potentially great devotee who has become a worthy "gun man" selected to shoot evil down wherever it lurks. No longer humbly asking that a greater power, by *its* will, judgment, and goodness, please move into a problem or suffering person, you have become arrogant. You no longer ask that the higher will be done but that higher consciousness should serve *your* will and perhaps ill-conceived purpose—like it's a hireling or slave.

The higher consciousness is very indulgent of beginners. It will continually encourage your growth in faith, even if you don't do everything correctly. As long as you're sincere, eager, *and humble*, higher consciousness will be accessible to you and help you grow.

However, if you become self-preoccupied, or try to dominate other people, you will suddenly find (but slowly realize) that *your power has been turned off.* Your higher consciousness will not aid in your arrogant projects or self-destruction. Your very loving higher consciousness will wait until you mature and again attune with it, in humility and appreciation.

In essence, consider what faith can do in your quest of higher consciousness.

You can turn on the switch of faith and everything you now need, or will ever need, to further your growth in higher consciousness will be made available to you. *Everything.* When you need an insight, through faith you will have it. When you need to know what to do next, through faith you will know it. When you need funds to further your purposes, flip the switch and you will have the funds. When you yearn to be of help to someone, flip the switch and you will be able to help. When you're tired and becoming less steady or persistent, flip the switch of your faith. A higher power will refresh you and make you strong. Higher consciousness—with its love, security, insight, peace, and power—will be with you always.

The main problem, it seems, is that people *forget to flip the switch*; they forget to allow light and power to express in their lives.

Remember, your expectations may not seem to be granted every time you "unleash" your faith. Your higher consciousness, which is more loving and wise than your normal awareness, chooses at times to manifest in different ways than your limited mind conceives. Nevertheless, higher consciousness expresses in the best possible way for you. Higher consciousness is one hundred percent *for* you in your growth. It is present. Have faith and turn it on.

But faith cannot further your self-destructive fantasies or desires for exaltation. Higher consciousness will not dominate others nor will faith enable you to use this great wisdom and power to dominate them. Your higher consciousness is concerned about the welfare of all people and will never be a tool for hurting others. When you flip the switch of faith, goodness—at a level which you can only glimpse—manifests each and every time. When you turn on the switch, leave it on until the difficulty or trouble in that particular area is transformed and gone. Don't turn it off with the thought, "Well, I guess it didn't work this time." If you, in faith, have turned on the switch, your higher consciousness will continually move in every area you designate.

We human beings have scarcely begun to develop in our understanding and use of faith. At present it seems there is *no limit* to what faith can do. ***May your faith be great!***

REFLECTION

Act on what you believe.
Why base your life on fear?
Say yes to life, and
Affirm the miracle.

III

PERSONAL RELATIONSHIPS
AND TECHNIQUES FOR
HIGHER CONSCIOUSNESS

21

STAGES OF RELATIONSHIP

Do you think experiencing higher consciousness involves shaking off your human limitations and donning superhuman garb? So many beginning seekers think that greater awareness necessarily entails becoming a "celestial wise cloud of light" and suddenly finding themselves relieved from being persons anymore. Such seekers do not accept—or have not considered—the possibility that higher consciousness has both a formless aspect and an extremely personal aspect as well.

Recently a minister on a fundamentalist TV station astonished his viewers and those of his congregation by asking, "Who would want to go to heaven, the heaven most people talk about? What Christian in his right mind would wish to live where streets are paved with gold, for example, or where people fly around playing harps?

"I would certainly not wish to go there," the preacher said. "If heaven's going to be like that, harps and gold streets, I hope the Lord will leave me out," he emphasized.

The internationally-known minister went on to say that the word *heaven* was incorrectly used by most people. His research into the word revealed that, in his view, the proper term for this place beyond death is *heavenlies.* He said the correct term is plural, and heavenlies refers to realms of life, planes of life transcending this one. Higher consciousness also involves planes of life experiences transcending normal life—but not splitting from, nor denying, normal life.

In the process of life people are striving to understand the world and themselves. Just as your heart may yearn to comprehend what heaven must actually be, so too, human understanding stretches beyond its capacity to comprehend when higher consciousness is the subject. Much guessing and presuming occur. There's considerable hope, and fantasy, too. Only the Lord knows the subject of higher consciousness thoroughly. The great East Indian master, Sri Ramakrishna (1836-1886), compassionately helped people who were locked into the idea they knew all there was to know about higher consciousness, or even that they had attained the highest experience of this glorious realm.

"There is no end," Sri Ramakrishna used to say. "There is always something more. Man is a *realizing* being." Whatever you realize, there is something more that can be realized, something more yet waits to be experienced. A life in higher consciousness is dynamic. It goes forward from realization to realization. Always, something more can be experienced or expressed from among the infinite possibilities of higher consciousness.

It *is* possible to experience yourself as pure energy and consciousness. You can enter a period of deep meditation and temporarily put aside the limitations of body, mind, and emotions to transcend regular human limitations into infinite or universal consciousness. Certainly, this is one of the marvelous aspects of higher consciousness. Free of the mind's chatter or any negative emotion, your consciousness soars beyond mortality for a period of cosmic consciousness, as it is often called. You are able to experience the source of life in its essence. You are able to transcend form and float free in the formless and infinite realm of conscious energy that is profoundly wonderful. Experiences of this nature revivify your whole being.

Coming back from cosmic consciousness into bodily awareness, you find your mind is fresh with insights and intuitions. Your emotions are washed free and clean, and deep calmness or joy easily establish themselves in a renewed heart. Breathing and circulation seem to work better, and you marvel at your body's increased strength and coordination.

Experiencers of this formless aspect of higher consciousness are indeed fortunate and very special people. Their insights and their vigor enrich all humanity. Their dedication to the underlying spirit, the source of life in all, enables them to be true brothers and sisters to humanity.

If you prefer to experience only the vast, formless qualities of higher consciousness, and if devotional, personal relationships with higher consciousness don't appeal to you, please skip forward to Part IV, *Agonies and Ecstasies.*

OTHER POSSIBILITIES

However, there are other possibilities, too. Great possibilities. You don't have to transcend form, or your humanity, to experience many kinds of higher consciousness.

Most people are dominantly emotional. That is, what represents happiness to them predominantly involves an emotional sense of well being and satisfaction. They yearn to be happy, to give love, and share love. They yearn to have constructive feelings rather than watch their moments of peace battered around by chaotic emotions. These seekers are not by nature yearning for flights in infinite, absolute spirit. They are ever so much more desirous that spirit and consciousness come into a *personal* relationship with them. They crave that higher consciousness fulfill them *as a person* and that they will become able to live each minute of their days in *continual interplay* with higher consciousness. Essentially, they don't want to become lost in, or *dissolved* in, higher consciousness. Each of these seekers wants to maintain a high state of awareness while actively being a person. They want a relationship with higher consciousness, not "sublime vacations," however beneficial such exalted trips might be. (Or, they may indeed like to have such transcendental flights but do not yet find themselves able.)

"I want to taste sugar, not become sugar," Sri Ramakrishna used to say in describing this personal form of higher consciousness. Sri Ramakrishna often said that modern people are very dependent on food and have a relatively short life span (compared with ancient wise men and women). Because of these "shortcomings," most seekers are not physiologically equipped for long periods of cosmic consciousness—transcendent out-of-the-body states. Sri Ramakrishna showed multitudes of seekers they could most effectively and delightedly experience higher consciousness through personal relationship—"in form," as he described it. He advocated several profound and extremely wonderful *relationships* which people could select and develop. He particularly emphasized that the form of superconsciousness you pursue in your quest must fit *your individuality*. By regarding your individuality in the quest for higher consciousness, you can most easily develop your relationship with it.

These relationships are called moods, or **bhavas**. You may experience a mood of higher consciousness sooner than you think. These personal relationships are *often* progressive. As you become developed and perfected in one relationship, you will enter a transitional stage and then a deeper, more advanced relationship will be formed. So it goes, on and on throughout your life, if you most easily experience higher consciousness through form.

Again, too, seekers around the world practicing their particular faiths or mystical philosophies may have a different vocabulary but they very often practice and develop these same relationships, or moods, as magnificent means to higher consciousness.

Likely, also, the majority of religious people deeply prefer these relationships to other kinds of higher consciousness. Relationship is one of the only ways to function in daily life while at the same time maintaining a higher state of consciousness!

Please do not feel, however, that you are necessarily one who would most benefit through these relationships. You may—based on your individual experience and makeup—find yourself more rapidly fulfilled through other means contained in this book. But do give yourself a chance. These upcoming, extraordinary experiences will likely enrich and transform your life! Read on to discover the *bhavas*, or moods, that can be experienced and, considering your nature, try to sense which of these is most appealing to you.

REFLECTION
Go Farther

A woodcutter lived in poverty. Often he had no food, no oil for his lamp. One day he met a wise man in the woods. The woodcutter treated the wise man with respect, and the wise man responded, telling the cutter two words, "Go farther."

The woodcutter pondered the words, "Go farther." He was unable to comprehend them and after several days he turned his mind to his regular worries and his hunger pangs.

But one day, during his backbreaking toil on the edge of the forest, he remembered the words, "Go farther" again. He dared to venture deep into the forest. And, he found a grove of precious sandalwood trees!

He gained enough wealth to buy a small house, to buy barrels of oil for his lamp, and he knew he would never be hungry again. He was happy.

Months later he awoke in the night. He said to himself, "The wise man said nothing of sandalwood trees, did he? All he said was, 'Go farther.'"

So, the woodcutter rose and went into the woods, past the scrub trees, past the sandalwood grove which meant so much to him. Then, amidst some boulders he found outcroppings of silver!

Now rich beyond his dreams, he became an important man in the city. He bought a large house—some would call it a mansion—and he married well. Enjoying himself, he forgot the words, "Go farther."

Several months later, he awoke in the night. Once again he pondered, "The wise man said nothing of sandalwood, or of silver, either. All he told me was, 'Go farther.'"

The woodcutter rose and went deep into the forest, past the scrub wood, past the sandalwood, past his silver mine.

He approached an unknown stream. Glancing down, he found gold. Gold!

Rich, powerful, and considered wise, the woodcutter again forgot the words, "Go farther."

Years passed. But, again one night, the woodcutter sat up in bed. He said to himself, "The wise man said nothing of gold, either. He simply told me to, 'Go farther.' What did he really mean?"

The woodcutter ventured past the scrub wood, the sandalwood grove, his secret silver mine, past his gold stream, and discovered diamonds!

This story goes on forever. But the main question is, "Who is the woodcutter?" And will you, "Go farther?"

22

AWE

Are you ready to explore the main relationships of higher consciousness? Then, one of these moods may be a natural for you.

Keep in mind all the relationships discussed in Chapters 21 through 27 are based on refined and pure emotions. While your mind and ego must cooperate, the goal in all relationships of higher consciousness is to get into a *mood*. You need to patiently establish an emotional flow, an attitude of heart.

AWE

To understand the first magnificent relationship, let us say you are developing, day by day, through faith and companionship. And, you are striving to be more conscious. At this point, you don't know quite what to expect, what higher consciousness will be like. You simply direct an appreciative flow of emotion toward your meditation object* or higher consciousness itself. You gather and direct your emotions to flow toward your ideal, again and again.

One day, in the privacy of your meditation, or during a quiet

---

* See Chapter 18, *The Good Will Witness.*

break from the activity of your day, rapture fills your heart and mind. Suddenly, the intense light, or power, or glory of the higher consciousness reveals itself. Blinders or curtains seem to be withdrawn and *you behold the intensity and the magnificence of this very real and palpable power.* You strive to contain your astonishment lest you lose your mood. *The experience is heavenly!* It's beautiful; it stops your throat, for the experience is ineffable. You sit mute and ever so *small* before what you are beholding. *Its immensity is truly mind-blowing. You are looking at, and feeling, wonder beyond comprehension.* Thus, you have entered what is generally the first relationship: *awe.*

People have different experiences, depending on which part of their nature is more developed. Often, light, blazing as bright as the sun, but ever so soothing to look into, is enchantingly beheld. However, most seekers in this state experience a "thunderous silence" which totally calms and stills their minds, as their consciousness is extended far beyond any dimensions they have ever conceived. Also, many seekers find the awe state as the "little" love in their hearts meets the *infinite source of love* and their whole self stands in shock. Light, thunderous silence, and expanded love are some of the principal ways this major relationship is experienced. The main characteristic, in all cases, is dumbfounded awe.

You return from this experience viewing all life and every living thing with a sense of deep respect and a lingering awe. Even the earth beneath your feet is sensed to have a new significance. Everything you see has an added dimension. You sense that the pure consciousness which you recently beheld has created and is sustaining all the physical forms and every person you see. You try to find words to approximate your experience, but it cannot be communicated. Only the similar direct experience of another person enables understanding.

In the days and weeks after your experience of higher consciousness you continue your daily life with an ongoing sense of awe. The afterglow of this incomparable state reorients your attitudes and perceptions. This mood or relationship of awe performs a most valuable secondary task: it makes you *humble*—it enables you to sense a reality greater than anything your selfish will or ego can possibly dominate or rule. In this relationship you get a sense of who is really the boss, or how tiny you truly are. On the other hand, as the relationship of awe develops, you pause regularly to sweetly muse that such a great reality, such a phenomenal being or existence, has lovingly revealed itself to you—as tiny as you are in comparison. You delight that little as you are, amid planets and galaxies, you are nevertheless capable of a relationship with something so astonishingly, enthrallingly grand.

This awe mood is extremely valuable because oftentimes people who practice techniques of higher consciousness tend, like most people, to get proud, or lazy, or even to take the best things in life for granted. This initial, totally silencing experience of awe can resonate throughout the rest of your life. Awe enables you to maintain a renewed sense of humility and thus be even more receptive to subsequent relationships.

Also, in this relationship of awe you realize that a higher power truly exists and really is capable of helping you with your life. The awe mood validates your devoted practice of faith and makes it very easy for you in your littleness to turn on the switch of your thought and allow higher consciousness to move and express wherever you are willing to receive that help.

If you were simply to remain in the relationship of awe without experiencing other relationships, you would nevertheless live your life with deep gratitude and a spectacular sense of well being. Needless to say, after the first experience of the awe mood you are often so totally impacted by it that you should spend a few quiet hours after the experience resting or walking, praying, or lightly meditating, allowing yourself to calm down. The awe relationship is governed by your higher consciousness and does not occur in unpleasant or inappropriate surroundings. Higher consciousness waits until you are ready, not only mentally and emotionally, but also in terms of your outer circumstances and schedules. Usually the awe experience is so profound that while you yearn to have it again, you are likely somewhat frightened that it *might actually* occur again! Your apprehension gradually diminishes in your growing consciousness of higher power and your sweet reflections on the surpassing beauty of your first awe experience.

When your apprehension has subsided and a continual flow of devotion returns, the awe experience will again come to you. Ultimately, awe can be experienced regularly. Its qualities will sparkle throughout your activities and even in your sleep. You will *live* in countless variations of the awe mood.

Awe is a precious experience which will occur only when you have prepared your heart, mind, and body. All you can do is prepare yourself, yearn toward the higher consciousness, and know you will be amazingly enriched when you are ready. May you be so fortunate!

REFLECTION

The wave dissolves in the ocean.
Is that the wave returning now?
Or, is it gone forever?

23

THE SERVANT RELATIONSHIP

People get lonely. When you contact higher consciousness you will—unless you are frightened of its immensity and power—want an ongoing relationship with it. You would probably feel miserably alone for years if you had only one brief experience of what you had been yearning for throughout your life. In your loneliness, you would live like a sentry, desperately scanning the horizons of your life for the sight of another saving, transforming relationship with higher consciousness.

People who are dominantly emotional yearn for continuous emotional satisfaction—not only occasional delights. They need to feel they have constant meaning and value to others. They want to give and receive love every day.

Now the relationships with higher consciousness become especially interesting. Your higher consciousness can fulfill you in deeply personal ways. While the experience of awe creates an ongoing well being and a tenderness of perspective for all created things, you, nevertheless, will likely ache for a more personal relationship with higher consciousness.

It should be emphasized that these moods of relationship may not occur in the sequence developed in these chapters. However, they generally do. Most often, one mood matures into another, and each mood builds upon the previous relationships. Most seekers find it impossible to have advanced moods without first having been developed in each earlier mood. Your progression in these moods means, in addition to receiving numerous other great benefits, that you will never be lonely again. Higher consciousness will not only prove itself a most thoughtful and delightful companion, it will also make your life and friendships with other people extremely interesting and enriching.

Please remember that all your relationships with higher consciousness always involve a mood or momentum of your refined emotional nature. As your emotions are freed from hatred, jealousy, and anger, and your various separate feelings are coordinated into one dominant tendency, then these relationships become possible. If your practice of any mood does not have emotional thrust and continuation, you will not experience a true relationship—not even if your mind thinks of countless, lovely images which it enjoys entertaining. While your mind must cooperate, these moods essentially involve a continuous flow of feeling.

At first it may be difficult to sustain one of these relationships for more than three or four minutes. An hour of a mood is truly a big event in your life, and if you normally have very scattered feelings, you may feel fatigued from the amount of energy required to maintain a beginning mood. Keep in mind, though, that with practice most moods are possible for you, and you can—especially after the awe experience—live in a mood. That is, your relationship can go on and on and on, day in, day out.

You will notice, when you experience the mood of awe and enter into this relationship with the higher consciousness, *scarcely any effort* is required to sustain the relationship—to live in a degree of awe and wonder. Your experience is so profound it frees you of petty emotions and thoughts; all you have to do is nurture the mood. You simply protect your mood from distractions or irritations which, for one reason or another, make you desire to live in fear, anger, or jealousy once again. With practice you learn to patiently ward off all potential disruptions of your emotional focus and return to your clear, strong mood.

MOVING FORWARD — THE NEXT GREAT EVENT

In order to prepare yourself for a more advanced and potentially gratifying mood, recall the awe mood, specifically. You first make the effort to be more conscious and develop faith through keeping good companionship—outside and in—and then suddenly your being opens into the first mood. You realize your relationship with the infinite, omnipotent, incredible source of existence. Beholding that greatness, being touched by such immensity, awe fills your being. The sense of awe humbles your ego, flooding your mind and heart with an astonishment which is exhilarating. You now know, more than ever before, there really is a higher power. You know its reality to the roots of your toenails. You know, vividly, that as small and limited as you are now revealed to be, you can nevertheless have a relationship with the higher consciousness. Your finite nature can have an ongoing relationship with the infinite.

As the *mood of awe* relationship continues you learn through experience the nature, love, and power of higher consciousness. This regularly accessible consciousness reveals such intelligence and wisdom to you that your mind feels infused with great ideas and increased clarity of thought. Confidence and a sense of worth develop within you. Also, your relationship with higher consciousness increases your emotional range and you become capable of deepening love. Each of your faculties is enriched through the rush of higher consciousness which you are experiencing. The awe relationship matures and develops you.

One great, exciting day you go *beyond* the awe mood. Propelled forward through the development of your awe relationship you become fit, and eager, to grow into the next mood of higher consciousness.

SERVANT RELATIONSHIP

Do you have a tendency to dominate others? In the quiet of your mind, would you secretly like to rule or control your part of the world? Even when you have little chance to dominate some situation, do you critically sit on the sidelines, your mind storming with your desire to control—to have matters done your way?

As the awe mood matures you, you will conclude the Lord of your heart, or the higher consciousness, is more able and wise than you are in your personal will and limited opinion. As you grow in relating to higher consciousness, it becomes progressively more obvious that higher consciousness is superior *to you* in many ways. You discover higher consciousness is more knowing, loving, and capable than you are, to say the least. In the humility which develops from your frequent experiences with higher consciousness, you also conclude you don't want to dominate others or be a subtle tyrant anymore. You no longer feel you're right, or fully knowledgeable, about almost everything.

In a way, you come to appreciate being little and you no longer expect yourself to be all-knowing. You enjoy turning toward your great higher consciousness with your problems and emotional wounds because you find you can be inspired with good judgment and your wounds are healed.

Humility changes you. One day, in your awe state, a powerful conclusion dawns in your mind—profoundly. You joyfully realize you would *love to serve your higher consciousness and its purposes.* You delight in the transcendental insight of responding to Infinity with your *humanity*—in a human way.

And why not relate in a more personal way—how else can you respond? After all, your whole being craves to respond to such light and love. You have never experienced anything in life which comes close to being so good to you and you ache to respond in some satisfying, deeply giving way.

Further, intuitive flashes while in the awe mood have proven right for you time and time again. Also, the satisfactions of expressing the greater wisdom of higher consciousness are so much more pleasing than those lonely and often anxious decisions made in regular states of consciousness. More and more, you find yourself developing a fondness to know what the higher consciousness wishes. Maturing in this relationship, then, on that special day, you'll turn to the higher consciousness and start asking, "What is the higher will?"

As days and weeks go by, you strive to realize and correctly interpret the higher will in your life. You find your life much improved, and your mind becomes almost worry-free. You gradually develop confidence in your aptitude to contact the will of the higher consciousness and to forthrightly do it. This is a most important time of your life in that you, through much development, give up asserting your egoic, personal will on others or on life itself. You seek to know a higher, more conscious, will; and you desire to live in harmony with it, serving it as best you can.

Finally, you may even go so far as to *choose to surrender yourself* —that is, lovingly, give over your life in service of this higher consciousness which is so important to you. *You live no longer covertly wanting to rule your world, but simply to be a good servant. You desire the higher consciousness to govern your life in its love and wisdom.* You yearn to be of service to the higher consciousness and to improve daily in your ability to serve it. The joy of your life becomes this surrendered relationship. You live to serve! As you look at other people, you see their essence tenderly and you yearn to serve them—perhaps materially, perhaps in a word or a thought, perhaps in an act of kindness or in a concerned prayer. You turn to your "master"—the higher consciousness—often and lovingly. Always sensing its presence, you seek to know what love and the higher wisdom wish of you from moment to moment, day to day.

This "servant to master" mood of relationship is not for the fainthearted, nor for those prone to fantasizing that the higher will is motivating all their personal desires and egocentricities. The servant mood is for the mature, those who are healthy and balanced in mind. Candidates for a servant relationship with the higher consciousness must have character, humility, and bravery. They need to be devoted and sane servants of the higher self, *while* being tempted to live selfishly once again, and *while* being menaced by those who stand against their values.

In this mood of service, extra talent and potential becomes immediately available to you, and more capabilities also are bred in you along the way. When you are consolidated in the servant mood, you seem to have twice the energy you had before. You tend to be able to outwork others so much it's embarrassing. Emotionally you yearn to feel you're giving the finest service of which you're capable. You feel keenly alive. There is dash, *pizazz*, in your actions, thoughts, and feelings. Your personality becomes magnetic and people who knew you before wonder what has happened to you. It's as if you had broken out of a shell!

In the servant mood, you're never bored and you're never lazy. At the same time you're devoted to your quiet, life-enriching times spent "alone" with your wondrous companion—your masterful higher consciousness. You feel your life has become meaningful and you have a genuine eagerness to know what's going to happen next. You're excited about what this loving and conscious higher self will want you to do. You have a joyous willingness to go to the ends of the earth or, perhaps, to stay in one town, village, or city, for the rest of your life—whatever pleases the higher consciousness.

Your steps have a spring to them, your mind is resilient. Problems don't have the impact they used to. You can bounce back from troubles to engage once again in helping to create a better world. Your motive of service mainly for a paycheck is gone. Certainly paychecks are important, but your *motive* is to please the higher consciousness. You strive to live in attunement with the higher will, considering and exploring how best to act. You seek, through study and fellowship with enlightened people, to become a more perfect and able servant. Most of your anxieties go away. You're not alone nor do you feel compelled to try to dominate circumstances and others anymore.

As your relationship develops, you find yourself becoming more and more the person you sensed you could be. You feel you are living by a deep, inner motivation now and not one that you presupposed or artificially constructed. When people flatter you, you secretly smile and realize they are giving you credit for something the higher consciousness has actually brought about. You humbly give the praise or acclaim to your higher consciousness and with gratitude go forward.

You feel, as you talk with others—especially loved ones—a deep wish that they could know the happiness in which you are now living. You have become a grateful *servant*.

REFLECTION

How poor I was as Master:
So lonely, always struggling,
Bound to ignorance
And its consequence.

In your higher wisdom
At last I find my freedom.

24

FRIENDS

The servant grows. But as you mature in the servant mood, you begin to feel there must be something more. While you find yourself much more fulfilled and successful as a servant than when you looked upon yourself as boss, your growing familiarity with the nature of higher consciousness impels a new understanding. Your higher consciousness reveals more fully as the days and months go by that it loves you very much and is more interested in your happiness than you ever were. Higher consciousness reveals it doesn't love you because you've become a good servant. *It loves you for yourself,* not because of services rendered—however deeply they are appreciated.

So you begin to perceive the servant relationship is extremely beneficial to your life but that the higher consciousness itself wants you to go on, to move forward in your relationship. Higher consciousness wants you to grow into a more dynamic relationship which has greater intimacy—one with more love, sharing, and communication.

FRIENDS

As you relate more appreciatively with your higher consciousness, an incredible friendship begins. Your relationship, which began in awe and then progressed into serving the higher consciousness, now moves forward another major step. Because of your accelerated awareness, *your higher consciousness wants to be your friend and enjoy the interplay of friendship with you. It wants to do more than tell you what to do.*

In the awe and servant relationships, you sloughed off old tendencies and became a more developed instrument of higher consciousness. As old habit patterns are released, your true personality and sense of identity gradually emerges. Being a servant has accomplished this new growth while at the same time helping you become relatively free of selfishness. You have a growing sense of what is important to, and deeply appreciated by, the higher consciousness within you.

Trained by the servant mood, your discernment has been greatly increased. You begin to distinguish your real self from false patterns of thoughts and emotions. You no longer think of yourself as incapable of good judgments. Your enlightened sense of self is emerging.

Caring so much about the nature and works of higher consciousness, you find its concerns and challenges are your own. Your interests are deeply shared. The two of you have much in common. In a natural tide of love, complemented with your developing individuality, you become a true friend and happy ally with higher consciousness. From your new coalesced individuality you share your personal thoughts, feelings, and battles with your friend. But, more and more, you *live* for the goals and delights of higher consciousness. At the same time, you sense higher consciousness is interplaying with you, sharing in all the significant events and commonplaces of your life. There's a delightful sense of give-and-take, of sport and fun. You share interests as well as concerns.

Still pervaded with a deep sense of respect and a permanent awareness of the greatness of your new companion, you are so aware of being loved that you do not hesitate to share your deepest thoughts and worries—or honestly confide your character flaws.

Of course, in the friend relationship you feel you are a different kind of being from your immortal friend. You humbly reflect at times that you are a mortal friend of an immortal, who very graciously loves you. You sense you have a very different nature from your benevolent companion.

The mood of close friendship with the higher consciousness can resemble a hilarious game of tag or a heavenly conversation—a conversation from the soul, and beyond words. Much as regular friendships enrich people in sorrow and delight, illness and health, poverty and wealth, hectic times and quiet times, your mood of friendship will be the treasure of your life. You'll discover higher consciousness to be loyal and true to you under all circumstances.

REFLECTION

I clasp this hand you offer me.
You walk in my time
And I in immortality.

25

FRIENDS OF GOD
And the Incarnation

Millions of religious people think of God as their friend. They often like to think of the higher consciousness as having subtle form, of being embodied. For example, many Christians feel that Jesus Christ in subtle form, an embodiment of higher consciousness, is their friend. They *feel* his presence. They can, when in a superconscious state themselves, perceive his subtle form. They walk with him and talk with him, as the hymn says. They feel Jesus to be their real, embraceable Lord and friend. They feel he is beside them at their work or especially when they are in difficulty. When they pray they sense they are not speaking to a distant, possibly diffused body of light and power, but that Jesus is there sitting before them or kneeling beside them in their room. They are certain they are not engaged in imagination although, they grant, many people may engage in imagination.

Friends of Christ find proof they are actually experiencing the higher consciousness because of the improved quality of their lives and the transformation of their previously uncooperative character. They see, in the physical, material, and other events of their lives, definite manifestations of the presence of their friend. They credit their friend for the greater opportunities which come their way. They recognize the handiwork of their friend in the increased security and peace in which they live. Very often they find help or inspiration bounding on the miraculous. These grateful friends observe their Lord entering into the relationships they have with other people and creating a pronouncedly different or improved state in those relationships. When in danger, companions of Christ often find the hand of their friend protecting all concerned.

Other Christians who prefer to live in a *friend to friend* mood do not think of Jesus being in superphysical form but rather formless— a formless friend, pure spirit or light. They find that Christ acts as their friend without having any "human characteristics," or dimensions, and are perfectly happy with this sublime relationship; however, it is difficult, due to our human frailties and needs, to maintain this ethereal relationship. It's much easier to forget the relationship completely at times if one is not predisposed to thinking of the Lord of one's heart *in form*, in a person to person manner.

Eastern religions have a word for this aspect of higher consciousness and spirituality. One who thinks of the Lord in form is worshipping and relating to what is called an *ishta*. This phenomenon of the ishta is extremely helpful to those entering into the friend to friend relationship and all subsequent moods of higher consciousness. The ishta concept can certainly be of help, too, in the previous mood of the servant relationship.

However, in considering the ishta, the human form of God, communication between people becomes difficult. Millions of people strongly assert there is no God at all: not in any form nor absolute state, either. Sincere members of some faiths are certain God exists but has no human form. They look upon worshippers of an anthropomorphic God with pity, or sometimes hostility. Devout adherents of some other faiths are convinced that God has one divine/human form—*and one form only.* And then large numbers of Hindus worship numerous gods with divine and human attributes—who comprise different aspects of the one infinite source of all: Brahman.

It's not easy to discuss God in form because people of some faiths condemn the religious, or spiritual, practices of those in other faiths. At times, including the present, lovers of God have been murdered for thinking of their Lord in a different way from what others insisted was the only way. Men and women who considered themselves dedicated and honorable people have imprisoned those outside their own religion. Also, as this spirit of self-righteous interpretation and opinion grows cruel from time to time, many people *within* most faiths have killed others who practiced the *same* religion differently. Witness the disappearance of the early leader of the Baptist Church in England who was very likely beheaded for questioning *the divine right* of kings, and for his views on baptism. Witness the mountains of bodies during the Thirty Year's War in Europe (1618-1648) when religious differences divided a whole population.

Any reference to history will help people realize how far we must yet travel to give true love and good will to one another—not only as individuals but as groups too, as nations and faiths. Love and understanding are especially needed when the world's religions are moved to share the Lord with others.

GOD AS MAN

Religious people who seek a mood of relationship with God almost always choose an Incarnation as their ishta—the *form* of God on whom they focus their minds and hearts. The concept of the Incarnation was initially an ancient Eastern idea (or realization) which moved West. You can trace the various Incarnations in different spaces of time and in different cultures by studying history and comparative religions. You can also observe the tremendous impact of the Incarnations on the overall well being of the civilizations which they served.

Devoted worshippers throughout the world are convinced God himself incarnated as man and is worthy of worship. Many people have been persecuted throughout the ages for believing in this tradition and seeking a personal relationship with the Incarnation of God—who is also called *avatar*, a descent of the Divine. Devotees who have a mood of relationship with an Incarnation, "God as man," ask doubters: if God is real and omnipotent and can create the whole universe including mankind, why can't he himself incarnate and walk the earth if *he* chooses?

It's extremely fascinating for a student of religion to find there is a tradition of the God-man, the Incarnation, in many civilizations throughout history. The incarnation tradition is further complicated and confused, however, because some ancient societies also called their kings divine incarnations.

WHAT ARE THE IDENTIFYING CHARACTERISTICS OF AN INCARNATION?

Specific characteristics mark those great beings who were hailed and loved as Incarnations. An Incarnation:

1) is preceded by messengers who declare His coming.
2) is born of immaculate conception.
3) lives among the lowly.
4) demonstrates God's grace alone is sufficient.
5) sacrifices His life out of love and as a propitiation for humanity.
6) clarifies the scriptures so that people can understand and practice them rightly.
7) adds something new which is particularly applicable to the era which He has come to serve and which will be of benefit to all future people.
8) cleans away the confusions in religious or spiritual practice caused by ignorant or incorrectly opinionated priestcraft.

Such Incarnations are Rama, Krishna, Zoroaster, Buddha, Jesus Christ, Chaitanya, and Ramakrishna. There may have been other Incarnations as well. These, however, are the main Incarnations recognized by millions and millions in the world today. (It's important to note that most Buddhists do not consider Buddha an Incarnation, but Hindus and mystics generally think Gautama the Buddha had the characteristics of an Incarnation.) Remember, some faiths do not recognize any Incarnations; and some people who recognize one Incarnation do not recognize any other Incarnation.

Commonly, those people who practice relating to higher consciousness through the different moods are dominantly devotional or religious. They find it easy and very natural to think of the Lord of their heart, the source of life, love, and existence, as an Incarnation. Millions of people around the world today choose to relate to God, the emanator of higher consciousness, through their chosen Incarnation. Their ways of loving their Lord and thinking of God are often extremely beautiful and charming. Some devotees chant the name of their Lord and friend while looking at a picture or sculpture which represents the Incarnation. These devotees lovingly chant his name or utter praises of love to him. Others think of the Passion of Christ and worship him, recalling his death on a cross, and lovingly wear crucifixes and say the rosary. Hundreds of millions receive the *body and blood* of Christ into their beings through communion, regularly.

Other devotees in their relationship with the Divine offer little plates of food before the Lord at an altar placed in a room in their homes, feeling that the Lord—in spirit and in form—partakes of the food and blesses it before they themselves sit down to eat. Meantime, some other devoutly religious people would call these practices idolatry and would not be caught dead daring to think for a moment of the Lord having form or being able to express so personally. And such differences of view and doctrine have often caused warfare, perhaps from the beginning of man.

Also, it's important to mention that millions of religious devotees think of the Lord as feminine, as well as masculine. They, by the millions, call upon the Lord as "Divine Mother." They feel that the Lord is unconditionally loving, as is often the case with mothers in this world. They equate the Divine Mother with the Christian concept of the Holy Spirit. They feel the Divine Mother is an ever-available *comforter* who will never reject her child, whether that child be good or bad. Similarly, Roman Catholics—in their relationship with God—often pray to Mother Mary and numerous saints. Mary Baker Eddy, too, the founder of Christian Science, often referred to the feminine aspect of God when she spoke of "Father, Mother God."

To clarify and sum up, the awe and servant relationships may—if you are so predisposed and able—mature into a new attitude, a new mood of the heart. Then you feel a soul-deep response to the call of higher consciousness which leads you to discover your true nature and value in the "eyes" of higher consciousness. A new and transformed person, you easily become a *friend* to higher consciousness. The two of you relate more intimately, friend to friend. You share life at a deeper level. While mindful of the greatness and amazing superiority of your senior companion, you feel free and welcome to chat and converse in rich dialogues with the higher consciousness—usually communicated superconsciously, non-verbally. In this friend mood of higher consciousness, you discover a greater capacity for intimacy and a person to Person relationship with the Lord.

Your relationship, being a true friendship, conducted at a higher level of awareness (not imagination), bears fruit in daily life. If you are not becoming a better person or a more able and competent person in your friend mood, chances are fantasy is dominating you. If your compassion for others is increasing and if your body and mind feel extremely blessed, then very likely you are experiencing the mood of relationship called friend to friend.

Remember, in this true friendship between the finite and the infinite, between *two* forms of higher consciousness (because now, you, a newly-awakened human being, have become a freely-expressive form of higher consciousness too), the marvelous aspect of *playfulness* occurs. Just as friends who love one another joke, tease, and inspire one another; just as they love to give presents and be of assistance to one another; just as they deeply enjoy being thoughtful of the other person and love the friend for this kindness; so too the higher consciousness and the devotee enter into much fun together!

Sometimes it may seem that your newfound friend is playing tag with you—running away and hard to find. At other times, in your career, for example, during particularly intense times, suddenly your special companion comes rushing into the room, filling it with light and a heavenly quality. Sometimes you suddenly feel touched and uplifted. Or, your heart unexpectedly expands with joy, realizing the unique friendship you are now having.

Ask any Catholic nun—that is, almost any nun—about her relationship with the Lord. If she is willing to share, she will charm you for hours describing "her" beloved Jesus. She may also, perhaps, confide her concern for many priests who seem to relate to God in an abstract manner and who talk about the Holy Spirit as if he's not a person. Jesus is friend, husband, and Lord to many nuns.

For some people, the natural outgrowth of their quest for higher consciousness is a sense of a personal friend to friend relationship. For others, it's just not conceivable and other possibilities seem more appropriate.

In the friend to friend relationship, both friends are important. The give-and-take is extremely valuable to the friendship. Although the higher consciousness is so much more aware, able, and infinitely more beautiful—at least it seems so to the new friend—both must contribute. Both must also be themselves. Both friends are essential to the relationship. Friendship cannot be one way.

You are extremely fortunate to move forward from a servant relationship into the embrace of friendship. You find a new way of perceiving the world, as well as realizing a new value for yourself. The awe and servant relationships, however, are still precious to you because they keep you from ever taking the higher consciousness for granted and they prevent you from taking unfair advantage of the new relationship. Humility and the readiness to serve must be constituents in your makeup in order for the friendship to go on.

But what a possibility! A completely satisfying, perfect, and undying friendship.

REFLECTION

To think that all I ever need do
Is respond to You and your love —
And that I shall never be lonely again!

26

MORE ADVANCED RELATIONSHIPS

Love grows. Love is not static. When there is love in a relationship it is dynamic; the relationship is a living reality. Love moves your relationship forward into ever-new and more subtle dimensions.

You find it thrilling to be a lover of higher consciousness. In a sense, one of the fulfillments of life is to be able to love and love and love. The ongoing love transforms you. Dynamic love enables you to see and experience life more fully and delightedly. Love becomes the cornerstone of your life. Faith has led you to this love and your experience of superconscious relationships. What more can be said?

Volumes can't adequately describe the relationships which now occur. Hopefully, the states mentioned in this chapter will soon be within your reach as you apply the principles of this book and enjoy the guidance of your special teacher. The most essential factor, henceforth, is your growing love. Love brings greater understanding and intimacy between the seeker of higher consciousness and higher consciousness itself. As love grows, so does the ability to give and share love at more superb levels.

In love, it is said, all things are possible. In love there are moods of relationship that go far beyond human ability to understand. We are incapable of thinking in such high terms unless we have a background in the awe, servant, and friendship relationships. Imagine being able to live your daily life, participating fully in the world, while delightedly developing from one level of relationship into another.

Please keep in mind that for perhaps thirty or forty percent of those who are seeking higher consciousness these moods are not suitable. Those who have a dominantly intellectual or willful (volitional) nature will generally prefer other states developed in other sections of this book. In particular, intellectual and volitional people will likely prefer to develop the sublime insight of witness consciousness rather than seek higher consciousness through moods and relationships. Then intellectual and volitional people usually go on to experience the higher planes of awareness which *grow* from witness consciousness and the expanded self.*

Generally, though, people of devotional, volitional, and intellectual natures will experience the witness consciousness and the expanded self in ways that are quite similar.

Are you dominantly devotional? Do you delight in giving and receiving love? Are relationships particularly important and gratifying to you? Let's explore the higher moods.

AS A SON OR DAUGHTER

The friend to friend relationship matures and, because love is so dynamic, another level of intimacy is begun. The awe, servant, and friend relationships mature *into a mood of love similar to that of a child with Mother or Father.* The interest of the seeker becomes so aligned—so attuned—with the interests of higher consciousness that there is a strong sense of becoming "part of the family." The concerns of higher consciousness have become yours; and you know your concerns have become the concerns of the higher consciousness.

In this intimacy your sense of who you are changes again. Your friendship has changed your nature. When you began the friend relationship you felt your nature was much different from that of the higher consciousness. However, as your friendship grew, you discovered yourself to be essentially of the same spirit as your friend. In this awareness you begin to feel more continually like a loving son or daughter of a loving, wise, and perfect father or mother.

* See Chapters 18 and 19, *The Good Will Witness* and *The Universal Self.*

Some individuals prefer to think of the higher consciousness as a father—loving, strong, provident and protective. Much as a father in regular life gives his child a sense of self-esteem, helpful guidance and an embracing security through many of life's adventures, fatherly attributes are readily found in the nature of higher consciousness, too. Many devotional people find they can easily establish a *child to father* relationship and enter an intimate mood of love.

However, because of the often manifest capacity of a mother to love her child, whether good or bad, with unconditional love and acceptance, many seekers prefer to think of the higher consciousness in the aspect of mother. That is, they feel the higher consciousness has the qualities of total acceptance, non-judgmental love, and eternally patient correction. While Daddy is often away at work, Mother is generally nearby night and day. While Father's corrections seem more stern or perhaps even threatening, Mother's corrections appear more calm and constant.

As mentioned, these stereotypes may not be true at all. However, many seekers find themselves predisposed at this intense high level of awareness to conceive of the higher consciousness as acting much as a mother would act—with unconditional love and patient correction. Through greater intimacy you become, as it were, a member of the family of higher consciousness, a son or a daughter who is at home with higher consciousness—perfectly comfortable. You become free to receive the higher faculties and greater power coming from your new mood of love—whether you prefer to focus on the father or mother aspect.

At this stage, you have been considerably purified and are progressively less able to use higher power for personal or selfish ends. As a son or daughter you are being prepared, groomed, for a mature life in higher consciousness.

In the child to mother or father relationship you know yourself to be young, not as powerful or as knowledgeable as the higher consciousness itself but at the same time beloved of it and intimately sharing in its nature and purposes.

Certainly it's fine for a seeker to imagine—or strive to develop —this mood without actually being in the achieved state. The ideals of this relationship are lofty and comforting. The *mood* itself, however, becomes *established* usually only after considerable purification through the awe, servant, and friend relationships.

Most scriptures strongly advocate that you accept you are a son or daughter, a child of the Lord. It's fine, certainly, to start your mood of love with this *child relationship* as long as you grow in the other attributes which will help you be a loyal and constantly loving child.

It's wonderful to think—in a religious sense—that the Lord is like a father or mother who is deeply concerned about the welfare and happiness of his or her child, and who will accept and love that child as part of its own being forever.

Indeed, the higher consciousness will guide and raise you up into the fullness of life. You'll find it most precious to have an ongoing mood, a momentum in your heart, which continually affirms such an intimate relationship with the higher consciousness.

AS IF MARRIED

Love continues, dynamically. Greater intimacy pushes you forward. You, the seeker, mature. You feel less a child and more an adult. Much like a nun who thinks of Christ as her husband, you begin to view the higher consciousness with the intensity and dedication of one wedded. The Lord of your heart is recognized as the love of your life, and the great satisfaction of *belonging* to the lover abides in your mind. You feel deeply loved and understood. You know you are eternally appreciated. You live for your beloved. Of course, you are still humble, and you wish to serve and delight your special companion—but the sharing is more completely open and natural. Few human beings ever know such love and the glorious state of being this mood brings.

In this "married" stage, rapturous joy easily moves throughout your being. In your ecstasy, sexual desire is greatly calmed down and your whole body feels a bliss, as if being satisfied at every level —physically, mentally, emotionally, and spiritually too. Those who are single generally feel much relieved from the pressures of sexual desire. Those who are married often find, when they are in this mood, a greater love and ability to satisfy, and be satisfied with, their dear mate.

Sometimes this mood of being a mature partner of higher consciousness can create problems in your home. If your husband or wife has a jealous streak, he or she may resent your joy of life and blissful attunement. He or she may fear losing out. Many problems will develop if communication is not particularly clear. Your love for others must be given great attention. Your beloved higher consciousness will, of course, help you to love people more completely than ever—especially your family members.

However, believe it or not, most of those who experience this exalted state of being—becoming a mate to higher consciousness—are single and celibate. Often nuns, priests, and mystics who have lived years of sacrifice find this extremely blessed and tender adult relationship with the higher consciousness. While those who are married can help one another bring about this invigorating dimension in their lives, they tend to be too busy and are also somewhat fearful of it. Yet by sensing the higher consciousness expressing through one another, an even deeper love is known. The love between man and woman becomes magnified in the Lord.

Just as man and woman together bring forth children, so too the seeker who lives in this exalted state—as if a husband or wife of the *ishta* (the form of higher consciousness)—finds spiritual children are engendered. Usually at the level of this relationship you become capable of teaching others about higher consciousness. Or, you become capable of inspiring others so much that they will sense the reality of higher consciousness and pursue greater awareness of it. Also, you may find that your talents can be turned to writing, art, or other projects which will uplift and benefit others. The ability to do something concrete, to serve the welfare of other people or humanity at large, becomes energetically inseminated, takes birth, and grows at this stage. Development of your work or calling may take some time. It may also be more a general service of good will to others in the course of daily life rather than a specific project or mission. However, at this stage of intimacy and love with the higher consciousness, you become a fit person to truly and significantly play a part in the loving outreach of higher consciousness toward all people.

THE FIANCÉ

More intense than the marriage relationship is that of the fiancé. What could be more dynamic? Please keep in mind human terms and concepts are used here, however inadequately, in order to try to describe an extremely subtle and powerful relationship between the individual and the higher consciousness—or, to say it in religious terms, the relationship between the individual and the Lord.

Have you noticed, either in your marriage or in the marriages of friends, that marriage partners tend to take one another for granted? They don't continually think of the well being of one another. Their attentiveness calms down. Now and then they have to consciously put time aside to pay full attention to one another and reestablish their expressions of love and tenderness. Sometimes they even have to fight in order to get realigned and working together again.

Intensity of your mood, while you maintain precise mental balance, is of primary importance in the next mood. Only as your love becomes more powerful can you go beyond the *husband to wife* relationship with higher consciousness. This lofty mood transcends the *as if married* relationship. It's called the *fiancé to fiancée* mood. This state is attained by very, very few seekers. Perhaps only a few dozen devotees in the world today are capable of living at this level. The emotional and mental intensity required is so great that unless you have developed your body and all your faculties tremendously, your health will break down. You will not be able to bear such love for a day, let alone live in it for months or years. Still, the fiancé to fiancée relationship will inevitably happen if you increase your physical, mental, emotional and spiritual health through exercise, honesty, and devotion.

The fiancé to fiancée mood takes its name from the behavior of young lovers and their extraordinary passion. Because love for the higher consciousness becomes *flat out* purified, unselfish passion, this sovereign mood is very much like that of fiancés. (In fact, this terminology was used in spiritual circles before society changed so much.)

WHAT IS THE FIANCÉ TO FIANCÉE RELATIONSHIP LIKE?

When people are deeply in love and preparing for marriage, the young man and woman can think of little else but their beloved. They have to make an effort to turn their mind to other activities or other thoughts. Even then, their minds continually drift into daydreams of one another, fantasies about their future, and phone calls. They love one another so much they are capable of sitting up all night talking and yet rushing off to work early in the morning, fresh and eager for the day to pass so they can be together again that night —and similarly the next night and the next.

Weekends are too short. These lovers are so intense about one another, so totally concentrated, that it seems to them other people only half exist. Normal humdrum words take on melody when coming from the throat of a fiancé. Little wishes, quite trivial perhaps, become extremely important in this blazing love. The world is seen fresh and new. Life has new prospects. The couple know their love is so deep they can withstand any test, any problem, and any erosions of time. If these dear lovers could be hooked up to appropriate wires, perhaps the force of their love would light a city for years.

This fiancé to fiancée relationship, observable in many high schools and colleges, among other places, is beautiful to see when the couple genuinely love one another in a healthful, wholesome way. They demonstrate caring and concern every day. Exposed and vulnerable to harm from scoffers and their own insensitivities, they fortify their trust in one another. Each is willing to take the risk and love completely, holding nothing back, whatever the consequences.

Many of these same qualities are found in the incandescent mood of love for the higher consciousness called *fiancé to fiancée*. Changed through faith and the progressive moods of awe, servant, friend, child, and mate, you become more *alive* than you could have previously imagined. Your flow of love is so powerful you become incapable of thinking other than of the higher consciousness. You relate everything else in the world to your relationship with your beloved, which easily has priority. You love, totally, and your love softens and sweetens the apparent harshness and menace of the outer world. Reciprocally, the world loves a lover and enjoys your zest. Greater opportunities and more good will come to such a lover.

In this ultrahigh mood of love, with your heart and mind so easily wavering from mundane concerns, you could become a menace when driving a car or doing an honest day's work. But as you experience this mood, you will find an obvious solution for your tendency to be absent-minded about the world. Simply drive, work, and attend to the details of your day with the attitude that you are doing them *for* your beloved. Feel it is for your beloved that you are doing the various errands of daily life. In this manner you can think constantly of your beloved even while doing something very complex.

Now your attitude and the greatness of your love create a new motive and a new power within you. You perform inspired service in a degree which far transcends the servant level, for example. Why? You *live* for your beloved. You have become an instrument, a constantly devoted companion of higher consciousness. Your life has become merged in higher consciousness.

However, so few people mature in this love that the *fiancé to fiancée* relationship is a rarity in the world. The few who live in this superhuman delight are mainly monks and nuns, priests, spiritual teachers. It's a shame many people turn from this intense mood of love because they are either preoccupied or afraid. Sadly, they dare not trust in a consciousness which would most capably help them but which, in its scope, frightens them.

Then, too, the *fiancé to fiancée* mood of love is often too intense to be maintained by most seekers, even if the earlier moods were established fairly easily. If your body shakes, or your nerves feel like they are burning, or you can't digest food, return to less intense moods and get healthier first.

Those who experience the exalted and thrilling fiancé mood encourage all seekers that to live in such a state is worth every patient preparation, even if you have to labor for decades—or lifetimes. These blessed ones live in an ecstatic joy, continually amazed that a human being can realize such love and fulfillment.

REFLECTION

I live in love,
And love transforms me.

27

SHALL WE GO ON?
The Highest Moods

Believe it or not, you can experience even greater relationships with higher consciousness. It's hard to believe but there's more—if you're interested and able.

There is a basic requirement: *your love must be so deep it changes you.* Your nerves have to be capable of maintaining what feels like many times the normal levels of energy. There are many analogies about the changes required. Some yogis have characterized the nerve change as: "A 110-watt bulb must become an *1100-watt bulb.*" Not only does your nervous system have to be transformed, the *fiancé to fiancée* mood must further strengthen your body, mind, and heart in order for you to enter these extremely advanced dimensions of life. As always, the science of yoga is particularly helpful in increasing your abilities.

Continuing your *fiancé to fiancée* mood, ecstasy fills your body from brain to toe tips. The bliss changes your cells so they can contain such a great rush of energy and devotion. Seekers who cannot handle the higher energy shake, tremble, weep, and sometimes roll around the room. Occasionally, their bodies leap up off the ground even when they are seated. While these involuntary actions can appear to be interesting oddities, or even signs of holiness to some, a nerve problem is indicated and your nerves must be toned so higher states can be held calmly—without jerking, shaking, or trembling.

Please keep in mind only a few dozen people in the world are capable of maintaining the level of consciousness we are describing here. We're not describing other phenomena which may also involve shaking, jerking, and the incapacity of the nerves to handle even a small amount of energy.

Your transformed body, developed through high states, is generally called *the divinized body*, spiritually made more subtle, able to experience and express higher consciousness. When this transformation of your physical vehicle occurs, it seems to emit a mellow glow, and the rush of ecstasy in your cells is continually felt. Sri Ramakrishna, for example, began to radiate so much light from his body that people used to gather around his doorway just to catch a glimpse of him as he went outside. On one occasion, when he asked Mahendra Nath Gupta about their extreme curiosity, he was told they had gathered there specifically to see the light shining from him. He immediately ran back into the house, saying he was disgusted with this kind of fame. He prayed that his effulgence be taken away, that he in no way wished to become some kind of marvel or curiosity. And, within a few months, his distinct glow was reduced —likely interiorized.

The next stage of intimacy with the higher consciousness can only be imagined when you are in the fiancé mood. The more developed you are in any of the relationship moods, however, the more you will be able to anticipate the nature of these new moods. Sri Ramakrishna was humanity's main teacher and demonstrator of these high moods. He said that at some future time people may commonly experience these relationships. But, it probably would take thousands and thousands of years—perhaps tens of thousands —before these moods were widely experienced. He, however, suggested that a few people in our time will be able to achieve relationships with the higher consciousness which are supremely intense and intimate. He did caution that people who are unprepared and who presume to live at an intensity beyond their capacity might well suffer health problems and even go mad.

Bearing his caution in mind, are you ready to engage your thought in something most wondrous and sublime?

KAMA RADHA—The Transformed Lover

Using Sri Ramakrishna's terminology—because of his knowledge and because his is the only available vocabulary regarding the extremely advanced higher states today—let your mind, in partial satisfaction, savor a marvelous progression: the possibility of becoming God's spiritual playmate.

You, surviving the fiancé mood, having successfully matured and been transformed by the intensity of your love play, now possess a subtly changed body in which to work and express. In a sense, you're a member of a new species or the next plateau of the human species. Sri Ramakrishna called these individual souls *Radha*. He used the term Radha because the individual soul is the beloved of God, just as the ancient devotee, Radha, was the beloved of the Incarnation, Krishna. So, by Radha, Sri Ramakrishna means you— the devotee, the individual soul.

Keep in mind, too, please, that by the time you have passed through the *fiancé to fiancée* relationship, incredible transformation of your sense of self has occurred. After all, you have surrendered yourself at the servant level and then a deeper, truer sense of self has developed through the friend relationship into the son or daughter mood. Then you went through the married relationship into the fiancé intensity. Thus, a great amount of transformation and self-surrender has already occurred. Now, in most senses a new being, you enter the Radha relationships.*

Before, your *physical* eyes, ears, fingertips were sensitive to the vast panorama of creation in very limited ways and were only capable of sensing a small portion of the spectrum of energy in which you lived. Naturally, to be aware of realities beyond the visible spectrum—which scientists are regularly able to measure and which they assure us do exist—you need to have changed eyes and ears. Also, you must have a capacity to *feel* far beyond the very limited range of normal human sensitivity. The transformation process through the previous relationships has accomplished a much increased awareness of the levels of electromagnetic energy (in the body and the universe) far beyond science's projections at this time. Hopefully these Radha moods of extreme awareness will reveal the keys by

---

* It should be noted that these Radha terms are used other ways in many fields of yoga and Eastern thought. These three Radha terms are being used in a special sense to meet specific definitions within Sri Ramakrishna's concepts.

which science, art, and religion will merge—each satisfying its own disciplines and each enriching the other two.

The main point is that a new being, a new you, is necessary for the Kama Radha relationship—*Kama* meaning *true fulfillment of desire*, or desire itself; *Radha* meaning *you, the individual devotee.*

The *fiancé to fiancée* relationship was so powerful it transformed you and, as you now grow in love, you are compelled by your new nature to love even more dynamically, even more intimately. And so, the Kama Radha relationship between the individual soul, Radha, and the higher consciousness happens.

Ramakrishna would urge that Kama Radha be recognized as a mood between the individual soul and the Lord. Sri Ramakrishna would also have a much larger vocabulary of subtle terms to use than our English language allows.

Endeavoring to approximate Ramakrishna's terms: in the Kama Radha experience you become such an intense, transformed lover you only care about one thing, you only live for one thing: the Lord and your love of him. He (or She) seems your all in all. You conduct your life only for him. You live or die for him only. Your actions are for him—your conversation, your exercise and study. You eat for him. Your thoughts are for him. You think only out of love for him. You have the conviction you exist for him only.

But believe it or not, there is a tinge of selfishness in the blazing love of Kama Radha—your spiritual desire for your Beloved. The selfishness concerns the *quality* of your love. However high you may be and however deeply deserving of the respect of all humanity, your love has a shortcoming. If your lofty love play with the Lord grows progressively, you are happy and all is well.

However, if your Beloved withdraws himself from the relationship for a time, and if you cannot experience your exquisite love play, *will you still love him?*

In Kama Radha, according to those who have been in it, you, the individual soul, stop loving and stop giving if for a prolonged time you feel there is no response, no appropriate love play from your Lord. You wonder why you have loved so long, and how the Lord could be so thoughtless of his devotee, the Radha. All this occurs at a very high level, however primitive the selfish response may seem to our minds as we strive to equate it with normal human emotional terms.

So, even at a sublime height, a person in Kama Radha, a mood which seems to be one of total loving and giving, there is, even in your reformed sense of self, an expectation or a demand which you are placing on the Lord. You become agonizingly frustrated and your heart feels stretched beyond its ability to stretch.

Your sudden self-preoccupation as a thwarted lover sometimes takes a long period of time to grow out of and the whole sincerity of your love, even at this colossal level, is brought into question. The entire progression of your love and intimacy through the moods seems a contradiction. You lament your Beloved's absence and endure while experiencing extreme suffering.

PREMA RADHA—The Joyous Lover

Though you live in anguish, usually you persevere and do not angrily spurn the Lord.

Then, in his own time, your nurturing Lord returns. In a while your love and play, soul to Lord and Lord to soul, resumes at progressively more wondrous levels.

However, you remember your sense of loss and exasperation when the Lord seemed absent, unreachable, and uncaring. Your love grows as you realize that, in Kama Radha, your love was not true self-giving but had a sharp hook in it. You subtly wanted to fulfill your self-centered desire for spiritual gratification, to control the Lord's actions and responses to your love. You were not asking for material things but you did expect the Lord to satisfy your intense desire for a delightful, all-satisfying relationship. Seeing this insidious fault clearly, you love the Lord more purely. You are able to love with greater self-giving. An even greater power of love grows. You dedicate yourself to the Lord without a tinge of selfishness. You rejoice in being able to love your Lord, whatever his response. In this state, *Prema Radha* begins. Never before have you enjoyed loving the Lord so.

The Prema Radha state is one in which you, the individual soul, enter into a mood of awareness something like this:

"I love you totally, my Lord. I deeply enjoy loving you. You may come or go. You may do as you please, but I enjoy nothing more than loving you. And in my enjoyment of loving you, my enjoyment alone is enough for me. I will love you whether you are present in my consciousness and we are in our love play, or if you go away for a thousand eons. Always, I will enjoy this constant state of my love. I can enjoy loving you whether you are here now, or whether I never see you again, my Beloved. And, if for some reason you choose to place me away from you, from this moment through all eternity, still I will enjoy loving you."

Who knows what number of people have attained this level of Prema Radha? Possibly fewer than two dozen. Sri Ramakrishna said hardly any mortals can withstand the rigors of Prema Radha.

Who could think there would still be a shortcoming, or flaw, in such a love as Prema Radha? Can you see what the flaw is?

Well, such a great love still has to be developed and perfected. So, once again, through the course of love, you develop a profound sense of separation. At some point you feel as if the Lord has gone away to some other corner of the universe, or perhaps to a different universe entirely, leaving this one to spin itself out.

"That's alright," you say, as a great devotee in Prema Radha: "That's fine, my Lord. I love you whether you are here or whether you stay away forever. I can still enjoy loving you. I love to love you. I love you, my Lord, whether you treat me well or ill. I enjoy loving you. My joy in loving you is not diminished. I don't need your response. I enjoy loving you so. Hide as you wish. I love you."

NITYA RADHA—The Eternal Lover

But, after a long time your joy peters out. You were capable of enjoying the love play so much that even when the Lord made you unaware of his presence or seemed to act contrary to your lofty expectations you could still love him. It was easy to be constant in your love mood because you *enjoyed* loving him so. But, now after a long time, your joy has worn thin so you stop loving the Lord.

"What was I loving him for anyway?" you wonder. "If he really loved me, he'd be here. What's the point in loving a Lord who's never around? *Why should I love him when I don't enjoy it?*"

As your joy flies away, a sense of profoundest desolation occurs.

"It's no fun loving a Lord who's far away from me. What kind of a Lord would treat me this way?" you wonder. "Certainly he is, after all, an unworthy lover."

It's common that human relationships are dissolved when one party in the relationship goes away, stays away and doesn't even communicate. However, it can be observed that in some cases there are people who continue to love the absent one even when he (or she) is far away, or uncommunicative, or even has done some evil to him or her. The love usually continues in the heart of the lover in these instances because he or she enjoys that love so much. The *enjoyment* of that love is extremely precious to the true lover.

So, too, at an extremely high and almost incomprehensible level does this occur in the breakdown of Prema Radha, when the enjoyment of loving wears thin due to the apparent distance of the Lord. When the joy goes, when the enjoyment of the love goes, then the love itself is gradually weakened and diminished. Now this great soul in Prema Radha finds himself or herself again, once again, but more painfully than ever before, alone. No words can describe the extent of this forlorn state nor the emotion of personal futility.

"What is the sense of a universe which has such an absurd recip-rocator of human love?" you cry. "Is the universe, and all that has unfolded in it, a preposterous joke? How can anything in this uni-verse have meaning if loving the Lord has no constancy or validity? Certainly all human beings should band together and parade the world with picket signs protesting their absurd treatment and refuse to go on!—unless better living conditions are extended from The Management.

"And, surely," you complain, "there is no greater fool than the one who aspired to and experienced Prema Radha. Perhaps reality itself is unreal! Surely it must be unreal because of these capricious actions of the Lord toward one who loves him and lives for him only! And then what of these mood experiences—all of them? Are they unreal too? Is everything nothing? Is all nothingness? Ohhhh."

In this dejection a great pivot point has been reached. What happens next? The weak seekers fuss and fume. But in due course the Lord returns to their awareness and their joy ultimately is built back up again. They resume life at the ferocious level of Prema Ra-dha once more. Of course, if in the future their joy falls away at times, so does their love.

But the strong ones, throughout history, continue to accept transformation—and "love" their way beyond Prema Radha. The dy-namics of love do not quit at Prema Radha mood. These few lovers look within themselves when Prema Radha love breaks apart. *They look at the frailty of their love rather than judge or condemn their Beloved.* They suffer, yearn, and ache but they endeavor to love anyway, despite the diminishing of their joy, despite the concomitant lessen-ing of their love. These rare lovers desperately investigate their love and determine what is really the problem. They hurriedly search their attitudes and behavior to find what is really wrong. While feel-ing so alone and so distant from their Beloved, they minutely ex-amine their all-precious love, searching for its fatal flaw.

In time the transcenders of the Prema Radha mood discover they are passing through yet another initiation, and are moving for-ward into even greater love. They discover the painful but obvious truth that even the great love of Prema Radha had a quality of selfishness. They can see their *enjoyment*—their personal, however magnificent, enjoyment—of their love relationship was a major part of their motive to love the Lord.

"Ah-ha! There is the flaw. My love is not even yet free of my selfishness nor my desire to dominate subtly," you realize. "I still have an expectation of joy. When my expectation is not fulfilled, then, sad to say, I love with less intensity and ultimately give up. Oh, what sorrow to know that my love is not a full giving, to know my love still has a hook in it. I am, even now, making a demand on my Beloved and loving him with an ulterior motive."

Gradually there awakens in this extremely painful self-revelation a new love ever so sweet and free, a love like a melody streaming through the space in your mind, filling your chest cavity. Your sense of existence is filled like the songs of a huge choir saturate a vast cathedral. Pure love moves forward. Pure love radiates forth.

"Now, my Lord, I love you whether you choose to stay here or leave me. Lord, I love you whether I enjoy loving you or not. I love you totally. If I enjoy loving you, fine. If I don't enjoy loving you, that is also fine. But I love you. I live in love. I love you and I can't help it. Whether I ever see you again, whether you ever respond again, whether my personal inadequacies make me feel sad or in agony, I don't care. I love you. I love you now. I live for you and your sweet will. I love you always—by your grace—no matter what!"

This perfected love is called *Nitya Radha*, the eternal love between beloved devotee and beloved Lord. You realize the seeming withdrawal of the Lord and his seeming lack of care was an act of love. The two of you brought it about to facilitate the necessary growth within you.

You needed to grow into being a person who can love so profoundly that your mood of love becomes eternal—beyond time, beyond space—incapable of destruction or impediment.

NITYA LILA—The Eternal Dance of Love

Your love relationship, now perfected through Nitya Radha, establishes a new way of life daily—an eternal dance of love between Lord and devotee: Nitya Lila. (*Nitya* means eternal, the Absolute; *Lila* means a play or dance. Lila also means the relative universe as manifest in time and space.) Sri Ramakrishna said at this level the devotee and Lord share together in the work of creation.

In Nitya Lila, the mood of love between the devotee and the

Lord is so perfect that the concerns of one become the concerns of the other. The Lord and his eternally loving devotee become, in a sense, co-workers. This is not to imply that the spiritualized devotee *is* the Lord.* However, sharing through love such deep, universal concerns, the devotee becomes ever so deeply compassionate about the welfare of humanity, for example—the development of values, the upliftment of the suffering, the comfort of the sick. Primarily the devotee serves at the level of raising human consciousness, recognizing most of humanity's wars and woes come from a beclouded awareness.

Now the devotee is at the height of his or her soul's expression and can be most instrumental in changing life's situations constructively. Will, love, intelligence, and power unite. Consider that all the advancements in civilization and the quality of life have occurred when people became more conscious. As people raise their consciousness they are not only able to solve many of their own problems, but they are also able to offer viable solutions for the world's problems.

The transformed lover in Nitya Lila sees the world situation clearly and, while acutely concerned, he constantly sees new hopes and possibilities for humanity. Even wars and bloodshed can be ameliorated. Some songs written by those who have experienced Nitya Lila say the "divine player" can suggest the creation of galaxies or universes and the Lord will fulfill his request.

As a devotee in Nitya Lila, you live in eternal delight, constantly thrilling to the ever-new dance with your Beloved. You share in the life and emanation of the Lord, while at the same time retaining your distinct spiritual individuality. The Lord continually shows his love and appreciation for you. While you delight in serving your Beloved, he delights too in serving you, his very dear lover. In Nitya Lila your love is fulfilled. In Nitya Lila finite and infinite fuse.

In Nitya Lila you have finally, after who knows how long, come home.

---

* Some religious sects and philosophies feel differently. They hold that God is the only reality and since God has created man out of himself, man *is* God. Further, they maintain man will only overcome or shed his problems when he realizes his divine nature.

REFLECTION

Our love is so intense we disappear,
Only to re-emerge and love again.

IV

AGONIES
AND
ECSTASIES

28

AGONIES AND ECSTASIES

In your daily, steady journey toward higher consciousness, there are agonies and ecstasies. It's so important to understand your daily struggles are tinged with promise and magnificence. Whether each of your days seems a battle or a tour of the sublime, you are growing toward higher consciousness and fulfillment. Whether your focus is character growth, your universal self, or a satisfying relationship, you will need to appreciate your highs and lows.

As you become more conscious, you see much more beauty around and inside you. You see everything in a fresh way—the breakfast bowl, the shape of the spoon. Perhaps the song of the birds seems so new and so beautiful that you wonder where the birds were prior to your adventures in higher consciousness. All your senses are sharper. Food tastes better. Your nose feels as if it's been turned off for years prior to your coming alive. Your sense of touch becomes greatly increased, and delightful. Your appreciation of shapes and colors rapidly expands. You find new depths in your appreciation of music. Your enhanced appreciation for melody and harmony may create in you a new musical taste, which thrills you.

You become more an artist of life—able to pay inspired attention to the subtleties, the fine details, and the extraordinary values

191

that make everything you experience or do seem more worthwhile.

There's more zip in your life. This added vitality sustains you and enables you to have progressively more meaningful moments in your life. You no longer feel, if you ever felt, that the project of life is just to get by and that the work of life has muscled out the joy. Instead, you now have the strength and energy to start creating a life more consonant with your inner sense of beauty and harmony. You find it easier to express your values in the outer world.

You live your life with periods of ecstasy, periods of sheer delight in being alive. You, likely and often, feel gratitude for the gift of life. You are eager to open this gift and discover all of its features.

Perhaps you begin seeing auras, bodies of light, surrounding people's heads or whole beings. Perhaps you even see these electromagnetic fields around your pets and the trees. Fortunately, scientists have verified that electromagnetic fields do exist around living things. They have also observed auras around inanimate objects such as coins. You may find, in the thrill and the ecstasy of your life, that you begin to see—through calm eyes—the light around people.

Your heart begins to be so full of love and kindness that you feel you are sharing in the life of those close to you. You are much less a stranger everywhere you go, and perhaps you even sense the pleasure of others in greeting you. Perhaps you also feel the delight of strangers in coming into contact with a happy person, a truly alive human being.

Breathing seems delicious. The air entering your nostrils delights you. On a clear day, the air flowing into your nostrils seems like rare wine. You also enjoy sensing your pulse which you can feel most anywhere in your body. You can feel new life and vitality throughout your body.

You live sensing the source of life. You live with the feeling that you are regularly in the presence of a higher consciousness. You thrill to be living your life in this presence which promises so much joy and so many possibilities.

THE AGONIES

But if there is ecstasy, there are agonies too. Moving toward higher consciousness and occasionally experiencing glimpses or tastes of it involves some downs, as well as ups. Sometimes, the agony and ecstasy take turns. And sometimes agony takes more than its share of your thoughts and feelings.

The main source of the agony will likely be your own emotions and your expectations. If they are particularly confused, you may at times feel that you are—despite your high quest and determination —visiting hell. Based on your past feelings you may, as you become more vital and alive, experience old emotional tendencies which remind you of your past frustrations or your low self-esteem. Your old emotions, which had free rein for years perhaps, will create a storm whenever given the opportunity. Your life force will easily flow in the old grooves, bringing up feelings from childhood and other feelings which seemed long forgotten.

When you are proceeding toward higher consciousness, it is natural to want to feel good and happy about it. So it's very disconcerting to think, at times, that despite your quest, you've been feeling rotten all day. Also, in your optimism and in your study of higher consciousness, you expect to achieve it soon, and in a delightful—perhaps even cinematic, ultradramatic—way. Then, as you proceed toward your goal, you realize it requires *effort* and the *transformation* of old tendencies into new tendencies; you find your romantic expectations are not being fulfilled. Instead, now and then, your conscience or some sense of inadequacy haunts you.

Your fears even torment you with the thought you will never attain higher consciousness, or perhaps your expectations were all wrong from the beginning. You fear the great hopes which you cherish so much may not be realizable by you or anyone.

Living with frustrated expectations for a period of time can also seem like living in hell. It is an agony to experience negative emotional momentums which continually hound you and sink their teeth into your dreams. It's hard to watch your desires die—or have to spend one long day, and then another, aching for satisfaction.

Also, your subconscious mind gets into the act and throws old memories, images of unhappiness or misdeeds, along with a few choice mistakes, into your daily thoughts. "What? You're planning to achieve higher consciousness? That's FUNNY!" your subconscious mind suggests in its acts of sabotage.

There are additional agonies—guilt, periods of self-doubt, an ongoing sense of inferiority or a painful, lonely arrogance which just won't go away. You also agonize that you should be more patient and yet you find yourself extremely impatient. Then you become impatient that you are not developing patience faster. It would be funny if it didn't hurt so much. But it does. It's agony.

Plateaus are often miserable experiences, too. Perhaps only a month ago you were doing fine. You made genuine progress and were experiencing many of the ecstasies.

"But where did the ecstasies go?" you ponder. "Nothing new has developed for weeks! I'm trying. I'm working hard. I'm doing my part! But goodness, what a barrier, what a plateau. Will I *ever* break through? Will I ever go onward and upward again? Is this the level I'm going to have to live on? I'm *stranded* between two worlds, between my old self and the impossibilities of my hopes."

Boredom is quite agonizing, too. When nothing new is occurring, while at the same time your friends are doing very well, it's especially difficult to deal with boredom.

"Something's supposed to happen. I'm making the effort. I've studied the book. I visited the Gurus and Masters. Nothing's happening. There's nothing to this stuff. I'd be better off playing solitaire," you moan at times.

Worse than the agony of the plateau or the boredom is failure. At times most everyone tries to move forward, tries to become more conscious. However, due to old tendencies, you discover frustration and blockage instead. You develop the feeling you cannot break through. You start to think everything you try "won't work." Your sense of self hurts, and your esteem goes down the tubes. You know, "for a fact," you're a failure. General doubts flood your mind. You wonder if you can ever, even if given a hundred million lifetimes, find your higher consciousness, make the grade.

Failure is agony. Not only is failure so painful, but other people seem so superior, so able, so successful compared to you. Your sense of failure adds to your sense of separation from them—often initiating jealousy and subsequent possibilities of hatred. While your failure looms larger and larger in your mind, the successful people around you seem to be a different and superior species.

Another agony is your conflict of direction. You may be trying to please everybody while also meeting the demands of higher consciousness. Concerned relatives who may think of higher consciousness as a worthwhile hobby perhaps notice that you are treating higher consciousness as something more important than boating or golfing. Your loved ones become worried. They've read newspapers and heard strange things about altered consciousness. While they've done strange things themselves, perhaps, they fear you may be doing something dangerous to your mental health or spiritual future. Poorly informed about what you are doing, perhaps even superstitious and unwilling to understand, they may make your life very painful. They may insult you or try to coerce you not to study and grow. It's fairly agonizing when people you love don't want you to do what you're doing. Conflicts may force a choice regarding what's more important—your aspirations or their respect. This ultimatum creates clouds of doom overhead and personal agony underneath. Higher consciousness could make you a much more loving, interesting, and happy companion if only your close companions would give you a chance.

Also, your own personal superstitions give you a rough time. Due to your lack of training, you don't understand the goodness or beauty of the higher consciousness. You fear high intuitions may command you to give up your career, to go fight such things as the tsetse fly in Zambia. You might also be afraid that suddenly you're going to project your consciousness out of your body and who knows where you'll go—and what if you can't get back into your body?

You may fear that, while you're out in the blue in elevated consciousness, friends will think you're dead and gone; undertakers might embalm your body before you're able to comment. This kind of doubt and ignorance is indeed agonizing, too.

Then there are the pressures of life. Everyday you have to make a living (most people, anyway). Somebody must pay the rent, food bill, utilities. If you have children it's necessary to see they get a good chance to thrive now and in the future. The pressures of career and all the activities generally required of you in order that you may look at breakfast on a regular basis impact your private dreams of higher consciousness. You feel torn between your duty in the world versus fulfilling the yearning of your heart, a yearning so important and deep that life seems entirely empty and worthless without that fulfillment.

Not only do the regular pressures of life seem agonizing at times, but there are so many unforeseen variables. For example, you strive to lead a balanced, goal-centered life but suddenly your car dies and you have to spend more time working to buy a new one. Or, you were planning a quiet evening but instead you have to work late or handle an emergency. Suddenly a problem comes up, people need your help, and your plans for a weekend in the woods evaporate. Perhaps a new expense requires taking a second job for a short time and your once leisurely evening meditations have to be tightly fit in before dinner. Or, you had counted on a few days of rest and study but somebody got the flu. Perhaps it was you. Constant variables can be agonizing unless you understand your quest from the viewpoint of *increasing your consciousness daily* as you face life's problems and challenges in a creative and forthright manner.

There's also the problem of being greatly misunderstood. For example, in your job you may try to serve your higher values and make life better for your clients. At the same time, your co-workers may feel you are striving to steal a promotion by looking good. Insecure managers may feel you're trying to replace them while you're simply endeavoring to be a more loving and efficient person. Or, when you go to the movies with a close friend, you may put your elbow way back on the arm so your friend can use the front part of the arm, the more comfortable part. Your friend gets angry. He feels you're making a territorial claim and are trying to prevent his use of the shared arm.

Big or small, numerous situations may occur in which you feel you're striving to perform a service and truly help somebody out; but the person you're trying to help, or another person who's watching, may feel you're striving to take advantage or even rip off the other person. The world lives with a conflict of motives. As you strive to grow in consciousness, your motives may often be misconstrued. These misjudgments are often a source of agony.

At first, it's hard to get a balanced life established. Sometimes you're so tired you don't have energy to do the study or the meditation you want. Activities run you ragged and you're too tired to try to better your life or consciousness in any way. Sometimes your concerns vary widely. Perhaps you don't ever seem to have enough money to lead a secure, balanced life. This may happen to you from time to time until you become consolidated in higher consciousness and prosperity becomes established. Until then, economic concerns can be a regular headache. At other times ill health may thwart or delay your hopes for progress. Most any delays—from fatigue, financial insecurity, or health problems—are private agonies.

You may know other agonies, too. People tend to fear the unknown. You may well seek the higher consciousness but probably have no idea what you would do with it if you received it. In your ignorance you are prey to wacky ideas. You may take seriously something you would not attribute any significance whatever—if it were in a field you were more familiar with. So you can easily become a victim of false ideas from false teachers, as well as false, unexamined experiences. You don't know what is true. You don't know whom to believe. You don't trust your experiences because they don't *prove out* in daily life. This confusion is agony.

Further, you assume at times you are not progressing. Based on your limited judgment, not knowing much about the situation at all, you can somehow assume you're qualified to gauge your experience as being successful or unsuccessful. Not yet being very subtle or very aware, you usually make false assumptions.

PSYCHIC EXPERIENCES

In the beginning you may fantasize what higher consciousness is like and then suffer when practices toward higher consciousness do not yield the hoped-for fantasies. Or, to make the agony of ignorance even worse, sometimes you get "psychic experiences." Psychic sights or sounds generally come into the mind during periods where you are not concentrating or giving attention to your meditation practices. Usually, psychic experiences occur when you are sitting back with your mind blank, perhaps feeling lazy or too tired to pay attention. Suddenly you experience lights, sounds, perhaps even visions of some strange or very celestial beings.

Psychic originally referred to the soul or spiritual realities but came to mean, in modern times: "1) of or having to do with the psyche, or mind; 2) beyond natural or known physical processes; 3) apparently sensitive to forces beyond the physical world," according to *Webster's New World Dictionary.*

Based on common usage today, psychic generally refers to "the psyche, or mind" and is distinguished—perhaps unfortunately or unfairly—from the spiritual. That is, some people do have genuine spiritual experiences but call them *psychic.* Or, often people who have no knowledge of higher levels of awareness brand all spiritual experiences as psychic, or mental, and dismiss them as imaginings.

In dealing with problems of terminology then, most modern yogis, mystics, and metaphysicians accept psychic to mean "of the mind." They place "psychic" awareness *between* the levels of regular objective/subjective consciousness and the higher level of spiritual awareness. Based on this usage of the word *psychic*, most adepts, gurus, and teachers *urge* their students not to indulge or encourage these intermediate, often incorrect, mental impressions from their psychic nature. The reasons for strong warnings and cautions about psychic experiences are the catastrophes which have often occurred in the lives of once-aspiring students. Students who become enamored with psychic experiences often rely on psychic impressions, which they don't understand, or which they misinterpret, to guide their lives. They base all their important decisions on these experiences—many times disastrously. Since these mental impressions are sometimes correct, students often become convinced their impressions are right so they ignore both reality and the helpful instructions of those who could extricate them from slavery to mental and emotional impressions.

Often students' psychic visions and other phenomena are triggered by their own subconscious desires to be great, or especially important to others. Such students have often throughout history become arrogant and, too many times, mentally ill. Also, as they often become convinced they are great leaders, or the Messiah, they attract small bands of like-minded people—especially where heavy drug use is also involved—and often become paranoid in the fear that an unreceptive world is "out to get them." And sometimes they do outright harm to others, their children, friends and strangers, about whom they get a negative impression.

On the other side of this extremely important issue, there are millions of people in the world who are, or learn to be, more sensitive than the majority of humanity. Their psychic perception is more accurate. They, because of their greater appreciation for others and life itself, often receive psychic images about future events, helpful hints to help others be happier, or to help ill people get well. It's a shame that these more-sensitive-than-normal individuals have often been tortured, burned as witches, or live in ignorant condemnation even today.

If you should have a psychic experience—i.e., see ethereal forms, hear voices, have tactile sensations about people beyond range of normal touch, smell fragrances others can't, see departed souls, glimpse possible future events—write it down. Don't try to interpret or understand it right away. Examine it in the light of your normal consciousness and scriptural writings. If you think it's important or affects you emotionally, discuss it with someone you know to be spiritually attuned. You see, the problem with psychic impressions is that sometimes they're right, other times they're wrong. Sometimes these impressions are only partial and woefully incomplete. Sometimes, too, your psychic experience is a vivid reflection *of what you want to experience*—a vivid fantasy. Gain a calm insight about your psychic impressions while pushing forward as fast as you can into higher consciousness. Go beyond the psychic. Consider it a transitional level of awareness through which you are moving.

It's also true that you should not totally disregard your psychic experiences. Consider the foreman of a crew deep within an African diamond mine who suddenly received the psychic impression that the mine shaft was about to collapse on all his crew. He ordered immediate evacuation. As soon as his men were safely outside, the shaft collapsed into rock and rubble. Was the impression from higher consciousness or an intermediate psychic level? It could have been either. Fortunately, the foreman didn't file away his impression for later study. He acted on his "intuition."

For the most part, examine your psychic experiences in the light of day. Act on them only if they seem appropriate while benefiting others as well as yourself. Always strive to distinguish between your psychic and spiritual impressions. And don't, if you would know higher consciousness, encourage psychic activity. Avoid making—or letting—your mind go blank. Don't seek psychic impressions of others or of events. Go beyond, seek your own reliable higher consciousness.

Mainly, keep in mind that psychic experiences—when encouraged—can lead you into a fantasy world, away from reality. If you rely on fantasy and direct your life based on what may be delusive impressions, you will gradually develop a weak will and mind. Acting mainly on psychic information you will lose control of your own life. You won't be able to know a true life-transforming vision from a psychic experience, even if your life depends on it. Your "misguided life" will, within a year or two, become a living hell. Another agony.

The point is, don't fear psychic experiences but don't *rely* on them. They may be wrong or right, which is really not much genuine help to you. However, the more pure the mind and subconscious are, that is the more free they are from egocentricity, and the more closely you draw to the higher consciousness, the more true intuition—"the voice of the soul"—will develop. Much protection in and of itself will be afforded you. For if you truly live in love, who can harm you? The Universe itself will move—with all its powers— to save you.

The main differences, by the way, between psychic experience and higher consciousness are:

1) Higher consciousness experiences prove to be right in the light of daily life. Psychic experiences can prove right, or they can prove to be entirely wrong.

2) Psychic experiences tend to flatter your ego and make you arrogant. They influence you to ignore good advice and your own common sense. Also, psychic experiences often portray what you want to hear, or what you fear.

3) Higher consciousness insights make you humbler; you feel honored and grateful.

4) Higher consciousness transforms you and empowers you, in fact, to *establish* a finer life.

5) Psychic visions are not as vivid or life-changing as those of higher consciousness.

6) Reliance on psychic experiences often makes your character weaker and your mind less clear. You may also become less stable emotionally. You can become progressively dependent on psychic experiences because your ability to think and discriminate erodes. Attunement with higher consciousness, on the other hand, develops your character and your mind. You continuously become a finer, more capable and independent person.

ECSTASIES THAT DON'T LAST

There's another form of agony which is important: the ecstasies that don't last. At times, especially in the life of the beginning and intermediate seeker, there is splendid life-enrichment. Your being is flooded with rapture and joy. You feel you could live in this rush of delight forever. Every phase of your life improves. But then, inexplicably, your precious ecstasy dies down and withdraws. Nothing you can do brings it back. You feel bereft. The ecstasy, the wonder of life, the sense of harmony, the fresh perceptions, vanish. You feel stranded, more than a little lost.

The main reasons your ecstasies come and go are:

1) Your nerves are not developed enough to maintain such an intense level of awareness.

2) You have not balanced your life to enable the momentum of your ecstasy to continue.

3) You have been preoccupied in other areas, so your life force has been redirected from an ecstatic state into the other activities that you have now focused on—*your heart is where your treasure is.*

4) Your body or health has been run down, perhaps due to fatigue or overwork, and due to this overextension, your body and nerves can no longer maintain the high level of energy which is involved in ecstatic states.

All in all, as a devoted seeker of higher consciousness you find yourself in an incomparable position. Not only can you experience ecstasies which transcend all other joys; your agonies are extremely beneficial, too. Your agonies can develop your character and under-standing, guiding you toward your sublime goals.

But there is much more to be learned: the two great techniques that deal with *all* the agonies and which will increase the duration and beauty of your ecstasies, two wonderful techniques that will further change your life!

REFLECTION

Somehow, again and again, I delude myself that I know what I'm doing. I limit myself and oppose, with my unenlightened will, the mystery of my awakening. Therefore, once more I remind myself to love, to respond, and to receive.

29

TWO PRICELESS SKILLS

How does a seeker of higher consciousness overcome agonies and maintain ecstasies? Detachment and Practice are two of the finest techniques. Based on your patient, day-at-a-time development in the early chapters of *Keys to Higher Consciousness*, you can likely do both of these techniques with excellent results.

DETACHMENT

Detachment here refers to a state of mind in which you witness, clearly and calmly, with good will, whatever you are seeing, hearing, thinking, enjoying, or suffering. Watch your problems, fears, and challenges as if you are not bound or preoccupied by them but viewing them calmly—a witness. With practice, your turbulent thoughts and negative emotions will lose their grip on your mind. They will not be able to *drive* you or distort your inner potential and well being.

In the Detachment Technique you first view the outer world with no sense of ownership. The concept of "mine" usually colors whatever you behold with an emotional intensity which keeps you from being detached. Often, simply sitting in a park, calmly witnessing the children, trees, and birds enables a pleasant clarity and freedom of mind which establishes detachment. Or, look around your living room and kitchen as if you are a first-time guest. See the furniture and appliances clearly—as they are—withholding mental comments or emotional reactions. Simply be a witness.

When you can witness external objects in a truly detached manner, free of mental/emotional turbulence, you will find you can close your eyes and look at a worry or painful memory calmly and clearly, too. In fact, *the inner detachment is the true test—and goal.* When you can witness people, events, and things in the outer world with great calm and clarity, you will find you can easily witness the play of your mind and emotions well, too—likely for the first time in your life.

The next level of the Detachment Technique, then, is to become a witness, a "first-time" compassionate and clear viewer of your mind.

Additionally, when you can easily witness any and all of your thoughts and mental images, turn your focus to your emotions. Become a detached witness of the rivers of your feelings.

The technique of detachment is fairly easy for most everyone with good mental health. All it requires is five or ten minutes practice each day and a patient willingness to get back into a "witness mode" each time the mind or emotions succeed in making your thoughts wander. Most people find the practice difficult the first two or three times they try. Detachment is, after all, a different way of viewing the world and yourself.

As your detachment develops you become even more subtly aware of your mental/emotional faculties. You gain greater understanding of your personality and true nature. Your memory improves. Your emotions become more integrated and constructive. Your perceptions of your life and relationships become more accurate and, likely, more satisfying. Your mind works better.

Detachment helps you become so free of mental/emotional turbulence you can contact your higher consciousness at will.

You can overcome most of the agonies listed in the preceding chapter through developing detachment well. Sincerely watch the play of your thoughts. Watch your frustrations from the calm center within your being. If you behold several problems or agonies, watch them all calmly. Don't let any thoughts or feelings destroy your quiet, clear view.

As you look at your conflicts, pressures, and challenges, your detachment will often enable you to perceive fresh solutions. When you can detach your mind from its chaos, you can attune with your higher wisdom. You'll be inspired with new possibilities!

An extremely important attribute of detachment is the freedom it gives you to *choose* your best actions and responses to life's situations. No longer will you merely react to the world because now your clarity of vision gives you greater understanding coupled with new abilities to decide more beneficial courses of action. You can abandon habits which previously caused you loss or suffering.

Some people are afraid of detachment. They think it will make them remote, whereas detachment involves getting out of the stampede of negative emotions and thoughts in order that the self-destruction stop. In entering the detached, "good will witness" perspective you can most directly see what your problem is and most immediately solve it. A detached state can give you insight which immensely accelerates your overall progress toward fulfillment. Furthermore, in the ability to be detached at will, you become able to get free of your longstanding biases and misconceptions, as well as the inner turbulence of thoughts and feelings.

Also, when you are in ecstasy, periods of detachment are invaluable. So intense is the ecstasy that sometimes you need to be able to calmly withdraw from it. Detachment also helps when extraneous thoughts and feelings—or worries—fill your awareness, diminishing your ecstasy; through detachment you can choose to reestablish the ecstasy. Too, unpleasant memories and old attitudes can come to mind at times, dominating your attention and making you ignore the ecstasy. Detachment helps you reclaim the ecstasy before you lose it. Or, you may mentally probe or try to manipulate your ecstasy so forcefully it becomes eclipsed by mental activity—and, again, you can lose the ecstasy unless you know how to detach. Through regular moments of detachment you can let your ecstasy remain with you—and grow. The clarity of detachment keeps self-destructive thoughts or feelings from blocking or diminishing your ecstasy. In moments of detachment your ecstasy expands and becomes more established. Your thoughts and feelings become anchored in higher consciousness rather than your subconscious spewings. Detachment enables you to open yourself to ecstasy, to receive and maintain it. Worth considering!

With a degree of detachment you can know your world and your friends more deeply and appreciatively. In every way, true detachment refreshes your faculties for a finer life.

PRACTICE

When you have calmly perceived a problem from your witness vantage point and have determined a better way to deal with the problem, then *practice* putting this new action into effect. Old tendencies will try to dominate. It takes regular practice to create a new, more ideal situation, free of old agonies. Patient effort and perhaps a number of failures are usually necessary until, finally, the ideal situation which you glimpsed in your detached state becomes firmly established and a new way of success is achieved.

This form of practice, as a result of detachment, is extremely important, but it's also very enjoyable. Whenever you are practicing dealing with any of the agonies you are cutting through old pains, old tendencies and habit patterns, to establish *new life*.

Generally, those who fail to *practice new attitudes and actions* fail to achieve higher consciousness. They allow the agonies and their turbulence in general to dominate them. They give up. They refuse to have periods of detachment or practice their ideals. They quit:

1) They simply change their minds. Something else has become more important to them.
2) They allow themselves to be pacified by a slight improvement in the outer world. As a consequence, they no longer feel they need higher awareness or greater well being. A bribe from the outer world, however slight, often suffices.
3) They allow other desires to become more important and to dominate. Thus they change their purpose and lose their desire for higher consciousness.

ENCOURAGEMENTS

If you take the help of Detachment and Practice, not forgetting how important faith and companionship are, you will find moments of ecstasy as you work your way forward. These flashes of ecstasy or light are encouragements, guiding signs that help you stay on track. They are indications from the higher consciousness of "Well done, my good friend."

These encouragements are not psychic but rather are genuine spiritual experiences:

A) In your meditations, and whenever you calmly close your eyes, pastel colors begin to be visible in your forehead. These pastel colors may form patterns like circles and spheres. Your mind has to be harmonious and relatively free of worry in order to experience this.

B) You may see flashes of light, like lightning flashes. You may think you are seeing fireflies at times when your mind is calmly pondering higher consciousness.

C) You may see soft, mellow light like that of the moon; or, you may see blazing light like that of the sun. These experiences are profound indicators of something marvelous ahead.

D) Also, centers of awareness in your spine and brain begin to open, giving you indications of the talent and potential within your being.

E) For example, in your spine in back of the navel you may feel a quickening of energy or a concentration of energy which makes your body feel warm—hopefully not too hot. (Heat indicates that you are pressuring your nervous system too much and you should simply relax and let yourself calm down. On the other hand, in the presence of a Master who is guiding the process, the heat may be an appropriate condition.) As this center, called the navel center, develops, you find yourself filled with courage. Your fears fly away and you also begin to notice that whatever you really need in your life comes to you. Whatever you need you can have.

F) Or, the center in your forehead, half an inch above your eyebrows, begins to pulsate and reveal brilliant white, yellow, or rich blue light into your mind. This light may flood your whole being. In this state, insight is rapidly developed. You find it very easy to practice detachment and, also, you find it progressively easier to attune with the higher will.

G) The ecstasy itself is wondrous. It may be a calm buzz of energy at localized points within your body or all over. Usually bliss begins occurring in the spine, the chest area near the heart, or in the brain. In the bliss you feel immediately in the presence of the higher consciousness. In bliss you find incomparable delight. Incomparable, that is, until it matures into an even more delightful ecstasy called *ananda*. In ananda your ecstasy becomes dynamic and expansive. It is an ever-new joy—endless and boundless—while being sweet and tender, not obnoxious or overpowering. The ecstasy—whatever its manner of abiding—helps you integrate your life. It enables your body, mind, and spiritual nature to work in closer and closer harmony. You will literally want to dance for joy. In fact, why not?

The main thing a seeker must do is hang in there! Neither ecstasy nor agony are as important as persisting. As one great saint, Lahiri Mahasay, said, "Doing, doing, done." Keep practicing, keep moving toward your goal, and suddenly you find your goal is accomplished.

REFLECTION

Doing, doing, done.

30

THE THRESHOLD

The seeker who doesn't have an enlightened teacher needs to be warned about two experiences along the way. This knowledge may not be necessary for everyone to know. However, when you don't have a teacher, it is essential to be forewarned. These two potential threats to your advancement are called the Terror of the Threshold and the Dark Night of the Soul.

If you've been progressing steadily and are deeply honest with yourself, you may bypass both of these events. You may not *need* them in order to overcome your blind spots. Your journey, because of your painstaking steadiness and continual growth, will likely spare you from these emotionally jarring times. It is especially true that you will bypass these events if you develop your whole being evenly. That is, a) maintain good physical health; b) do not waste or dissipate your life force; c) develop emotional balance and consistency, maintaining a sense of well being; d) develop a clear, efficient mind; e) develop devotion and a humble ego.

Having made it clear then that you may never know these two frightening experiences personally, and may wonder why some people are going through them, let's explore "The Terror."

TERROR OF THE THRESHOLD

Usually you embark on the path to higher consciousness with some very good opinions of yourself. You know you're not perfect but you're certainly as good as others—perhaps a little better. You've often observed many times in life that you were the correct one or did the right thing. Perhaps you've been misunderstood but you've generally, nevertheless, been in the right. Most often, you feel, people have hurt you, or outraged you, far and away more than you have hurt or outraged them.

Proceeding for a few weeks or months down the road toward higher consciousness, you may begin to get the hunch you're not as *okay* as you first thought. In fact, there are times, you now recognize, you behaved like a creep. At other times you did the right deed but for the wrong reason. Your motivation seemed to be kindly but it was—you know within your heart—covertly selfish. You recall you often tried to take the advantage, even with your friends. Indeed, you begin to see you have pretensions of goodness at times without the substance of goodness inside.

Becoming more thoughtful, you easily observe during your daily life that there are times you're ashamed or embarrassed by your old feelings of jealousy or unreasonable anger toward another person. "No," you tell yourself, "perhaps I'm not as great as I like to think."

Your reflections and observations intensify in the cold light of truth.

Suddenly, in the middle of the night or during meditation, you, in your search for truth, have a frightening experience. It's called the terror of the threshold, and the word terror is apt. Striving to enter into a higher realm of consciousness—striving to enter the portal of greater love, truth, and beauty—you, all at once, in one total impression, find yourself gazing into a horrifying sight. You perceive your evil. There, ever so vividly, your cruel and thoughtless actions stand revealed to your inner sight. You see these ghastly images, while feeling deep pain. Remorse wells up; but in your terror you cannot stop the sight of such selfishness, such foul thinking, such egocentricity. Your emotions seem so base, you feel you're looking at an animal. Yet, in all the terror, you know, inescapably, you are seeing *yourself*. That's the terror of it.

You clearly see yourself, in myriad examples, as an *enemy of light*. You have, for your own purposes, limited or denied goodness. You have hurt others. You have, for some personal gain, conspired against good people—or blocked them. You have spoken ill of others. You have tormented people with your insults. With tears you realize you have often been given a choice of light or darkness and you have, *sometimes eagerly*, sometimes slowly after great pondering, chosen the darkness. Oh, the revulsion of it all! You see your evil in such detail, with so many proofs.

"Oh, what a horrible person I've been!" you say from the agony of your soul. "So manipulative! How conniving! How like a cunning animal! How unlike a human being. How unlike my dreams and pretensions of my true nature have I behaved! In thought, word, and deed I have stood against life and goodness itself. It is undeniably evident.

"Oh, I'm terrified," you cry. "A thousand years of remorse will still not relieve my guilt about what I have done to others, to myself, to my Lord. How silly are my pretensions to goodness. How foolish to conceive of myself entering higher consciousness. I tremble in shock, convicted."

Much weeping happens. Your whole body sobs. You have a growing sense of helplessness due to the acknowledgement of your allegiance to evil thoughts, words, and actions. You feel you stink at every level, and oh, how putridly.

Then morning arrives and you go about your daily life *smiling*, doing your job, but feeling empty inside—empty and very clean. In your terror of the threshold and your profound remorse, many longtime personal blockages and obstacles are released. In your admissions of self-centered evil and insufferable pettiness, your inner cleansing is so great that a new life can begin. Through the terror of the threshold, months, perhaps years, or even greater time spans of limitations within your mental and emotional nature are released. You become able to think and feel love at extremely subtle and satisfying levels. Your remorse and terror make you very humble and ever so appreciative of that grace or goodness which sustains your life—even though you have been an opponent of life.

Convicted, and also purged, you vigorously turn to a higher life. Your condemnation of others is totally gone. Your reliance on higher mercy and a new way of life is readily enforced.

You become, through the terror of the threshold, humbled and all the readier for the pursuit of higher consciousness, even if it should take you forever to find it. Abhorring what you have seen in yourself, you actively seek healing. You will do anything you can to become a better person each day.

Sometimes men and women are not capable of beholding the whole terror in a two or three-hour period. In these instances, the terror experience occurs five or six times, perhaps, over a period of several weeks with the process fulfilling itself in specific stages. Each stage relates to a general area in which you have denied yourself and others the fullness of life.

The terror experience is so powerful that your hair seems to stand on end. You have to be in a very healthy state of mind for such a powerful event to occur. Those who are suffering some degree of mental illness are denied this experience because it would be too crushing. Instead, they live with the sense there is an explosive guilt welling up within them. They need the tender lancing of a professional counselor.

Through your personal terror and remorse, your emotional nature becomes so free of condemnation of others that you are capable of a greater fellowship with all people. The heart, often so full of negativity, deeply needs to be cleaned out if love is ever to dwell in it for any length of time. Certainly, if your love is to be ongoing and a constant state of relationship is to occur, a clearing away is absolutely essential.

The ordeal of your private terror brings renewal. You are mentally, emotionally, spiritually, and often physically refreshed. Through the Terror of the Threshold a new, humble, and eager seeker steps from the dark way, from old tendencies, into the light, and into a life of light.

REFLECTION

The truth I fear
Is my only hope.

31

DARK NIGHT OF THE SOUL

"Dark night of the soul" sounds like a threatening and much to be avoided experience. Yet perhaps a quarter of the seekers on the road to higher consciousness will pass through the dark night. In fact, they may pass through several until they experience the profound joy of their true nature.

Many seekers would encourage the dark night experience if they knew what it was. However, to one engaged in the dark night, suffering seems unending.

The dark night occurs after considerable advancement toward higher consciousness. Indeed, the dark night usually occurs like an initiation before one of these special seekers is admitted into regular relationship with higher consciousness. The dark night also occurs to those who do not seek *relationship* but *immersion or unity* in the higher consciousness. While the term *dark night of the soul* is used broadly, its general meaning—in the field of higher consciousness—is *a lengthy and profound absence of light and hope.* In the dark night you feel profoundly alone.

The dark night usually develops this way—

You, as a genuine seeker, have gone through many significant phases as you progress toward higher consciousness. Your faith is

212

strong. You have kept loyal companionship with fellow seekers and perhaps you have already found a special teacher. You've experienced indications of the reality of higher consciousness and yearn to be more deeply in communion with it. You see the principles of a higher power at work in your life. Yet, all in all, you find yourself somehow painfully on the outside. You feel caught between your old way of living, your old tendencies and associations, and this nebulous, unreachable realm of higher consciousness.

You feel an exile in both places. You don't belong in the old pastimes, in the old empty or numbing way of life, yet you somehow can't fit in or feel at home in the fellowship of those who talk naturally of the higher consciousness and its reality. They are experienced, they are absorbed in it. They are loving, giving people. But you are unable to live, with full heart and mind, the way they do. They're able to apply the principles of higher consciousness easily, yet it's so hard for you. They have manifestations and proofs on a regular basis. You only stretch like a human mule after a receding corncob while pulling the heavy weight of your old tendencies behind you.

You try to be good, and often you can't. You try to be loving and find at times your heart is hard like stone. Sometimes your projects fall down around your ears. You keep struggling and still you don't break through. You understand the path is one of joy and yet your life seems to have been barren for a month or two, perhaps longer. Where did that early joy and zest go?

Up to this particular time there was joy, there was delight. But now there is only a hanging on, a dogged hanging on. You persist because you can't conceive of going back to your old way of life. That seems impossible now. That would be like going to prison, living as if with a transorbital lobotomy.

You deeply want to have joy and fulfillment, easily manifest prosperity, but something's not working. You don't know what it is but something's awry, and your meditations have lost their luster. Sometimes, during rare meditations, you do experience brief moments of peace. Your agonizing mind and heart rest from their turbulence and even these fleeting times of calm are so deeply appreciated. Your light dance of life, which had gone on for some time, is now a trudging in what seems a devastated and alien land.

Your fellow seekers look at you and show their concern. Their words of kindness are valued but you feel you're somehow incapable of responding well. Your heart is numb. At these times your friends try to cheer you up. They invite you to dinner. You seem to perform fairly well, despite the emptiness you feel inside. What else is there to do? You wonder if you have any right to be in their fellowship at all. You think of leaving town, but where would you go? What good would diversion be?

A number of your friends in the fellowship of this great path know what you are going through for they have been through it themselves. They feel the main thing to do is encourage you to go on. They know if you keep it up and do not quit you will succeed. They know if you quit you will be a self-reject and will return to the old life, forever a foreigner, being neither at home with it nor at home anywhere else. They recognize that your own higher self, out of love, is lifting you up into its embrace. They see you are being drawn into your dark night because 1) your inner potential has great stature; and 2) your crusty, old ego requires you go through the dark night in order to be transformed.

Other seekers, for various reasons, do not have to pass through the dark night. However, the dark night is your way.

Your night is a very difficult time. While others may one day envy you for the marvelous growth you experienced in such a short, intensified period, you will, because of the pain of your experience, always feel profound compassion for those whom you one day see going through a similar night.

Being caught between the old way of life and the new possibilities, your sense of alienation intensifies. Your sense of inadequacy and not knowing what to do next becomes gnawingly constant. You feel you would do anything to get out of this state, yet it is only your ego which is keeping you in it. However, this insight is impossible for you to grasp while going through your long night.

And you feel so totally alone. Sure, you have friends and you appreciate them, but you are keenly aware they are not capable of feeling what you are feeling or knowing what you are going through. Sometimes they seem like clowns, sometimes they seem empty-headed, caught up in meaningless pursuits. They do not understand, you think, how much you are suffering or how you cry out and pray deep into each midnight. You try their advice but it doesn't seem to touch the heart of the matter.

You begin to enter the dark night in earnest when you feel *completely stranded*. In the fullness of the dark night you don't know where you are spiritually. You're separate from God and man. You do not know where to turn. Your friends love you and wish you well but your condition does not improve.

The dark night is a very private matter. The person in the dark night is generally able to function quite well despite inner suffering. Often your acquaintances never suspect that you are going through the dark night—they probably do not even know what it is. Only people close to you—especially friends along the path—can recognize your pain.

You feel like a hollow person doing the activities of life with no motivation except expediency. Your eyes seem deeper in your head. You are profoundly aware of the suffering of humanity and the cruelty of one person to another. You feel that cruelty and negativity far outweigh love and constructive action.

Alone, and not wishing to be, unable even to express yourself to others, you enter midnight and the greatest intensity of the dark night. Here you have finally come to the time of sovereign solitude. In this precious time, which has no apparent prospects of love or happiness, you clearly perceive that nothing in the outer world has proven adequate to heal your condition. Nobody, not even your dearest friends and loved ones, can make you whole. Even if they have tried, and love you enough to try loving you forever, they can't give you peace.

You eye your books and consider all the benefit you have gained from these extremely wise vessels of truth. Yet not one book, not one thought, goes deep enough inside you to where the affliction abides.

You look at your possessions, your money container. No material thing has been able to help you. No material means have worked. Nothing, no one, in the outer world has enabled you to come out of this dark night.

In your loneliness, you next—in a seemingly random process— notice that none of your thoughts have proven adequate to your suffering. Not one—even repeated fifty thousand times—breaks the inner storm and lets in light. God and higher consciousness seem so far away that perhaps they are unreal. Neither one has, despite your protracted exposure of yourself, done anything to ease or remove your agony. Nothing appears efficacious. Nothing works.

Clearly, there is nowhere to turn. There is nothing to be done. All actions you considered have been tried. There is nothing to think, nothing to feel, nothing to do, nowhere to go. It seems you have to accept this defeat—or, you can persist in struggling against it. For awhile longer, you go about thinking, feeling, and doing other options that occur to you. But you realize in the midnight of your soul that you have tried every option you know of.

Helpless, totally helpless, as well as ever so alone, you abide in this condition. And you accept your predicament. You accept that there is really, except for a murmured prayer to a remote Lord and a remnant of a shredded faith, nothing else left.

Suicide would be absurd. Suicide would be an act of arrogance and vanity. You have grown far beyond such primitive responses to your private agony. No, nothing to do. Nothing remains in this lonely helplessness. There is, without question, nothing you can do.

You abide. You accept your state. How have you gotten to this place? That's insignificant. Musings and feelings aside, you wait. You feel you may have to stay this way forever, doing the regular day-to-day things, but in this mood of emptiness. Nothing. Nothing.

Then, it happens. A holy presence comes into your room—sweetly, softly. You feel it filling you. Your mind is filled with mellow or bright light. Your heart, your still heart, is permeated with peace. This peace moves through your body like a cold spring of mountain water. It flows in your spine, your brain, and under your skin. Everywhere.

Also, this presence, this comforter, moves like a breeze across your arid mind and numb heart. Then, or a few days later, the fire of joy begins to smoulder. Here, abiding with nothing more to do, *your ego drops away!* Your ignorant, arrogant, fearful sense of self falls away from you. You stand in light—a new being, a free being—transformed.

Believe it or not, that's what the dark night is all about: transformation. Your ego, your limited sense of self, your inadequate complex of ideas about who you are, had to be dissolved. Your ego was, you begin to see, eclipsing higher consciousness and your true nature. Your old sense of self was inadequate to your new hopes and proper state. Your suffering intensified because of a major misapprehension. You were too used to thinking of yourself based on inputs from your previous experiences in life. On and on through life, you gathered information and responses from the world which indicated to you what kind of person you were and are. These superficial units of related inputs became integrated in what is called the ego—your sense of self, your sense of who you are. As long as you allowed this inaccurate or only partial sense of who you are to dominate, you could not know or abide in your true nature.

Your ego sense is so powerful—you invest it with so much of your thought and feeling—that your attitudes of life become based on an egocentric perspective. The ego gains a progressively greater foothold on your entire life because your basic attitudes about your existence and essential nature are strongly linked with ego.

Then, your ego sense, due to your suffering or your limitations in life, wants to have more power over circumstances, and a more pleasant life. The ego sense often becomes motivated to seek higher consciousness and, thus, greater ability to dominate in life. Not always, but often, it is the ego sense which most eagerly pursues higher consciousness. It wants to be in charge; it wants to manipulate events and make life come out more to its satisfaction. But, as long as your ego dominates, it is on a collision course with your true nature and your higher consciousness. There's going to be a showdown. There has to be a confrontation sometime if your higher consciousness is ever to emerge, if you are ever to know truly who you are and what your human capabilities are.

Furthermore—and this is extremely important, especially in understanding the dark night of the soul—your ego, as it develops from childhood onward, has the conviction that *it is the doer*. Generally, your ego assumes that it chooses what your mind will think, and chooses what your heart will feel. It feels it selects the various actions and activities you are going to undertake. Your sense of self, being convinced it is the doer, feels it accomplishes anything and everything in your life. Do you see, then, how the dark night develops? A false sense of self has been ignorantly and manipulatively standing in the way of enlightenment.

Additionally, until you are **consolidated** in higher consciousness, your ego can return and reestablish control if you let it. Sometimes when you're fatigued or when you have special, new opportunities in life, you are vulnerable to the reestablishment of your ego and its opinion that it is in charge of doing everything. It will again eclipse the higher consciousness until you recognize what has happened. Then you must courageously and consciously reaffirm your true nature, and deal with the upstart, old ego. Otherwise, another dark night phase will again develop.

A person seeking higher consciousness is, in effect, and with intensity, seeking the transformation of his own ego. He is seeking to end the tyranny of the ego and abide *in his true nature*, instead of a false nature concocted through experiences and emotional inputs during the process of life. While it is true these inputs have a value in subjecting you to new experiences and so offer unique learning situations, they often give you a delusory sense of self. You are not your mistake. Even a murderer can change and become a new being.

Still, as you progress toward higher consciousness, your ego may not be humbling and daily transforming itself. You may, instead, have a highly developed ego which is sure that it is causing the events of higher consciousness to unfold bit by bit. Your ego, after all, can be very interested in the attributes of higher consciousness, in meditation and association with enlightened beings. Your ego feels gratification and satisfaction in moving on down the road toward higher consciousness.

Your ego may also have the opinion that, because of its grasp of matters, it will one day establish or—by its thought process and feelings—bring about enlightenment and awakening. It is convinced that it will *achieve* higher consciousness. This is ironic because by the time of the dark night, the ego is the *main obstacle*; it is the obstruction of the light of consciousness. It stands between you and your fulfillment. In fact, the length of your dark night is *based* on the truculence and cunning of your ego. It can fight a very lengthy battle if it fears it's going to be destroyed or will have to give in to something so much greater than it knows itself to be.

Incredibly, your ego wants to be in on the act of enlightenment. Ego wants to bring about higher consciousness by its own dramatic means. Certainly, it doesn't want to be granted fulfillment by a power outside of itself. Convinced that *it is the doer*, your ego holds on for dear life—until that event called the dark night of the soul, when your ego awakens to the profound fact it cannot cause or bring about higher consciousness.

Ego cannot, by its will or any other skills whatever, create the wholeness of heart which will end your deep suffering. In a sense your ego recognizes itself—in the dark night—*to be* the disease. It recognizes that its foothold on your mind and heart has, at an advanced stage on your path, proven a great numbing agent and a high stone wall against the light. Ego stands against the fulfillment of your faith and the realization of your profoundest yearnings. Finally your ego has found something it cannot do and, in the dark night of the soul, it becomes totally convinced it is inadequate. It cannot deal with your suffering or the fulfillment of the heart's yearning. Nothing it can do, think, say, buy, or travel to, will in any way suffice.

Here in this dark night, the lifelong ego sense dies: impotent. Having fulfilled its part, now weak and incompetent, it is dissolved —transmuted. From a higher sense now awakening within you, you slough off your false sense of self. You now know yourself to be a different person than you thought you were. Your ego was merely experiencing some of the attributes, some of the qualities, of your true nature, while at the same time obstructing others.

You, in passing successfully through the dark night, enter the realms of higher consciousness. You've been cleansed of the most deep-rooted sickness: your ignorance of your true nature and your inadequate, often totally wrong opinion of who you are. You now cease your inner conflict and abide serenely in your true nature. The night is over. The dawn of a new life in higher consciousness transforms your bleak life of the past few months into one with a heavenly nature. You have been delivered of the intolerable bondage to ego.

Henceforth, you will walk the earth seeing others afresh, living a new life, and abiding in your true nature. You have become a son or daughter of higher consciousness. Now your words and actions will be attuned with your true self. Now you express inspiration and comfort.

The dark night has passed. It is over.

REFLECTION

What must the caterpillar do
That it may one day fly?

V

MASTER
AND
INITIATE

32

KEEP AN EYE OUT FOR THE MASTER

As you progress in your exploration of consciousness and discover more and more of the other nine-tenths of yourself, you may become fascinated by the spiritual aspects of life. If so, you are preparing to be a fitting companion for an enlightened friend. A Guru, or spiritual teacher, can accelerate your awakening by light years. He will not only help you discover the higher consciousness more rapidly, but enable you to consolidate your life and live as an enlightened person.

WHAT IF YOU SEEM UNABLE TO FIND YOUR GURU?

Don't be discouraged if the years pass by and you can't find that incomparable awakener of higher consciousness, that merciful man or woman. It's very important you never give up in the quest for your compassionate personal guide. Also, your own higher consciousness will stand as your Master and uplift you day by day until you find your true Guru.* Then, too, it's possible for you to

---

* In respect, I will observe the tradition of capitalizing Master and Guru throughout this *Master and Initiate* section.

experience higher consciousness without personal training from a living Master—possible but vastly more difficult.

WHY CAN'T YOUR HIGHER CONSCIOUSNESS ALONE BE YOUR GURU?

Your higher self, or spiritual essence, *is* the ultimate Guru. But early in your development lack of training, impurity of mind and emotions, and the regular opposition of your own ego, keep you from reliable and frequent contact with your inner Guru. Breaking through your inner barriers to a discovery of "the Guru within" usually requires the help of an enlightened person—one who shows the way to your personal awakening—a Guru or Master.

WHAT EXACTLY DOES *GURU* MEAN?

While the term *Guru* may be specialized in its exact meaning, the reality and importance of the Guru is widely recognized in both East and West. The phenomenon of an enlightened being empowered to convey awakening or higher consciousness to others who are worthy is commonly found throughout traditions of religion, mysticism, metaphysics, yoga, and various philosophies.

Some time ago a medical doctor, Maurice Bucke, became intrigued with the subject of higher consciousness.* Exploring the lives of especially aware people of his time, he came to the conclusion that higher awareness—which he called cosmic consciousness—is generally experienced in the presence of one who already has it. Almost always there is an *extension* of light rather than the creation of it. One who is "aflame" shares the fire through touch or by being present in the life of the seeker.

Then the newly-awakened seeker usually abides in the heavenly experience for a few weeks or months and the experience goes away. The seeker pines for the return of higher awareness but cannot induce it to come back. What becomes necessary, as Bucke observed in many instances, is the formerly "on fire" seeker must then tackle the problems of his life and character and, over a period which may last for years, prepare his life to become capable of again receiving *and maintaining* the special flame. Then, when his, or her, life has been aligned with strong character, good will for all, and a universal spirit, cosmic consciousness returns. It stays for longer and longer pe-

---

* See *Cosmic Consciousness* by Dr. Maurice Bucke.

riods, its presence often becoming continuous.

Bucke maintains that these people of higher consciousness, or *cosmic consciousness* to use his term, have been the main "forwarders" of civilization throughout the ages. He determined that there are so few of them they could meet together in a large living room. However, he goes on to say that, in his opinion, there has been a development of human faculties over the ages.

For example, man can very likely perceive more colors now than thousands of years ago, and Bucke feels man's sense of humor has developed from being very primitive to being more subtle. Bucke feels that the next major human development is in the field of higher consciousness and he foresees an age when men and women will so refine their character and understanding of one another that *most of them* will be able to live naturally in cosmic consciousness.

Bucke's conclusion is that mankind is evolving spiritually and the *majority* of men and women will become cosmically conscious! They will live heavenly lives in love and peace with one another. They will strive to understand and share the planet nobly with people of different views who are also matured in their development— all experiencers of cosmic consciousness. This transformed society will come about as one enlightened being awakens another throughout the world.

IN JUDAISM

There are similar traditions of enlightened persons awakening sincere and worthy seekers in Judaism. Oftentimes Hebrew scriptures speak of a man of God, a prophet, conveying knowledge, wisdom, or experience of God to a worthy aspirant. For example, Elijah and Elisha. Elijah gave his mantle to his disciple, Elisha. Both Elijah and Elisha brought people back to life and, also, faced false prophets victoriously. Elijah and Elisha spent considerable time in the wilderness perfecting their spiritual faculties and came among men to serve. Elisha had many disciples during his life.

Another "awakener" was Baal Shem Tov, the seventeenth-century founder of modern Hasidism. Many traditions of awakening and enlightenment resulted from the spiritual work of Baal Shem Tov and his followers. His name means "master of the name of God," or "master of the good name." Enlightened on a mountain, he started the Jewish Hasidic tradition of intense prayer, joy, and love. He was called a wonder rabbi—healing people and turning enemies into friends.

IN ISLAM

Similarly, Islam has a tradition of revering true teachers who practice what they preach and live in personal piety, a personal awareness of God. The highest example of such a one is the Prophet Mohammed himself. Muslims, the believers of Islam, revere the Prophet Mohammed's 100,000 followers who are called his "companions." The companions of Mohammed went out from him and circles of followers gathered around many of these companions of Mohammed. The followers of the companions were called *tabi'is*.

During the time of the tabi'is, according to Dr. Muzammil Siddiqi, director of the Islamic Society of Orange County in California, a special movement started in the Islamic work, a mystical movement called Sufism. Deeply pious men and women within Sufism became known as Masters, or teachers. These Masters attracted a large number of followers. So, around each Master developed a circle of followers called a *halaba*.

Seekers of greater surrender to the Lord come to these Sufi Masters, usually seated in the mosques, and ask a particular Master questions or listen to spiritual teachings—how to develop themselves spiritually, how to create sincerity in their faith, how to improve their awareness of God—and the Master shows them what steps to take in their personal development. These Masters also help guide the sincere believers through certain states of higher consciousness and stations of higher awareness. (In Islam, these stations are known as *maqamat* and *ahwal*, which develop into states of deep surrender of both ego and selfishness called *fana* and *baqa*.)

As in several other traditions, Islam emphasizes that the Masters and even Prophet Mohammed are not divine but *reflect* the divine presence.

IN CHRISTIANITY

Spiritual Masters are common in Christianity as well. Christ, in addition to being the redeemer of humanity, functioned also as Guru; He awakened his disciples and others to God's glory. Study of his life and relationships with his disciples will give you much help if you are seeking to understand the nature of the transference of higher consciousness and the awareness of God. It's extremely beneficial to study the Gospel of John in this light.

Detailed study of many Catholic saints such as Vincent de Paul is also very helpful in becoming familiar with this phenomenon of "awakening" in the field of higher consciousness. Vincent de Paul became one of the greatest human beings ever to walk the earth. A priest who had been through many heroic experiences, he had been much honored, even in Rome; he appeared a man of God—"doing the right things," living in a way appropriate to a priest. He, however, really beheld huge obstacles within his own mind and heart.

Vincent observed his life did not fully accept or reflect the presence of the Lord. Over the years he observed a priest named Father Berulle who showed every evidence of being deeply intimate with Christ. The life of Father Berulle was an inspiration. One day Vincent beseeched Father Berulle to become his, Vincent's, personal spiritual guide. He said he recognized Jesus Christ expressing and moving in the good priest's life, thoughts, and words. Vincent, after pressing his request with intensity, was accepted by the humble Father Berulle. Vincent pledged himself in complete obedience to the senior priest. He pledged to do whatever Father Berulle would ask of him, knowing that Father Berulle's instructions would be as Christ would give them and would be very specific in terms of Vincent's daily walk with God.

Vincent then lived for years doing exactly what Father Berulle told him to do—at least almost always. He did the work Father Berulle told him to do: he became parish priest at Clichy, and undertook other missions as instructed by Father Berulle. He conducted his daily life as Father Berulle instructed. He disciplined his thoughts and also studied as directed by Father Berulle.

Though Vincent became more and more widely known for his holiness, he disobeyed Father Berulle on one occasion and ran away. Vincent felt pride taking over his nature. He fled to the humble church at Chatillon to serve the poor parishioners there, rather than the prominent aristocrats who loved him so. But Father Berulle instructed Vincent to return to his duties after several months and Vincent willingly did so.

Vincent, with the help of his spiritual mentor, his dear "Guru," overcame his obstacles to the life of Christ. The presence of Christ infilled him and abided within him constantly. In the light of Christ, knowing that his resurrected light was now freely moving through him, Vincent lived a life of extraordinary service and achievement. Because he was also very brilliant, he was able to help millions of people. He saved—physically saved—tens of thousands of lives during the Thirty Year's War. He also rescued many abandoned babies from church steps and garbage heaps.

At the stage where the spirit of Christ constantly abided in

Vincent and his higher consciousness was consolidated, Father Berulle lovingly pronounced Vincent healed of the confusions of the world and ego. Father Berulle saw Vincent was free, truly free, and released Vincent from the vow of obedience to him. They continued as dearest brothers in the Lord for the rest of their lives.

There are dozens, and likely thousands, of examples of this Western tradition of the transference of higher consciousness from one who has been so awakened to another who yearns and has prepared himself for that awakening. Protestant ministers have often spoken of meeting a great man of God to whom they turn for teaching and correction. They speak in strangely Eastern terms of wishing to bow down before the Christ in a great brother or sister. They deeply value the laying on of hands from Christian brothers or sisters. Being called to serve the Lord, they seek to be more and more Christlike shepherds of their congregations.

Certainly western mysticism *is* a tradition of the transfer of higher consciousness from those who have it into the lives of worthy brothers and sisters—those who have prepared their character and those who will not abuse greater power. Most all schools of thought which speak of awakening have a tradition of transferring consciousness.

Certainly, many eastern religions and yoga emphasize the great importance of the aspirant becoming prepared for the great meeting with the Guru who will convey the spirit of enlightenment to a truly worthy and able candidate. The word Guru comes from Sanskrit and its root words are *gu*, meaning darkness, and *ru*, dispeller. A Guru is an awakened man or woman who has personally, through the help and invaluable transfer of consciousness from a Guru before, become able to transmit higher consciousness to the aspirant. An aspirant who is accepted by a Guru and who is considered to be worthy to be initiated is called a *chela*, meaning devotee, or a *sisya*, meaning disciple, one who accepts the discipline of the Guru.

The Guru function is mainly a spiritual one. A true Guru never claims to own or *originate* the spirit of higher consciousness which he conveys. He considers himself only an "instrument" of love and light. As his life has been immeasurably helped and uplifted by the Lord of his heart, he willingly conveys higher consciousness and awareness of the Lord to a worthy initiate.

While strange and bizarre events today are confusing the great beauty of this Guru/Chela relationship, and while sensational individuals who call themselves Gurus and Masters live in a hype similar to the Beatles' invasion of America, the tradition, nevertheless, goes on. A *few* Gurus are still in the world today. There are so few, perhaps, because of a lack of interest. Many people are not desirous of improving their character. They don't want to look at their problems, let alone correct them. But without becoming a worthy aspirant and truly being eager to overcome ego and other personal flaws, one cannot *abide* in the higher consciousness, and so one is not capable of becoming a Guru. Consequently, there are not many Gurus in the world today—that is, defining the Guru as one who has experienced higher consciousness himself, abides in it, and is willing and able to extend that awakening to qualified aspirants.

Moreover, there are problems in the tradition of Master and Initiate today. Some great Gurus, nearing the end of their lives, have become infirm or senile and are no longer capable of functioning as transferrers of higher consciousness. This circumstance is contrary to ancient writings but it happens today. In a chaotic world "smogged" by drugs, greed, violence, and self-gratification, these super-sensitive souls have more difficulty maintaining their health. Gurus, who of necessity take on the sins or karmas of their chelas, have great burdens to bear in these most difficult of times, and the self-indulgent culture often wears them out quickly. A Guru teaching in a metropolis is not unlike a soldier on a battlefield, subject to battle fatigue. Most Gurus of old had more peaceful times. That God sends Gurus eternally is his greatest blessing to man, and all Gurus should be valued for the love and service they give and for the goodness they embody in the lives of their beloved chelas.

Certainly one who seeks the Guru today must be selective and discriminating. You must be willing to search forever, search to the ends of the earth for the Master, as you concentrate mainly on developing yourself for the day that your Master—your great companion—will be attracted to the time and place where your initiation is received and your new life becomes established.

In your search for the Guru, keep in mind that often by the time a person becomes qualified to be a Guru, old age is approaching or firmly established. Many Gurus accept thirty, or fewer, initiates— sometimes only seven. Some Gurus, due to their early advancement, perform the initiating/awakening function for numerous decades. Some Gurus are qualified and able to transmit higher consciousness and God-realization, or self-realization, to thousands and thousands of people.

Different kinds of Gurus, depending on their nature and their development, specialize in specific *ways* of realizing the higher consciousness. Some Gurus transmit consciousness which serves all people of all paths. Certainly a blessing from any Guru will help you on your own path. However, some Gurus focus on enabling the aspirant to realize the soul, the higher self, God within. This is called *self-realization*, where *self* is not meant to be interpreted as ego but as the Lord who dwells within. Other Gurus focus on enabling the aspirant to enter into and realize profound and lofty relationships, or moods of love with God, as described in Chapters 21-27. Others focus on enabling the aspirant to experience God as pure spirit—essence. They may also focus on enabling the devotee to realize the Absolute which is the one reality out of whose being everything exists and is sustained. In all these different ways, and with the aspirant's help, Masters untie the knots and blockages which stand in the way of the aspirant's realization.

DO YOU HAVE TO GIVE UP THE WORLD WHEN YOU FIND YOUR GURU?

It's common for both single people and married people to receive initiation and realize higher consciousness *in the manner most suitable to their nature.*

Just as a few people in society wish to enter a monastery or convent, it is possible that some Gurus—certainly not all—will agree that some exceptional candidates, who want to renounce worldly life and surrender themselves with their goods, enter a monastic or convent facility. Approval of such a decision is rare, however. Most initiates strive to be better people while actively pursuing their careers in the world. Through planned morning and nightly meditations they—like a priest or nun—can develop the capability of realizing and sustaining higher consciousness or finding their personal relationships with God.

In a society which mocks most everything, it is perhaps healthy that the Guru/Initiate relationship be mocked too. At a time when the young naïvely and hysterically follow and idolize so many different entertainers, it may be useful that the naïvely inclined think twice—or ten, fifty, or a hundred times—before seeking a Guru. There are false Gurus who do not abide in higher consciousness and who are not capable of transmitting it, nor of consolidating it within the devotee. And these men and women, too, are usually unscrupulous as well. You should be alert and not treat the matter frivolously or commit yourself for emotional reasons only.

Nevertheless, when both parties—the Guru and the Chela—are genuine, the Guru/Chela relationship is the most sacred and complete human relationship—short of the moods of higher consciousness. United in spirit first, their relationship is sustained through all the ups and downs of daily life. Having a deep respect and reverence for one another, and knowing their reverence is founded in God himself, they thrive. Their appreciation of one another always grows. It cannot recede when each is doing his, or her, part.

As the spirit of love and light becomes a steady blaze in your life as an aspirant, you will perceive who the Guru and the chela really are. You perceive the Guru as a spiritual being and yourself also as a spiritual being. When your ignorance and ego are overcome, and your enlightenment becomes steady, your Guru dances for joy. Your Guru's work is a labor of love, a challenging and often fatiguing service. Above all, the Guru yearns that your awakening be *established*, and that the Guru/Chela relationship be matured into an eternal friendship of equals. In fact, the Guru, through love, wishes his every chela become superior to him in awareness, in wisdom, and in love.

WHO ARE TYPICAL SEEKERS OF THE GURU?

The characteristics seekers today have in common with one another are the *same age-old marks* of the seeker. Their world, however pleasant or unpleasant, has proven deeply unsatisfying to them. Whether rich or poor, healthy or sick, man or woman, they yearn to experience something more, something finer from life than the outer world in all its glitter has been able to provide. They ache to find more meaning and purpose in their existences. They don't want to play superficial games at the office or at home. They want to cut through the sham and emptiness of their lives—however successful they may be materially—and experience "X."

For some, "X" is God. Others have had a tragic or insipid experience with religion; they are hostile to religion and the idea of God. They often seek lasting fulfillment or self-esteem. Others seek to know their own soul in self-realization. Others seek pure Spirit, the "Absolute Reality," or ego-effacement in Nirvana. For some, "X" is transformation.

Most all true seekers are ready to change. They want to give more of themselves, to love more. Their personal pain or emptiness *propels* them to seek wherever possible, and as long as necessary, the satisfaction of the call of their hearts. Their world proving at best incomplete, they are driven toward a finer life—inwardly and outwardly.

Seekers of the Guru can't be satisfied with small prizes or temporary pleasures. Attentive students of life itself, they seek to solve the mystery of their existence. They are determined to know, to *experience*, their true nature and express it—whatever that means. Highly motivated, they are energetic, magnetic people who live with their long-term goals constantly in mind.

But another factor in the modern world makes matters challenging for both Gurus and bona fide seekers today. There are so few able and genuinely earnest seekers of higher consciousness. Many of those who seek Gurus merely have the desire to escape from the problems of life. They are also extremely reluctant to behold their own character flaws and mistakes from the past. They often prove defiant and unwilling to change their old tendencies into new ones.

Many seeking the Guru today have slept through high school. They have also burned up many precious brain cells through the use of drugs. These cells are particularly important to the awakening process. Many candidates' nervous systems have been hurt badly. Often their memory is poor, their ability to think clearly, or reason, is gone. And social skills—the abilities to relate to others—are minimal or even aberrational. Often the candidate today has not been true to anything for more than a year, moving from one interest or fascination to another, leaving behind a trail of unused dreams.

While some heavy drug users, past and present, are doing exceptional humanitarian service or are millionaires running some very successful businesses, many former drug-explorers have extreme difficulty in getting and maintaining a job. Often they forget important functions and endanger their employer or fellow worker so much that they are let go again and again. They then rationalize there is something wrong with society and they yearn to live in another world.

People with this complex background comprise about forty percent of the people on the path to higher consciousness—a very substantial number. They have good hearts and are in many ways wonderful people. The state of many is a tragedy—perhaps a major tragedy of our time, ranking in scope with the losses of lives in World War II and other wars of the twentieth century.

Still, the few available Gurus will convey initiations to those who demonstrate persistent yearning and a willingness to do what the Guru recommends or even directs them to do. Many people alive today are considered high souls even if they have done considerable damage to their lives and nervous systems. Many have a predisposition to higher consciousness which makes them strongly motivated seekers.

Another group of aspirants, which comprises about forty to fifty percent of those who seek Gurus today, are "straight people." These people have developed socially, mentally, and emotionally. They can be any age. Somehow they have bypassed the rampage of self-destruction. They are capable of holding down a high-level job. They are more alert about others and actively strive to relate to reality as a way of life.

Development under the instructions and with the blessings of a Guru inevitably reveals each devotee has some advantages over other seekers, and also some disadvantages. Often, former drug takers feel superior to those who have not chemically opened their minds. At the same time, the other devotees feel superior to these drug-burned men and women who "can't possibly" find higher consciousness. The whole matter is essentially quite simple. With the right tendencies and aspirations bodies and minds can often heal to a considerable degree; and *nothing* on earth, or in your mind, can keep you from your Guru and your fulfillment.

The Guru considers each applicant with love. One day he is shocked to see how many initiates he has as they sit together on the beach. "Oh, Lord, what have we done?" he says in gratitude and he smiles.

REFLECTION

Who is the friend of my soul?
Am I?

33

DESIRABLE QUALITIES

The Master/Initiate tradition is an exciting one. As you progress and develop in faith and fellowship, becoming a fit companion, you will perhaps have a number of teachers—special and very able teachers—who will help you more deeply to understand your quest and your nature. These special teachers can give valuable instruction and inspiration. In the East they are often called *Upa-Guru*. It is very likely that Joseph, Jesus' father, was an Upa-Guru. A seeker may have none, one, or many Upa-Gurus. Each Upa-Guru helps prepare you for the ultimate meeting with the *Sat Guru*, the Spiritual Master. (*Sat* means truth or reality; the Sat Guru permanently awakens the seeker to truth. The term *Guru* usually means Sat Guru.)

The Sat Guru is the man or woman of God, an instrument of the Lord, who will quicken the enlightening process. He or she enables you, the seeker, to overcome your ego and delusion—not only gaining realization of higher consciousness but enabling you to *live* in higher consciousness. Your Master's mission is to transform you into a realized being who stays that way. Since higher consciousness often comes and goes at first, the kind Master, the Sat Guru, will work with you until you are so fulfilled you will not go backward. In fact, the Master's work in *establishing* you in higher consciousness is, in many ways, more important than the initial great awakening. Just as the birth of a child is very important, the continuing life of that child is extremely important too; so the Master is particularly concerned that you not only awaken but *stay awake* in higher consciousness.

Your good Master is primarily a *servant.* It's his secret. While he seems to be telling you and all his initiates what to do, in effect he's quite dependent upon his initiates to do what they've agreed. (Of course he's already found what *he* most yearned for: the realization of God.) Your Master can inspire, bless, even scold, but you must do your part. You have to do what you agreed to do in developing your character and in performing your spiritual and meditative practices faithfully—with the right attitude of devotion every day, even when outer circumstances are chaotic.

When you stand before a Master, seeking to be accepted, the Master hopes he will see some of these main qualities in you:

1)   profound interest in God and spiritual values.
2)   readiness to seek higher consciousness devotedly.
3)   a friend.
4)   capability to maintain growing consciousness.
5)   stable personality.
6)   willingness to see your own flaws.
7)   willingness to let go of the bad—or to transform the bad into the good.
8)   willingness to persist, no matter what—whether happy or sad, dull or inspired, never quitting.
9)   willingness to lead a good life, and a happy one.

If you possess many of these qualities, you are a good candidate. If you are severely lacking them and wish to proceed spiritually, begin now to develop them so your "light" will attract your true Master.

REFLECTION

What am I living *for*?

34

THE MASTER/INITIATE RELATIONSHIP

The Master and initiate are essentially a team. They must work together or the initiate will not achieve and maintain higher consciousness. Teamwork of a high degree is required. The way you, the seeker, conduct your daily life—in thought, word, and action— is vital to the success of the team.

Initiates often like to acknowledge that their Master's love and grace alone is awakening them and accomplishing their lives' fulfillment. They often think their Master is like the moon, having no light of its own but capable of reflecting the light of the brilliant sun directly into the night of their ignorance. And while a beginning seeker is physically *incapable* of beholding the splendor of God (goodness and higher consciousness), the Master reflects that Divine light in a muted manner—a divinely shining personality that testifies to a greater light. While the importance of the Master cannot be overestimated, the Master is not the only factor in an initiate's ultimate delight. Essential, yes. But not the only essential.

The following exchanges have often occurred in Masters' homes over centuries:

A devotee who is not doing very well sits before his Master.

"How are you doing in your spiritual practice?" the Master asks his mentally-scattered initiate.

"I'm doing fine, Master, just fine," the young man or woman replies, "all I need is your blessings, more and more of your blessings."

"You have God's blessings. You have my blessings. But what you do not have is *your* blessings!" the Guru replies. "For you to succeed spiritually, all that is missing is your blessings!"

When this same dialogue occurred in the ashram (home) of the great Master, Paramahansa Yogananda, he added that the Master/ devotee relationship involves fifty percent the blessings of God, twenty-five percent the blessings of the Master, and the remaining necessary twenty-five percent from the initiate himself toward his own life and path.

Merely being in the presence of a Master does not assure an initiate success, Yogananda warned. Rats and mice lived on the property but the rodents, he often observed, were making no spiritual progress.

Masters are unique in their way of quickening higher consciousness. Each Master's method creates hundreds of inspiring—and sometimes amusing—anecdotes. Usually their words have the spark of genius, of an inspiration that can be savored and developed through all time.

The Master/Initiate relationship is one of love. There is a respect and good will between the aspirant and his beloved Master. Both have a high opinion of one another and deeply respect the part the other plays in the success of the team, each being essential. The Master often prays for his devotee each day, and does everything he can to inspire the initiate to do his part. If the initiate does not do his part he or she will ultimately live in great sorrow and unfulfillment, caught between two worlds—the physical world and the spiritual world—an alien to both.

Whenever any initiate succeeds, the initiate is given loving acknowledgement and great respect. That initiate who does his or her part becomes a great soul.

"MAY HE PROTECT US BOTH"

This invocation was sung in ancient days by the Master and his devotee. They often began their study, or work day together, or their evening class, with this invocation translated from the Sanskrit:

May He (the Lord) protect us both. May He nourish us both. May
we both work together with great energy. May our study be thorough
*and fruitful. May we never **hate** each other.* *

Yes, hate. While on the path of love the devotee goes through
many changes, sifts through old attitudes and tendencies. Most everyone has the tendency of hatred. When the disciple is blocked or
frustrated, or told to do something he or she believes impossible, or
is told to obey in some practice which seems childish, the capacity to
hate rises up powerfully in the mind and emotions. The initiate's efforts to become more conscious, coupled with the purity of his or her
life, give more vitality and power to think and feel. Because of this
power, the initiate's negative passions, if indulged in, are mightily
expressed with much vigor.

When you, the initiate, do not deal with your negative emotions in a positive way—yearning for growth and trusting in the
goodness and the guidance of your Master—then the teamwork can
(and does) break down. The all-important project will not succeed
until you begin to deal with your character flaws.

The Master—assuming we are speaking of a true Master—never
hates the devotee no matter how cruel or evil a failed devotee may
become in this lifetime. The Master has already found what he
wants. He already knows the Lord of his heart, he already abides in
higher consciousness. It's only out of love, compassion, and a commission from the Lord that the Master is willing to be part of the
team.

So, because of the immaturity of the initiate, who does not persistently face and strive to overcome negative tendencies, the team
may become divided. The initiate may become antagonistic to the
Master who was so much love's fool he accepted that devotee.

To the initiate who is not willing to deal with his flaws, the
Master often seems to be an authority figure who stands in the way
of the initiate's fulfillment. The initiate may even construe that his or
her own will is more in tune with God's will than the Master's will.
The initiate may eventually look down on the Master. But the initiate
usually feels guilty about harboring contempt and irrationally con-
demning the Master. These complex feelings can lead to hatred, too.
As guilt builds up, it creates even more intense hate problems. The
wedge of the initiate's poison endeavors to become a wall.

* *Kathopanishad*, translated by Swami Sarvananda (Madras, India: Sri Ramakrishna Math, 1973), page viii.

An example of this "failed relationship" was Judas Iscariot. Judas was an initiate—a direct disciple—of Jesus. Judas expected, according to some historians, that Jesus would create an army and—through military and other means—establish a kingdom of heaven on earth. At the very least, Judas is said to have thought, Jesus would force the Romans to leave Israel. Instead, Jesus performed miracles, preached about faith, and in no way turned to materialistic power to bring the kingdom of heaven to earth.

Judas kissed Jesus and betrayed him into death.

While Masters have many problems with devotees, the true initiate must beware of the "false Guru." These pretenders sometimes enjoy self-importance and power. In an arrogant state, they lose whatever attunement they had with God. They are incapable of being the Lord's instrument of awakening. The bridge along the path to higher consciousness stinks with the lives of treacherous initiates and false Masters.

Keep in mind that a true Master is one who is consolidated in the higher consciousness and who, by definition, does not fall. Sometimes, however, a very advanced person who is not yet qualified to be a Master may be commissioned by God to act temporarily as a teacher in some ways, preparing his junior brother or sister for the true Master yet to come. This guidance from an advanced and true devotee is not uncommon because there are so few true Masters in the world today.

Looking generally at spiritual and religious communities, one is often saddened by the intensity of the hatred and cruelty practiced in the name of love and obedience to God. The Master/Initiate relationship, therefore, *absolutely requires the good will, respect and obedience of the initiate*. The relationship also requires that the Master be a truly enlightened and constant instrument of the Lord.

Before forming such a bond, the Master and initiate want to be sure that they can be a team together. While it's true that those who function as Upa-Gurus (spiritual guides who *teach* some aspect of higher consciousness rather than *awaken* one into spiritual realization) can give minor initiations quite liberally and casually without much contact with the initiate thereafter, this relationship is only a helpful phase in the aspirant's life. Through the help of an Upa-Guru, the seeker grows into a ready and worthy candidate capable of entering into relationship with the Master. And now the initiate and Master need a period of time to get to know one another.

Because the Master/Initiate relationship is of a life or death importance spiritually, certain qualifications are usually required by the Master of the aspirant. Most Masters look for initiates who feel life is not worth living unless they can discover their true natures and go forward. Do you feel life would be an empty thing, a sham, a vanity, if you do not find its true meaning, or discover your true nature and potential?

Still, there are other significant qualifications. In order to meet the vital qualifications, you must prepare yourself. At the same time you prepare, you should deeply consider whether you trust your prospective Master. Is he or she truly qualified to serve as the Lord's instrument and awaken you? Consider well, because you will need to enter the relationship with full faith—and maintain full faith. Without faith, or a sincere willingness to seek faith, you will fail. Failing in faith, you will in time feel the higher part of yourself is dead.

While considering a Guru, you should study with him if you can. You should observe him in his manner of thinking, feeling, and acting. You should determine, to your satisfaction, that the Master is living in God-consciousness, that he is a lover of God and such a deep experiencer of God that God can use him for his high Sat Guru purpose.

You, a prospective initiate, should keep in mind that you will, at or before your initiation, be required to agree, or formally make a vow, to obey the Master. This obedience is in two fields: 1) regarding your character; and 2) regarding your spiritual practice. That is, before becoming an initiate, you will have to agree to do what the Master instructs regarding your spiritual practices—whatever is necessary in the development and consolidation of your higher consciousness. For example, the Master may require you chant a *mantram** a few hundred times each day, or direct your life force up and down your spine one hundred and eight times daily. You may be required to keep your body healthy. You may be required to read or study various scriptures or to faithfully attend regular classes— whatever manner of consciousness-evolving practices the Master requires. While you enter the relationship voluntarily, entirely free of duress, and while this is a relationship of love, you will be required to do your part. Your obedience in spiritual practice and character development is fundamental to your success.

Remember, the Master does not have to serve any initiate who

---

* Mantrams are words or syllables which, when chanted properly, lift you from normal awareness into higher consciousness.

is not happy and eager to see him. An initiate is duty-bound to keep his head on straight and deal with personal ego storms. He or she must behave maturely enough to be continually appreciative of the instruction, love, and insight of the Master. The spiritual well being of the initiate is at stake.

Regarding character, the Master has a right and duty to correct you, the initiate, whenever he is so moved. You, the initiate, are not only duty-bound to do what you have been told to do but *must* do as instructed *with good will and love*—even if you totally disagree with him. At the same time, there are few fit candidates for the Master/ Initiate relationship in the world and most Masters will explain themselves and strive to deal most reasonably with the initiate's protests and questions. A true Master has no desire whatever to dominate anyone, especially an initiate, and would rather be elsewhere than tell another person what to do. It is only out of love that he will give correction. Usually, today, he will not give correction unless it is readily appreciated.

Further, obedience to a Master in no way extends to lowering your morality or your being required to sexually satisfy him or her. A strange world precipitates these strange aberrations. When a supposedly great teacher asks such a thing, it is obvious he or she is *not* a great spiritual soul.

No one on earth is as fortunate as the initiate of a true Master, a Sat Guru. With devotion and persistence, you will become more fulfilled than any human being can. To live without daily, deeply felt gratitude for the presence of your Master is sheer tragedy—and colossal loss.

Remember, most Masters do not accept many devotees. However, a few Masters initiate liberally, usually as they near the end of their lives. They pour out their love and life force, usually dying within a few years. They voluntarily undergo an astonishing depletion of their life energies. When his body no longer has enough life force to maintain itself and various diseases develop, the Master, lovingly, with a smile and benediction, departs his body. He remains an inspiration from heavenly realms but is profoundly missed by those who are not subtle enough to communicate with him.

Too, there are other classes of *descended masters*; the East Indians spoke of them as *siddhas, isvarakotis, avatarans*, or other already enlightened beings who seem to come to earth as if born for the purpose of being Sat Guru to many. These holy ones are able to initiate as great Masters, initiate liberally, while at the same time maintaining their bodies for many years. But often they will not admit that they are Masters or Gurus, requiring that prospective initiates be particularly perceptive. These enlightened Masters usually have other holy missions in addition to awakening worthy individuals.

Some seekers have spent years searching in the East for their Guru. Often they leave unsatisfied. In every instance they are unprepared for the Guru. When they are truly prepared, they will find their Master without fail—and usually not have to travel far. "When the devotee is ready, then the Master will appear," is an often-said aphorism. "When the devotee is ready to travel even to the ends of the world in search of his Master, then the Master appears nearby."

Summing up, when you enter into the Master/Initiate relationship and receive initiation, you agree to be true for life. You agree to be faithful until the day your Master—in person, not in psychic or astral form, or through automatic writing, or from an itinerant teacher of a psycho-mystical fad or other path—pronounces you consolidated in your enlightenment. On that greatest of days your Master is most deeply pleased and honored to be present for your spiritual graduation. You will transcend the Master/Initiate relationship. In your new freedom, established in higher consciousness, the requirement of your obedience is released—it being no longer necessary, since your life is now constantly attuned with the higher will. Your Master is released from his service to you. Fulfilled in your quest, you and your dear companion enter into eternal friendship.

REFLECTION

Love Is Self-Giving.

35

HOW TO QUALIFY

You can likely find many people and a number of institutions willing to tell you, for several hundred dollars and a little of your time, that you are an enlightened being. Then you can go through life behaving very strangely and irresponsibly while assuming your behavior is a genuine aspect of higher consciousness.

If you seek enlightenment and the incomparable help of a Master, you generally have to qualify. Sometimes qualification is amazingly easy. Once Sarada Devi, a Master herself, in addition to having a special role as the wife of Paramahansa Ramakrishna, was riding in a train through the Indian countryside. At one station she saw a boy who had spiritual signs. While the train paused, she compassionately went to the young fellow, accepted him as a chela, and initiated him. This kind of qualification and acceptance is rare but is possible.

More than ninety-nine percent of the time, the Master requires the candidate to prove his or her devotion and earnestness in meeting a number of well-considered qualifications. Different Masters stress different qualifications.

The goal of this chapter is a better understanding of the Master/Initiate possibility. Its purpose is not to recommend that you seek a Master. Many seekers are not so deeply interested in higher consciousness that they wish to be transformed by it. They are not sufficiently prepared—or interested—to have a relationship with a Master. Then again, you may be a suitable candidate. You may already be nearly qualified.

Whether you have a mild or intense interest in Masters, you can gain much growth toward higher consciousness by knowing the qualifications for the Master/Initiate relationship. To the extent you have, or develop, any of these attributes, your life is more unified, more powerful, and sweeter.

QUALIFICATIONS FOR INITIATION

Since different Masters focus on specific qualifications differently, you will have to ask the Master you seek what *he* or *she* feels is most important. The general qualifications for being initiated by a Master are:

1   UNCONDITIONAL LOVE

Unless the initiate and Master have unconditional love for one another, there will not be enough love in the relationship for the achievement of the initiate's ultimate goals. Knowing this, you have to thoroughly consider whether you can strive to commit your love, unconditionally and totally, to your Master. While only a realized person can truly give unconditional love, you, a candidate for initiation, agree to try—day in, day out—with your very utmost, to practice unconditional love. In developing unconditional love for the Master, you become so changed and so giving that you are purified enough to receive the total and awesome love God and the Master have for you. Your giving becomes a great receiving. But unless you can love, you cannot be filled.

The Master is not a god. He is a human being who has been so changed by the Lord that the Lord can use him as a servant, as your awakener. Thus, your Master, being human, will have flaws and personal likes and dislikes which an unloving initiate may condemn. Through ill will, an unloving devotee grows into an antagonist. If you wish to be a true and successful initiate, you determine, prior to initiation, that you are not going to aim *any* ill will at your good Master. Rather, you will be vigilant and careful that no ill will ever go out from your mind, heart, or words against your chosen source of transforming love. This yearning to be constant in love for God and the Master is the ideal of all true initiates.

But if you should nevertheless happen to fail, and you find yourself directing anger, fear, or jealousy toward your Master, *never give up*. Accept the deep remorse which comes from blocking such love and do everything humanly possible to right the wrong. Correct the problem: deal with the character flaw which so harshly intrudes in the grand project. For example, if you are deeply angry with your Master, devotees from all ages urge you not lash out at him or her, but proceed something like this:

"Beloved Master, I am having a problem with my anger. Will you help me with it?"

Then the Master and initiate, as an invincible team, work on the anger together. Your character flaw, through love and grace, is eradicated. Endeavoring to have unconditional love and being persistent in it is a tall order for those who have scarcely ever governed their emotions in this life. Its practice is, nevertheless, essential for a successful fulfillment in higher consciousness or God-realization. Even if it takes much extra work and extra thought and extra prayer, an attitude of unconditional love must be engendered. Your determination to persist in selfless love must be a *strong passion*. That is, much of your blessing on your own quest, "your twenty-five percent," involves your unconditional love—for God, the Master, and yourself.

Your endeavor to persist in unconditional love *has to* involve your *determination* to live in unconditional love even when you're feeling lonely, depressed, frivolous, or smarting from correction. Whether you feel good or bad, happy or sad, your unconditional love must grow!

2   YOU MUST DESIRE THAT ABOVE ALL ELSE GOD COME FIRST IN YOUR LIFE

While it is impossible for an aspirant to focus *perfectly* on God every day, your focus must *become continual*. Your ego or daily circumstances cannot ever be allowed to overtake or undermine the priority that God come first. Even when you fail to do this, you must pick yourself up and direct your life Godward once again.

In entering the Master/Initiate relationship, you must fully understand that you will never give up.

Divergent desires will flood your mind. Whichever desire preoccupies you usually dictates your mood and actions toward fulfillment of that desire. Perhaps yesterday you wanted a new career.

Today, you feel you need a new car or different friends, perhaps great fame, or no, a mushroom pizza will do. For now. Your desires for others, your children, your colleagues, your countrymen, flood into your thoughts and emotions, too. Most people are a mass of desires—each desire an anarchist dominating for a brief time. Because of the tremendous number of desires—and their constant conflict—you find it difficult to fulfill most of them. Possibly, you cannot accomplish even your most important desires due to the sabotage of other conflicting desires.

What is the way out? How can you make the most of your fleet years? Desire God above all else—and be constant in that one desire. In this fixity of purpose, goodness will fill your life. In becoming fulfilled in your most central desire, many other important desires are often satisfied as well. Above all, if you do not put God and higher consciousness first, you will never be able to find them.

In entering the Master/Initiate relationship, fully understand that your main desire must be God. Be so dedicated you will never divert your mind and heart until God is truly established throughout your life as the Lord of all. (It should be noted here that the word "Lord" is not meant to limit those who seek to realize the Absolute or Nirvana. In this case, the seeker agrees that the Absolute, or Nirvana, gets the most priority and this focus is discussed with the Master.)

3   OBEDIENCE

You, as an initiate, agree to obey the Master regarding:

A)   Your spiritual practices and other activities relating to your spiritual growth. (For example, your studies or your constancy in faith and good will.) Such instructions from your Master rarely intrude on your family life or career. If you have any questions about what you are expected to obey, talk with your Master *before* you seek initiation.

B)   Your character. Your Master must have your cooperation in helping you overcome character flaws—or forget about higher consciousness. He must have the freedom to correct your inappropriate behavior if and when he sees fit. Remember, he loves you and has good will for you. The error in consciousness in back of the flaw he mentions is apparently very significant because he chooses to mention it. It's important you be appreciative and thankful for his corrections, although your ego may rise up against the whole process. Your ego and ignorance, after all, are the villains of this teamwork.

Appreciative obedience is one of the most important qualifications.

4   PERSISTENT ASKING

Usually you have to ask to be an initiate many times before you are accepted. The practice of persistent asking gives you a chance to reconsider, to pull out, or to explore other avenues before you enter into a relationship so profoundly eternal.

That is, the Lord himself creates and sustains a Master/Initiate relationship. It's correct to infer that if you spurn the Master, you are spurning the Lord who sustains both the Master and your own soul, the divinity abiding within you. Nothing is more serious. No cancer or broken back can ever as deeply affect the fulfillment of your whole being as much as an initiate's spurning of the Master.

As some enlightened initiates have declared, "Beloved Master, here at your feet is my only hope." They were speaking from their higher consciousness. They knew the significance of abiding in the love and instruction of the Master.

So, persistent asking enables each candidate who is considering being initiated to think about the matter very deeply and seriously. Perhaps, at your present point of advancement, you may decide it's best not to seek entrance into so sacred and important a relationship. Initiation may not be appropriate. You may not be able to fulfill your part of the teamwork.

On the other hand, persistently asking the Master for initiation and the Master/Initiate relationship may help make your mind and heart more certain. You can sense your soul's wisdom as you ponder. Your frequent prayers help you weigh factors buried deep in your psyche. As weeks go by, you deal with your doubts and anxieties about initiation. During the period of asking you get to know the Master better. You can also analyze how much priority you truly place on your spiritual path—and how strong your devotion really is.

5   READINESS TO ABIDE IN THE CONSCIOUSNESS OF THE MASTER

The Master/Initiate relationship, as we have said, is primarily a spiritual relationship. While it is desirable to be in the physical presence of your Master whenever you can, his physical presence will not replace the more important factor: living day in, day out, sensing the presence of the spirit, consciousness, love, and blessings of your Master.

In considering your qualifications for higher consciousness, the Master needs to see indications you will remain in attunement with him wherever you happen to be. Over the years it may not be possible—due to your schedule or his—for you to be physically in his presence every week. Some Masters have to do much traveling or observe long periods of solitude. Nevertheless, the Master/Initiate relationship needs to be maintained so well that it grows and grows. Your part is done primarily through keeping the Master in your thoughts, sensing his love and guidance in your heart. You must be willing and able to do this however far away you may be from him physically. Wherever you go and whatever your activities in life, you feel your Master is there beside you or within you. You live in the progressive sense of the nearness of your Master.

6   HELP YOUR MASTER ENTHUSIASTICALLY AND COMPETENTLY

Since the Master gives you something so utterly precious and indispensable to your fulfillment, naturally you respond to his love.

Will you love him deeply and try to assist him in his work, or in some other service he asks of you? While he freely gives his love, and will likely accept you even if you are emotionally crippled, he hopes you can love and give of yourself in time for your own sake. The path of higher consciousness itself requires that you grow in love and become a joyful, prosperous giver. A profound principle on the spiritual path is involved. Truly, unless an initiate is willing to give of himself and his resources, he (or she) has a hard heart and cannot receive much of anything. Even the sweetest love and the greatest blessings from the Master will have little impact on you if you are petty or lacking in generosity. Your eagerness to share usually involves voluntary contributions, however small, but also consists of contributions from your heart, contributions of your care and love. Throughout spiritual history, service to a Master usually includes physical work, a few days of labor each year, some wood chopping perhaps, helping with administration, or cooking for retreatants.

This giving of yourself must come from your heart, through your love. If you don't have the inspiration to serve in a helpful, attentive way, you are, without question, not ready for initiation and should wait until another time when you can see more deeply that spiritual giving is the *basis of awakening* and also the *law of true prosperity.*

However, even if you will likely gain substantial benefits through your service to the Master, your thought needs to be one of simply giving; you do not desire or require benefits or recompense in kind. The benefits you receive as you travel your road to higher consciousness will be spiritual, mental, emotional, physical, and material in nature. Of course, you should be cautious—there are self-declared "masters" who want your money. Nevertheless, if you are a sincerely loving initiate of a true Master, you will readily find the benefits you receive far exceed any contribution or service you have given—or are capable of giving.

You will find, in your love, you can never outgive God or Master. It is literally impossible.

7 MODERATION IN SEX ACTIVITY

What an easy life Masters would have in this sexually permissive society if spiritual awakening had no relationship with sex activity! But, most all seekers of higher consciousness today readily concur that sex activity requires the use of considerable life force.

Generally, Masters and devotees throughout the ages have not considered sex evil or vile. "Sex is holy, it's from God," they affirm. In the past, roughly half the world's prominent enlightened men and women were married; and half were celibate. Yet, most of these agreed that a devotee's sexual moderation is not only vital, but also very valuable.

Achievers of higher consciousness do much more than think about superconsciousness now and then while in pleasant moods. They direct their life force, their energy, toward their ideal.

If you seek to direct your precious life force toward higher consciousness—and it takes a great deal of energy—you have to be, of necessity, sexually moderate in order to achieve higher consciousness and God-realization. Without moderation it's unlikely your nerves will become subtle enough to maintain the awakening energy. Instead, your nerves will feel like they are burning up when your spiritual energy is awakened.

But if you merely restrain yourself and do not redirect your life force wholeheartedly toward higher consciousness, you will repress your energies. Symptoms of repression and failure in moderation are: irritability, timidity, cruelty, jealousy, anger, fear, skepticism, sarcasm, poor concentration, confusion, sickness, and intolerance.

The precious benefits of moderation are: a clearer mind, serenity, improved memory, vigor, more positive emotions, sweeter disposition, better concentration, greater ease in entering higher states of awareness, and greater well being. A longer life span is also claimed where moderation is practiced.

Because of these findings throughout the ages, the physiological factors of awakening necessitate moderation. Further, the benefits are considered worthwhile by all who give themselves, and their loved ones, a chance.

If you have problems with moderation or repression, you can learn a number of marvelous transmutation practices. They will also help you overcome intense sexual desire and the debilitation from overly frequent sex.

Here are a few simple practices which may help you redirect sex energy, increasing vigor and serenity:

A)   Before retiring at night, wash all your body openings with a cool, damp washcloth. Then, as you sleep, your energy will move more naturally in your spine and upper body and tend to reduce the pressure in your senses and sex nerves.

B)   If a doctor has told you that your heart and lungs are definitely healthy, learn to do deep, full breathing. Whenever you are feeling sexual pressure, practice full, slow, even breathing, with emphasis on making a longer exhalation than inhalation. Don't breathe rapidly, as this exhausts or hurts the nerves in the chest area. Through the deep, full breathing, more energy will be activated in your upper body and often the intensity in the sex nerves diminishes significantly. In this practice, as you do it well, you'll begin to feel greater vitality and warm, radiant love universally moving out from your chest to all humanity.

C)   When you are haunted by thoughts of the attractive, physical body of another, appreciate its beauty or handsomeness but strive to think of the person more deeply. Strive to sense that person is a soul or spiritual being and wish him, or her, well with his, or her, life and goals. Often this approach will give you the freedom to choose whether to become involved with that person or to go forward with other goals that you have chosen.

D)   Study yoga. While not foolproof, yoga is the best method for controlling and redirecting all forms of vital life force, including sexual energy. Yoga can help you transmute sexual desire if you are determined. However, yoga can also help you improve your sexual functioning in many ways if you are suffering sexual problems.

8 WILLINGNESS TO LEAD A CLEAN AND HEALTHY LIFE

A strong, healthy body and clear mind are extremely helpful. If, however, you have serious health problems while nevertheless being extremely devoted and worthy in other ways, the Master will generally accept you.

In any case, you, a prospective initiate, are required to lead a constructive life, being as positive, happy, and helpful as you can. Use of street drugs, alcohol, or practice of other dissipations which hurt your mind, body, or emotional balance are "no-nos." Higher consciousness can only be realized *and maintained* by those who have good will for themselves—or are willing to develop it.

Now you know the main qualifications and attitudes necessary for your acceptance as an initiate by most Masters. Your period of asking may go on for months or, in some cases, years. Sometimes the asking cannot be done in person but is done by letter. If you are particularly prepared, your Master may accept you rapidly.

In many ways, it's up to you!

REFLECTION

The essentials:
     God's Blessings
     The Master's Blessings
     And *Your* Blessings.

36

INITIATION

If you persist in asking for initiation, and show the Master that you are sincere and genuinely motivated, usually the Master will give you a task.

You then perform this simple task, faithfully and well. The Master may ask you to do a specific form of meditation, once or twice a day—or perform humanitarian errands, for example. If you are able to do your assigned task steadily and well every day, without fail and without excuse, your Guru-to-be will observe: 1) you respect his instructions; 2) you can do what he asks faithfully and well; and 3) you are likely mature and responsible enough to do advanced spiritual techniques.

In addition to performing your task, your cheerfulness, common sense, and attitude are studied by the Master. As you do your part faithfully and competently, the Master is pleased to go to the Lord prayerfully in your behalf.

When all continues well with you for a time, the Master will accept you as his own dear devotee. He accepts you unconditionally and forever—beyond time. Your period of asking is fulfilled. It's a wondrous day for Initiate and Master.

Your beloved Master then states a specific, auspicious time

when he will initiate you. The devotee is initiated personally, in almost every case.

During your period of asking, and between the time of acceptance and initiation, the Master studies you further. He determines and selects the best possible spiritual practices for your needs and your nature. He chooses practices which will most felicitously speed you toward higher consciousness and God-realization.

THE INDESCRIBABLE DAY

On a special morning or evening—but usually a morning—you, a newly-accepted initiate, shower thoroughly, dress in clean clothes, and come to your Master's place. An initiate usually brings flowers, fruit, and an offering in an envelope. Oftentimes other recently-accepted candidates sit in the waiting room beaming and in moods of devotion. One by one each goes to the Master and is initiated.

When your name is called, you enter the room where your Master is seated. He or she tends to look extremely beautiful in the love of the Lord and you. And you tend to look already saintly due to your aspirations and good will.

Usually you bow before the Master as a symbol of your obedience and also your willingness to receive God's love and grace through the Master into your life. You offer him your flowers, fruit, and the offering in the envelope which he either accepts into his hands or gestures that you should place in the basket nearby.

He asks you how you are. Then he repeats some questions he has asked earlier regarding your understanding of your new commitment and responsibilities. He asks these questions so you will, as you remember your initiation, recall the solemn promises and agreements you made on your initiation day—mainly to practice your techniques faithfully and be a loyal devotee. He gives you the opportunity to leave, if you wish to change your mind.

If you choose to go forward and be initiated, your Master will likely do some purification practice, perhaps chanting some mantrams or prayers as a preparation for transference of spiritual light. Often, you, the initiate, join in these practices of purification which usually take a few minutes.

Then your Master asks your help in invoking, through prayer, the presence of God. The two of you sit quietly, meditatively. You are sitting a few feet in front of your Master.

Your Master then lovingly conveys your personal technique for enlightenment. It may be a word or phrase for you to chant and concentrate on; it might be a breath control practice; or, perhaps, you will be given a specific technique for awakening spiritual centers in your spine and head. Initiated techniques are usually personal, according to the seeker's individual strengths, and very diverse.

The Master patiently does the practice over and over until you understand it. Then you, the initiate, repeat the practice over and over until the Master is satisfied you can do it properly. Sometimes an initiate, while first doing the practice, becomes superconscious or enters levels of higher consciousness immediately. The devotee sits in sweet samadhi, a flowing state of higher consciousness, or a wondrous bhava, a mood of spiritual relationship. The Master lovingly watches you to be certain all is well and developing smoothly.

Sometime during the initiation the Master, through a touch or a mantram, or in some other way, conveys his consciousness. That is, a seedling of his awareness is initiated into the consciousness of the initiate. This marvelous infusion of higher consciousness has to be ever so carefully established in the mind and heart of the beloved initiate. As you sit performing the practice, the new infusion of life force develops and grows within you.

During your initiation the Master will also lovingly take into himself what is called your "karma." (Usually this refers to the future painful consequences of your past actions.) The Master will take into himself the suffering which you have "contracted for" by your past actions and attitudes. Out of love, your Master will suffer for his initiates, making their lives easier, reducing their burdens so they can more easily and quickly find fulfillment. Masters, after giving initiations, are often very weak and it takes awhile for their vigor to return. Throughout their lives their bodies empathetically share in whatever suffering their initiates may be going through.

Not all Masters practice this sharing of the initiate's suffering. In fact, a few Masters feel no man can suffer the karma of another. However, most Masters do. Because of their love, Masters find it unavoidable to help their devotees in any way they can—even if their assistance involves personal pain. But, remember, Masters have amazing resilience and phenomenal ability to recover.

Your initiation then concludes with the Master giving you further instructions and arranging the next appointment for checking your development.

You depart, feeling heavenly. You spend the day enjoying your new practice, having a light lunch and relaxing. You allow the new life to abide in you.

The seedling, your newly "planted" higher consciousness has to be watched over very carefully by the Master. You will have to return several—perhaps many—times to be checked. Your Master wants to be sure your practice is being done properly and your newly infused higher consciousness is steadily growing—if not thriving.

Sometimes it takes months for an initiate to do the practice properly. But both Master and initiate are a team and they work together very well.

YOU WILL PREVAIL

Now your blessed life as an initiate becomes *relatively simple*. You do your duties in the world while keeping God and Master utmost in your mind. You follow your Master's instructions and do your initiated practices with faith and steadiness.

Your life moves on. You *simply maintain your devotion* as you go through the daily events of your world. Circumstances may rock you a bit and tend to make you unsteady in your new life. But, with devotion, you apply those spiritual practices which are designed to enable you to be steady, devoted, and continually growing. You now have, through your initiated practice, a means for truly dealing with the vicissitudes and the paradoxes of life. You have something to do. You know how to do it, and you are doing your part on the team.

Of course, many times the violent ways of the world or your ego will make the path seem more complex, or perhaps even impossible. But your team is able. With the help of your Master and your own effort at maintaining your spiritual practice, your character develops and you find inner strength. No storm of confusion or fear has the power to thwart your progress, not a one. Nothing can separate you from God. You will have victory over every frustration and obstacle. With your Master, you will prevail.

Still, there will be other storms from inside. Waves of old jealousies and memories, waves of pettiness, anger, and cruelty may flood your mind and heart from time to time. So, you *simply* do your spiritual practices, keeping God and your Master foremost in your mind. Like oil floating on the surface of water, your love is naturally uppermost. Whether you have spiritual experiences or not, you have, above all, a relationship with your Master and the extraordinary blessing of knowing a specific means to realize higher consciousness. You're one of the richest people in the world already. You have what you truly need for the fulfillment of your life. In a sense, you have everything. Whether life brings outer storms or inner storms, you *simply persist* with sweet love and appreciation, knowing each day you are closer to realization of higher consciousness.

Also, you know through faith and growth you will enter into continual awareness of God's presence. You will prevail, even though there are times you might forget this. You will prevail.

Know that your Master is alertly watching as higher consciousness manifests in your life. He eagerly awaits the day when he will see the clear light of God looking back at him through your eyes—the eyes of his beloved initiate.

He will walk with you eternally through the ups and downs of life, through all your ego storms and fears, until at last you are free of impediment. With joy the Master watches as you let go of your false self, with its limiting preoccupations, and enter into your true nature. For both you and your Master there is no greater joy on earth.

REFLECTION

Who will dispel my darkness,
My misperception of everything?

VI

AWAKENING
AND
ENLIGHTENMENT

37

DAWN COMES

Awakening begins.

You proceed patiently and persistently, with devotion and faith, striving to be a friend of all.

From the deep yearning of your heart you put forth every effort. Fulfillment in higher consciousness requires the focus and energy of your whole being—short of strain. (You recognize strain creates resistance to success. Your developing self-acceptance enables you to distinguish between application and strain.)

Perhaps you have a Master, perhaps not. If not, you strive to your utmost to understand and take the guidance of your higher consciousness through your meditations and prayer, and through your studies. Ideally, you have a special teacher or even better, a Sat Guru. However, if you do not, remember the Lord is with you and is always adequate in providing whatever is needed. In your unfolding into the light, you will receive all the help you truly need.

Inevitably, as a result of your sincerity and devotion, the dawn of your awakening comes.

Awakening is individual. Your particular sequence will be the very best one for you. It is arranged through the instrumentality of higher consciousness itself. You must give yourself a chance and not interfere with your awakening. Using guidelines from this book may be helpful, but to use these principles in order to *set your will* on how your awakening is *supposed* to occur will greatly inhibit you.

However, while awakening comes to each person differently, some stages of realization are nearly universal. These stages and signs recur again and again in the lives of awakening aspirants. When you experience any—or many—of these stages you are greatly fortunate. Your understanding of these signs will prove extremely beneficial, providing you encouragement and validation of your personal awakening.

Many seekers have experiences they don't understand, and they live far away from qualified teachers. Often, these sincere seekers are having genuine enlightening experiences but since they cannot comprehend or evaluate what is happening to them, they do not recognize or build upon their tremendous blessings. To uninformed seekers, one experience seems as important or unimportant as another.

Many times, spiritual awakening is confused with psychic states or a flood of vivid impressions projected from the subconscious mind. It's a "precious and rare thing," unless you have a Guru, to know where you are coming from and where you are going as awakening begins. Awakening events can occur to you for years but you probably will not give them the attention they deserve unless you have a basic familiarity with the road ahead.

You may lament you are not becoming enlightened while indications of your awakening are all around you. It's essential, if you wish to make gratifying, lasting progress, that you understand the dawnings of higher consciousness and what they signify to your life-enrichment.

As you proceed, be alert.

THE FIRST SIGNS OF AWAKENING

The first sign of awakening is usually a growing reverence for life. You find you are immensely appreciative of being alive. Life itself is revealed as a wonder or a miracle. In your reverence for life you delightedly value the lives of others and of yourself. You perceive life as extremely precious, such an extraordinary phenomenon. You find it easy to conceive in your musings that incredibly great consciousness and energy is at work wherever there is life. With awe and enthusiasm you often turn your mind to consider how great must be that higher consciousness which gives life and sustains it! In life itself there is enough to wonder at *forever*. In your unique heart you see enough to explore and develop for much more than a life-time. What is life? Who can say? But you, the awakening aspirant, wholeheartedly treasure being alive and love to watch that life force animating each person; indeed, you admire all living creatures.

You become aware that you may have many negative qualities but, nevertheless, you have an extremely positive and undeniable plus—you have life. You are an expression of that higher conscious-ness which maintains and sustains life. Life is a marvel. You see it. You know it. You abide in wonder.

You find, with these realizations, that you begin to value other people a great deal. Whether they value themselves and have noticed the miracle of life or not, you perceive uniqueness and significance in each one. You have become enabled, as your eyes of higher con-sciousness open, to see life well. You can easily understand why Albert Schweitzer said that it's fine to cut the grass in order to grow a garden, but on the way home from the garden do not drag your scythe and needlessly kill one blade of grass. This now makes great sense to you.

You also clearly understand "Do unto others as you would have them do unto you." You know all people are, in reality, sharing life together. You deeply yearn that everyone will see the preciousness of life and not hurt, deny, or strive to destroy the life in another.

Your awakening to life's richness also prompts a profound con-sideration of your own conduct. Your interactions with others more deeply reflect your respect for their concerns and feelings. You ac-tively strive not to harm people or cause them any suffering. You practice, "Do unto others . . . ." You seek to be constructive and helpful to fellow human beings.

CAUSE AND EFFECT INSIGHT

Being appreciative of life you understand it more clearly. Your reverence for life gives you deeper levels of wisdom and more op-portunities for fulfillment.

Another excellent sign of your awakening is your heightened awareness of *cause and effect*. You see that the *events* of your life are the *results* of *causes*. You recognize that what happens to you each day is not based on random, irrational fates. Rather, your thoughts, attitudes, words, and actions most significantly *cause* and influence your personal experiences of life. While some events in your life remain perplexing and inexplicable, more often than not you can understand why other people and life in general treat you the way they do. You gain the insight which enables you to examine your good experiences and create (cause) more of them.

Further, you stop ignoring your bad experiences if you are truly awakening. Whenever something painful or otherwise negative happens to you, you seek an insight about what caused such an unpleasant effect. Then, in your thoughts, feelings, words, and actions, you strive to *cause* a preferred effect, a more satisfying and ideal result.

You notice the good you do for people, or for the world in general, comes back to you in kind—not necessarily directly from the people you helped but by some perceptible means your "good returns good" to you.

You see harm, or evil—either in thought, feeling, word, or action—often comes back to its originator.

Each day you appreciatively watch cause and effect relationships going back and forth, on and on, in simple or complex combinations. No longer does life seem to have no rhyme and reason, or seem *absurd* as many existentialists regularly exclaim.

In your reverence for life you find that life itself is like a two-edged sword. If you use your life in a negative way you can hurt someone; but, inevitably you too will find yourself cut—perhaps not by the person you hurt but by some other precise means. The cuts come back, each and every one, in detail. Evil returns suffering; good returns good.

You also discover that your increased awareness and reverence for life make profound changes in the way causes and effects act in your life. You become progressively free from negative experiences and revel in new causes.

Hindus call this cause and effect reality of life, *karma*. Western paths also emphasize this phenomenon. Teachers of many paths not only think cause and effect an interesting factor to observe, but a law of life—a law that operates within life itself. Christ spoke of this law, and the nature of love, when he said: "Do unto others as you would have them do unto you."

Often formalized thought makes *cause and effect* a bizarre philosophy of punishment for being alive and a rationalization for every unfavorable occurrence. However, you will see cause and effect, in your awakening, as a creative process—beautiful, exciting, just, and very helpful. Becoming more responsible for the condition of your life and attitudes, you take part in a regenerative process. You realize that a new life, one ever more to your liking, awaits you.

In essence, as your awakening begins you will very likely perceive more meaning and purpose in your life. You will become more fulfilled and able to accomplish your goals as you see a relationship between cause and effect, between your ideas (and feelings) and events in the outer world. You now know that *your good returns good*, that being evil is cosmically stupid.

But you have even more to experience. The days and years of awakening and enlightenment rush toward you. The five stages of mental/emotional quickening in higher consciousness beckon you to new discoveries. Dawn has come! Let's begin!

REFLECTION

I am free to generate
New causes and change my world.

38

STAGES OF MENTAL/EMOTIONAL
AWAKENING

Practice makes you perfect. Success on your quest is inevitable if you put aside fancies, cowardice, and laziness. However, success is impossible if, no matter how many hours and years you practice higher consciousness techniques, you do those techniques incorrectly or selfishly.

Experience of higher consciousness comes sooner than expected to those who proceed with devotion, good will, faith and a balanced mind. Doing, rather than fantasizing or talking about the techniques, is the key. As you proceed earnestly you experience several unusual, utterly delightful levels of awareness. You move through "levels of the heart" and through numerous planes of consciousness.

This chapter begins a whole section of possibilities and delights for you—if you are a sincere seeker. (And why not be a sincere seeker? What have you to lose but myriad frustrations and sorrows?) As you give yourself a chance and practice the chapters throughout *Keys to Higher Consciousness*, you will discover the nature of awakening, "becoming aware of," your own higher consciousness. Proceeding in your awakening you will, on one unforgettable day, receive *enlightenment*, a permanent realization of higher consciousness which enables you to *live* in your true nature.

In order to awaken to your true being and live as an enlightened person, you pass through the levels of mental/emotional development. Whatever your unique path or method, you grow dynamically. Likely, you already have begun your ascent.

LEVELS OF MENTAL/EMOTIONAL AWAKENING

1 THE DARK STATE

Normal consciousness is often given the term "darkness." Masters of higher consciousness throughout the ages have expressed—often with great passion—that not knowing higher consciousness is a state of ignorance. If you are unable to see the brilliant light of your inner self, if you cannot contact higher wisdom or your creative intelligence, if you cannot experience spirit directly and do not know the bliss and ecstasy of your true nature, you are living in ignorance. You are *ignoring* personal fulfillment and any degree of lasting satisfaction.

In the dark state of ignorance, or the *dark heart*—as it is often called—*you think the physical world is the only reality.* That is, you live *bound*, in your experience and opinion of life, to what your senses communicate to you about the world and about yourself. Your thoughts and feelings are mainly based on sense data and your personal history of thoughts, feelings, and actions. Of course, you accept the information and input of other people and numerous studies about the physical world through your senses and mind as well, but the masters hold that you are blind and numb. That is, until you discover your higher faculties of awareness, until you perceive your higher nature well, you are ignoring what your life and your world can be.

Certainly the teachers of life encourage that each person be as adept as possible in using the senses, the mind, and the feeling nature. However, they urge that each person consider the other nine-tenths of the legacy bestowed on him or her at birth.

A person in the dark state "sees everything incorrectly" because the senses are very limited to a small and often inaccurate view of the electromagnetic spectrum. Your senses can easily be fooled. For example, new car scent—a few chemicals brewed in a spray can—may well influence your decision to purchase a car by satisfying your sense of smell that a particular unit is fresh, in great condition, and (therefore?) probably has a very good engine. In fact, many people assume a car is in good shape if the ears hear a "solid" sound when the doors are slammed shut. Manufacturers, knowing about your ears and your usual mental reliance on sense information, often spend extra money on car doors and scents to induce you to assume the rest of the car is very well built. So, because few of us can adequately evaluate an engine or transmission, we often blindly rely on our limited senses.

Even your sense of touch can be fooled. Put on a blindfold in an unfamiliar room and notice how misleading your tactile sense can be. College initiations and Halloween tricks are often based on easily deceiving the mind through the fingertips. Somehow peeled grapes do feel like eyeballs and jello can take on sinister qualities when touched in the dark. Also, even with your eyes open, you can sense two sharp points lightly touching your palm but on your shoulder blade, are you really feeling one point or two? Often you will not be able to tell; the nerves are more numerous and closer together in your palm than over your shoulder blade.

Your ears, if you are average, can only hear sound activity from a frequency of fifteen cycles per second to eighteen thousand cycles per second. So, our ears are easily deceived, too.

A brief study of sound effects likely will amaze you. The symphony is probably not playing beside the blissfully roaring surf. Rather, technicians are running water through a bucket to create a surf sound—the technique is called "white sound." Cannon sounds are made by "thumps" of various kinds. For example, dropping a barrel into an empty swimming pool can give a better cannon sound than most cannons can. Your ear is being consistently fooled every evening as you watch television and thrill to the action and realism of electronic magic.

Do you know, regarding the effort of the senses to represent reality to you, that if your nose closed and you had to rely strictly on your taste buds, you would not be able to distinguish between the juice of a potato, onion, and apple?! Try it.

And vision. Vision is our most relied upon sense, but behavioral scientists and psychologists in any university near you can demonstrate how easily the eye is fooled so that it misjudges what is perceived, due to mental/emotional interference as well as the inadequacies of the eye.

All the masters and most of the disciplines of the path to higher consciousness urge you not to ignore your senses but rather to make the senses keener and sharper in every way so they will present their transmissions to the brain as *reliably* as possible—not further increasing their limitations, nor wearing out as you grow older. But you should also strive to keenly attune your mind and emotions in such a manner that your mind does not misjudge the information received through the senses nor confuse misinformation with reality.

The person in the dark state thinks the physical world is the only reality and everything not related to matter or the senses is imaginary. Believing that the non-physical world is illusory and not worth exploration, the ignoring person does not feel any reason to turn within and consider what enables his mind to think or heart to beat. He is not intrigued by questions like:

- What is the source of my consciousness which enables me to think in the first place?

- Am I mainly a *body*, or am I essentially the *dweller within* my body?

- Why are some people brighter than others? Or more successful? Or more artistic?

- How is lasting satisfaction attained?

- Where does love come from?

- Where does matter come from? The world? The oceans? The sun? Stars? Galaxies? Light?

- What is the difference between a live person and a dead one?

- What happens at so-called death?

- What is life?

If such questions have fascinated you over the years and if you have thought about them a lot, you are already called or prompted to move beyond your ignorance and the dark state. If these questions have no interest to you and seem to be mere dry, philosophical or theological speculations, you would very likely be wise to ponder the next four levels of awakening and spend a few relaxing minutes each week exploring your inner potential. You might find something you've been looking for your whole life long.

However, most people in normal sense consciousness do not even suspect that there is a higher consciousness and are not interested in investigating the source of their daily awareness. Rather, they wish to focus their awareness and energy on greater accomplishments in the physical world which seems so real, stable, and, in most ways, unalterable. Exploration of higher consciousness does not appeal to people in a dark state. They feel those who seek other realms of consciousness or spend time in practices of the path are foolish and perhaps even wasteful.

As long as a person permits himself or herself to have the attitude that the physical world is all there is, then he or she will likely maintain such an attitude for a very long time. Such a habit of thought and feeling is rarely given up by anyone unless, and until, his or her world affairs and hopes are one day *smashed*, falling apart in a manner most painful to the materialist. Rarely does anyone leave the dark state or even consider other possibilities unless pain or a profound sense of dissatisfaction goad the dark-hearted to look elsewhere for fulfillment—or even the minutest *possibility* of satisfaction.

For the most part, people will remain in the dark state as long as they feel physical existence satisfies them; or as long as they have faith that the outer world will, on some distant great day, satisfy them. Usually the death of a close relative, a painful physical injury, or the collapse of professional life have to occur before the inhabitant of the dark state rattles his or her bars and seeks to exit the prison of ignorance.

2   THE PROPELLED STATE

Mental/emotional awakening begins and the search for higher consciousness becomes established in your life when you doubt the outer world can satisfy you in any lasting way through your senses, mind, and emotions. You are about to become *propelled*.

Do you find yourself saying: "There's got to be something better than this! This is not what I want from life! My life has no meaning. Why do things always fall apart? Why is this happening to me?" All these are typical cries of an unsatisfied dark heart which is about to become propelled.

Whether the substantial doubt comes from the conflict between your dream states and the appearances of the outer world, or from heartbreak and near desperate yearning for happiness, you intuitively sense that the external world is not as solid and real as it used to appear. The outer world, the world of the physical body and the senses, along with your mental/emotional commentary, seems to be some sort of great dream, however vivid it may appear. And, however much the dream may have contented your senses with its presumed substantiality, suddenly or gradually you're driven to find answers that *satisfy* and fulfillments that *last*.

In the propelled state you are not merely philosophizing about the meaning and the truth of life, you are propelled, *literally propelled,* to search until you find what you seek. Your heart aches for understanding and meaning. Events in the outer world lose much of their significance and their power over you. You feel an ache, a burning ache, to solve the mystery of your life and to know, in a convincing way, the meaning and purpose of your existence.

Are you propelled? Do you find you are willing to seek every day, for the rest of your life if necessary, in order to get even a little bit closer to your personal realization of truth and meaning? That is, even if you were to know now that you can't possibly succeed in your quest for meaning, would you nevertheless be propelled to conduct the search simply because there is no other way to go—the outer world having lost its charm or its promise in your eyes? Then, you are propelled.

Unless you are driven to find higher consciousness and vigorously go about it with persistence and consuming interest, with deep, balanced, focused attention, you are not yet propelled.

A lot of people are dissatisfied from time to time in life. However, they are not propelled if they are merely complaining or speculating. A propelled person cannot be put off. Every day is an action and a focus toward ultimate realities. A propelled person can't conceive of giving up or being satisfied by some attraction or bauble from the outer world, even if it be a tremendous business promotion or a very cute glance and implied promise from a member of the opposite sex. Nothing will satisfy the propelled person other than the fulfillment of his or her deepest yearning. A call from deep within the soul has to be satisfied and nothing short of the realization of your true nature, your highest consciousness, will suffice.

Many seekers to your left and right will be interested in other things next year. Will you still be propelled next year? Will you be propelled until fulfillment? Will you live in peace and friendship with the world but, despite any daily duties—which you will do conscientiously and well—will you be true to your call? Will you seek forever if necessary, across the heavens if necessary, until you come home to your true nature and live in your true estate?

YOUR SUCCESS IS INEVITABLE

You see, if you are truly propelled and will simply abide in a dedicated way in this propelled state, *you will succeed. Your success is inevitable!* You will definitely achieve fulfillment and realization, without question! Your propulsion contains the power that you need to pass through all the obstacles and realize each and every state of awakening. Once you are propelled, all you have to do is honor your motive and the sense of its importance which you are feeling right now. You will have to say no to the bribes and sleeping pills of the outer world. Your dedicated propelled state is one of the greatest gifts any human being can ever receive.

While you may feel miserable until the resolution of your quest, nevertheless you should value that you are one of the few truly motivated people on the face of the earth who is honestly and sincerely responding to your as yet unglimpsed true nature.

It is often in this propelled state that you will attract and come into close companionship with a bona fide Master who will, because of his love and experience on the path, show you how to proceed toward the satisfaction of your praiseworthy quest. Often at this stage the Master initiates you and conveys an inner spiritual light to you by which you can rapidly and with a sense of blessedness move forward in your awakening.

3   THE STEADY STATE

While in the propelled state you may think many divergent thoughts and have vastly varied emotions in your heartfelt search, still, there comes a time when the propelled state enables you to become *steady*. That is, your propelled state enables you to understand yourself and the various aspects of the path more clearly and well. You begin to find what techniques and specific areas of study most facilitate your growth. You also discover that you are easily able to choose the best and most effective teacher to help you fulfill your quest for higher consciousness.

So, the propelled state, which may have taken you many places, resolves to a series of selections by which you determine where and how you wish to conduct your inner quest. Perhaps you must travel many miles in your search for the fulfillment of your driving yearning. Perhaps you are blessed to come into the community of a Master and receive initiation, along with instruction about what to do next. Perhaps you don't have to leave your neighborhood.

In steadiness a deeply gratifying emotion and sense of well being fills you. The frequent sense of desperation or perplexity which often occurs in the propelled state is shed, let go of, no longer being essential to your quest. However, the power of your aspiration, developed in the propelled state, is stronger than ever. Since your *propulsion* is not being consumed in many divergent directions and philosophies, you now have a greater sense of what you're doing and how to do it.

The steady state is also often defined as "abiding in your initiated or baptized state." That is, having sought far, and now having found your Guru, for example, all you have to do is maintain the initiated state and be true to it throughout the vicissitudes of a still quite restless mind and heart. All you have to do, at the point of being steady, is follow the spirit of your "inward turning" (repentance, or initiation). Be true to it throughout each day, despite any negative or otherwise impacting experiences from the outer world or from the chaos of a still somewhat turbulent mental/emotional nature.

Proof that you are in a steady state is:

- Constancy in your spiritual practice.

- Being punctual and courteous to others, in a natural, unfeigned manner.

- Appreciating the instructions and techniques you've adopted, or been given by your special teacher, and practicing them daily.

- Experiencing a sense of complete freedom from the temptation to roam to other places, either by moving your body there or by allowing your mind and heart to dwell elsewhere than your blessed state and your relationship with your Master—or your spiritual ideal, if you have not yet found your Master.

Steadiness is an important state of well being. The propulsion, having moved from a stormy seeking and wondering state, now becomes a sense of confidence and a natural faith that realization and fulfillment are near at hand for you. In the steady state you find it easy to do what you commit yourself to do. You find it only natural and vitally important that you keep your word. You are also steady enough that you can meditate and pray easily. You are often free of confusion or mental/emotional turbulence and in this calm, balanced state you are able to sense the reality of your inner self.

While you do not have a deep realization or experience of your inner nature, you do, at times, see pastel shades of light in your forehead. Now and then you have wondrous feelings of love and expansion in your chest. You are calm enough to feel greater empathy with other people and at times understand thoughts that move within their heads or the feelings that dwell unspoken in their hearts.

In the steady state you are a rare human being already. You keep your agreements and do not want to harm anyone. You are able to be true to your quest in a calm and natural way, no matter what outward temptations or menaces strive to impact or affect your life.

Maintaining an appreciative mindfulness about your blessed state, you cannot fail to go forward and experience the next awakening.

4   THE DEVOTED STATE

As steadiness matures, you sense your inner light, love, and wisdom very deeply. You become devoted to the interests, the insights, and concerns of your inner self. Not only steady but loving and appreciative in the presence of your higher self and in the blessings of your Master, your heart sings with happiness. You now find it easy and natural to love. Your deeds are now more spontaneous and vigorous—actions from a love which you feel very deeply.

Now, not only propelled toward the higher consciousness within you, and not only steady in your pursuit and attitudes about it, you gain intimate contact with your true nature. You live, thrilling in the experience of giving and receiving deep, transforming love.

You are not only true to your Master and ideals because you *should* be, as in the steady relationship, but you are true to your Master and your quest because of great joy, satisfaction, and the delight of being *faithful to what you now know.*

In this devoted state you are also capable of perceiving and dealing with your old selfish nature. You are capable of honestly and sincerely observing the wrongs you have done to others and to yourself. You see the manner of ignorance by which you have blocked awareness of your true self and denied the Lord of your heart. You see how desires, personal pride and fear, as well as envy, have tormented your life up to this point. In a state of love, compassion, and good will, you look at your life and those of others with new eyes— eyes which have seen the truly beautiful and eternally existing reality.

In the devoted state there is a transformation of what you are living for. You have sensed the reality of higher consciousness, the true self, and are coming home to it. You live for the higher consciousness and its interests rather than old, egoic, selfish preoccupations and mechanical tendencies dictated by sense experience in the outer world.

Established in a devoted state of heart, you now clearly perceive what to do and how to overcome these negative, self-centered, arrogant tendencies from your past which emanate from your deep state of ignorance and former confusion.

You have become a devotee of Love, Light, and Truth.

5   THE CLEAR STATE

Wouldn't the devoted state be the highest? What could be higher than devotion? The clear state, which is also called the clean state, naturally follows from the devoted state. Indeed, the clear state is a fruition of devotion and is one of the greatest levels of awareness that could ever happen to you.

In the devoted state you began to see the reality of your inner self. In fact, you may find what some metaphysicians and *jnana* (wisdom) yogis say: that in the devoted state all ideas are internal ones and that the outer world is an expression or manifestation of ideas that exist within you, within the consciousness which is your essence. However, this view is not held by a number of masters and yogis of other forms of inquiry.

The clear state, in a nutshell, is one in which you are enabled and empowered to shed, to let go of, your old nature. You drop your old thoughts, tendencies, and emotions. You're capable of dismissing them, releasing them to oblivion, no longer to hound you or bother the attitudes and perspectives of your new awakened life—of love, wisdom, and attuned will.

Delightedly abandoning your old nature with its selfishness, pettiness, and worries, you finally stand free. You stand clear, and clean. Now clear, you can easily turn toward the brilliant effulgence of your true nature and humbly accept that light in every cell of your body, in every tissue of your mind, and in every throb of your heart. Clear, free, and *empty at last*, you become fully *infilled* and *indwelled* by your true nature! Your inner self, freely chosen in an act of love and free will on the part of your outer self, now permanently enters your mind, heart and senses. No longer only an "inner self," *it abides throughout your being*.

CONCLUSION

In your new state you wonder at the miracle of your transformation. You see how you moved from being an ignorant, materialistic, and selfish individual into a propelled state—usually precipitated by heartbreak and doubt. You thrill to note your propelled state was truly magnificent in its impact on your future happiness.

You see that in being true to your propelled state, you found your teacher and manner of proceeding. You found your way of study, meditation, and prayer. You became steadfast and pleasantly enjoyed well being and a one-pointedness which enabled you to progress rapidly toward your enlightenment. You observe how steadiness enabled you to become aware of your inner self, its true existence and nature.

You recall how naturally you became devoted to your inner self and lived for its inspiring purpose and ideals. You adored it and loved it.

Then you became able, in your devoted state, to distinguish between your old nature and your higher consciousness. You could distinguish the way of light from the way of darkness and selfishness, the way of faith from fear, jealousy, and anger.

Then you became clear. You grew to the point that your inner light empowered you to release, to banish, to put aside for once and all, your old nature—your old tendencies of thought, emotion, speech, and action.

How beautiful! Your doubts and frustrations have become your propulsion. Now your propulsion develops into love. And love transforms you.

Washed clean, washed clear, having abided in the blessings of your quest and the initiation of your Master (if you were so fortunate), you freely and humbly allow the light and life of your Creator to flood and permanently indwell you! You know the Source of existence and the essence of love.

REFLECTION

Is my mind my soul's window
Or the mirror of the world?

39

TRANSCENDENTAL CONSCIOUSNESS

To become enlightened you will very likely need to develop transcendental consciousness. When you have developed your faculty of transcendental consciousness, you will find it relatively easy to move through the stages of the heart and also experience the planes of consciousness revealed in the next chapter.

Transcendental consciousness is a faculty which you can develop and which readily makes your higher consciousness accessible. While a few aspirants on the path are able to find success without developing transcendental consciousness, most people who ultimately *abide* in higher consciousness have mastered the three levels of transcendental consciousness (called *samyama*): concentration, contemplation, and *samadhi*. Samadhi is roughly defined as pure awareness, free of mental, emotional, and physical turbulence or distortion. Samadhi means "the thing itself," literally. Development of transcendental consciousness is very enjoyable and enables you to easily direct your awareness to life improvement at will.

Because modern commentators disagree on the interpretation of Patanjali's ancient yoga sutras (aphorisms), some masters define the process of samyama—the three ascending levels—as being contemplation first, then concentration, then samadhi. But, the classical perspective of transcendental consciousness is the sequence of: 1) concentration; 2) contemplation; 3) samadhi.

By means of transcendental consciousness you can make your mind, emotions, and ego-sense subtle enough to experience your higher consciousness and your true nature. In transcendental consciousness you become able to concentrate your mind at progressively higher levels. You will find that your consciousness seems to have many veils. These veils distort your perceptions of life. Through transcendental consciousness you are able to remove one veil, then another, then another, then another, until your perception of life and reality is perfectly clear and ever so enthralling. You will likely come to the conclusion that in normal mental, emotional, and egoic consciousness you are *misperceiving everything*. That is, compared to the perspectives of your higher consciousness, your regular view of life is very partial, limited, and often distorted.

Another way of considering transcendental consciousness is that you have habitually directed your awareness outward to be particularly aware of the physical universe and in order to do this you have used the grossest, or densest, level of your psyche. You have needed to use numerous veils in order to maintain the awareness that the physical world alone is real. Ignoring higher consciousness, spirit, and the conscious energy which maintain the universe, you have lost out on many invaluable perspectives, opportunities, and an all-important sense of wholeness—of unity and harmony—in your life and world.

Those who have mastered the subject of transcendental consciousness liken its development to the progressive freeing of the individual from the prison of delusion or misconception. That is, as you remove the veils through which you are perceiving your world, one by one, you will find that you are increasingly aware of a more subtle identity. You are also aware of awesome calmness, ecstasy, and insight as you unveil your true self. Through transcendental consciousness, a state of liberation or perfect freedom, truth, and majestic well being results.

As you remove the veils of your consciousness and approach your true identity, you find that you can meditate on more and more subtle objects. Your initial practice of transcendental consciousness will likely be on a physical object which you gaze at with your calm eyes. Then, when you have perfected this ability to be perfectly aware of a physical object, you will be able to select an object—a point of concentration and meditation—*within you*. For example, it may be a light you behold in your forehead, or the movement of energy which you feel in your chest. This inner object (the light or the feeling) becomes more developed as you focus your mind more perfectly.

So, you will normally begin your development by concentrating on a gross external object and then on more refined and subtle inner objects. You proceed toward focusing on aspects of higher consciousness itself—peace or wisdom, for example—and beyond. With practice you can concentrate on the *source* of higher consciousness.

To experience transcendental consciousness one must understand, and achieve, its three main levels.

1   CONCENTRATION

Concentration means "with centeredness." You will find that all three steps in the development of transcendental consciousness involve focusing your awareness well and being able to poise your mind on the object of your meditation—whether that object is a gross physical object or a very subtle interior one.

Consideration of transcendental consciousness *begins with an awareness of the* **content** *of your mind*. Notice, as you watch your mind, how many thoughts and feelings flood through it—related thoughts and feelings, unrelated thoughts and feelings, images based on what your senses are telling you about the world or what they told you about the world yesterday or ten years ago. Memories and feelings flood up from the subconscious basement where you store the events of your life. Plans about the future also are part of your mental content—happy plans and views, as well as dreads.

Watch your mental content. You will likely find, as most do, that the mind is very turbulent and is messier than any child's room. This observation of the mind is called conscious "mind drift," and is a wonderful way to know what is going on inside you. By watching your mind drift for a few minutes each week you can know what you dominantly feel about life and yourself. You can be clearly aware of your fears as well as your hopes.

You will notice your mind is particularly turbulent unless you are aware of your character flaws. Whenever you try to concentrate, your mind drift gets worse unless you face and deal with your flaws faithfully.

Consider, too, that since you live in your mind drift, all the activities of your life are conducted in spite of or because of the turbulent flow of images and feelings that pour through your mind.

In a nutshell, the process of transcendental consciousness is one of guiding the content of your mind to become easily focused on one thing and then that one object of focus is made progressively more subtle.

Watching your mind in your normal waking consciousness you will likely find that numerous components make up the present content of your mind. For example:

. . . . My son . . . . The rose . . . . .
. . . . . My sore knee . . . . Tension in my jaw . . . .
. . . . The phone . . . . The pen . . .
. . . . The desk . . . .
. . . . The horse I rode when I was a kid . . . .

Now, in concentration you choose to patiently focus your mind until your mental content *is only one object.* That is, other objects are told not to interfere or enter your mental content for the period of your meditation. Of course, as your meditation becomes more subtle, you will be able to meditate in a much more discerning manner on much more refined objects—inner light, energy centers, and visions, for example. You will even become able to meditate without the need of an object; your mind will be perfectly focused and responsive without having to have an object. But, to develop the essential skills which enable you to have loftier meditations later, start with a simple object that is easy to view with eyes open, and easy to hold in the mind when you close your eyes. The object needs to have a unified look—too many features, or lines, encourage the mind to wander rather than focus.

Let's say, for example, that you choose to practice concentration on an apple which you set on the desk before you. The goal of a beginner in this practice is to hold the mind to the territory of "apple" thoughts. Your mind is allowed to wander or think about aspects of the apple but is not to stray into any mental content which is not directly related to the apple before you. At this beginning stage of the practice you are free to mentally reinforce what you are doing by chanting the words, "apple, apple, apple," or by reasoning about the apple, thinking of its kind and quality and freshness, for example.

Now your mind content may look something like this:

.. Apple, apple . . . McIntosh . . . . . . apple tree . . . .
. . . the desk . . . . the pen on the desk . . . . the bills
that await my study and payment . . . . errands I must do
tomorrow . . . . oh no! I want to pay attention to the
apple . . . . this apple . . . . apple, apple . . . .
. . . oh, I can't do this . . . . apple, apple, apple . . . . . .

You will succeed with practice—and that's all it takes—patient,
kind practice. You need to be kind to yourself because getting frustrated or angry adds more turbulence and further disturbs your mental content.

Probably you will notice you cannot concentrate very well unless you are aware of your character flaws and are striving to do
something about them. Often, when you try to concentrate, your
character "shortcomings" will float—or flash—into your mind, unless you have the peace which comes with the effort to be a better
person: a kinder, more constructive, efficient, responsible human
being.

You begin—usually after a few days—to relax more and give
more undivided attention to your fledgling attempts at transcendental consciousness. Now your mental content looks more like this:

. . . . . apple, apple . . . . desk . . . . apple, apple
. . . . pen . . . . apple, apple . . . . . . pen . . . .
apple, apple, apple . . . . desk . . . . apple . . .
. . . . . . sore knee . . . . apple, apple, ... apple
. . . . desk . . . . apple, apple . . . .

With practice, you find it is not too difficult to choose the content of your mind. That is to say, you find you can *borrow* your own
mind at times, borrow it from oblivion and wild turbulence, to do
something constructive and pleasant with it. This practice alone
greatly reduces the "worry time" that most people clock into their
lives.

You will notice as you do this practice that your feelings are
quite important. A pleasant feeling about the apple and the practice,

as well as about yourself, enables a more cordial and constant concentration. On the other hand, if your feelings want to play elsewhere with yearnings or frustrations of days gone by, your mental content becomes less steady and more chaotic.

Also, you find it's important to sit in a manner that is alert, upright, but not tense.

Soon—how soon, depending on your patience in working with your mind's contents, as well as how much mental discipline you have developed throughout your life—you will be able to hold the apple, or any simple object, clearly in your concentration. Other items and concepts won't push their way like terrorists into your awareness.

At this point you will greatly enjoy the practice of concentration and feel your "effort" was all worthwhile, despite appearances to the contrary at earlier stages. You will also feel fifty to one hundred percent more alive each day now that your mind is learning to become your ally rather than your sabotaging foe.

You now move forward to the next level of concentration which is the ability to hold your mental content on one object without having to mentally chant, reason, or use any verbalization to maintain the object in your clear and focused mind. This stage is indeed wonderful.

It should be mentioned here that your mind has a faculty something like the clutch in a car. Whenever you move from one level of concentration, contemplation, or samadhi to the next level above it, you will likely experience a changeover. For example, if you chanted the word "apple," and reasoned about the apple as you strove to hold your mind constantly on the apple, you likely experienced a moment when your mind went blank. In essence, you moved from "verbalizing concentration" to concentration without the need for verbalizing or reasoning; you passed through a brief period of "contentless" meditation. This temporary blankness is an activity of your higher self which switches your mind from verbal meditation to nonverbal meditation. Somehow your higher self clears the way for higher levels of meditation by freeing the mind of all content.

You will find "contentlessness" somewhat like being in a plane in partly cloudy skies. As you proceed through the sky you enjoy the beauty of the landscape and the way the sun reflects off the gorgeous clouds. Then suddenly your plane is inside a cloud. For a brief time you cannot see the landscape below or any other clouds. The beautiful view is "suspended" as you pass through the cloud.

When you come out of the cloud, you once again behold the beautiful landscape and can see a great distance before you.

But, in transcendental consciousness, you come out of the contentless "cloud experience" into a new *dimension* of awareness, not a resumption of the old perceptions. The new vista is markedly different and more glorious.

You will probably find that brief periods of contentless concentration occur, not only now at this beginning stage but every time you are about to move into a higher stage of transcendental consciousness. But bear in mind, because it's very essential, this brief time of contentless meditation is not a time to be mentally passive. You maintain full alertness. You are about to enter into a higher state of awareness and will need to be even more aware, more subtly aware, if you are to experience and achieve the next level. One vital rule of not only concentration but all forms of meditation is *never be passive*, never merely relax and take potluck, because then not only will your subconscious have free play to suggest whatever it wants to your mind, but also the astral or psychic world can easily invade and confuse your transcendental practices. Even for contentless meditation you must be very alert; only enjoy that a transformation is taking place in your mental content.

In time you will be able to meditate without the need of an object! Your mind will be perfectly focused and responsive without outer or inner objects.

As you develop in your concentration and the content of your mind becomes one-pointed, you are ready to move to the second stage of transcendental consciousness. However, keep in mind that with practice you will be concentrating on progressively more subtle inner objects: light in the forehead, love in the heart area, for example, rather than apples.

2   CONTEMPLATION

When the object of concentration shines in the mind without interruption you are, in the opinion of many masters, in a state of contemplation. For example, your mind is easily aware of the apple; no other thoughts intrude or interrupt your perfect flow of consciousness as it steadily holds the awareness of the apple. The apple, the meditation object, shines and abides in your mind. You are aware that you are contemplating the apple and nothing intrudes or distracts you from the very pleasant, near-exhilarating perfect use of your mind. Your mind is not rebelling, fighting, or resisting. It is serenely and very cooperatively maintaining the content which you have chosen.

Now the content of your mind looks like this:

Apple . . . .

In time, as you are consolidated in this lovely experience, your higher consciousness will enable your acceleration to a higher level of contemplation. Likely it will do this by first releasing the apple and you will abide in a contentless state for a few seconds or a few minutes. If you maintain your alertness you may suddenly experience a universal or extremely vast perspective of the apple—of its meaning, of its essence. Often perfect concentration on a specific object goes on to become, when the contemplation is also perfect, a realization of universal aspects or attributes within the object of meditation—in this case, the life or essence of the apple. Your mind simply becomes more subtle, vastly more aware, and specific objects are seen in their universal aspects.

ANOTHER VIEW

Now to make an enriching, important digression: it's important to note that some scholars and adepts believe contemplation instead of concentration should be the term used for the first activity of transcendental consciousness, that concentration *follows* contemplation.

In their analysis, the average seeker—especially in the modern world—has a particularly turbulent mind. In many cases, even after many days of practice, it is nearly impossible to concentrate the mind on an apple or an elephant with success. The aspirant should not give up hope but should instead first become familiar with the object by observing it in a friendly way and asking the mental content to become more focused through a contemplative process such as asking oneself, "What do my senses tell me about this apple?"

The aspirant then considers what the eyes, ears, nose, sense of touch and taste reveal to him about the object which he is striving to focus upon one-pointedly.

Another question then follows after the first has been considered fully: "What do my mind and memory tell me about this apple?" Present and past thoughts about the apple are then brought up and duly noted.

Another question is asked: "What do my feelings and emotions tell me about this apple?"

Similar questions are raised until your whole being—mentally, emotionally, physically—is focused on the apple. In this process the mental content becomes readily gathered and focused on the apple. This process of gathering and reflecting is what several masters and scholars call *contemplation*.

These masters go on to say that when the mind is so gathered, it most easily holds the meditation object—the apple—still. And when the object becomes perfectly still in the mind, the one-pointed mind, these masters call this one-pointed stage *concentration*, or mind poise.

So, you see, the differences about the progression of transcendental consciousness are important, thoughtful, and quite helpful. In the first method, based on concentration, one tries to hold the physical form of the apple in the mind. In the second method, based on contemplation, one asks questions about the object, gradually centering and *settling* the consciousness on the object. You must determine which process is easiest for you. Don't try to do a hard process if you can do an easy one. Either start with concentration as we used it first in this chapter, or start with contemplation, as mentioned most recently, and get on your way.

Likely you should also be told about one more consideration. The meditation object does not necessarily have to be still. While stillness is generally desirable, some people have a particularly difficult time concentrating on a still object. They find it easier to concentrate on the movement of the breath, or to think of a bird flying through the sky, or a fish swimming through the infinite ocean.

If you have difficulty maintaining your mental content on a still object after two weeks of trying, then you may wish to change your object to a moving one; and the motion of your awareness may enable you to more easily avoid distractions and disruptions of your thought.

Hopefully, mentioning the two views of the first steps of transcendental consciousness, as well as the still or moving object, will help you find the best way for you. Later on, when you have learned transcendental consciousness, you can enjoy the richness of these abilities by focusing on different objects over a period of several years. The beauty and joy of meditation are great rewards, in addition to the practical value of having easy access to your higher consciousness.

During contemplation (that state in which the object of meditation shines in the mind), the object is the *one content* which stays in the mind easily—without interruption, distraction, limitation, or distortion. You are aware you are contemplating and your experience is beautiful. Your mind easily maintains the apple, the meditation object, and has no inclination to wander or halt your contemplation.

What yet remains to occur? After all, your mind is clear and undisturbed. Still, there remains a very definite problem, a big barrier to transcendental consciousness. Can you see what it is? Let's go forward.

3   SAMADHI *(THE THING ITSELF)*

In contemplation you are subjectively aware you are meditating. Believe it or not, your sense of self and your emotional nature *intrude* on your experience of meditation. In fact, your sense of self, with all its limited past experience, stands as a barrier to the direct experience and superconscious perception of the meditation object. You are very limited in what you can know of your meditation object or your higher self. The quality of meditation must go forward if you are to experience your awakening and find yourself enlightened. That forward step is called *samadhi*.

Through very alert and appreciative contemplation, plus a willingness to allow your higher self to lift you up to an even higher plane of perfect awareness, samadhi must occur. Samadhi means "the thing itself," free of your egoic and subjective perspectives, opinions, and possible errors. Samadhi is not a different process from contemplation or concentration. It is a natural improvement in the quality of your alertness, of your attention and attunement.

As you maintain your contemplation and the object easily shines in your mind, free of interruption or distortion, there will be a magnificent change in your meditative process. You cannot make this change happen. The ego, as long as it's active, defies and thwarts samadhi. All you can do is cooperate and allow your alertness and attention to increase (without straining—straining will frustrate the process too).

Also, if you try to reason your way into samadhi you will discover you are inhibiting and preventing the process from occurring.

After samadhi you will have the distinct knowledge you experienced it. Particular characteristics occur. If, however, you are thinking of any event, object or sequence while you feel you are in samadhi or while entering into it, you will be having a false experience—as many beginners do. By mentally trying to bring about or control the process they merely experience a psychic or partial and delusive state of awareness. But what are the characteristics of samadhi?

What happens is this: *In samadhi the object of meditation, the person who is meditating, and the act of meditation become one. In the state of samadhi you temporarily suspend your sense of separateness from the object of meditation. You merge with it and know it deeply and intimately. You also lose consciousness that you are meditating—because of your total awareness of the object.*

In samadhi you are experiencing the faculty of geniuses who become totally absorbed in what they are doing and completely forget themselves or any self-conscious considerations of technique or their appearance: they are rapt, engaged completely and totally in their music, art, or inventiveness. They bring to humanity the wealth of higher consciousness, the inspired answers, solutions, and inventions from superconscious realms.

You will experience the greatest thrill of your life—excepting possibly the exalted moods of relationship mentioned in Chapters 21 through 27. The thrill is indescribable. It is pure being, free of false, egoic opinion and egocentricity. It is total apprehension of the object meditated upon, which in most cases, as you can assume, will not be an apple.

This indescribably blissful period of freedom from the tyranny of the ego and the mind, while experiencing the pure source of consciousness itself, is life-giving and ever so regenerative. You sense in samadhi the possibilities of life which are available to every human being when the barriers of mental, emotional, and egoic chaos are temporarily suspended.

Various analogies are used to describe samadhi. None of them are adequate. However, as Ernest Wood, author and teacher of higher consciousness observed, samadhi is like that point at which separate notes become music. It is similar to the point at which two separate gases—oxygen and hydrogen—are fused together and an entirely new and different substance, which is the product of hydrogen and oxygen, suddenly comes into being as water.

In samadhi, ignorance and loneliness are suddenly let go and a grand sense of well being and of one's true nature are finally discovered! Truly the notes of one's life, the separate thoughts and actions, all the events, major and minor, suddenly merge into a meaning and purpose undreamed of! A significance, a unity of all the loose ends occurs.

St. Thomas Aquinas, considered the greatest intellectual theologian of his time, spent most of his life writing a vast treatise on God and the universe. Then, at a mass in Naples in 1273 A.D., he actually experienced a vision and a great samadhi. Later, he said, "I cannot go on . . . all that I have written seems to me like so much straw compared to what I have seen and what has been revealed to me."* At last he was seeing from his true nature. His writing had greatly missed expression of the reality he now beheld. The "notes" of his life had become music.

THE MAIN FOCUS

These threefold steps—concentration, contemplation, and samadhi—comprise the necessary faculty of the mind for your discovery of higher consciousness. After developing these three aptitudes, you will find that ignored levels of awareness within yourself become revealed and very likely the focus of your meditation will become your soul, your inner self. You will make your inner self, or a symbol of that inner self, your meditation object. In becoming skilled at moving through the levels—from concentration through contemplation and into samadhi—you will find that you can *realize* your soul!

You will know your true nature, and (through samadhi) have a direct, unburdened, and clear experience of your Creator. You will see the essential consciousness and energy—the spirit—of this universe. Through a series of samadhis on progressively subtle objects, you will one day realize your true nature and stand free from the bondage to ignorance and ego. As one master says, "When you have transcendental consciousness, you realize you have *everything*."

It is also possible to practice the relationships mentioned in Chapters 21 through 27 and you will, through that development, be able to easily gain the faculties of transcendental consciousness. However, many people prefer to develop transcendental consciousness by the three steps developed in this chapter. Further, the Good Will Witness state and the Universal Self, as discussed in Chapters 18 and 19, are experienced mainly through concentration, contemplation, and samadhi.

It's up to you! It depends on your nature and how you may most quickly progress toward your delightful fulfillment.

* *New Catholic Encyclopedia*, 1967, Volume 14, pages 108-109.

REFLECTION

The object of meditation,
The person who is meditating,
And the act of meditation
Become one.

40

THE PLANES OF HIGHER CONSCIOUSNESS

On the day you thoughtfully turn the direction of your life toward higher consciousness and yearn to discover the consciousness that created and sustains you, you will begin the greatest adventure of your life. On that day the motive and the quest of your life are both changed. You no longer live for yourself but for something greater than you. You no longer are driven by the motive for personal gratification but for lasting fulfillment and personal transformation.

Your adventure in higher consciousness will test you, as well as thrill and satisfy you. Many times you may feel fearful as you stand before unknown dimensions of higher consciousness. Your mind, trying to guess what is about to happen, will never be adequate. Its presumptions are too limited and too predicated on previous experience in the outer world. Your emotions will be stretched beyond the normal comfort level, stretched until they can maintain universal love and revel in the ecstasy of pure being.

Your adventure requires your courage—more courage than you think you've got. You will also have to endure, to hang on and persevere, longer than you think you can.

You will need faith. At times it may seem faith is the only thing remaining to you. You will be tempted to let go of your faith and slide back to the turning point where you can forget about higher consciousness and your quest.

There is a need to be kind, especially to yourself. Your harsh judgments about yourself and the path can cause too many doubts and certain failure.

You need to be energetic and strong. The weak do not persevere and they give up pitifully early.

You will also need to be humble. There are times you may feel you don't have enough strength and wisdom to continue, times you desperately need inspiration, guidance, and strength from above.

Your journey through the stages of the heart, as it grows from the dark state to the clean, has been described in Chapter 38. It's very important to keep these stages of the mental/emotional awakening in mind as reliable guideposts of your voyage. However, it's also very important to know the following levels of awareness which you will likely experience as you come home to your higher consciousness and become enabled to live in it as a new person.

As soon as you turn within and begin your adventure you experience an all-important realization which hopefully you never forget:

FIRST LEVEL

Having made the significant redirection of your life, of your purpose and goals, you experience, in the quiet of the night, or looking out at the world through calm eyes, that the material world is essentially spirit. The material world is essentially conscious energy. While the world seems very dense and solid, this solidity is only a beautiful power of spirit and higher consciousness to make itself dense, "to crystallize" itself and occupy time and space. You, by one means or another, receive the conviction or revelation that the external world is made up of an essence or an energy which you can perceive or feel. This essence is also the primary substance, or the essential reality, of everyone and everything that exists. You realize that your nature, your personal nature, is essentially conscious energy or spirit. This you behold with your own superconscious sight; and the world, you find, has never seemed so beautiful as it now appears. You see both the hard, physical forms and the subtle plays of essence and energy within and around all living things and every object, big or small.

Realizing for once, and hopefully forever, that the physical world is truly what physicists say—energy—you have a new attitude about the entire universe. You realize how fluid and how change-able your world can be with the right application of consciousness. You see that your thoughts and feelings are plays of energy and that they do have an impact, an interplay, with the vast universe. Your thoughts and feelings, as well as your actions, are interrelated with the way the world is now and the way it is becoming in the future.

Many people, you realize, take hallucinogenic drugs in the hope of catching a glimpse of this energy and consciousness which you now—with the feeling of being at home—behold so calmly and naturally.

In this perception of the essence and energy within all living things and within all objects, you perceive more deeply how faith works. Faith brings about a change in circumstances. It causes change because all things and all people are rooted in, have their essence in, this same energy ocean. Here, in the unity of spirit, each person directs his convictions and activates his faith about a life and world that *can* be. A prayer or act of faith becomes a powerful move-ment in one part of the ocean of consciousness which then (or simul-taneously) acts upon the consciousness and energy in another place, person, or situation.

You also see how important it is for your health to relax in the consciousness of the higher subtle energy so this dynamic force may most easily heal and rejuvenate the body which, after all, is truly a product of consciousness and energy.

Many who have this first experience of higher consciousness consider themselves enlightened and cannot conceive of higher levels of awareness beyond this staggering view of reality: that everything is consciousness and life is essentially conscious energy.

SECOND LEVEL

When you feel at home with the shocking and breathtaking real-ization of the universe as a play of energy or consciousness which you are able to behold through your heightened senses and subtle mind, you enter into a state of indescribably sweet serenity. Your serenity is so deep that it seems to pervade not only your bones and body but the air around you. The energy in your room, or car, or wherever you may go, has a beatific quality. Others may love to stand near you and many dogs and cats may wish to abide with you in the new atmosphere which radiates from your new level of consciousness.

In this state of serenity you are able to feel free from old habits, free to choose new and better ways to express yourself or spend your time. Your serenity enables greater freedom of choice and greater ability to be constructive than you have known before.

While perhaps the first level of higher consciousness is the most shocking—to behold the entire world, yourself, and life in an entirely new light is certainly mind-boggling—it is also quite surprising to find that the body and mind feel quite uncomfortable with serenity at first. While the serenity is so sweet and pleasant, there is a tendency from old thoughts, feelings, and perceptions of the world to avoid what is so wonderful. There is resistance at first which tries to *prevent* the serenity from occurring. And, if the serenity nevertheless occurs, there is then a reluctance about staying in it or in allowing it to go on.

Further, there is a treacherous residual malice which strives to deprecate, deny, or criticize the serenity, to limit it or make it go away. There is the haunting feeling that to be serene is not "patriotic" or human; or some such rationale floods the mind in its desperation to tyrannize your organism once again with its conjectures, doubts, apprehensions, and wild free play of fears from those days before the dawn of higher consciousness.

It takes practice to accept the insights which you have gained about the world as consciousness and thus reestablish yourself in a serenity which enables you to thoroughly align your thoughts and feelings with your new state of well being. You may find it hard to accept serenity as a natural state because hardly anyone you have ever met has been serene. Often the temptation will be to think of yourself as lazy when you wish to attune with your inner self and enjoy the gleaming inner light.

However, with just a little observation, you will notice that in your new serenity you are more active and efficient than you have ever been before. You also relate to others more easily, and you can perceive and achieve goals more successfully.

In this serene level of higher consciousness you make choices and decisions about forming your new character, letting go of destructive flaws, and accepting and creating tendencies of character which are *supportive* of your new perceptions of yourself and the universe.

THIRD LEVEL

Your realization of higher consciousness now inspires you with courage. You begin to know that all the strength you need to succeed in your quest will be instilled within you. This gift of courage from your higher consciousness is fully accepted and you feel very strong and powerful but are perfectly aware you do not own this courage, that it is bestowed on you as a gift through your loving surrender and attunement. In this state of courage you sense that whatever you truly need you will always have—or know how to attract it or achieve it.

In this state of courage you are finally able to let go of deep insecurities that plague most everyone: greed and covetousness. In your new security you find you do not have to be greedy, and the tension and misery you used to feel is released as you throw greed away. It is no longer a necessary part of your makeup. You also find you do not *need* to desire anything anyone else in the world has. You sense in your courage that whatever you truly need will be yours, without question. Your ally, higher consciousness, will enable true fulfillment. Further, you don't feel so much of a need for material things. They can be great tools but they are no longer important to you as symbols of accomplishment or self-esteem.

It is at this point in your adventure that your courage will be tested many times. Having the conviction of true courage, as well as freedom from greed and covetousness, your life will very likely put you to the test. This testing is a subtle agreement between your higher consciousness and your world somehow. You will be given many opportunities to find out if there is any residual greed hiding within you. Again and again you will be made to feel lacking—without some object or situation that would be very helpful to you. At that point you will find out whether you feel greed or perhaps even wish to have the monies and objects someone else has. You will be tested many times, and may fail several times before you go on to the next level of the adventure. What has to be established within you is a courage that prevails against any challenge. Certainly it's alright to have fear, but true courage is involved in facing that fear and succeeding in spite of it, not allowing it to diminish your courage in any way.

The quest will determine whether you want to use your old-fashioned, cunning ways, developed before the dawn of higher consciousness, or whether you mean it when you say you wish to live a life in higher consciousness and that it truly is capable of sustaining you.

So many people talk a good game and cite many miraculous events of the higher consciousness helping them out. However, all too many aspirants have given up and broken faith with their higher consciousness, their true nature, when their life situation was critical, when the results were very, very important, and when no help or inspiration seemed forthcoming. These "edge-of-the-precipice" experiences, as some people call them, are the true builders of character and the real transformers of devotees.

It is at this third level that many initiates in higher consciousness pause for a very long time and gratefully recede into fleeting moments of serenity rather than face the unknown and go forward.

It would not be correct, of course, to maintain that one simply relies on the higher consciousness to do everything. The adventurer seeks to attune mind, body, hands, feet, words, everything, with the higher consciousness and seeks greater common sense, among other things, to know how best to serve the higher consciousness in the practical, day-to-day matters of life. The person who is passing this test of true courage is not sitting somewhere in a dark room waiting for somebody to throw a loaf of bread or a gold brick through the window. He or she is actively moving about in life but living that life from a sense of deep inner satisfaction and a willingness to cooperate with the great inner wisdom and goodness.

When true courage is accepted and it becomes part of your nature, and when greed and covetousness have truly fallen from you—no longer being your tendencies, however deeply hidden—then another level of higher consciousness makes its appearance.

FOURTH LEVEL

In this level your sense of self expands. Having grown in higher consciousness, you are now bestowed the ability to let go of your egocentric drive. Releasing the tremendous self-preoccupation that most people have, your sense of self lightly and easily expands outward from you, moving out beyond the confines of the body, extending and extending not only to the horizon but beyond the horizon. There is a rush of awareness that you are conscious energy yourself, pure awareness, and that you are not confined to a body. You can extend your being, your essence, not only as a general glow or radiance but this marvelous light of your being, this marvelous power of your being, can extend to infinity—and it does.

This infinite, vast experience is filled with ecstasy and delight. It is called *cosmic consciousness* by many people. You realize your cosmic, or universal, self. You realize what mystics through the ages have experienced through their profound meditations. You are alive as never before.

Usually these expansions last about half an hour and then you return to physical awareness and feel that once again you are abiding within your body. The nerves have to be strengthened in order for this experience to occur in the first place and if you are to have expansions that last more than twenty minutes to a half hour, then your nerves will have to be very strong because the rush of energy is very powerful.*

As a result of this expansion you feel deep empathy and attunement with all people. No one is a stranger to you. Everyone you meet somehow feels like a relative, a person from your family, from your circle of friends and acquaintances.

This cosmic consciousness, or expansion, is not without its tests and difficulties. Very often you will find you are about to have the experience but you choke. That is, you clutch, you hold back, you do not dare let go of your self-interest or your attachment to your body. It is often difficult to expand even a little bit, let alone allow the process to extend to seeming infinity—which is indeed what can happen.

So, many aspirants balk at this point. They are afraid to let go of their body and to experience a change in their perception of who they really are. It's scary, and it is not known to the beginner what is going to happen. There is a fear of losing oneself, or of dying, of being very unsafe. What should happen if one is out there and the phone rings or somebody comes into the room? Perhaps one won't be able to get back in the body. All these fears have to be dealt with by a patient acceptance of the higher consciousness and a willingness to work with it and to understand it—to the extent one is ever able to understand something so great.

Sometimes it takes a person over a year to be willing to trust this expansive pressure that lovingly builds up, usually in the chest area. Some people who begin the experience and then, through fear, stop it, give up the spiritual path and live in quiet terror that the expansion might happen to them sometime. They find the feeling utterly horrible, their sense of self being altered so. Often one needs the help and inspiration of a Master/Guru or adept who routinely experiences

---

* Usually, the nerves are made stronger through mental/emotional health, a wholesome diet emphasizing fruits and vegetables, daily physical exercise, and the practice of happiness.

this state. Such guidance encourages the aspirant to be patient and to be pleased when the expansion tries to happen.

The difficulty is based entirely on the strength of the ego and its predilection for self-centeredness. The higher consciousness will not overwhelm the ego. It awaits the time that the ego is willing to experience something beyond itself, willing to welcome a new state of love and freedom to occur, and willing to surrender control to the higher power, the greater wisdom, and the true love within.

Many seekers do not understand and do not have what it takes. They try the expansion a few times, find themselves unwilling or unable to cooperate with the outward thrust of the self. They return to the fork in the road where higher consciousness began and they willingly take the other road: the road of self-confinement.

On the other hand, those who persist and understand that the problem is the thickness of their ego—the intensity of their ego-centricity—find the experience so wonderful they yearn that it not end. And each day that goes by thereafter they yearn to experience the expansion again and again and again. They feel, both in the expansion and in the afterglow of it, that they are surrounded by blessedness. They behold everything as tinged with a sweet ecstasy. The serenity of the second level has been totally replaced by an ecstatic and dynamic play of consciousness. It is thrilling to be alive in every tissue! Every moment, every second, has a delight in it for the one who meets with this adventure and dares to be changed in so fundamental a way.

FIFTH LEVEL

Having experienced the exaltation and also the transformation of one's sense of self in level four, a very pleasant and necessary state now occurs. The aspirant, in his growth in higher consciousness, gets *comfortable* with the new state of expansion and is able to sense the freed and expanded ego—the transformed ego—quite easily throughout the day. A quality of calmness and an ability to perform well in daily life now occurs.

It is obviously a necessity that one not be so preoccupied with one's ecstasy that one sticks one's hand in front of a saw or drives crazily down the road into other cars. While such empty-headed incompetence is very unlikely, it is nevertheless a possibility. So, the ecstatic states of the previous level are generally experienced in the quiet of one's apartment or meditation area. In this following stage, that magnificent exaltation becomes so consolidated within you that you become calm enough to live in a degree of this higher awareness night and day. You gain the ability to maintain a higher level of consciousness while in the outer world. You also feel great ease in entering meditation and going into a more intimate experience with higher consciousness as well.

So, in this state you become deeply calm—*very, very calm*. You are also able to maintain this calmness while you are extremely busy. The keynote of this advanced stage in higher consciousness is "calmly active, actively calm." Whether in motion or at rest, you have a calmness that enables the ecstasy and blessedness of higher consciousness to abide with you in your job, home life, and any other activity.

SIXTH LEVEL

You are now tempted and rather severely tested. The question is: Whose will is to be done in your life?

You realize that you could probably direct your energy to heal people, to create millions of dollars for yourself, or to benefit yourself in some other particularly handsome way. You could become quite famous. You very likely could be considered a saint—and a great one. Probably you could develop occult powers and read minds or project your astral body to distant places. You could predict the future very likely. In fact, at times you seem not to be able to keep yourself from knowing what's on another person's mind or from being very "lucky" in your career world.

It's a difficult time, in fact. You don't know to what extent you should use your higher consciousness to benefit yourself or others. After all, there are so many needy people in the world! You may feel like a pitiless monster—or an arrogant scrooge—if you don't use all of your higher consciousness to help those who are suffering or who are less fortunate than you are.

These trials often send people back out on the road away from higher consciousness. It's amazing, but even having experienced so much of the higher consciousness many aspirants, at this point, get the opinion they are now empowered to play God and it is their calling to run about the planet using their higher powers to *zap* and influence people and situations. "After all," they ask, "did we get this higher power, this higher consciousness, only to do nothing with it?"

This series of trials may go on for ten, twenty years, or a lifetime. It's a state easy to talk about, but hard to deal with when one is in the testing and tempting phase. Many fail. Many decide that they are authorized and empowered to run about playing God.

However, those who *appreciate* the higher consciousness do not have much of a problem. They simply seek the wisdom and guidance of their higher consciousness about what they should do next. They know it is only by the power of the higher consciousness they progressed from one level to the next. They recall it's only due to an inspired sense of need for the higher consciousness that they ever *began* the path. It's only the grace of the higher consciousness and the Lord within that has enabled them in any way to *stay* on the path. For such devotees it's quite simple. They submit themselves to the higher consciousness and seek its will. They don't want to do their own individual will. They've observed that many times in their lives when they've tried to use their limited thought, insight, and power they often hurt themselves or others. Such aspirants seek, through their gratitude and appreciation of the higher consciousness, to attune their personal will with the higher will—with the wisdom of the higher consciousness which they have learned to love and trust.

And so they go past the many hurdles and precipices that other seekers find difficult to deal with. These seekers of the higher will are blessed to be trained, through life, to attune more and more readily with the higher will. They learn how to recognize it, how to distinguish between the higher will and their old-fashioned, less adept will. They find the higher will is easily revealed and expressed through them. This alignment of one's being with the higher consciousness brings immense satisfaction and a sense of being a sharer in the ongoing creativity of this universe.

These wise aspirants seek to humbly, through their prayer and meditative life, further the act of creation, further the expression of goodness, in their daily lives. They feel no conflict between their personal will and the higher will because they have completely submitted their personal will to the higher will. They seek to live in attunement. As some saints say, "I am the instrument. You, O Lord, are the operator of this instrument."

These are but the mere beginning levels of enlightenment. After these basic tests and triumphs there are ever-new and ever-more delightful experiences in store. There is no limit to the adventure and the reward of intimacy with your higher consciousness and your Creator.

For some of the greatest insights about awakening and enlightenment—inspired and fascinating realizations from around the world—read on!

REFLECTION

I was as if dead;
Now, I am alive!

VII

DIFFERENT PATHS

41

DIFFERENT PATHS

Religious leaders, yogis, mystics, and metaphysicians urge us toward God and a new way of living. Daily, they exhort people to put off their old ways of thinking and feeling in order to live lives of faith and greater understanding. They encourage us to put aside our anger and fear and enjoy lives of confidence and love. They guide us to long-term considerations and away from selfishness—which is shortsighted and usually leads to disaster. They reveal pathways that lead to true well being. In many ways, these spiritual men and women enable people to experience higher consciousness.

In this section, *Different Paths*, you may find the help you have been looking for all of your life. Something shared by one of these dedicated persons may touch your heart so deeply that you will never be the same, and your path of unfoldment will suddenly appear to your immediate gaze. Or, perhaps you will gain a hundred or a thousand insights which will help you invaluably on your personal path. Then again, you may quickly gain a deeper understanding of the differences between people regarding important religious issues. In your appreciation of these differences, you may experience a greater compassion within you. You will likely rejoice, too, in observing how much people of different views have in common: in every path there is a deep concern and respect for life itself and an eagerness to be friends even with those who do not share a particular view. These spiritual leaders have a great willingness to reach over walls and across chasms of differences.

Interviews of these concerned human beings took place over a period of three years in Southern California. Most of the leaders are widely known in spiritual circles. They are listed alphabetically here by religion or path:

• Reverend Mahathera Piyadassi, Harvard-educated senior monk at the Vajirarama Forest Hermitage monastery in Sri Lanka. Reverend Piyadassi is a dedicated Buddhist. See *Buddhism*, Chapter 42.

• Reverend Elwin Pelletier lovingly represents much of mainstream Protestant Christian thought. A Baptist missionary for thirty-five years, twenty-five of which he prepared pastors for the field ministry in what is now Zaire (formerly the Belgian Congo), he is now a Chaplain at the University of California-Irvine Medical Center in Orange, California.

Reverend Pelletier and his wife Lois share their Christian love and experience in *The Baptists*, Chapter 44.

• Archbishop Tomas Clavel of the Diocese in Orange County, California. He was formerly the Archbishop of Panama and joined Pope John Paul II in the Holy Father's visit to Central America. He is Vicar for the Hispanic Community of the Diocese of Orange, California.

• Also, Bishop John T. Steinbock, who was the auxiliary Bishop of the Diocese of Orange in Orange County, California and formerly a priest on skid row in downtown Los Angeles, California. He is now Bishop of the Diocese of Santa Rosa, California.

The Archbishop and Bishop are known internationally for their ministries among the poor and undocumented people. Both share their views in Chapter 45 on *Roman Catholicism*.

• Professor Satya Pal Sharma travels the world on behalf of Hinduism and his quest for understanding between different religions. To enjoy Punditji Sharma's views on humanity and Hinduism, see *Hinduism*, Chapter 46.

• While some people may hold the view that Islam is not widely known or practiced in North America, Reverend Muzammil Siddiqi, Harvard-educated director of the Islamic Society of Orange County, California has several thousand members in his congregation. Serene and happy members enjoy spiritual lives around this Islamic Center in Garden Grove, California. For Reverend Siddiqi's candid and fascinating comments, see *Islam*, Chapter 47.

• Rabbi Frank Stern ministers to a very large congregation in Southern California also, at Temple Beth Shalom in Santa Ana, California. Very knowledgeable, he questioned my questions and we had a wonderful afternoon together. We ranged the world from spiritual experience through Jewish history and modern psychology. For Rabbi Stern's comments, see *Judaism*, Chapter 48.

• Rabbi Stern sent me to see Rabbi David Eliezrie for a greater understanding of Hasidic Judaism. Rabbi Eliezrie of the Chabad Community Center in Anaheim, California is one of the main spokesmen for Hasidic Judaism in California. For inspiring and perplexing spiritual stories and deeply profound insights, see *Hasidic Judaism*, Chapter 49.

• Reverend William Hornaday is internationally known as one of the world's leading metaphysicians and teachers; he also did personal service with Albert Schweitzer in Lambarene, Gabon, in Africa. Reverend Hornaday is a spokesman for Christian metaphysics, metaphysical religious thought in general, and the Church of Religious Science, a leader in metaphysical thought worldwide. See *Religious Science*, Chapter 50.

• Swami Swahananda joined the Ramakrishna Order of the Vedanta Society in Calcutta in 1947. He's spent over thirty years of his life studying and teaching Vedanta in India and the United States. He became the Director of the Vedanta Society in 1976. The basic position of Vedanta, the Swami says, is "man in his ultimate nature, nature in its ultimate nature, and God in His ultimate nature are all the same." To know the basis of this religion from India which is practiced worldwide, see *Vedanta*, Chapter 51.

• Yoga is not a religion but has many spiritual aspects. The author, who is a Guru of yoga, metaphysics, and mysticism, describes rudimentary and advanced aspects of *Yoga* in Chapter 52.

These lovers of God and mankind are doing acts of extreme good will by participating in a manuscript which they have not read. Of course, each person interviewed has had a period of time to study and comment upon the chapter based on his particular interview. And, I'm so grateful for their comments and clarifications.

Further, each of these good people were encouraged to speak from the heart and let the chips fall where they may. Our goal was to understand each path in terms of higher consciousness. All those interviewed have spent many years in dedicated service of the Lord and humanity.

These chapters about different paths are, of course, too few but are meant to be a guide to deeper understanding and greater experience of the world's major paths—and a few smaller ones which focus on higher consciousness.

As you read these chapters, you may find it fascinating to observe how many of these spiritual leaders protest against the word "religion" being applied to their particular path. Most of them deeply object to the politicization of their precious spiritual values in such a manner that people of one faith hurt and even kill members of other faiths. One gets the feeling in conversing with these leaders that they're *all* making a significant change in the world.

In conclusion, what is it these men know that makes their faces shine? What gives them such confidence in times of adversity? What makes their minds so sharp, and yet their hearts so full of love? Why do they seem so much more alive than most people?

What is this power? What is this light? What is this great dimension?

May the multitude of fascinating and sometimes very divergent insights now inspire you in heart and mind!

42

BUDDHISM

Reverend Mahathera Piyadassi arrived at my house in reddish-orange robes and brown sandals. He walked erectly from decades of meditation and discipline. Slightly above medium height, his head was clean shaven, his thin face shadowed with a hint of gray whiskers. Dark, intelligent eyes studied me. He was in his sixties perhaps and his expression seemed stern except that his lips were generous with smiles. He gestured gently as he spoke, his voice soft and rich, "This is a gift for you."

He handed me a heavy object wrapped in blue silk. I opened the cloth to discover a crucifix fashioned in metal by a master craftsman.

"I knew you would like it," he said, noticing my delight.

"I like it very much," I replied, and admired the shining form of Christ for several minutes. Then my secretary placed the crucifix on a special shelf.

Educated at Nalanda College, the University of Sri Lanka, and Harvard University, Reverend Piyadassi is the senior monk at Vajirarama Monastery in Sri Lanka—a most beautiful country island on the southeastern tip of India. The equator passes near Sri Lanka.

313

Every other year this holy man travels around the world sharing the light of Buddhism, and he had paused in Southern California to make a series of loving lectures.

Reverend Piyadassi likes to be called "Bhante," which is a name similar to "Swami," or renunciant devotee.

We considered a number of possible snack foods and Bhante ultimately chose to have a little sliced fruit. We sipped juice and he consented to answer my questions about Buddhism. I was asking the right man because Bhante Piyadassi is the author of *Buddhist Meditation*, *The Virgin's Eye*, and *The Buddha's Ancient Path*, a significant discussion of Buddhism's great teachings.

"Bhante Piyadassi, what is Buddhism, please?" I began.

He gestured gracefully, "Buddhism is not merely a religion; it is also a whole civilization with its historical background: it's literature, art, and philosophy. Buddhism touches all aspects of human life—the social, economical, ethical, intellectual, spiritual, and mental development leading to enlightenment and nirvana. That is the goal of Buddhism—nirvana, or perfect peace and happiness."

I reflected how hard it is to take any of the world's religions and make them fit into a simple box. Obviously, a religion which is alive and helping humanity becomes deeply involved in all aspects of a society.

"Bhante, in essence, what are Buddha's teachings?"

"Buddha's teachings are summed up in what came to be known as the Four Noble Truths. That is what the Buddha taught—the Four Truths." He stopped, as if for emphasis.

"One, the fact that there is suffering in the world—that is to say, *unsatisfactoriness* or conflicts. The truth of suffering. Secondarily, this suffering has its causes. Suffering is not causeless—without cause. The Buddha, like a scientist, showed the cause of these sufferings. The cause is more *subjective* than it is objective. That is, man's *craving* —his greed, hatred, or ill will and ignorance or delusion. These are the root causes of all our suffering."

How similar these sufferings are to the views of ancient yogis, I thought. The great master Patanjali wrote that when a man ignores his true nature, he then experiences the five-fold suffering—ignorance, egotism, craving, fear, and possessiveness or greed.

"How can one deal with this suffering?" I asked.

Bhante's forehead creased slightly, "Suffering ceases when craving is stilled or removed. Then follows perfect peace or happiness—that is, the cessation of all suffering. This is the third Noble Truth.

"And the fourth truth is the *path* which leads to the cessation of suffering. This path consists of eight factors or eight limbs:

1 Right Understanding
2 Right Thought
3 Right Speech
4 Right Action

5 Right Livelihood
6 Right Effort
7 Right Mindfulness
8 Right Concentration

"These are the eight factors of Buddhism in practice," Bhante smiled, then went on.

"Suffering and conflicts are like an ailment. There is the cause of the ailment, the cure, and the prescription. Buddha told his disciples, 'I am like a physician, not for bodily ailments, but for mental ailments, mental maladies, of beings.'

"But," Bhante added, "the recognition of this universal fact of suffering, however, is not a total denial of pleasure and happiness. The Buddha never denied happiness in life when he spoke of the universality of suffering. In Buddhist scriptures there is a long enumeration of the happiness that people are capable of enjoying. But all pleasures are impermanent, not lasting. A dispassionate study of Buddhism will tell you that Buddhism is a message radiating joy and hope—not a defeatist philosophy of pessimism.

"So, one who thinks deeply will interpret these Four Noble Truths as: One, suffering and conflicts to be understood; Two, the causes of suffering should be removed; Three, the cessation of conflict—nirvana—is to be realized; and Four, the Noble Eightfold Path is to be practiced or cultivated."

How beautiful and how succinct, I thought. "You are saying, then, the goal of Buddhism is nirvana?"

He nodded. "The goal of Buddhism is nirvana—deliverance of the mind. That is the final goal and cessation of all sufferings and conflicts—supreme happiness. But, also, the Buddha emphasizes the importance of the present life. In Buddhism we find the economic, social, ethical, intellectual, and mental or spiritual aspects. Buddhism emphasizes these aspects and the Buddha teaches all aspects of human life."

How similar to Judaism, I thought, with its numerous directives about how to lead a spiritual life.

Bhante Piyadassi reflected a moment, then continued. "The Buddha speaks not only of a goal and life after death, but he also emphasizes (even more) the present life. For the Buddhist, this is not the only life.

"According to the Buddha, there were lives before birth and there will be lives after death. This is what we call re-becoming (or rebirth). We don't use the word 'reincarnation.'* When one attains nirvana, there is no more re-becoming."

"Bhante," I was fascinated with his answers, "how is a Buddhist fulfilled, or saved, or realized—whichever term you prefer to use?"

"You attain the goal by following the eight factors, the eight limbs. Buddhism, one may say, is a 'do-it-yourself' religion. The Buddha said: 'You yourselves should put forth the necessary effort and work out your deliverance.' The Buddha points out the way. It's something like this: a man walking the road is suddenly confronted with a parting of the road and is unsure what to do. He looks around and sees a signboard and fingerpost and these give him directions. It's left to the pedestrian—to you—to keep walking. So Buddha says, 'I am like the signpost. I am a pointer and I show you the right path.'

"It's left to the individual to follow the path," he explained. "This path is the Noble Eightfold Path.

"Or, again, when you get sick you go to the physician. The physician will diagnose and find out the cause of your illness. Then he will give a prescription. It is left to you to see that the prescription is taken correctly."

"I see. And what is the process of fulfillment for a Buddhist?"

"Buddhism is a gradual process," he answered. "The attainments do not come all at once; there is a gradual unfolding.

"You start," he said, "with morality (sila). That is the starting point. Morality is the ABC of Buddhism. All ethics and morals have one function—to control the speech and action of man. Taming the tongue and controlling the bodily actions. That is the function of all ethics in Buddhism. So, you see, ethics is not an end in itself, but a means to an end.

"The second stage is developing the mind. We call it meditation or concentration (samadhi). We need a sharper weapon to tame the mind; so, established in morals or ethics, we go to meditation and concentration of the mind.

"Meditation is two-fold. The first, samatha, or samadhi, is calming the mind—taking an object of meditation and concentrating on it. This helps the mind to get calm, to collect itself, and to concentrate.

---

* Bhante explained to me later that "Buddhists do not believe that there is a permanent entity or 'I' self to take birth or reincarnate."

"The second aspect of meditation is *vipassana*, or *panna*, true wisdom or insight. This meditation helps one to see things as they really are, not as they appear to be. To see things in their true perspective—looking *into* life and not merely looking *at* it.

"So, there are three stages in the process of fulfillment: the first is the *ethical stage* which controls speech and action; the second stage is *calming meditation*, or *concentration*; and the third stage is *wisdom* or *insight*. These teachings, Buddha said, are excellent in the beginning, excellent in its progress, and excellent in its consummation."

How interesting, I thought. From the ethical, to the calming of the mind, to wisdom.

"And what are the stages, levels, or states that you pass through as you become enlightened?"

Bhante spoke very seriously, but at first I thought he was teasing. "There are four stages," he answered. "The first stage is sanctity, the second stage is sanctity, the third stage is sanctity, and the fourth stage is sanctity."

I raised my eyebrows.

He smiled. "Let me explain. Human beings have so many defilements. At the first stage certain defilements are removed. One, unnecessary rituals and ceremonies are gotten rid of. Two, many doubts are also removed: doubts about Buddha, the teacher; doubts about the teaching; and doubts about the taught, the disciples, are gotten rid of.

"The man who attains the first stage of sanctity has no doubts about these three—the teachings, the teacher, and the taught. The suspicions and doubts are removed. One gets rid of the 'I' notion or the personality belief.

"Then in the second stage of sanctity, the person will cut down and attenuate, or lessen, the desire for sensual things, as well as hatred.

"In the third stage of sanctity there will be complete removal of sensuality and hatred.

"And in the fourth stage of sanctity one gets rid of the desire for higher worlds and the desire to be born in higher realms. Pride and conceit are no more. Restlessness is no more. Ignorance, the crowning corruption of all our madness, is also removed. One experiences perfect peace and happiness," Bhante smiled lovingly at me.

I recalled the life of Gautama the Buddha: how Buddha was born a prince and lived in luxury, but felt compelled to seek enlightenment when he attentively observed the common sufferings of humanity—sickness, old age, and death. I remembered that Buddha renounced the world at age twenty-nine and, after six years of spiritual discipline, experienced his enlightenment—*nirvana*—which literally means *freedom from bondage or corruption*.

When I was in India, I'd had the privilege of visiting Bodh Gaya. After enjoying the beautiful serenity of the descendant of the Bodhi tree under which Buddha had received his enlightenment, I'd visited a number of the temples placed at that holy area by Buddhists from many nations. I recall being so happy that I broke into a dance while wandering from one temple to another and attracted a crowd. I had understood it was commonplace for devotees to dance in India and was surprised to find that a simple little dance could cause a lot of commotion and spectacle. In fact, contrary to what I had been told before going to India, I did not see anyone dancing informally about the countryside.

It was interesting to be in India where most Hindus call Buddha an incarnation—a divine descent of consciousness—while all the Buddhists insist that Buddha was definitely *not* an incarnation. That was quite a pleasant perplexity.

I took advantage of my opportunity and asked one of the world's greatest spokesmen on Buddhism to enlighten me about the Buddha.

"Bhante, do Buddhists consider Buddha a divine incarnation?"

"No," he said, "a noteworthy characteristic that distinguishes the Buddha from all other religious teachers is that he was a human being. Not just another man or philosopher, but an extraordinary man, a unique being, a man *par excellence*. The Buddha cultivated his mind to the highest possible state. This is called enlightenment. The title of *Buddha* means *the enlightened one*. Buddha means 'he is immune to all evil.'

"The Buddha was known as *Bodhisattva* before he became a Buddha. Bodhisattva means 'one who is aiming at enlightenment, one who is bent on enlightenment.'

"So, before he became the Buddha he was a Bodhisattva. He took birth for many, many, many lives. He had to go through and cultivate ten essential qualities to a high standard before becoming the Buddha. These ten qualities are:

Generosity	Forbearance
Morality or Virtue	Truthfulness
Renunciation	Determination
Wisdom	Loving Kindness
Effort	Equanimity

"These are called the ten *paramita*, or ten essential qualities—virtues of high standard. These are the ten qualities that a Bodhisattva cultivates life after life. To attain enlightenment he must cultivate the ten paramita. This is why we say he took birth again and again. As you know, we do not use the word *reincarnate* because Buddhists do not believe that there is a *permanent entity* or 'I' self to take birth. Buddhism uses the word *re-becoming* rather than reincarnating—coming again life after life.

"So, one cultivates the ten qualities to become Buddha. The Buddha is not an incarnation of God or Brahma or any external agency. As the Buddha was a human being, his teaching was anthropocentric, or man-centered, and not theocentric—God-centered. The Buddha is not a God, or Creator, who punishes the ill deeds and rewards the good deeds of the creatures of his creation.

"The Buddha attributed all his attainments and achievements to human effort and human wisdom or understanding. Through personal experience he understood the supremacy of man."

Bhante's remarks made me understand how difficult it is for people of the West to be fair to Buddhism and strive to understand it deeply. It is difficult to conceive of an openly man-centered religion unless one studies the ten essential qualities and the eight limbs of Buddhism.

"Bhante, I've long treasured a walking conversation I enjoyed with a Zen Buddhist at Bodh Gaya in India. Here in the U.S., we are fascinated with Zen. Please tell me, Bhante, what exactly is Zen?"

"The word *Zen* sounds Japanese, but Zen came from India," Bhante answered. "We have a word in the Pali language—Pali is the language Buddha used—*jhana*. And in the other ancient language of India, Sanskrit, the word is *dhyana*. *Jhana* or *dhyana* means meditative absorption.

"So," he continued, "when an Indian Buddhist monk called Bodhi Dharma went to China, the Chinese people pronounced the word not as *jhana*, but as *chan*. Even today, Chinese say *chan*. Now, when this *chan*, this way of meditative absorption was taken to Japan, the name was Japanized and became *zen*. So, the original word is *jhana*; in Sanskrit it is *dhyana*; Chinese call it *chan*; and Japanese call it *zen*.

"Good," I said, "then Zen is a method of meditative absorption."

"All meditation," he replied.

"Now, what is the difference, if any, between Zen and regular Buddhism?"

"Mainly," Bhante leaned forward, "Zen is a meditation sect. It specializes in meditation and aims at enlightenment. But in Buddhism, generally, before coming to meditation you must cultivate morality. It's a gradual process, a gradual training, and a gradual doing. First morality, then concentration, and then go inside to meditation. In Buddhism the aim is enlightenment *and deliverance*, while the aim of Zen is enlightenment."

"But wouldn't enlightenment in Zen bring deliverance, too?"

"It can," he nodded slowly, "but only the collected mind, the contented mind, can see things as they really are and not as they appear to be."

"So," I responded, "a person practicing Zen might not have enough development to experience full realization."

"In Buddhism," Bhante reiterated, "you first have to bring your speech and action under control—that is morality. Then you go to the calming meditation; and, then, proceed to the inside meditation. Through inside meditation you find your true wisdom, your right understanding which leads to deliverance and enlightenment."

"Zen doesn't do a gradual process. That's the difference, Bhante?"

"Not a gradual process," he smiled at me. "They try to get enlightenment from the very beginning. Of course their aim—in itself—leads to some purification. Zen is a meditation sect.

"The books written about Zen by Daisetz Teitaro Suzuki are very good," Bhante added.

"And, dear Bhante, what is a Buddhist's attitude toward other religions?" I asked.

"All religions, major and minor, have their origin in the East. Today there are five world religions: Buddhism, Christianity, Hinduism, Islam, and Judaism.

"Buddhists do not belittle other faiths in order to extol their own. Even the Buddha, when he had time, visited other religious centers and had friendly talks and discussions with them. Two hundred years after Buddha passed away, King Asoka of India wrote in his inscriptions that, 'People should respect other religions.'

"If you wish to keep religious harmony, it is better not to interfere with the doctrinal aspects of religion but find out the common factors. In other words, we must find out the areas of concern which the religions share in common. For instance, peace, social justice, removal of poverty, protection of the natural environment from destruction by pollutants and industry, etc. Representatives of different religions should meet and discuss and discover the essential similarities and differences between the religions."

How succinct, I mused, wishing all could hear what Bhante was saying. "Two more questions, Bhante, and then we must leave. First, what is the Buddhist view of man?"

"Of course," Bhante responded, "in Buddhism the pride of place is given to man, because it is a man who becomes a Buddha. All can become Buddhas provided they cultivate the necessary qualities that go to make a Buddha.

"So, Buddhahood is not the prerogative of a chosen few. The Buddha seed is in all men, so each man is like a box of matches. In a box of matches you cannot see the flame but you can, through friction, get the flame. Man works out his deliverance through effort, and bringing out the light.

"Human beings can reach the highest or go down to the lowest. That is each man's lookout. It is left to man to go up or down. There is no compulsion or coercion in Buddhism. It's a free religion. Buddha gives the first charter of free inquiry in a special discourse, called the *Kalama Sutra*. Buddha says you have the right to inquire, to scrutinize, and to examine."

In Bhante's discussion he had not mentioned the relationship of God to man and I wanted to fully understand how God functioned in Buddhism. "What is the Buddhist view of God?" I asked.

"When you speak about God, there are two types. One is the Creator God: the permanent, everlasting God. Then there are what are called the *deities*, or celestial beings, or *devas*. In Buddhism we speak about the deities. They are not permanent or everlasting. The God that theistic religion speaks of is a permanent, everlasting God and it is this God who punishes the evil deeds and rewards the good deeds of the creatures of his creation. This concept is not in Buddhism.

"In Buddhism there is a belief in the deities, or celestial beings. The Buddha was not against the word *God*, or *soul*, but he does not approve of anything permanent or everlasting. Only nirvana, which is Supramundane, is permanent. Looking at it from a purely scientific standpoint, nothing *is* permanent in this world."

I told Bhante I was going to strive to quote him as accurately as I could and trust that his words would bless those who entered into the chapter on Buddhism appreciatively and with open hearts. While I so appreciated his clear explanations of Buddhism, I knew Bhante was sharing a view of life which only much study, discipline, meditation, and direct experience could truly reveal.

Reluctantly, I asked my last question, "Finally, how do you, Bhante, see a more peaceful world occurring?"

Bhante Piyadassi gazed thoughtfully at me for a while and then his clear, mellow voice replied, "To bring about peace and harmony in this world, my viewpoint is this: people have peace conferences, discussions, meetings, and all sorts of activities, but the whole thing is really in the hands of a few powerful people in powerful countries. There should be a radical change in the hearts of the people who are at the helm of affairs, otherwise you cannot bring about peace. We may talk about peace and have conferences everywhere, but what good are conferences unless the powerful people give a thought to world peace? Only they can bring about peace and harmony. We can write about peace and have discussions, but the whole thing is with these few powerful people.

"I understand that when people went to Albert Einstein and asked, 'What do you think about the Third World War?,' he reportedly answered, 'I don't know about the Third World War, but I'll tell you about the Fourth.' They asked him, 'What is it? What is it? What is it?' Einstein said, 'When you go to wage the Fourth World War, it will be with sticks and bows and arrows. We'll be back to primitive man.' Einstein explained what the Third World War is going to do—complete devastation.

"So, all this peace and harmony can be brought about by only a few powerful statesmen of the powerful countries of the world. Only they can bring about peace and harmony."

Bhante stood. It was time to go. He put on his cloak and rode with me to his lecture. "Ninety percent of Buddha's teachings are about the mind," he told his audience. He went on to say that the goal of Buddhism—whether Zen, Mahayana, Tibetan, or Theraveda—is the enlightenment called nirvana. "As a result of this supreme state of higher consciousness, ignorance, arrogance, fear, and anger fall away. One no longer distorts one's vision of life or of the self," he emphasized. Bhante explained that all these different schools of Buddhism followed the same Sakyamuni Buddha.

All life's problems, Bhante said, can be reduced to one simple problem, that of *dukkha*, suffering or unsatisfactoriness, or conflicts. The solution put forward by the Buddhas or Enlightened Ones of all ages is the Noble Eightfold Path. The efficiency of the path lies in the practice of it. The Buddha's path still beckons the weary pilgrim to the haven of nirvana's security and peace.

But, he smiled gently, "Buddhists do not spend too much time inspiring others about the greatness and glory of nirvana. The mind, ego, and emotions are totally unable to understand the reality of that sovereign, wondrous, illimitable freedom and well being!"

When he finished speaking, I thought about nirvana, about that great and total *no-thing-ness* into which every being would ultimately dissolve. Bhante had made me feel its peace. And, I remembered how the Buddha, the prince of compassion, had said he would not enter into nirvana till every creature had been liberated. I savored the thought of the beautiful Buddha and I thanked Bhante for his great wisdom.

43

CHRISTIANITY

"Take up your cross and follow me," Jesus Christ said to the young man who asked what he should do.

Later, at the Last Supper, Christ said to his disciples: "Go ye therefore, and teach all nations, baptizing them in the name of the Father, and of the Son, and of the Holy Ghost."*

At the time Jesus Christ began his mission upon the earth, the term "Christian" was applied to his followers. It was often a derisive term and in many times throughout history it has been extremely dangerous to be called a Christian. The Romans crucified Christians and set them on fire. And many eras of bloodshed and danger were yet to come for the followers of Christ. Historians estimate only ten thousand Christians existed in the world at the end of the first century A.D. Now there are more than one billion Christians around the world and 126 million in the United States. They have taken up their cross and followed the living example of Jesus Christ. Throughout the centuries they have endeavored to go forth into all the lands preaching the Christ, His life and message.

There are eighty-five main Christian denominations. These

* *The Holy Bible*, Matthew 28:19.

denominations make a distinction between Catholic Christians and Protestant Christians. There are 926,164,600 Roman Catholics and 332,016,400 Protestants in the world. Most Catholics are Roman Catholics; there are 78,991,000 in the United States. Protestants in the U.S. number 52,893,000 as of 1986.*

What is the second largest Christian denomination in the United States? The Baptist Church is the leader with 19,678,000 members.† Next in numbers are the United Methodist Church and the Presbyterian Church.

Christian denominations are many and diverse. Some churches proclaim Christianity is the only true religion. Other churches emphasize that only their own denomination—or, perhaps, denominations closely affiliated with them—practice true Christianity. However, many denominations hold that *all* other Christian churches, in addition to their own, are also valid. Further, many Christians today state their recognition that religions *outside* of Christianity are also God-given and true.

According to Dr. Fred Register, a minister of the Southern California Conference of the United Church of Christ:

> "The United Church of Christ affirms, and always has, the beauty and truth of diversity. Traditionally this has been seen as a wide range of diversity of belief and practice within the Christian context. However, as we are now in a time when many of us are more aware and appreciative of the great religious traditions of the world, we affirm the validity of these many great paths which may be ventured on in the journey of spiritual development."

Enjoy these chapters! First, the Baptists—the largest Protestant denomination in the U.S. And, then, Roman Catholicism. Catholics are by far the largest church in America, and in the world.

---

* According to *World Almanac*, 1989.
† *Statistical Abstract of the United States*, 1986.

44

THE BAPTISTS

In recognition of the strength and popularity of the Baptist church, I arranged an interview with Reverend Elwin Pelletier, a Baptist missionary for over thirty-five years and now a hospital chaplain.

Reverend Pelletier is a kindly man of medium height with gray hair and glasses. In his gray suit, he could easily have been taken for a family doctor or a successful businessman, but he exuded kindness, attentiveness, and concern. Everything about him emphasized he was a spiritual man, a servant of God.

Now in his sixties, he looks well and healthy despite having won a miraculous battle with near-fatal meningitis.

Reverend Pelletier's wife Lois, a dedicated Christian who served many years as a nurse and teacher in the Belgian Congo, welcomed my assistant and me and served our favorite kind of herb tea.

Reverend Pelletier explained that while he was sure we had many different views about a number of subjects, he was very happy and pleased to take part in an interview. Further, he said he was definitely not a theologian and would do the best he could—with my understanding of his theological limitations.

I replied that a man who had been a missionary for thirty-five years certainly qualified to be in *my* book—that I was striving to speak with people who had lived their spiritual values, and that I wanted the interviews to be a personal sharing of their years of religion in practice.

"Reverend, I want to explore the way Baptists think and feel about God, life, and the world," I began. "I want to note the characteristics of higher consciousness found in the way of a Baptist Protestant Christian. If you would, kindly tell me first something of your background."

He nodded, "I went first to Europe to study French in 1946. I arrived in the old Belgian Congo in 1947 as a missionary of the conservative Baptist Mission Society. I spent twenty-five years involved in preparing pastors for field ministry in what is now Zaire—the name has changed—and my wife and I both taught in that school. My wife, Lois, is a nurse." He glanced at her, eyes shining, "I was in pastoral training and she was, too.

"As time went on, I became a professor in an inter-mission seminary for a year and then ended my career in the work of field administration for five years in the city of Goma in eastern Zaire. So that was a total of thirty-five years in Africa.

"Then my wife and I came back to America for health reasons. I was treated at University of California-Irvine Medical Center. That's how I became a chaplain at UCI Medical Center."

Somehow it seemed ironic that the Reverend had spent twenty-five years preparing pastors for the field ministry and yet modestly felt himself unqualified for our interview.

As we sipped tea, I told Reverend Pelletier and his wife a little of my background and also the nature of the book on higher consciousness. I encouraged him to speak out on any issue and to feel free to share the particular or distinctive views of the Baptist church.

I plunged into the interview, asking, "What is Christianity?"

"I think," he replied, "the simplest way to say it is that Christianity *is Jesus Christ.* We don't really view Christianity as a religion. We view Christianity as the person and the ministry of the one to whom we refer as the Lord Jesus Christ. This involves, of course, that we have a historical personage who was supernatural, who brought to us the final, complete revelation of God, which is inscribed in *The Holy Bible.* We accept him as the redeemer (of mankind) and there are theological implications as well, but I believe I've answered your question."

"What is the goal of Christianity?" I asked.

"I think the goal of Christianity is to make Jesus Christ known. The word of God as we see it, in the Bible, in the Book of Acts, says there is no other name unto heaven given among men whereby you must be saved. So, therefore, upon the basis of the word of God, we feel that we should go into all the world and make disciples, as Jesus commanded us to do in the twenty-eighth chapter of Matthew, the great commission."

I asked the Reverend what he meant by the term "saved," so that we might be clear about his definition. He explained there are two main considerations: death and life. Death, by Biblical interpretation, is a state of separation from God. The Bible says that man is born as a mortal, as a sinner, and that the consequence of this condition of man is death, or separation from God. However, through Christ, God gives man the gift of life—an abiding in the presence of God, in the nearness of God. This state of life is eternal, beyond time, bestowed on man through Lord Jesus Christ.

"I don't think there could be anything worse than to be eternally separated from God," Reverend Pelletier said. "To be *saved*, then, is to be born again, to believe in Jesus. The Bible says, 'He came unto His own and His own received Him not. But to those who received Him,'—invited him, accepted him into their heart—'He gave the power to become the sons of God,' to those who were born not of the flesh but of the spirit of God. So this *being saved* is the reality of being saved from judgment upon our sin and entering into a new and eternal life in the knowledge and in the fellowship of God through Jesus Christ."

I asked, "Could you describe the nature or characteristics of a son of God?"

"Well, the *ian* of the word *Christian* is the diminutive of the word *Christ*, so a Christ-ian is a photocopy, a carbon copy, of the Christ. That is, he, the new son of God, must have the qualities of the Lord Jesus Christ.

"The Christian receives these qualities not because of his human ability to recreate himself but the Bible says that if anyone be in Christ, or a believer, a saved individual, 'all things are become new.' Old things are passed away and the individual has become a new creature.

"Now, the qualities of a Christian should be progressively more similar to the qualities of the Lord Jesus Christ, who was full of compassion, love, purity, holiness, righteousness, and other virtues. Each book in the New Testament, which is written as a theological treatise is always—at least twenty-five to thirty and sometimes forty percent—an explanation of how to apply the theology, or doctrine, into the life of the Christian. So, if you want it in detail, you can read any of the four Pauline epistles and you'll get that. Paul summed it up in Romans 12, though: 'I beseech thee, therefore, brethren, by the mercies of God, that you present yourselves a living sacrifice, holy, acceptable unto God, and be not conformed to this present world but be transformed to the image of Christ.'"

I explained to Reverend Pelletier that I was going to be including in my chapter on Christianity an interview with two Roman Catholic priests and that I would like to have a clarification about the nature and definition of the Protestant church in general.

"Well," he replied, "Protestantism was a label given to us by those with whom we differed because in the early days the so-called Protestants conflicted with the Roman Catholic hierarchy in emphasizing, 'for by grace are you saved through faith. Salvation is a gift of God, not of works, lest any man shall boast, for we are created by God unto good works.' (Ephesians 2:8,9)

"So, salvation by faith was one of the great doctrines that impressed Luther, that it wasn't a matter of storing up benefits, and other things, before a holy God, but rather that initially there is this inner state and grace—because of the death and resurrection of Jesus Christ—that we (Protestants), accepting his sacrifice in our behalf, may be presented to God as righteous. Dressed in his righteousness, not our own. That is the inner state and grace. We differed with the Roman Catholic hierarchy on this point."

"You're saying then that the first Protestants emphasized God's grace through Christ's death and resurrection as the way of man's salvation—rather than through our own efforts, charity, and good works," I added.

"We also speak of the outer serving grace which has to do, for example, with the Book of James. As Jesus said, 'By their fruits ye shall know them.' If one is truly born again, his life, his walk, his characteristics, his manner of life and deportment, will give evidence of that rebirth, of God's life within him." Salvation by grace and the outer serving graces are the essential bases of what came to be known as Protestantism, according to Reverend Pelletier.

"The goal of Protestantism, I would say first of all, is to make Jesus Christ known. This is evangelism. Secondly, our goal is to present God's Word, which we feel is the true Word, wherever man is found. Thirdly, we must establish churches or groups of Christians, organized bodies of Jesus Christ. Then, good works are necessary—

wherever man is in need, to minister to those needs whatever they may be, whether it is hunger, illness, lack of education—whatever. We strive to minister to the whole man."

"What is the Baptist faith as different from other Protestant denominations, and what are the goals of a Baptist?" I asked.

"We are evangelicals: we are Bible-oriented; we are conservatives. We're not radical Fundamentalists. We are conservatives, and we are Biblically-oriented in our teachings. We accept the Bible from Genesis to Revelation as, in fact, God's holy Word—the revealed Word of God—and that's where it all begins. We believe in the Virgin birth; we believe in the miraculous conception; and we believe in the Trinity. By Trinity I mean that we believe God exists in three persons—the Father, Son, and Holy Spirit.

"Secondly, we are called Baptists because we are members of a Protestant denomination which holds that baptism should be given only to believers *after* their confession of faith. And that baptism should be given by immersion, not sprinkling." Reverend Pelletier smiled and paused. "Well, there's more to it than that, but we got the name 'Baptists' because we considered ourselves Biblical Christians, baptizing by the method of immersion as in the Bible. Actually, the word *baptism* originally meant immersion."

"Could you tell me what the significance of the baptism itself is?"

Reverend Pelletier nodded. "Certainly. First of all, the individual has passed from death unto life. We were dead in our trespasses and sins. Now we are, through baptism, alive unto God because we've received Jesus into our hearts. In the immersion we become one with Christ in his death. Christ died on the cross for our sins (our sins put him there) and in the act of immersion we are one with him. This is called our union with Christ. So, in baptism, we are united with Christ in death. And, we are united with Christ in the power of his resurrection unto newness of life! This is the meaning of baptism and this is why we feel our being *immersed* into the water is a better symbol of the death and the resurrection of Christ— the Christian dies to sin and is then born alive unto the newness of life.

"But we do not believe in baptismal regeneration," Reverend Pelletier emphasized. "We believe baptism is a *symbol*. We have many friends (in other denominations) who are sprinkled. We don't make an issue of this. In fact, our group of hospital chaplains is affiliated with sixty different denominations, many of whom do not baptize as we do. We do not feel baptism is a saving action. We are saved by grace, unmerited favor, not something we worked for but something we receive as a gift from God. Baptism, then, is a form of public confession. The person who is baptized is publicly confessing before all that Christ is his or her saviour and will walk in the newness of the Christian life."

I was surprised at Reverend Pelletier's wide acceptance of different methods of baptism as I recalled the many times in history when Baptists were martyred for emphasizing the importance of immersion or were so often run out of the towns and cities of Europe. I recalled how Baptist forefathers in America were often abused in the New England colonies and how on one occasion the doors of their worship hall were nailed shut by people of the majority denomination.

I asked, "Are you saying that what may have been life-threatening and dangerous differences regarding baptism way back when have been changed in the perceptions of religious people generally? Or are you saying that there was just a lot of hysteria at times in Christian history and there isn't now?"

Reverend Pelletier leaned forward. "Of course, when you have religion which is made into a state religion or religion which is involved in politics you will always have extremes. We saw this in the early days of the Catholic church and we saw it in the early period of the Protestant church as well. When you have a *politicized* church, then you have extremes. I think that Protestants and Catholics, for example, now are both reading God's Word, *The Holy Bible*. We find Catholics bringing a Bible into the hospital; we find Protestants bringing a Bible into the hospital. If I read God's Word, and if another individual reads God's Word, then there's bound to be some blessing, some harvesting of special help and comprehension from that Bible which will be similar. And we find Catholics talking about being born again and so forth. We find we're coming together, not in affiliation, but in *relationship* to Jesus Christ—as fellow believers. So, I don't think that baptism at this point is an issue about which we would quarrel.

"Now, if I were a pastor and one became a member of the church where I was pastor, I would insist upon their entrance into that body of Christians via baptism—if they hadn't been baptized— in order to become a member. But in my cooperation and affiliation with other Christians, I cannot require the Baptist form of immersion of a Presbyterian, or Methodist, or Catholic, or someone else. If a person's relationship and faith in Jesus Christ is real, then he's a brother in the Lord and we cooperate."

"So the problem is politicism, not zealous bigotry. Politicism is not of Christ, is it?"

"No," Reverend Pelletier said very seriously. "We have lived in Africa during the period of eighteen years—almost nineteen years—when we had dissident Christians (around us). You have to live near such Christians to experience what they really are. They have a politicized church in which a 'Christian brother' will say to you that if you don't do what they want you to do, your head will roll down the bank. That isn't a very lovely Christian solution. You have to understand the extremes and perversions of 'politicized Christians.'

"You know," he continued, "if you have a politicized church, you can have a crusade or religious war. I talked to an Irish person in the hospital the other day. She said, 'Chaplain, don't you believe for a minute that this war in Ireland is a religious war. People have used the terms, taken the terms, Catholic and Protestant, and voluntarily imposed these terms on groups of people. But it is not a Christian war in Ireland. It's a political war.'"

"What a tragedy," I reflected. I wanted to get back to the Baptist's walk with God and asked, "What is the goal of the Baptist? Is it different from other Protestant Christian denominations?"

He shook his head. "The goal of the Baptist is similar or parallel to the goal of the Christian in general. We seek to make Christ known wherever man is found and to establish the body of Christ wherever Christians are, through an organized worship. In other words, we believe that we should win souls to Jesus Christ."

"How do you do this?"

"We present to people what we call the simple facts of the Bible truths: man is estranged from God by sin. Though man is estranged from God, he may be brought into fellowship by receiving the gift of salvation, by putting his faith in Christ. So we present God's Word to individuals, where they are, whenever we find them, just as we find them, and try to bring them into realization and acceptance of Jesus Christ as personal saviour.

"Sometimes people have read the Bible for years but have no sense of the reality of God in their lives. A lady I visit had given her father a vow that she would follow in his religion but she never did keep that vow. I said to her, 'Did you ever read the Bible?' She said, 'No, I've tried many times but it doesn't mean anything to me.' I asked her, 'Have you ever in your life either come to the point where you had the assurance that Jesus was your saviour, or was there a point where you made a definite commitment to Jesus Christ or accepted him and invited him into your heart?'

"She said, 'Neither of these have been a part of my experience.'

"I said to her, 'Would you like to pray what we call the Sinner's Prayer?' I told her what the prayer was: 'I confess that I am a sinner. I believe that Jesus died for my sins and I accept him. I invite him into my heart as my own personal saviour.'

"The lady did say the Sinner's Prayer. She's had cancer for twenty-three years. She's still alive. And it's almost nine months now since she said the Sinner's Prayer. And for the last nine months something has been happening. The prayer seems so simple, and yet we believe that Jesus Christ, by the Holy Spirit, entered her life and heart and became a resident in her life. Although she is emaciated and very distraught physically, her heart is filled with peace. And her mind—you can see—is filled with serenity from trusting in Jesus Christ. She reestablished fellowship with God by receiving Christ on the basis of his word. It's not a matter of philosophical or intellectual ascent. It is a matter of a definite act—confession, and admission, and acceptance of Jesus Christ into the heart."

After a serene pause in our conversation, I said, "Please explain sin. What is your definition of this condition that keeps people from the Lord and keeps them from sensing the presence of God?"

"The Bible says that one definition of sin is 'missing the mark.' Another way the Bible expresses sin is that it is falling short of the glory of God. To fall short of the glory of God is to be found wanting or short of the demand which God places upon men: and sin is enmity with God," he said.

I continued, "Then, how does a Baptist Christian become fulfilled, or realized? Use whatever term you'd like to use."

"I think the best term of all is that a Christian is fulfilled in *fellowship* with God. Now, fellowship with God, to me, is consistent reading of God's holy Word, the quiet time, meditation, and prayer. Fellowship is the daily contact with God. I know no other way than the daily reading of God's holy Word in prayer and meditation. This is a necessary part—fellowship with God.

"Secondly, obedience to the revealed will of God as we find it in the scriptures. We must witness, giving of our resources (some call it tithing, some say giving), demonstrating the love of God to others, helping others, participating with other believers in worship, assembling ourselves together."

Reverend Pelletier explained, "We believe that the Bible is the living Word of God and that it isn't by error or mistake that it was called *The Holy Bible*. We believe it is God's revelation to us. So, when we read God's Word, wait and pray, and meditate and listen,

God speaks to us through His holy Word. He warms our hearts. We know that he is there, that he is with us. This is called fellowship, fellowship with God."

"When you say fellowship with God, I should ask you what you specifically mean by *God*."

"Well, the Bible describes God as the Creator, the ruler, the builder of the universe, the One to whom all men, every living soul, is responsible."

"What do you mean by *responsible*?" I asked. "Are you referring to the levels or states involved in the process of responsible, maturing fellowship with God?"

He shook his head again. "I don't think we would use those terms: levels or states. I know what you're talking about. I think we would put it this way: As the Bible indicates, a new Christian, as a newborn babe, desires the sincere milk of the Word. So, the Bible says there are different strata of growth. First there is the new Christian and he understands to a certain degree. There is also a teenage Christian and he understands a little bit more. And in the Bible it says that the mature Christian eats the meat of the Word. He gets into the deep understanding. This, of course, is parallel with the growth of the Christian. We call it the process of sanctification: being cleansed and forgiven of sin and growing to be more like Christ. It's a growth process. Christian life is a way of walking in fellowship with God, the knowledge of God, and being continually made over in Christ.

"I have a prayer," he added, "which is, 'May we grow in the grace and knowledge of Christ, to know His power in our lives, to be in the process of being transformed, becoming more like Christ.'

"Of course, conversion is the initial step. Conversion is when a man turns from his sin to Jesus Christ and accepts Him as his own personal saviour, and Jesus Christ takes up residence in that heart. Now, growing in Christ is a way of living. It is keeping in contact with God through the quiet time each day, through the reading of His Word, through meditation and obedience to His Word. There is a growing consciousness and a growing comprehension of what life is all about.

"Then, there comes a time when the Christian has, comparatively speaking, a mature understanding of what the Bible teaches, or what God expects of us as followers or disciples.

"It's important to add that we never become perfected on earth," the Reverend emphasized. "The Bible says that when we see him in heaven, we shall be like him for we shall see him as he is—in his beauty, in his complete, divine holiness and perfection. But you and I will never attain that in this life. We do not believe in sinless perfection. We don't believe the Bible teaches it. As long as I am in this mortal body—in the flesh, as we say—every day I ask God to forgive me for the sins I have committed, and rejoice that the love of Jesus Christ continually cleanses me from all sins.

"The Christian has a personal relationship with Jesus Christ. That's the main point. And if you can get God into your picture, then God will help you, the individual. What you can't change in your own heart—alcoholism, for example—God will change in your heart. God will remove the desire for alcohol. And God, within your life, will enable you to become an overcomer. A Christian has invited Jesus Christ to live within him."

I asked Reverend Pelletier if he'd like to comment further on any of the points we had covered so far. He declined. I then asked, "What is the view of Baptists regarding other Christian denominations, and also the other faiths outside Christianity?"

"When it comes to the various shades of Christian religion— Catholic, Protestant, Methodist, Baptist, Pentecostal, etc.—we feel that if people believe the call of the Gospel, that Jesus is the Son of God, the Son of Man, that he is deity, that he was born of a virgin, that he's a member of the Trinity, and that he died for us on the cross and we can know him personally by accepting him, that puts us together in a unity. As it says in Romans 17, 'Those who would properly relate to God vertically through Jesus Christ can also find fellowship horizontally.' This is referring to other Christians.

"Now, as we come to the other, the pantheistic view of God, for example, that I may build a temple on a hill with ten or twelve —or whatever—entrances and that we can all come in through any door to be with God because there is only one God; we do not subscribe to that view. We do not feel that Christ is one religious leader among other religious leaders or that Christianity is one among other religions. We feel the Bible teaches that Jesus is the *only* way. That's why there are some Christian groups who hold the index finger up to signify the one way and that Christ is the one and only way.

"Christianity is exclusive in this sense. We say that only by the Gospel of Jesus Christ can a person be saved: 'There is no other name unto heaven given among men whereby we must be saved.' The Bible doesn't say that we can *choose* to be saved. Christ is the saviour and the redeemer."

"In other words, Christ chooses us?"

Reverend Pelletier nodded. "So, this means that whether we are with Buddhists, Hindus, Muslims, or any other religions, we feel we have a message to present to them—that Jesus is the way, the truth, and the life, and as he said: 'No man cometh unto God but by Me.' Jesus is not just a prophet, as Mohammed was a prophet, for example. Jesus came, as a historical person, to proclaim a message. History proves that Jesus died on a cross and on the third day he rose again from the dead. For this reason we believe that eternal life may be known only in his name.

"Now, as far as having friends and loving those who disagree with me, *that's the least I can do!* I have many Muslim friends in Africa who came to our house. And we went to their houses. We have many Hindu friends. We have many friends of other faiths."

"Is there anything else you'd like to say about this question?" I ventured.

"Well, this is the impetus and the dynamic of the Christian mission, or missions, per se. We don't really agree with the viewpoint that God is at work in every religion to bring man to Himself. We believe that God is at work through Christianity and through Jesus Christ, his son, whom he sent to die for us on the cross. We believe that Christ is at work to save man and to bring men under the knowledge of Himself through his son. But I don't have to go to war about it."

His remarks formulated my final question, "How do you see a more peaceful world coming about?"

He frowned. "I have a problem with this question because on the one hand, humanly, my heart says that if people would just determine and make up their minds to get along, they could get along. But, the fact of the matter is, the Bible says the heart of man is desperately wicked.

"And then it says in Matthew 24 and 25, there would be wars and rumors of wars, earthquakes, and all the rest. It's what the Bible says. And I don't think there ever will be, that we will ever achieve, real peace on this earth. Look at Belgium. You have the Walloons and the Flemish people who for a thousand years have been feuding. They're international award winners in science and so forth but they are still feuding. And look at the Africans, they are feuding. Look at Mexico and Central America. Still you have the differences of the various groups. And you have it throughout the entire world. You have the Arabs and you have the Jews. Look at Northern Ireland. I do not look for utopia on this earth. But in the Bible it says Jesus will come and set up his kingdom of a thousand years and that it will continue on through eternity, with Jesus Christ as our ruler. Then I would expect peace."

"Please say more about this," I urged.

"Well, the Bible says for the first thousand years Christ will set up his kingdom on this world. And after that the Bible says, in Revelations, a new heaven and a new earth will be established, whatever that means. I don't like to be totally fatalistic and totally pessimistic. I'm glad for all the coming together—of our President and the Russians—and I still live on this earth and I still enjoy it here. I have children and I would covet for them peace on earth, but I'm afraid Armageddon is out there somewhere."

Then, in words that seemed a summation of Reverend Pelletier's whole life, he said, "I prayed that God would make me a blessing to you people, and an inspiration, because that's the only purpose we have for being here." He stood and we shook hands. I left the Pelletier home feeling grateful to have such a clear, succinct explanation of the Baptist faith.

45

ROMAN CATHOLICISM

Bishop John T. Steinbock sat near a crucifix and regularly looked at the image of Christ on the cross as he thought deeply and responded to my series of questions.* A thin man of medium height, he has dark, thinning hair and dark brown eyes. In his forties, he wore a short-sleeved black shirt and a white Roman collar. His manner is humble, his countenance peaceful. He speaks softly and simply, calling himself "just a parish priest."

My assistant, Chris Rodriguez, a former magazine writer, interviewed Bishop Steinbock at his office in Orange, California. Most of this chapter is based on his recorded answers and Chris's remarks.

Bishop Steinbock has spent his whole ministry among the poor. He studied for the priesthood very early in his life. He began his

---

* I've yet to meet Bishop Steinbock. Both of us were so busy we couldn't arrange a meeting despite several tries. When he was later transferred to the Diocese of Santa Rosa, in Northern California, I went there in hope of seeing him; however, a death in Bishop Steinbock's family required him to leave abruptly. I'm grateful that my assistant was able to ask the Bishop my questions, share her observations, and that Bishop Steinbock reviewed the draft of this chapter.

service in East Los Angeles and then served on skid row in downtown Los Angeles for eleven years. His apostleship was mainly with the men and women of the streets, families living in the U.S. without immigration documents, and people with broken lives. At the time of this interview he was the Auxiliary Bishop of the Diocese of Orange in Orange County, California.

The interview originally began in the offices of Archbishop Tomas Clavel who sent us to speak with Bishop Steinbock. Archbishop Clavel preferred we discuss these questions with someone who had a better command of the English language than he did. However, Archbishop Clavel was very eloquent in his own way and I include several of his comments at the end of this chapter.

"What is Christianity?" Chris asked Bishop Steinbock.

"I'd say the first thing that distinguishes Christianity from other major religions is that most other religions, I think, are searching for God," he said. "Christianity, we believe, is *God reaching down and revealing himself to man.* This is an essential difference between, say, Christianity and other major religions. We believe that God has revealed himself, both through the Old Testament, the prophets of old, and finally through the Lord Jesus, his own divine son. We believe that Christianity is God becoming man and showing us the way to eternal life. He shows us the way to truth, peace, and love in this world—through the example of his own life and his call to follow him. I believe that's basically what Christianity is."

"Do you believe that people can experience this descent of God to man in a very personal way?"

"Yes," the Bishop affirmed. "I believe you certainly can experience this in a very personal way because the basis of Christianity is a relationship, a personal relationship with the Lord Jesus whom we believe is our personal Lord and saviour, who reveals Himself to us not simply through the Word of God in a holy scripture (especially the New Testament) but he reveals himself in the happenings and events of our every day lives—and through the people around us. We come to a very deep realization and consciousness that through his Holy Spirit Jesus' very presence will be received into our hearts and lives."

"What, then, is the goal of Christianity?"

"I believe the goal of Christianity is what the goal of God is for man—to have union of man with God and union of man with one another. When we call God our heavenly father, we have this call that we live as brothers and sisters, one with another, in true love, unity, and peace. And then, the final goal is—as we follow the Lord

Jesus in this life and try to live in love, unity and peace with our brothers and sisters—that we come to eternal life."

"And, how does one have union with God?" Chris asked. "Fascinatingly, yoga is often defined as *union with God* and man, also. So, please tell me, how do you have union?"

Bishop Steinbock replied, "Through faith in God and faith that he has revealed himself. In confidence that his spirit is with us in our lives, we have union. Then, through taking all those means that God gives us to realize his presence with us. Times of prayer are so important, for example. In prayer we try to be led by the spirit of the Lord; and being alone with the Lord enables us to see him present in those around us."

"How do you know if you've had union with God?"

"Through faith. A person may or may not have an emotional experience of that union, which we believe would be, certainly, the grace of God. People can have times in their lives when they feel the closeness of God but other times they just live through the everyday routine part of life. Faith means this union is with us just as much during the routine times as when we personally *feel* his presence. That's what faith is all about."

"And what is Roman Catholicism?"

"Roman Catholicism," he repeated. "Well, we believe that the Lord Jesus in this world sent forth his apostles to continue to teach and preach in his name. He founded a Church, and we believe that Roman Catholicism is the Church that's been brought down to us through the centuries, to this very day. We believe that the Lord Jesus continues to teach and preach, alive in our midst, especially through the visible sign of the church and the visible signs within the church which we believe Jesus gave us himself—particularly the sacraments which we have in Roman Catholicism. Not only the visible structure which we believe has developed from the apostles, but also the sacraments, enable us to keep faithful to the teaching of the Lord."

"And what are those sacraments?"

"The sacraments are visible signs that the Lord Jesus has given to us to enable us to realize his loving presence within us. For example, Baptism: a person receives baptism through water, a visible sign, to realize the eternal life and the new life that we receive through the Lord Jesus. Communion: under the signs of bread and wine, we believe we are nourished truly with the very presence of the Lord Jesus coming to us. And so we have within the church seven sacraments that have always been within the church since the time of the apostles. The sacraments continue as visible signs of the invisible presence the Lord has with us through his spirit."

"The sacraments help the people be more aware of their union with God?"

"Definitely," the Bishop replied. "That's the whole idea of the sacraments—to help us realize his living presence with us, through visible signs. The seven sacraments are:

1) the waters of baptism;
2) being nourished through the communion;
3) being confirmed and strengthened in our faith;
4) the sacrament of penance—*confession* as it's called—to enable us to realize the loving forgiveness and mercy of the Lord Jesus in our lives that we may begin anew;
5) the sacrament of matrimony where two people become a visible sign of the very love of God to their relationship, one with another;
6) the sacrament of Holy Orders where a man becomes a priest, again through the signs of laying on of hands by the Bishop to continue the whole sense of bringing God's forgiveness, through the sacraments, to his people;
7) and the seventh sacrament is the anointing of the sick, that they be strengthened and comforted—again by the laying on of hands and anointing by holy oil—to realize the help and healing of the Lord Jesus in our lives."

"Is it necessary for a person to experience a number of these sacraments in order to have union with God?"

"Within the Catholic faith," Bishop Steinbock explained, "one is naturally going to be receiving some of these particular sacraments. It's part of being a Catholic. But if we are talking about other people who are not Catholics, I think God reveals himself to everybody in this world. Everybody is able to realize the existence and the love of God through the created things around them. So people who are not Christians certainly are able to experience the presence of God in their lives in many other ways. The Holy Spirit works in this world not simply alone through the sacraments, but he reveals himself through everything created. He reveals himself to us through other people around us, in many different ways."

"How would God reveal himself, say, through somebody else?"

Bishop Steinbock spoke tenderly, "I would say the main way I came to know God's love is through people loving me. And the way

I came to know of God's forgiveness is through people forgiving me. And so, in turn, through my forgiving other people, I think those other people will know God's forgiveness, too. We experience the Lord through people in our lives."

"Is it your belief, then, that people of all the various faiths are touched by the Holy Spirit in some way?"

"The Second Vatican Council of the church was very strong in the spirit that God would reveal himself in many, many different ways in this world. God isn't limited by the structure of the church which we believe he founded himself; but God doesn't limit himself to the structure of the church," the Bishop explained.

As I later wrote this chapter, I wondered why the whole world wasn't dancing in joy about the great love expressed in Vatican II.

Chris continued, "Please go on, what are the specific goals of Catholicism?"

"The goal of Catholicism is, first of all, evangelization—to bring the knowledge of Jesus to all peoples of the world. We also have the goal of the ongoing evangelization of those who themselves are Catholics; we have a continuing eternal conversion of the heart to bring us into union with God and follow God's will in our life—and then we seek union with one another, living as brothers and sisters in the world."

"You mentioned 'conversion of the heart.' Do you mean becoming a better person?"

"Yes," Bishop Steinbock agreed. "Becoming a better person, overcoming hardness of heart—hatred, envy, jealousy, selfishness. A Catholic struggles with this, seeks to have internal conversion. Also, Catholics wish to be able to live more in love, peace and forgiveness with their fellow man and woman."

"How does a person overcome these negative states?"

"In Catholicism a person believes that Jesus is with him or her and is trying to be led by the will of God. He or she tries to come to know that will of God, especially through the scriptures, the holy Word of God—especially the Gospels in the New Testament—to know how Jesus acted, what Jesus said, how Jesus directs us as we try to follow him. In trying to follow the Lord Jesus and in trying to let his spirit enter into us, we are enabled to have a continuing conversion of the heart to overcome our problems and limitations in life. The power of God enables us to do this; not our own human power. This is a very important point. If we are left to our own human power, there is very little hope for mankind. It has to be the power of God that really changes people's hearts."

"And, how can you have more of the power of God in your life?" Chris asked.

Bishop Steinbock gazed at the crucifix. "I think one comes to realize the power of God in one's life the more one lives in the consciousness of God's living presence. For us Catholics, one is only going to have the consciousness of God's presence especially with him through the sacraments, through personal prayer, public prayer, and communal prayer—all the different kinds of prayer in our life. If we don't have a time of prayer—*aloneness with God*—it's going to be very difficult to realize God's presence in a world that's so hectic." He smiled.

"And then, how does a Catholic become fulfilled?"

"By following God's will and loving God and his fellow man and woman."

"But how does a person know God's will? This is the constant question of so many seekers on so many paths."

"Again, as I said before," the Bishop smiled, "through the scriptures, through the teachings of the church, through their own conscience which God gives each man and woman—through *conscience*. Being led by conscience and by what we believe about how God has revealed himself through Christ and the scriptures . . . ."

The question arose naturally, "Would you say that God's will for each person is some specific thing? That God wants each of us to do something very specifically, or do you mean something more general, like becoming a better person?"

"I think it's both," the Bishop responded, "I mean, each person in his own circumstances is called to bring the knowledge of God and God's love to those around him, or her. So it becomes very specific when you think, 'Who's around me? Around me are my family, my children, my wife, my husband, the people I work with.' Thus, it becomes very specific that God wants people to manifest his love, goodness, kindness, and forgiveness, and to try to work for justice in this world amongst those who are deprived in so many ways— whether economically, politically, or socially."

"Please, what is the process by which a person becomes fulfilled or gets to live in God's will?"

"The process is living in faith, faith in God: trying to be *led* by the Word of God—scripture—personal prayer and prayer within the church; also, hearing the Word of God proclaimed and spoken and explained, and trying to reflect on these things in your own personal life. You should consider how God is trying to lead you in your particular circumstances of life."

"Are there different levels or stages that people go through as they get more of the power of God in their life?" Chris asked. "The lives of Catholic Christian saints—Teresa of Avila, John of the Cross, and others—indicate that Catholicism has much to share about spiritual stages and states."

"Old-time writers in spirituality brought out that there are three stages in spiritual life. We don't hear much about them nowadays but they're more or less still there in our people's lives. First is the purgative stage. Then the virtuous stage. And the third stage is the contemplative stage.

"In other words, the idea is that the first stage of the spiritual life is purgative. At this level you are really trying to root out sin from your life—selfishness, greed, avarice, and all these things.

"Then, in coming into union with the Lord, struggling hard to pass through the purgative way, you enter into the second stage: virtue. Once you've rooted out a good amount of sin within you, you begin to live more in a realization of God's presence. You live with the idea of virtue in your life. The first stage's emphasis is overcoming evil. Then the second stage is one of living more with virtue in your life—whether it be kindness, patience, forgiveness, or other virtues.

"And then, if you continue and grow spiritually, you're going to come to the contemplative stage where you realize even more the presence of the Lord Jesus and his overwhelming love. You live more consciously in the presence of God. This stage is one of greater joy as you become aware of the continuing presence of the Lord."

"What are some signs that a person is in this contemplative stage?" Chris asked.

"Ah," Bishop Steinbock reflected, "through aloneness and quietness with the Lord, they *really* realize his presence. First of all, they're going to have prayer every day of their life. It's not something they do once a month or once a week, but prayer is in their daily life. They just have an openness to God. The spirit of the Lord is with them and that sense of God's presence and pervasiveness in their life enters into everything they do or say. It enters into their total life. It's a spirit that begins to bring joy into everything."

He went on, "A characteristic, I think, of a Christian is that he's meant to be a joyful person. We are redeemed by the Lord Jesus, our hope is in eternal life. We realize the love of God. Someone said that joy is the echo of God's love within us, and joy is comprehensive of everything in one's life. You know, all kinds of sadness—tragedy, hurt, pain—enter into everybody's life. But these are not expansive things which can enter into the total being of the person. On the other hand, joy enters the total being of the person. When tragedy or times of sadness come, they're not comprehensive or expansive but only fill a small area of life where suffering can be felt. These sorrows do not pervade the whole person's being. Love and joy do."

"And does everyone have an opportunity to go through all these stages?"

"It's first of all!" he raised his voice. "*Growth* in one's spiritual life is first of all. But, everything in this world is a gift of God. Our very being is a gift of God, and everybody's life is different. Some people's lives aren't even going to have the possibility of going through those three stages because there are many, many problems in this world. It depends on how a person is brought up and what that person has experienced. God's grace goes to every man and woman but a lot of people's lives are bound by their environment and many other things. It could be very difficult for many people to grow through those different stages; many people are cut off in their lives, through tragedies or in different ways. So, certainly, people are not necessarily going to go through all three levels. But growth in spiritual life is most important.

"We believe God's love goes out to every man and woman wherever they are. God loves the sinner as well as the person that can pray and contemplate, too. That's why we have the Lord Jesus. Jesus didn't come because we're good; he came because we needed him, because we are sinners. *Jesus is God's love known*. We know that he came for us even when we were not worthy of his love."

"What do you think of other religions? Do you feel that everyone in the other faiths has the same opportunities of, say, going through these three stages of spiritual life?"

Bishop Steinbock smiled. "The very first thing I said was that I think the difference between Christianity and other religions is that other religions are searching for God while I think in Christianity God is searching for man. But I believe, certainly, that God's spirit works in all religions, and even though man is searching for God in so many other religions, at the same time God is searching for man too. And God's spirit is going to be working through all religions. There is only one God. Whether we worship him with different names, there's only one God, the Lord and Creator of everything.

"So, what do I think of other religions?" He beamed, and spoke slowly, "I think other religions are beautiful, and wonderful. I think God's spirit is working through them. At the same time, I believe very strongly that God reveals himself through the Lord Jesus who came into this world and wills all men to come to eternal life, or to the Father through the Son—even though a lot of people may not know the Son. So, a lot of people die in this world never even hearing of the Lord Jesus, perhaps. But at the same time, we believe that through the Son's death and resurrection that those very people who never heard of him will come to eternal life if they're trying to understand God and love God in their life—however their own religion may lead them."

"Turning to another subject, what do you think are the main problems of the United States? And from your perspective, what solutions do you see?"

"I think the main problem of the U.S.A., the number one problem, is God has been put aside. God having been put aside, some very basic things in life are forgotten—like the sacredness of marriage, the permanency of the marriage commitment, and love. Also, values like forgiveness and patience, which are so essential in a marriage that's going to be a life commitment, are put aside. I think the breakdown of the family comes from this.

"With the breakdown of the family, which comes from a lack of faith in God, I think we're seeing a lot of related problems in our society. There is the problem of drugs, drinking, and everything else. I mean, I experienced an awful lot of misery, pain and hurt in skid row, both in the lives of those who are drinking and those who are taking drugs. Because of my experiences on skid row, I saw an awful lot of the abuse of people by other people. People are not following God's will so much as they are seeking their own self-interest and their own self-will. When you seek your own self-interest and will, you use and abuse people. You do not respect people.

"I think self-interest and self-will have infiltrated into our American society, and that's the reason we have so much abuse of people, so much closing one's eyes to the hurt and pain of so many people who are deprived economically and socially. Basically, it all goes with loss of faith in God, and this starts touching everything in society, naturally.

"From these problems stem an awful lot of prejudice and poverty in our country," he continued. "I think our country is beautiful and wonderful and I'm one hundred percent for America. There's not a better country in the world, but at the same time we can't close our eyes to the evils and ills within our society. That would be living with blinders. I think we have to constantly emphasize that people respect other people and be open to the hurts and pains of others."

"Do you think that faith in God will be the thing to help turn us around?"

"Faith in God, *with an openness to God's will.* Somebody can believe in God (some say that even the Devil believes in God) but I mean you have to want to follow God's will, too," the kindly Bishop answered.

"Lastly, how do you think world peace could be achieved?"

Bishop Steinbock again studied the crucifix. "I think world peace is only going to be achieved, first of all, through internal conversion of people's hearts. We're not going to achieve world peace simply through political means. We've been trying to use political means to achieve peace since mankind has been here, and political peace is only as good as the people. People are prone to forget what they say and selfishness starts taking over. So, I think, first of all, that world peace is only going to come through God's doing.

"Unless people have an internal conversion of the heart to God, we're never going to build peace on politics. Politics is essential for working toward world peace but really, people have to try to have an openness to other people: respect, care, love and concern for others. Otherwise, world peace will only be words. Peace has to come from people working for justice and trying to bring justice into this world; people trying to be open to God's love in their life. That's the only thing that's going to bring people together at once."

I'm grateful that Archbishop Clavel directed me to Bishop Steinbock who in all likelihood could inspire the whole world if given the chance. However, the Archbishop himself, despite his modesty about his English, is widely known as a great man of God.

Archbishop Tomas Clavel has a broad, unforgettable smile. His hair is dark with flashes of gray and rich brown eyes glint beneath bushy eyebrows. Clad in a black suit with Roman collar, a special copper ring given him by Pope Pius XII adorns his strong right hand. In his fifties, he is about five feet, seven inches tall and bears authority confidently.

Archbishop Clavel lives among the poor, in a simple house in Santa Ana, California. At the same time he is a world traveler and has been a close friend of Pope Pius XII, Pope John XXIII, Pope John Paul I and Pope John Paul II.

Archbishop Clavel's work is mainly among the three hundred thousand Spanish-speaking people in his diocese in Southern California. People come by his house night and day. They simply knock on his door. He strives to help those who are fleeing economic and political persecutions in Mexico and Central America to find food, shelter, clothing, and proper documentation from the authorities. Through the help of two Catholic hospitals, he also arranges medical services which are badly needed.

Last year the Archbishop and his staff were able to give four million pounds of food to the needy. The demand is increasing and so are Archbishop Clavel's concerns and duties.

Archbishop Clavel is the former Archbishop of Panama and was President of the Bishops in Central America. He knows firsthand the problems of Central and South America. He also joined Pope John Paul II and traveled with him on the Holy Father's visit to several Central American countries.

Archbishop Clavel said that people in Central and South America really don't want communism. "They want freedom, freedom. The poor don't want to be communists."

He went on, "I have been involved in many things, and in Panama we worked with the poor, too, but the communists are very strict in the discipline and in the work. When I was in my diocese I helped some boys who were revolutionary communists to go to Cuba. Later, they came back because they didn't want to be communists. They had thought it would be an easy life in Cuba—that they wouldn't have to work. They felt they would have money and be able to enjoy life. It's not true. In Cuba there is a tremendous discipline and a lot of work. The Cubans work and work. I have a boy with me from Cuba. He said he was working for one hundred fifty Cuban pesos a month, and that the people in Cuba are working all day long but have only a little food with which to live."

Archbishop Clavel feels that the United Nations should become more involved in Central and South America. For whenever democracies are established, the communists and leftists use the freedom within the democratic society to organize their guerilla bands and to press their aims through violence. It's a very common story that in Central and South America, as well as worldwide, the leftists tend to de-stabilize any democracy. Archbishop Clavel feels that Americans who try to go forth and do something to assist democratic nations are regularly criticized and scandalized, even by American citizens, and that for this reason the assistance to democracies should be done through the United Nations; the United Nations should be given some power to help governments to maintain true democracies and respect for democracy.

The only way the Archbishop sees hope in overcoming the pain and bloodshed "is to assist and protect the democracies."

Also, in Latin America most people are thought to be practicing Catholics. The majority of religious people in Latin America are, after all, called Roman Catholics. However, Archbishop Clavel says that vast numbers of people who are considered Catholics are not practicing Catholics at all. They were baptized as infants but many millions of them are not truly practicing their religion.

Also, many non-Catholics express the opinion and conviction that there is a Roman Catholic conspiracy to take over the world through Catholic propagation. The fear is that Roman Catholics, who are so prohibited in their practice of birth control, will one day be the vast majority in any country they're allowed to live in.

The Archbishop remarked, "We don't say the number of children that a man or woman should have, but we say that you should *only have the number of children that you can support and educate.* And if you cannot support and educate your children, you should practice birth control and wait until you are able to look after them.

"We have no problem with the idea and practice of birth control. But we do have a problem with the method. We recommend the natural method and say people should not use artificial birth control. However, we understand it is necessary to control the population.

"But, the population is usually not the problem and birth control is not the only solution because sometimes people have plenty of money for other things but not for their family. The rich people are using the birth control, not the poor. The poor don't want to use it."

I turned to another subject, "As you look at the world, do you see any emerging hope for people who love freedom to have a better world—a world where people are eating every day and have a place to sleep? Do you see emerging possibilities? Is life getting better or worse?"

"I think that while I am not a pessimist—I don't want to be a pessimist—I don't see any solution," the Archbishop answered. "Only God could send us a solution. Only God, because I don't see much from the people."

"If you don't see any immediate solution or any long-range solution," I persisted, "have you a clear view of what the problem is? Why is it that we can't find a solution? What is the main problem, as you see it?"

"The problem is the corruption," Archbishop Clavel replied. "It's not really the ideas, the philosophies that communists are fighting for this and the democrats are fighting for that. There is the same problem in the capitalist countries as in the communist countries—

materialism. Everything is resolved by money, by business. All the exploitation today is by business. Everything is business. And they are destroying the children, the youth, the women—abusing and taking the women as instruments of sex. So that is why the corruption here in the democratic countries and the corruption in the communist countries is the same—the materialism of life. So, the solution is to come back from materialism."

"What's the conclusion, then, Archbishop Clavel? What can people who seek to be of service to others and who are awakening their consciousness do?"

The Archbishop spoke with great force. "The conclusion should be that all religions, all the different religions, have to be united in one point. We should not fight about theology, about our differences. No, everybody should believe in what they really believe. But we have to be united in the way that's necessary to bring people to God and to enable people to love one another—and understand one another. It's so important for religious people to respect each other. We need to respect the best things in many religions.

"But we are fighting and dividing ourselves—like the Arabs and Jews who say they are fighting for religion, and the Irish who say they are fighting for religion.* And, in other countries there is the same problem." He spoke sorrowfully.

"So," he looked into my eyes and then, raising his gaze in a contemplative manner, went on, "we religious people around the world—all of us—must always think about what we should respect in one another. All of us, in all the religions! We have to be united together in one main way—to love God and to love one another," he exclaimed.

"If we could *join* in love and respect, we could help humanity. We could help the world! Together," the Archbishop concluded, "together."

Yes, Chris and I nodded. It was the only way the world could be helped.

Unfortunately, Archbishop Clavel passed on shortly after our interview, but he left me with a very warm memory, for he had said to me of this book, "What a wonderful thing for the world!"

* See also Reverend Pelletier's comments on politicized religion in Chapter 44.

46

HINDUISM

It's nearly impossible to find a Hindu spokesman in Southern California. Phone calls placed throughout the area revealed very few possibilities.

After several months of searching, Chris and I were fortunate to learn of the lectures being conducted by Professor Satya Pal Sharma at the East-West Cultural Center in Los Angeles. Professor Sharma kindly consented to an interview.

Professor Sharma is in his late fifties, but he moves actively and vigorously like a youth. A man of medium height, he has straight, black hair, horn-rimmed glasses, and a broad smile.

He complimented us for being on time. We removed our shoes and entered his apartment. Hindus are famous for their hospitality. Professor Sharma insisted we first have a cup of tea. He explained that he had lectured around the world on Hinduism, so I felt very comforted that I had finally succeeded in gaining a chapter on Hinduism. He also mentioned that he had served as a Hindi officer in the Ministry of Education in India, in addition to being the Professor of Hinduism at St. Paul's Theological College in Nairobi, Kenya. He is the author of *Know Your Religion*, among other books.

With tea pleasantly completed and an atmosphere of good will filling the room, we began.

"What shall we call you?" I asked.

"Punditji,"* he answered.

"Punditji, it's a pleasure to interview you today." I asked him to begin with a thumbnail sketch of his background.

"Now I am fifty-seven years old," he began. "When I was only eight years old I was sent to Kurukshetra which is in Haryana, then I went to Gurukul University in Brindaban (also, Vrindavan), which is the birthplace of Krishna."

"I've been there," I said.

"You've been there?" He seemed pleased. "The difference between the modern education and the ancient education is that in ancient education the disciples or students went to live with the teacher. But nowadays the teachers come to the students."

Professor Sharma, in explaining the ancient tradition of education used the terms *Gurukula* (Guru, or teacher, school) and *shishyakula* (student school). His explanation, in turn, caused him to comment that the English language, and most European languages, came from ancient India.

Somehow we also began discussing religious persecution during the second World War and he said quickly, "What I think is people should not blame any religion for all these (persecutions)."

"What should we blame?"

"A person," he answered.

"Which particular person?"

"According to Hinduism, don't blame even the person—blame the *bad habits* in that person. A person is not bad or good, it's only the habits. When the habits change, the person changes."

I brought him back to the original subject. "So, we left you at this Gurukul Institute."

He nodded. "The Gurukul Institute that is in Brindaban. I studied there for fourteen years and the studies were done in Sanskrit— no other language, only Sanskrit. I studied grammar, the Upanishads, philosophy, the Vedas, everything in Sanskrit. Now I am again digging down in these studies and see them in a new light. I don't say that Hinduism is the only way to get this new light."

He waved his hand, "So, after fourteen years of study, then I became an officer in the government of India in the Ministry of

---

* *Pundit* means a learned man, schooled in the spiritual scriptures of India. The suffix *-ji* is a term of respect.

Education. Then I took retirement."

"I see. So you spent your career as an administrator?" I noticed a gap of information between his becoming a government officer and then retiring.

"Hindi officer," he responded.

"So you were a Hindi officer in the Ministry of Education. That was your career?"

"Yes, after the government I went to Nairobi. I worked in the religious seminary there and for four years I was Professor of Hinduism at St. Paul's Theological College where people are trained to become Catholic priests. I taught them Hinduism."

"That's wonderful. Wonderful. And then after four years at Nairobi . . . ?"

"Four years there and then a lecture tour. I went to Canada, to England. I spoke on Hinduism and gave lectures in English and Hindi and Sanskrit. And then we had a very good interfaith conference in Pietermaritzburg in South Africa. That is the capital of Natal. Then later we had interfaith conferences in Canada, and now in Los Angeles."

Satisfied that I had succeeded in getting a thumbnail sketch of this well-traveled and much-studied scholar, I asked: "Would you please tell us what is Hinduism?"

"Hinduism. There is one root word in the term 'Hindu.' It is called *hidi*. Hidi means a man who moves on the path of spirituality, and who neglects all the worldly pleasures and other passions for that spiritual upliftment. He is a Hindu.

"Now, when people ask me, 'What do you mean by *Hindu*?, I say there are five letters in the word Hindu. H stands for honesty, I stands for integrity, N stands for nobility, D stands for devotion, and U stands for unity. And, I say any person who strives for these ideals is called *patasheela*, which means five good things.

"You may believe in any cult you want, any path you want, but do you believe in honesty, do you believe in integrity, and nobility, devotion, and unity? If you do, you are a Hindu.

"So this is why we say to people of other religions, 'Go and convert others, as you like. Christians, go and convert. Islamic people, go and convert others.' But Hindus never convert anyone because anyone who holds to these five values is a Hindu by birth. Why should I try to convert you?"

Seeking clarification, I asked, "Would other Hindu people agree with your definition? I just want to be sure that this is a common Hindu view." I recalled being admitted to some Hindu temples and literally being bounced out of others.

Professor Sharma then opened a book by S. Radhakrishnan, a great philosopher and former president of India. Either reading or paraphrasing from the book, Punditji said, "Hinduism has no creed by which it may be said to stand or fall. But it is convinced that the spirit will outgrow the creed. For the Hindu, every religion is true if only sincerely and honestly followed."*

"That's very beautiful, beautiful," I said.

Professor Sharma nodded. "And one thing more. Even in Hinduism there are those who are outlaws, who have not seen the new light. And there are those just like Dr. Radhakrishnan who have lived in the tradition but have also seen the new light. A person who wants to evaluate his own religion without coming to the new light, he cannot do that. This new light sheds real light upon his own original thinking."

"What do you mean by 'the new light?'" I asked.

"There are very few people who can understand the religious books and their real interpretation. When there are so many branches in Christianity, the Bible has not been interpreted in the correct way. Similarly, those who are not studied in Indian philosophy or Indian culture misinterpret the Indian philosophers. But, as we think in the spirit, then that spirit brings us to a higher level. It speaks to us. So, I read whatever philosophers have spoken from the high level of spirit. Spirit sheds new light on what I studied in Sanskrit."

"Are you saying," I tried to understand, "can I put it in these words—please use your own words if you prefer—are you saying that God is bringing about a collective revelation to humanity? Are you saying there's a change that's necessary because it's an act of God, or spiritual fact, that one must have this new light regularly, throughout the ages?" I struggled for words.

"I am saying there are souls who think that the time has come when this struggle, this strife, all these quarrels, should be done away with."

We sipped tea thoughtfully. I went on with my next question, "In the new light of Spirit, what *is* the relationship between God and man, if any?"

"In Christianity there is only one son of God. According to Hinduism, every soul is the son of God. We are all children of God, and

* From the book, *Religion of Society*, by S. Radhakrishnan, published by George Allen and Unwin.

that is why we call ourselves *arya*. Arya means 'the son of God.' We are all sons of God."

"Are we all sons of God whether we know it or not?" I asked.

"Whether we know it or not. A son is a son."

"What's the difference between a son who does not know he's a son of God and one who does know?"

He smiled. "Suppose there are two sons of one father, and one son obeys his father. He follows the path of his father. Suppose this father was a very saintly person. Then, that son becomes a saintly person. But the other son—who does not know and does not obey—does not follow the path of his father. He will go to hell. The son who followed his father goes to heaven.

"Similarly, whether we know it or not, we are sons and daughters of God. But I do not say *daughters* particularly because the soul has no gender. It is neither a male nor female. So, we call the soul a child of God. I hear some say, 'Jesus is the son of God, the only son of God.' Am I not the son of God, too? And, can a woman not be the son of God, too? So, we Hindus say we are children of God."

Then Professor Sharma and I discussed the subject of sin.

"Some religions say," Punditji thought a moment, "that if I commit a sin and go to church, or go to the heavenly Father, and I confess, 'Oh, Father, I have committed sin,' that I shall then be free from that sin. We Hindus think this is wrong. Because once I have committed that sin, natural law is against me and I will get punishment from that natural law—which is being operated by God. Even if I pray to God, He won't help me. So, what does Hinduism say? Don't think that by praying to God, by going to the temple, you will be free from the punishment for your sins. You will be punished. This is natural law."

I was surprised, having studied the views of many eastern saints—many of them Hindus—who say that God is forgiving, like a mother to her misbehaving child.

"But, do you not have forgiveness and grace in Hinduism?"

"Grace is there, but grace doesn't mean forgiveness," Professor Sharma explained. "Grace doesn't forgive. But, how does the grace work? Suppose a son, a small child, goes against the orders of the father. The father beats the child. That is the natural way the father should prevent the child from doing that bad thing again. But, at the same time, the father loves the child. He tells the child, 'I told you not to do that act, but you have done it.' He makes it clear why he has punished the child. The father then says, 'Don't worry,' and the father gives love to his child. That love makes the child forget all the punishment.

"Similarly, when God punishes me for my sins, he gives me love with which I can endure that suffering. And so, I do not succumb to that suffering or forget the love because of the suffering. This is by his grace."

"What is the goal of Hinduism?" I asked, moving to my next question.

"Perfection," he answered.

"What do you mean by perfection?"

"To become the perennial child of God, to become *arya*," Professor Sharma answered.

"When you are a child of God, what are you like?" I asked. "What are your characteristics, what is your nature? What are your thoughts?"

"For one thing, as it says in the *Bhagavad Gita*, 'Don't think what is right, don't think what is wrong. You will be confused.' So just say, 'Whatever God has said in his scriptures, I shall follow that.' And what is this scripture, what is this knowledge given by God? It is the *Veda*. It is called the Veda. By Veda I don't mean *the book*. Bible literally means *book*, but Veda does not mean book. Veda refers to *the knowledge*."

"But which knowledge?" I asked.

"The knowledge which is ever with God. It never perishes. And that is why the people ask me, 'Christianity has been founded by Jesus Christ and Islam has been founded by Prophet Mohammed, and so all these religions have founders, who has founded the Hindu religion?' And my answer is, there is no one man who has founded Hinduism. The founder of Hinduism is God. And all these people— Rama, Krishna, saints, and *acharyas* (great masters)—all these people, they never founded Hinduism.

"They were just tributaries of this main stream. They came and they explained all the principles and initiated people in the Veda— the knowledge of God which was necessary for that time, for those people. These great ones *explained* the Veda to the people in detail. That's all. The great ones gave different explanations of the knowledge—the Veda. They were not giving any new religion."

"So, the goal of Hinduism is perfection—becoming the perennial child of God?" I sought to understand perfection more deeply.

"What is perfection?" he countered. "Perfection means to make the soul the real master. It means to be perfect spiritually—to be above the senses, to be above the passions, to be above other concerns. It means to be oneself—one's true self. The pure and true self, that is perfection. Once you attain that perfection, you go and be part of the will of God. Without being perfect, your ego says, 'Oh, God, help me. I'm coming to you.' God says, 'Be *purna*; purna means perfect.' If you want to *achieve* that purna, *become* purna. After becoming purna, you say, 'Yes, my father, now I am above that mask of ignorance and ego. Will you accept me?' And God says, 'Come in, my child. I'll accept you.' That is Hinduism," he concluded.

"Is there a view in Hinduism that you cannot become perfect without God's grace or God's help?" I asked.

"Two things must be there to become perfect," Professor Sharma explained. "The first thing is not only do you need God's grace, but you need God's help. God must be with me. And then, the second thing is my efforts."

"You're saying, then, that perfection is achieved by God's help and also your personal effort. Is there anything else?"

"Study," he answered.

"Anything else?" I asked.

"That's all. These three things."

"Studies, personal effort, and God's help," I summed up.

"Right," he answered.

"And perfection is achieved?"

"Yes."

"And perfection is where the soul is the master of the mind: the soul is the master of body, emotions, and the senses?"

"Right."

I wondered what the Professor's definition of the vitally important soul was. "Since you say the soul, being the master, is the whole essence of fulfillment, could you tell me a bit more? What is the soul? What is its nature? And why doesn't the mind pay attention to the soul? Why does the soul have to become the master? Why isn't the soul automatically the master?"

"If I want to go to the other bank of the river, I must go through the water. I should swim . . . or find a bridge. This world is like an ocean. It is called *samsara*, by the Hindus, meaning that which keeps moving on. The way for the soul to go to God is through the world only. By going through the world the soul gets to God. The soul has come into this world to achieve closeness to God.

"But, as the soul goes to God, what happens? Now comes the second test: temptation. The temptations come and occupy the senses. And, if the mind is caught in the passions—the temptations—

it becomes a slave itself and it enslaves our emotions and senses. People call this enslavement *maya*. Often maya is defined as illusion. But, really, maya is not illusion. Maya is not an illusion. Don't think God is a cheat to create this maya. It is only you, you are cheating yourself. The mind is so mighty that once it discards the passions, it can easily make the soul its master."

"So, what is a better word than illusion?" I asked.

"There is no illusion at all!" Professor Sharma said very strongly.

"There is no illusion here?" I felt the surprise, having heard the term for so many years.

"No, no illusion. Everything is real," he explained.

"Are you saying that man misperceives the reality?" I asked.

"Only when man becomes perfect does he see the reality. But before that he sees only partially. As the sun dawns in the sky, we get a little light. Then as the sun rises more, we get more light. It's like that. When a man starts to go on the path of perfection, step by step, step by step, he sees the light. And then the light, those rays, guide him and he moves forward to the perfect light. So, we do not say that in our beginning efforts we don't have any light. We do have it! But in small measure, in small quantity."

"People who read this chapter may have a difficulty which I'd like to speak about now," I said. "It sounds like rising above the passions so that the soul may be the master is too hard for people—especially for husband and wife. What do you think about this difficulty and what does it mean in terms of most people ever experiencing the mastery of the soul? Is it possible to experience spiritual fulfillment while married, for example?"

Punditji smiled at his wife. "Suppose these married people say, 'Oh, God, please make me so that I can see you.' Then suppose God actually comes to them and says, 'Yes, I have come to you. I want to take you with me. Will you come with me?' Then these people will say, 'Oh, not now! Not now! Let me see you at the end of my life—let me tend to my children and my grandchildren, then I shall come to you!'" Punditji laughed.

"So, there are very few people who are really interested in getting this spiritual perfection," he said. "They want *some* light but *not* spiritual perfection. Why? They like temptation and desire. They think of perfection in worldly terms—as money. They want all these things—good money, a good wife, good children.

"Most people are not bothered about spiritual perfection. Why? Because in order to have spiritual perfection they have to leave all of their attachments. And, once they leave their attachments, still they will say, 'We have been deprived of something, we have lost some great pleasure.' The way out for these people," Professor Sharma continued, "is they should try to feel the soul. They should try to feel that bliss, in their prayer and in their meditation. They should enjoy things which are not worldly things."

He gestured, "But really, you can look at it this way. A man should grow from whatever state he's in. He leaves one state and moves to another when he's perfect in the former state. It's like this: a child who studies in class one learns and masters class one; then he passes to class two. That is, when he's perfect in class one, he goes to class two. When he's perfect in class two, he goes to class three. And so he goes through school. Similarly, here also, the husband and wife grow and develop in household affairs. They learn how to be a good husband and a good wife. They receive spiritual benefit and light as they grow, becoming better and better husband and wife, father and mother.

"So life is God's class one, God's class two, God's class three, God's class four . . . like that. If I go on learning the lessons and attaining perfection in one state, then I will be moved to the next position, and that perfection itself will lead me to the whole perfection," he waved his hand.

Professor Sharma's explanation of perfection led very naturally into the problem of salvation and I commented, "I've asked other religious leaders this question which I'm about to ask you. Often the problem is one of vocabulary, so I'd like you to feel free to choose words that you prefer. How does the Hindu become fulfilled, or saved, or realized? Some religions say you must be saved, some say you must be realized, others say you must be fulfilled. Using whatever words you like, how does a Hindu become fulfilled, saved, or realized?"

"Saved by whom?" Professor Sharma asked me back.

"Well, how does a Hindu find complete and perfect satisfaction? Is that a fair question?"

"Complete satisfaction . . . ." Professor Sharma reflected.

"Perhaps I could ask you this way: How does a Hindu abide in God? What I'm trying to do is ask similar questions of different religious leaders. And if you can't find words here that we can use, we'll have to . . . ."

"I see." He smiled. "About the word *saved*, we don't believe in that."

"You don't believe that you have to be saved?"

"God does not save me. I will have to save myself," he said with conviction.

"About the word *realized*, how does a Hindu become realized?" I asked.

"Realized by whom?" he countered.

"*Realized*," I persisted, "usually means, especially among yogis and devotees of other eastern paths, that one realizes or recognizes one's spiritual reality and thus realizes that God is the Lord. This realization is not just mental but it's a totally transforming experience."

"Right, but then it is not God who is to be realized. It means that I should realize my own true self," he said.

"What you're saying then is that the Hindu viewpoint is, 'I should realize my own true self.'"

"Right. Realize my own self, and after realizing my own self, I shall try to realize God. That is realization."

"And you don't particularly like the word *fulfilled*? It doesn't have much pertinence to a Hindu?"

"I do not see how it fits in Hinduism," he replied.

"Fine. Do you use the word *enlightened*? How does a Hindu become enlightened—if we haven't already covered that?"

"Enlightenment happens anytime," he explained. "Perhaps you might have also experienced sometimes when you sit down and you want to do something. There is an insight, something inside you which says, 'Do like this.' That is enlightenment. And that light comes not from the soul or from the intellect or from within—it comes from God.

"So, if we sit in meditation and join ourselves—our own self with God, which is called yoga—automatically that light which is with God comes to me. It flows through me. That is enlightenment."

He continued, "When I join myself to, or make contact with, the divine power, then the divine power itself flows through my self, and that self within me is called *shakti*, which means that the soul is getting the power from God. And that power is what Hindus call enlightenment."

"Is that a major goal of Hinduism, enlightenment?" I asked.

"No, it is the *means*. That's all," he explained.

I reached for words. "Enlightenment is the means by which the soul becomes the master and by which perfection is realized or attained? In other words, enlightenment enables . . . ."

"Enlightenment enables the soul to be perfect, and then after becoming perfect, to achieve God."

"Could you explain the process by which a Hindu finds, realizes, or knows, perfection? I know we've talked about God's help and man's effort, along with the study of the scriptures, but is there a day-by-day or year-by-year process by which this perfection happens?"

"Yes. We seek to become free of desire, then free of ego. How do you feel that you've become perfect? When you're perfect you do not feel suffering, you do not feel pleasures. If you do not feel any attachment and if you feel yourself stabilized in all these circumstances which are normally against you, it means that you are going on the correct path. You can get the process in the *Bhagavad Gita*, chapter two."

"Which verses?"

"Chapter two, verses fifty-five through seventy-two." (Which read as follows:)

"The Blessed Lord said: When a man abandons . . . all the desires of the heart and is satisfied in the Self by the Self, then is he said to be one stable in wisdom.

"He whose mind is not perturbed by adversity, who does not crave for happiness, who is free from fondness, fear and anger, is the Muni (sage) of constant wisdom.

"He who is unattached everywhere, who is not delighted at receiving good nor dejected at coming by evil, is poised in wisdom.

"When also, like a tortoise its limbs, he can withdraw the senses from sense-objects his wisdom is then set firm.

"Sense objects drop out for the abstinent man, though not the longing for them. His longing also ceases when he intuits the Supreme.

"The excited senses . . . impetuously carry away the mind of even a wise man, striving for perfection.

"The yogi, having controlled them all, sits focused on Me as the supreme goal. His wisdom is constant whose senses are under subjugation.

"Brooding on the objects of senses, man develops attachment to them; from attachment comes desire; from desire anger sprouts forth.

"From anger proceeds delusion; from delusion, confused memory; from confused memory the ruin of reason; due to the ruin of reason he perishes.

"But the disciplined yogi, moving among objects with the

senses under control, and free from attraction and aversion, gains in tranquility.

"In tranquility, all his sorrow is destroyed. For the intellect of the tranquil-minded is soon anchored in equilibrium.

"There is no wisdom in the fickle-minded; nor is there meditation in him. To the unmeditative there is no peace. And how can the peaceless enjoy happiness?

"Just as a gale pushes away a ship on the waters, the mind that yields to the roving senses carries away his discrimination.

"Therefore . . . his cognition is well poised, whose senses are completely restrained from their objects.

"That which is night to all beings, in that the disciplined man wakes; that in which all beings wake, is night to the Atman-cognizing Muni (the Self-realized wise one).

"Not the desirer of desires, but that man attains Peace, in whom all desires merge even as rivers flow into the ocean which is full and unmoving.

"That man attains Peace who lives devoid of longing, freed from all desires and without the feeling of 'I' and 'mine.'

"This . . . is the Brahman (the Absolute, Pure Spirit) state. Attaining this, none is bewildered. Being established in it even at the death-hour, a man gets into oneness with Brahman."*

"So," I said, "among the things that happen are, you give up desires, and you give up ego. What are some of the main techniques for getting rid of desires and ego? Techniques, attitudes, or practices?"

Professor Sharma laughed. "Do the work without having any desire or any selfishness. Live in that state. To do that work is your duty, and it is the work of God you are doing. If you think this way, automatically you will reduce your desire."

"By work you mean not only a job but—"

"Any work. Any activity."

Too soon, it was time to ask my penultimate question: "What is the Hindu view of other faiths?"

* *The Bhagavad-Gita*, Chapter 2, verses 55-72, commentary by Swami Chidbhavananda, published by the Secretary, Sri Ramakrishna Tapovanam, Tirupparaitturai, India. Used with the permission of the Vedanta Society of Southern California.

"We believe in all faiths," he said. "As I said earlier, we believe all these faiths are various ways and paths going toward God. We believe in all the ways that stand for honesty, integrity, nobility, devotion, and unity. But sometimes, what happens? Some people say, 'Only those who come to this church will go to God—nobody else.' The thing is, I should follow the correct way, the straight way, which leads me toward God. I ask you a question: How many straight lines can you draw between two points?" he asked.

"One and only one," I laughed.

"Only one and one only," he said. "So, we cannot say that all these different paths are straight and go toward God. There may be many ways and paths going toward God but not all of them are straight. And because of that, we have to find out the one straight way."

I looked at him surprised. "How do you find out one straight way? Are you saying, for example, that Hinduism is the only way?"

"No, no, no, no. I'm not talking that way. What I say is, to acquire the knowledge of God, the knowledge which has been given by God, know that. Follow it. That is the straight way. That's all I'm saying. Be a child of God, have that knowledge, follow that knowledge. Don't follow the path given by people. Follow the path given by God," he spoke with enthusiasm.

"You're really saying then that people's interpretations, or 'personality cults,' should be avoided?"

"Right, right, because all these paths and ways that are created by men, not by God, they deviate us. They confuse us and mislead us so that we may go the wrong way," he said. "One more thing I want to add . . . ."

"Please go ahead," I encouraged.

"What our Hindu scriptures say was written down by *rishis* (enlightened men and women). Rishis were those people who were selfless. They were not like ordinary beings. Whatever they spoke, they were explaining the knowledge of God. If you want to see that knowledge, go through the books of the rishis—the *Vedas*, *Upanishads*, *Darshanas*—and you will find the direct way."

"Punditji, how may we have a more peaceful world?" I summed up my questions.

"I told you: have one God, one religion of humanity, and let all the people have one straight line which takes us to God," he said.

"How can we possibly do that, with so many different views and different power structures?"

"This is why my aim in life is to bring all these religious leaders together at one forum and find out the one religious stream going through all these religions and ask each of them to join this religion and nothing else. Nowadays religion itself is in danger. If the religious leaders are not awakened now, if they are as selfish as they are now, if they are fighting with each other as they are doing now, the new generation is not going to accept religion. The new generation says that it is the different religions which have brought war into this world and created great international unrest. The new generation says different religions claim to teach love and affection, but what are they doing? Fighting with each other, fighting among themselves. Religion is a divided house everywhere. If religious leaders do not develop the power of tolerance now and if they do not try to love their neighbors, they will be doomed."

I frowned. "What exactly do you mean by doomed?"

"Religion in this world will not be loved or practiced by the new generations. People have to start loving God and stop loving churches. We so-called religious people say to mankind, 'Have tolerance, love one another,' but to do that you have to sacrifice something—your prejudice and your prestige—for the sake of humanity. Then you can go in harmony."

I left Professor Sharma's company with the hope that his passion, and the love of many other religious leaders, be shared globally. I hope the yearning hearts of all people can find understanding and finally agree. Enough to get along with one another. Enough to seek world peace together.

47

ISLAM

Islam means "the way of commitment and submission to God. Islam is the name of our religion, and Muslim is the person who practices our religion," said Dr. Muzammil Siddiqi, Director of the Islamic Society of Orange County in California.

A kind, soft-spoken man in his mid-forties, Dr. Siddiqi has dark hair, a moustache, and a generous beard with hints of gray whiskers. Spirit shines through his dark eyes.

He greeted me very cordially when we met in his small, simple office in Garden Grove. In his subdued tweed jacket and light shirt with the top button open, he seemed relaxed, truly happy.

While born in India, Dr. Siddiqi received his doctorate in comparative religions at Harvard University. He was happy to relate to me the Islamic tradition of higher consciousness and spirituality.

We sat comfortably around his book-laden desk. I began my questions about higher levels of consciousness.

Dr. Siddiqi readily understood. "Islam is a way of peace and perfection, and a Muslim is a person striving toward that way. A Muslim is working toward peace in the full sense of the word—not just absence of war—peace, meaning wholeness, completeness, being without any defect, without any inadequacy, being perfect, being full. A Muslim is not claiming that he is perfect, but he is *striving*, struggling within himself and with the society around him, to reach to that goal, to that aim that he has before himself. Islam is a continuous struggle, a continuous work."

"What is the way, or method, of Islam?" I asked.

"The way of Islam? Within Islam itself, every Muslim, every believer, has to practice certain worship, some personal practices, and five prayers every day. Every male and female is expected to perform prayers five times a day. Also, we fast during the month of Ramadan. Fasting is a very important, highly spiritual practice that you can go through, along with prayers and devotions at night during the month.

"We also emphasize that each believer earns for himself, for his own livelihood, and that a believer should work hard. The believer, the Muslim, strives to live simply and humbly and do some charity to others. Charity and simplicity are important because they also purify greed from the heart, which comes from the mind."

Spiritual truth is indeed universal, I thought, as I briefly contemplated that most religions recommend charity and simplicity in order to make the heart pure.

"We emphasize trust in God, patience, and constancy," Dr. Siddiqi added.

"Please continue," I urged.

"As a result of the devoted life in frequent prayer, devotional activity, simplicity, charity to others, humility, patience, and constancy, the believer becomes more whole, more filled with peace, love, compassion and awareness. These virtues, as they become living attributes in each devotee, develop into a state of higher consciousness called *fana*."

I smiled in delight and fascination as we entered into the discussion of higher consciousness.

He went on, "Always the highest thing that teachers and masters would work on in helping a believer is what is called a state of fana. Fana means that you totally forget yourself. You forget who you are. You feel that you are not doing an activity but rather that the action is being done through you.

"So," he underscored, "in all your activities, you commit yourself completely to God. You give yourself to God, and *that's what Islam means*. Islam does not take its name from any person—as Christianity takes its name from Christ or Buddhism takes its name from Buddha—or Hinduism receives its name from the Indus River and Valley of India.

"You see," he leaned toward me, "the central basic point of Islam is consciousness of God."

"Do you pass through a number of levels to arrive at fana and greater consciousness of God?" I asked.

He nodded. "Your state changes from one level of consciousness to another. Through your spiritual work, through your practices, you try to attune with the next level, and as you develop, the next level becomes your station. Then you move to another higher station, and your consciousness grows and grows. As you grow you become an instrument of God, so you have no pride in yourself, no arrogance, no sense that 'I am doing this.' You forget this 'I' which is a deception," Dr. Siddiqi responded.

"But," he added with emphasis, "the scriptures and masters say that even at this stage, fana, a believer should not think too much about this negation of himself." Dr. Siddiqi cautioned, "At this level the ego, the I-sense, can feel that it is doing the job of self-negation and thus remain very strong in itself, very strong in its opinion that it is controlling the spiritual development. So, you have to *negate the negation of yourself—truly humble yourself*—and then comes the state of *baqa*, the preservation of the person."

Fascinating, I thought, the Muslim strives to totally negate himself or herself before God, and then comes a truly humble state which reveals baqa, the preservation of the person.

"So," he waited for me to return from my thoughts, "the exalted state of fana, along with its marvelous sense of freedom, spiritual attunement, and well being is not the goal because it does not represent complete submission of oneself to God. Fana is a state leading to the highest state of baqa. When the believer is totally living under the presence of God, then one is *preserved* by God and *lives under the consciousness of God*. This is the highest state of knowledge: *ma-rarifa*. Ma-rarifa means knowledge, or highest consciousness. This state of baqa is not consciousness in any abstract sense. It is the consciousness of God."

"Ideally, then," I asked, "how does a Muslim view the world and other religions?"

"Islam is a very God-centered religion, so emphasis is always to recognize that everything that is here in this world God has brought into existence. A Muslim sees God in everything. We say, 'See God in everything, don't see yourself.' Sometimes this has led to pantheistic ideas but really there is no pantheism in Islam and cannot be. We don't point our fingers and think that, 'This is God or that is God.' Once you point at anything and say, 'This is God,' you are doing polytheism, which becomes idolatry.

"So," he continued, "you cannot point to any person or any figure and say that he or it is God. God is always beyond. But whatever exists exists because of God, so God is present in everything. At the same time, nothing exists in this world without God. It is God who is the Cause of causes. It is God who is the Ultimate Cause, but God himself is transcendent. He is beyond. You cannot point to him, you cannot say that 'Here is God' because the moment you do that there is some danger of, a risk of, idolatry—taking some person, some being, some object, as divine. A Muslim wants to become an instrument of God and live under God's consciousness, forgetting this 'I' which is a deception."

I asked Dr. Siddiqi if, in this state of complete submission to God, there was any merging or sharing of the divine nature by the Creator and his beloved believer?

"God is God, man is man, but there is a very close relationship. There is no identity, no merging of the two, but there is a very deep closeness. The Prophet Mohammed was told by God, 'Give the answer, tell them (the seekers) I am near.' Now, God didn't say how near. You cannot measure that closeness in inches or in feet or in yards. But God's nearness is something that everyone has to realize for himself or herself. How very near God becomes to you. He is closer to you than your own jugular veins. He is closer to you than your own self. God is closer to me than my own self.

"So, God is near. But still, one should not point to any person and say, 'This is God.' This becomes idolatry, this becomes polytheism, and then people turn away from the worship of God to the worship of other things. Other things and other people.

"The Muslim surrenders his ego, his deceptive ego, and finds himself in the nearness of God. He finds that God is nearer than his own jugular vein, nearer than his own self."

Dr. Siddiqi then asked me, "Have you heard the word *jihad* in today's media, especially newscasts, where the term is translated as 'holy war?'"

"Yes, I've heard the term Islamic Jihad—'holy war'—many times and have wondered deeply about what Muslims mean by it," I answered.

"Jihad," he explained, "means the struggle, which is basically the spiritual struggle, against the forces of evil."

"That's what I have understood, too," I replied. "I once listened to a Muslim who was starting a mosque in Philadelphia. He sat in his wheelchair and said to all gathered in the mosque that 'If you see darkness in another, and if you are in darkness, then all there is is darkness.' The Muslim leader had said it's the duty of all persons—especially Muslims—to be light and to see light. 'In this way,' he said, 'there will be light.' He urged that people must look upon one another and other peoples in the world from a point of light." I stopped, then went on. "This furthers my question. How should a Muslim look upon people of a different faith?"

"Islam gives a sense of great commitment to God. The Muslim knows that Islam is a way that is shown by God—the way of *truth*, the way of *kindness*," Dr. Siddiqi emphasized. "A Muslim's duty is to live according to that commitment, *truth* and *kindness*. Also, the Muslim is to show other people this path of goodness and guidance, without judging the other people. A Muslim is not supposed to say that all these other people are going to hell."

"That's what I was wondering," I commented, as my mind filled with images of political Christian, Jewish, and Muslim devastation from the Mideast.

"Yes, a Muslim is not supposed to say other people are going to hell. But a Muslim should always say that 'This is the truth that I am shown through Prophet Mohammed. This is the message of truth that has come in the Koran, and it is my duty to live according to this message myself and to tell other people—because this message has to be proclaimed.'"

Dr. Siddiqi leaned forward. "I have to declare this message to people. I have to tell the people, and then it's up to the people to accept the message or not to accept it."

"What happens if people do not accept the message?"

"Then it's between those people and God. God will judge them according to their sincerity, how sincere they were in rejecting his message. Did they reject it because they did not understand it? Did they reject it because they were not convinced of it? Or did they reject it because of their arrogance, because of their pride within themselves, or because of their vested interests?"

"What are the basic tenets of Islam, please?" I asked.

"The basic points of Islam, which we emphasize, are really three: One is the belief in God, the oneness of God. Second, we recognize that there is guidance given by God and that each Muslim must live according to that guidance. This guidance came through Prophet Mohammed in its final form. A Muslim recognizes Prophet Mohammed as a Prophet, as the final Prophet, and is willing to live according to the Prophet's message. The third important aspect of Islam is that my life here in this world is a temporary life. I'm living here only for a short time. Islam doesn't say that this is the only life. There will be another life after this life. After death there will be resurrection. There will be judgment and I will be questioned according to my deeds: whether I did behave properly and honestly; whether I lived according to the command of God, or did not live according to the command of God. And eternal life depends on that.

"So," he looked into my eyes, "these are the three basic points. If someone accepts these three basic points, then he becomes a member of the Islamic group. He or she becomes a Muslim. A Muslim's duty is to live according to the truth, and to explain this truth to other people, without forcing anyone. We're not allowed to force anyone to accept this religion. God himself doesn't force people.

"We are white, black, brown, yellow, all kinds of colors. All of us believe in the oneness of God and we have realized that Islam is our way of life. We try to live according to that way."

I left Dr. Siddiqi deeply impressed—with Islam and with him. My heart was in tears that religious leaders were not sitting down with one another enough to communicate and gain deeper understanding. Also, many members of most faiths are, apparently, killing people of other faiths without reflecting on their own scriptures and listening to their own leaders.

I long for a world of *truth* and *kindness*, too.

48

JUDAISM

Rabbi Frank Stern of Temple Beth Shalom in Santa Ana, California is a tall, confident man with a resonant voice. He has dark, curly, thinning hair, a moustache and short beard—like a Vandyke but rounded under his chin—and appears to be in his forties. He was dressed casually, gray slacks and a white shirt, with the top button open.

Rabbi Stern is an attentive man with intense concentration. His speech quickly reveals his keen mind and his deep dedication to his values. He walked down the corridor of the synagogue with my assistant and me and showed us into his large office. Light streamed into the office through a big window as we pulled our chairs near one another. I explained my book, along with its concept of higher consciousness and told him what my main questions would be: What is Judaism? What is the goal of Judaism? How does a Jew become fulfilled? What are the levels or states of this fulfillment?

"What is the goal of Judaism?" I began.

"I'm going to answer that in just a moment," Rabbi Stern replied. "But since you were kind enough to share the questions with me beforehand, I would like to make a few comments on your questions. The first is, while you're asking all of these questions of each

371

religious group—and that's an appropriate way of dealing with these issues so you can have a process of comparison—the fact is that what you're doing is boxing every religion into the same mold. I want to make you aware of the fact, from the outset, that Judaism doesn't quite fit the box you've put out."

"That's fine," I said, and encouraged him to help me find a better way to proceed.

"I will answer your questions and try to give you the areas of comparison," Rabbi Stern went on, "but I want you to understand from the outset that what will emerge will be a stilted configuration of Judaism."

"Would you prefer this interview go another way?" I asked.

"Not at all," Rabbi Stern replied. "No matter how we proceed we're going to run into some of the same kinds of problems."

"Would you give me an example of this problem?"

"For example, you talk about levels of religious consciousness. That's not in Jewish tradition. There are different kinds of experiences within Judaism which you might characterize as 'levels of consciousness' but it's not like rungs of a ladder."

"How would you prefer to characterize these experiences?"

"I'll be happy to answer that when we get into this area. And one more thing I want you to know is that personally I accept the notion that there are many roads up the mountain and I see Judaism as one of these roads. I see there are lots of other roads which are appropriate also, so I want you to be assured that I'm happy to cooperate in this kind of endeavor in which you're involved.

"Further, I also sense that in Judaism there are many ways in which one can experience God, and when you talk about the term 'higher consciousness,' I'm not sure whether that's God himself, or whether that's a consequence of your experience with God."

"I understand." I agreed with his concerns.

"My own personal belief," said Rabbi Stern, "as opposed to any kind of authoritative Jewish position—because there is no such animal and I will talk about that if you want me to—but my own personal belief is that our experience of God does something to us as individuals, and 'higher consciousness' might be a way to describe what happens to us. To apprehend, to understand God's characteristics or qualities, or Her characteristics or qualities, or however you want to describe it, that's just beyond human ability, as far as I'm concerned. It's like trying to describe infinity. You know, you can approach it, but you can never comprehend it."

"Right," I said.

"But there are things that happen to us that we cannot comprehend. In my own mind, that's what I would understand by 'higher consciousness.' It's not that somehow we *understand* God and we now can comprehend him, but that whatever it is of God that we experience *affects our lives in some way*. But I'm not sure there are levels that build one upon the other. It's not like Maslow's hierarchy of consciousness, you know. I'm not sure that I personally buy the kind of an image that you start off at one level and then you achieve or fulfill that level and suddenly you're open to another level. Rather, I think people can have peak experiences *without being prepared for them*. I think it helps if you're prepared for them in your knowledge and background, but I think people can be transformed by experiences they're entirely unprepared for. Having a child can be that kind of experience in our lives. So, it doesn't have to be a mountaintop experience, but it can nevertheless be a peak experience."

"What are some of the ways in which Jews have peak experiences and mountaintop experiences?" I asked.

"I think that there are many ways of experiencing God, and in my own teachings I've looked in at least four directions that I find quite natural. I see God as a force which operates within nature, not as an extra-natural phenomenon which somehow interrupts nature to make himself visible or vivid. So I see the God force operating in nature and I see us able to apprehend that force or become one with that force in at least four different ways.

"The first way, and perhaps the most obvious to people who are part of a religious tradition, is to plumb the depths of what you've been given—in the traditional sense. We have a vast literature: we have the experiences of our forefathers, of the sages, of other people of Jewish tradition. We can read their accounts; we can understand their ideas. We can plumb the experience of God through the traditions to which we are heir. Study then becomes one pathway to God.

"A second way would be to look at the resources we have within ourselves as persons. I think we can become conscious of God because of what we find within ourselves. For example, the kind of awe we feel at times, the sense of goodness we feel within ourselves, the outreach we have, the sense of dignity and worth that we feel within ourselves. In other words, there are things within us that are beautiful, special, and precious. These inner qualities somehow move us to some kind of higher form of behavior, higher consciousness, whatever you want to call it. So another pathway to God is to somehow get in touch with and express the finest qualities we find within ourselves.

"A third pathway to God is to do precisely the same with respect to others. I find God—I recognize God—in other people. And I can come into contact with God through my relationships with other people. If they are loving, if they are supportive relationships, if they are relationships that achieve some kind of joy, if I see other people blossoming as a consequence of our relationship, somehow I experience the presence of God. So another path to God is through other human beings.

"And then the fourth way would be the natural world. There are times in our experiences with the world around us that we become aware of forces for good, and beauty, and harmony—and whatever other adjectives you want to use—but we call those forces a name: God.

"It's not that one pathway is somehow better than the other," the Rabbi added. "They are all pathways. Like opening one of four doors and that door gets you ultimately to the same conclusion. They are all available pathways to us. What I find is that some people are more receptive to one pathway and some people are more receptive to another, and they should journey on their particular pathway."

I found his straightforward answer very inspiring. I continued, "Please tell us, what is the goal of Judaism?"

"The goal of Judaism," he answered, "is to somehow carry out the ideals—the values—which man apprehends to be godly *in our lives*. So the goal of Judaism is to live lives in harmony with God."

"And how do you do that? I recognize you have these four pathways but . . . ."

"That's right," he said. "What Jewish tradition and experience has offered us are insights into all four pathways. Ultimately, *belief* is not the significant achievement or criterion of Jewish consciousness. The ultimate criterion is: what impact does one of these four pathways have on your behavior, how do you live your life as a consequence of whatever experience you have had? The Jewish concept of love, for example, is a good image in that regard. Love as a feeling is not enough in Jewish tradition. If you sit in your living room in front of the fireplace and you extol and exalt about how you love God but that love does not implore you to go out and do anything about your relationships with your fellow man or the world in which you live, or in developing your own talents and abilities, then somehow that love is insufficient. *Spiritual experience has to somehow create differences in your behavior, have an effect on the way you live.*

"And the same thing is true regarding love for your fellow man.

If you say to your child, 'I love you and I am compassionate,' but you don't listen to what that child has to say, or you don't go out of your way to help the child, or you pay no attention to the child's desires and wishes, you are really not showing love. You may feel the feeling of love but somehow it doesn't translate. It's when love translates into behavior that it becomes love fulfilled—or love in any real sense. So, loving your fellow man means you behave toward other people—members of your family, your neighbors, members of your community—in certain kinds of ways that express these godly inspirations. And it's not just a feeling or just a sense or just a belief.

"So," the Rabbi concluded, "Judaism translates, ultimately, less into a system of belief than a system of behavior."

"And you get the appropriate behavior through these four pathways?"

"Through your apprehension of God," the Rabbi responded.

"Through your apprehension of God," I repeated. "But what part does faith play?"

"Faith is one way. See, it's interesting that in Jewish tradition there is no Hebrew word for *religion!* The reason for this is there isn't such a concept. If there were a concept, there would be a word for it. We've been around a long time. We've got words for everything else. We are very articulate peoples. We had no word for religion because that's not a concept in Jewish tradition. That's a Hellenistic notion."

What a thunderous idea, I thought, *no* Hebrew word for *religion*?

"You see," he said, "everything in life is under religion because everything is impacted by your experiences in this world. So, Judaism makes laws about sexual conduct, relationships of parents to children, business relationships, how to plow your fields, what are the proper clothes to wear, how you observe holy days, when you should sleep, when you should bathe. There isn't an area of life that isn't touched in some way by these ideals—ideals of faith."

I asked, "As a consequence of knowing how to treat your children, when to bathe, and various observances, what happens?"

The Rabbi paused and thought. "I pause because this question isn't Jewish. The presumption that something is supposed to happen is an interesting presumption."

"Then you don't have to answer it," I said in surprise.

"I'm not sure that I can."

"When I ask about the goal of Judaism, I mean is it not also Jewish to think of some realization of the reality or presence of God?

As a very distinct experience which does occur?" I endeavored to reach toward a Jewish question.

"I think the experience of God is a very distinct and concrete experience. Yes, it's something you can sense that happens to you, and it's even something you could attempt to talk about." He smiled.

"Would you, please?"

"Obviously, the more you talk about it, the less it becomes. Coming from a mystic tradition, you understand that kind of a concept. There is a whole stream of Jewish philosophy that says you can say nothing about God—because the minute you try to say something about God you categorize, constrain or confine God, and you've lost whatever it is you want to talk about. Jewish religious experience is not like talking about 'X-ism.' The minute you start talking about it, you don't have the same thing anymore.

"You see," he went on, "I personally had experiences where I felt the presence of God. I know members of my family have had those experiences. We have an adult education study program where just a week ago the whole theme of the get-together was personal experiences of God and how a person can share these experiences with others. There were thirty people attending the discussion and I was amazed that not one of them said they had not had these special kinds of experiences. Every single person there had some kind of personal experience of God—of different sorts and different natures. But not all of them translated their experiences in the same vocabulary: 'I felt the presence of God' or 'Some special course opened in my life. I felt the Divine Presence,' or ecstasy, or whatever it might be."

"What are some of the common attributes of these varied experiences? For example, you mentioned the word ecstasy . . . ."

"I think ecstasy is one of those attributes of the experience, or one of the consequences of the experience," Rabbi Stern replied. "I think the heightened awareness of abilities, skills, potentials, that exist within persons is one of the consequences. I think often a new sense of priorities and values is a consequence. Very frequently a person's life direction is changed from such an experience, and he begins to do things he wasn't doing previously—or he re-focuses his life.

"There is a kind of consciousness of being chosen, of being special in some regard, also. There's a sense of awe and wonder, too. There's a sense of purposefulness in terms of the order and harmony of the universe, usually. Perhaps there is also a sense of special relatedness between yourself and other people—and other things.

"But, yet, when you begin to tear it apart this way, all of these are but parts of the same experience. However, these are some of the ways a person can try to start talking about spiritual experiences."

"But," I smiled, "in striving to talk about these experiences, what phrases are often used? What do people coming from this experience say?"

"Well, you see, again, your question is not quite a non-Jewish question. You're asking a perfectly legitimate Jewish question except not many Jews ask it," he laughed. "Judaism has a mystical tradition but it's a minority tradition and suspect, to some degree, historically. So, most people haven't talked about these experiences. To this day, most people don't. All of the people who were with me at that study program last week had probably never shared their peak and mountaintop experiences before because this is simply not the kind of thing one goes around talking about in Jewish tradition. It's not that it's forbidden to do so, it's just not our way.

"For the most part, the experience is left as an eternal, individual kind of thing. It is the *behavior* which becomes articulated.

"So, when you ask me what most Jews say about these experiences, most Jews don't say anything!" The Rabbi shrugged.

"What do those Jews who *do* talk about it say?" I asked curiously.

"There are some Jews who do talk about these things," Rabbi Stern responded. "One of the most articulate modern philosophers of Jewish mysticism was Martin Buber, of whom I'm sure you're aware. His most vocal American exponent was a man by the name of Maurice Friedman who translated many or most of his books from German into English, and who had them published in the United States. Most of what we read of Buber today translates through Maurice Friedman.

"Maurice Friedman tells a story of a student who came to his New York apartment and asked Dr. Friedman to explain Buber's 'I/Thou' relationship. Maurice Friedman said, 'I'd be happy to do so,' and took the student for a walk in the park. They walked side by side for quite some time—quietly. It was a lovely day. Eventually they meandered their way through the park and finally, as they were nearing the edge of the park, the student turned to Dr. Friedman and said, 'Well, I'm waiting for your response.' Dr. Friedman said, 'I've been answering you for half an hour now.'"

"That's very profound," I said.

"So, Friedman obviously comes from the school that said you can't talk about these things, you can only experience this reality.

But Dr. Friedman also said, 'Maybe I can help you experience it. Come, take a walk with me.' Okay?" the Rabbi gazed back at me.

"Others, who are modern in their point of view," Rabbi Stern continued, "would use contemporary fulfillment kinds of terms—self-fulfillment terms, authenticity terms, peak experience terms—the kind of jargon that has grown out of Gardner and Maslow—some of these kinds of people.

"The only other group in contemporary Judaism that talks in terms of ecstasy would be the Hasidic Jews, and I'm just not familiar enough with their literature in that regard. I would suggest that you either talk with Hasidim or that you read their literature to see the kind of vocabulary they employ."

The Rabbi sat back in his chair. He continued, "But the Hasidic Jews have a word in Hebrew tradition called *Shekinah*. Shekinah is a Hebrew word which means the presence of God, or God force—however you term it in English. Shekinah is that part of God which we apprehend in the course of our existence, and there are lots of lovely notions about man's relationship to the Shekinah, how we experience the Shekinah and what that does to us, and so on."

I had wished he would discuss the Shekinah, but I saw he did not intend to so I asked, "This is probably a non-Jewish question which I would like you to clarify, if you wish, or feel free to state the question in a different way, but how does a Jew become fulfilled?"

"Fulfillment in Jewish tradition means carrying out God's demands for your life as fully and as completely—and as joyfully—as you can," the Rabbi answered.

"And you know these demands from the scriptures?"

"Well, that's one way to discover them," he responded.

"You know these demands by the other pathways, also?" I asked.

"That's correct," Rabbi Stern replied. "Obviously, if you look at human relationships and you sense what brings joy and fulfillment to other human beings, then you sense that that is what you ought to do and encourage. On the other hand, that which hurts and degrades or denies other human beings is not good. Or, when you talk about Jewish study, there is no one direction you would study. You've read enough of the Bible to know that there are large sections of the Bible that deal with communicable diseases. There are large sections of the Bible which deal with religious ceremony. Other large sections of the Bible deal with family relationships. Any one of those places are places to start, and if you begin to fill God's demand in one area, this keeps leading you farther and farther and farther into an interconnected universe in some way."

"And would you call this carrying out of God's demands a relationship with God? Would that be a fair term for this?" I wondered.

"That's a very popular kind of term," he said.

"But do *you* like it?"

"I like it, yes," he said, "except in my own philosophy or experience. I feel that God is a constant. So, my relationship with God is more up to me than it is up to God. God's always there. I have to make my effort. I have to open myself and become, somehow, conscious. A rabbinic legend illustrates this.

"The story is told that the day Moses experienced the burning bush he was not alone on the mountaintop. There were other shepherds herding their flocks in the same area and the bush was burning. Any one of them that turned and looked would have had the same experience of God. But they didn't turn and look. Moses was the only one who was open to that experience. And the conclusion is that the burning bush is burning still." He smiled.

I thought about what he'd said. "That's magnificent. So, you mean by fulfillment that a person, as much as possible, does the demand of God in a growing and developing way? Obviously, the term 'demand of God' is not a very popular phrase out there in much of religion—I've rarely heard anyone use the phrase 'demand of God.' What do you mean by *demand*? And, how do you know this demand?"

The Rabbi answered me with a question. "What is it that impels a mother to protect her child, or a father to guard his child against attack?"

"This is what you mean by the 'demand of God?'" I asked.

"There is that sense that you don't have any choices. You have this internal force that compels you to move in a certain direction. Now, there are some mothers who neglect their children, and some fathers who brutalize their children, and parents even abandon their children. So, it's not automatic, and yet I think most parents can understand the feeling they have of wanting to respond if they feel their children are somehow endangered. In a sense, this is the same kind of push, the internal push," the Rabbi explained.

"Or," he continued, "how do you explain the feeling of ecstasy one achieves in a sexual relationship? Or the feeling of pride a parent has at a child's accomplishment? Now, these are all very simple kinds of things we sense all the time. Most parents have had these experiences, but trying to put these things into words somehow doesn't do them justice. However, it doesn't mean they don't exist.

"Well, God's demand is much the same kind of thing. Feeling the presence of God or experiencing God in some way pushes you onward—whatever that push is."

"And if one does not respond to that demand, what happens?" I asked.

"That's an interesting question," he said. "I'm not sure that a person who is open to the experience of God can refrain from responding to the demand. I think a person who refrains from responding to the demand doesn't experience God."

"Then, suppose you are not experiencing God and you are not doing his demands . . . ." I tried to form my thought.

"Let me give you an illustration," he offered.

"Please do."

"Again, you know enough Old Testament tradition to know that almost all of the prophets who were called by God resisted."

"Yes, even ran away!" I recalled.

"They didn't want to do what they were called upon to do. Well, they had no choice. Ultimately, whatever it was that they felt inside *compelled* them to move in a certain direction. The demand of God is that kind of sense. Most people don't even get to the point where they hear the voice of God—they're so busy doing all kinds of other things."

I began to be concerned about defining terms. "What do you mean by 'God's voice?' For example, do you have to be able to hear God's voice before you know his demand?"

"Only in the sense of Biblical prophets," he answered. "If I were to ask you with which of your senses do you apprehend love . . . ?" He paused.

"I would say no sense and all senses, probably. I would say one loves with a deeper sense, something beyond the regular senses."

"I accept that," Rabbi Stern said. "Except that in Biblical terms they use words like 'and God spoke,' or they saw a 'vision.' I'm not sure that God's speaking or a divine vision implies certain human-like qualities. In other words, this doesn't mean that God had a body, you know, or that kind of thing. These terms are just the box that human beings are in when they try to articulate something in their language which is essentially emotional. Every word has constraints to it. The minute you give a word to something, you've also set its limits, and that's the human box we're in."

I wanted to approach what he was saying another way. "As a

Jew, does one pray and seek to know God's voice and God's demand on oneself?"

"Yes, sure."

"Is that part of the way of a Jew?" I asked.

"Yes, that's one way," he answered. "Study is another. Decent
human behavior is another. Prayer isn't any more a way—or prayer
isn't any more a demand—than any of the other ways. In fact, if
anything, the Jewish concept of prayer is that prayer is directed toward oneself as much as it is directed toward God."

"This is an intriguing idea. Would you please explain it?" I
thought that I would love to spend all my afternoons talking with
profound people like Rabbi Stern.

"Well, let me give you a couple illustrations and then I'll explain the concept. Prayer is obviously directed outward toward God.
One of the prayers that is recited frequently in the synagogue begins with, 'Hear, O Israel, the Lord is our God, the Lord is One.'
Well, it seems somewhat ludicrous to have to keep reminding God
of that," he smiled, and I laughed.

"So, to whom are we articulating this prayer constantly? Obviously, we are articulating it aloud but we're really talking to ourselves.

"Or, there's a marvelous quotation from the Book of Deuter-
onomy which is found in almost all Jewish congregational worship
services: 'You shall love the Lord your God with all your heart, with
all your soul, with all your might,' and so on. It goes on for several
paragraphs. Well, are we really saying, 'God, we want you to love
yourself with all your heart . . . ?' What we are saying aloud to God
is something we're trying to remind ourselves to be doing!

"So, those are illustrations of typical prayers. Even the Hebrew
word for 'pray' is a reflexive verb. A reflexive verb is a verb that acts
upon the actor. The verb 'pray' says you pray and somehow it comes
back and affects you. That's the notion of Hebrew prayer. So, prayer
is as much directed to us as we direct it to God."

I felt very grateful he'd granted me the interview and said,
"Rabbi, you've been very generous with your time. But you have
fascinated me with an earlier point and I'd deeply appreciate your
clarification. From what you were saying earlier, you have no term
'religion' in the Jewish vocabulary. Does this mean that you have the
view that there is one religion—an individual's relationship to God
—and that religious groups and sects and schisms get in the way of
that one religion?"

"There is no word for religion in Jewish tradition because everything is touched by religion. So, by talking about religion, you're talking about everything. There's no way to distinguish between religion and anything else."

"Is there only one religion?"

"The answer, historically, is probably no, but not on a philosophical level. Judaism, obviously, recognizes the reality of different religious systems and has gone so far as to say that while God makes certain demands of all beings—certain ways in which all human beings ought to behave in response to the best within them, or within God—those demands translate sometimes differently for Jews than for non-Jews. For example, Judaism does not believe that non-Jews have to keep kosher. Jews have to keep kosher. Judaism does not believe that non-Jews have to observe the Sabbath. Only Jews have to observe the Sabbath. Non-Jews don't have to have a Passover; only Jews do.

"But all people have to treat each other decently. Nobody has the right to steal. Nobody has the right to commit murder. Nobody has the right to be adulterous. So, there are certain universal demands on everyone, and then there are other demands for us who are Jews because we have a particular tradition."

"But those who are not Jewish," I asked, "do they have equal access and opportunity to be with the Lord in every way?"

"Absolutely," Rabbi Stern said powerfully. "Noah wasn't Jewish, although there are some people who make Noah Jewish according to their view. And certainly the Bible says that Noah walked with God. There is no problem."

As we parted, Rabbi Stern smiled, took my hand, and said, "Good luck to you. God bless you."

I left the Rabbi's synagogue feeling truly blessed, and very happy. I asked myself, "When will the whole world listen to such men and, free of bias, take to heart the love and great help which is so sincere and abundant?"

49

HASIDIC JUDAISM

"Why are we going to the Hasidic Rabbi in Anaheim instead of the one in Los Angeles?" I asked my assistant, Chris Rodriguez.

"Rabbi Eliezrie is one of the main Hasidic spokesmen here in Southern California," she replied. "He's one of the chief public relations men for the Hasidics. I guess they're so often misunderstood." She grinned playfully, her dark eyes sparkling.

"It's a strange world," I thought aloud, "when people who go into ecstasy are misunderstood and need to appoint public spokesmen."

Rabbi David Eliezrie, Director of the Chabad Community Center in Anaheim, California, beckoned us into his office. A frank, straightforward, and very kindly man, he shook hands. He was medium height, with short, dark hair and dark brown eyes magnified by glasses. When he spoke, his voice was soft, gracious. He wore regular clothing—a shirt and pants—not the braids or hat I was expecting. I found him an intellectually rich man who thought very quickly. Later in our interview, when he placed a phone call to his beloved Rebbe who was giving a talk in New York, and he heard the Rebbe's voice, Rabbi Eliezrie revealed a sweet, beaming happiness.

However, let's begin at the beginning.

Rabbi Eliezrie explained that Hasidism is a dimension within traditional Judaism. "Really, you don't have to label Jews as different kinds of Jews. We see Jews as Jews. We see Jews who perhaps use different tools or different mediums within Judaism to grow spiritually." Hasidism is a medium which helps an individual "reach to a level of spiritual perfection, spiritual development," he explained. "You will not necessarily find that there is a card-carrying Hasidic Jew, but rather Hasidic philosophy helps an individual have a greater awareness of spirituality and godliness. We hope that this awareness will serve as a catalyst for a greater sense of observance and commitment.

"I mean there's a lot more to it," he said. "This is a simplistic introduction. There are some Hasidic groups which are more emotional, focusing more on emotional aspects, like Belz or Ger. The emotional forms are found in Hasidic groups that evolved in Poland.

"*Chabad* or *Lubavitch*, which are really two interchangeable words, is a much more intellectual approach. It evolved in Lithuania, which was the center of Jewish intellectualism and scholarship two hundred years ago. The works of the great rabbis of Chabad are considered to be classics of Jewish philosophy and theology. These classics are studied in many universities and almost every center of academic studies, as well as Biblical studies. You'll find the works of Chabad philosophy studied by a significant constituency. There are many people who, while they are not Hasidim, find they're interested in Hasidic philosophy.

"Now, our Chabad focus is basically on developing an intellectual awareness and understanding of spirituality," Rabbi Eliezrie clarified. "Then, through that awareness we develop a sensitivity to godliness which affects our day-to-day living." He explained that the Jew observes six hundred and thirteen commandments and is obligated to fulfill his role in sharing basic values of belief in God and morality with all of society.

While many people enjoy the study of Jewish philosophy, "to study the philosophy without doing anything about it doesn't bring the philosophy to its purpose," he underscored. "We see the six hundred and thirteen commandments as a manifestation of God's will in the physical world. And the *Torah*, the body of knowledge which tells us how to do the commandments, is a manifestation in this world of God's intellect. We unify ourselves with that intellectually through the study of his Torah and, more spiritually, through the fulfillment of his commandments—*mitzvahs*—by doing these actual deeds."

"Mitzvahs are . . . ?" I questioned.

"Mitzvah means commandment, but philosophically it means the bond of unification, a connection between man and God. The relationship is like six hundred and thirteen pieces of twine that all tie together into one rope. Each one of these little thin strands represents one piece of twine and they all link together and become one. So, this is what binds us, connects us, with God—the six hundred thirteen commandments.

"So, in Chabad," he went on, "we focus on spirituality, and on intellectual awareness of God, according to man's ability. But, human intellect being limited and God being infinite, we can only understand things within a finite context. We can't understand what the essence of God is. We know what he does, but do not know how he does it. So, the goal of Hasidism is to help people—Jewish people particularly—to realize their spiritual potential," he summed up.

"How do you help them realize this?" I asked.

"Well, the key, we believe, is study—study of Hasidic philosophy—which talks at great lengths about spirituality and godliness.

"In Chabad, the key which opens the door is prayer. The key which Rabbi Schneur Zalman developed was a system called *Hit Bononut*, which means contemplation. We study a work of Hasidic philosophy that deals with spirituality and godliness. Then, before you sit and pray, you contemplate a particular idea from Hasidic philosophy. After you contemplate, you pray and the emotion flows within the structure of the prayer," he explained.

Rabbi Eliezrie clarified that all the ideas of Hasidic thought are not new ideas to Judaism, but rather that the Hasidim—those who practice Hasidic Judaism—reemphasized ideas that often existed already within Jewish philosophy. The Hasidim developed a number of these ideas, revealing them more to the average public. The concepts, ideas, and philosophies of the Hasidim have existed throughout the Jewish mystical tradition. However, what the Hasidim did was to popularize these ideas and make them more widely known because there was a spiritual need in the Jewish religion.

"There's a story told about a *Hasid* (a Hasid means a follower of a Rabbi, mentor, or spiritual leader who is commonly called a *Rebbe*) who went to his Rebbe prior to Bar Mitzvah at thirteen. He asked the Rebbe to give him spiritual direction. The Rebbe told the young boy that every time he made a blessing—before he ate, or whatever—he was to think to whom he was making the blessing. That was in the

1840's or 50's. Some seventy, eighty years later, people who traveled the many miles to meet this man who had become so spiritually great would ask him, 'What made you so spiritually sensitive?' The holy man would reply, 'I listened to the words of the Rebbe when he told me as a child that whenever I make a blessing to God I should think who I am making that blessing to,'" Rabbi Eliezrie smiled.

"When a Hasid directs the emotion in the prayer, what happens then?" I asked.

"Then a person reaches a certain level of spiritual ecstasy and opens himself up spiritually. He has thought about godliness; he has thought about spirituality; he has thought about the things that God accomplished in the world; then he focuses his prayer on the greatness of God, the spirituality of God. Then he comes out of the prayer with a tremendous feeling of upliftedness," the Rabbi explained.

"Could you give me some examples of states or characteristics which occur in this ecstasy and upliftedness?"

"Characteristics . . . ." He thought a moment. "I think, mainly, there is an *awe-ness* of God. I think it is a realization by a person of what is important and what is secondary. You look around the world . . ." he reached for words.

"You are saying there is tremendous insight? Would that be fair?"

He tried to explain. "I'll take it a step further. You look at the world around us and you see the physical. Judaism tells us—and in Hasidic philosophy we emphasize the idea—that the physical is only an extension of the spiritual. The story is told about one of the great Hasidic masters in the last days he was alive. He said, 'I don't see the physical wall. I can only see the spirituality in the wall.'

"Another story is told about Rabbi Schneur Zalman of Liadi. He was sitting and praying and he was saying, 'I don't want this, I don't want that, all I want is God himself.'

"You develop a proper sense of priorities. You realize what is primary, what is important and what is not important. You have the realization that the essence of this world is really spiritual and that the physical only hides the true qualities of the world."

"What conclusions, then, does one have about oneself?" I asked.

"That we have to work a little harder with ourselves. For Hasidim, there's a tremendous emphasis on self-analysis—what we've done till now, what we need to accomplish, what we need to rectify. There's always this theme that you can accomplish more. You've got to challenge yourself. You've got to motivate yourself. A person can't be docile. He has to be moving in some spiritual direction constantly," he said.

"What conclusion does one gain about one's relationship with God?" I inquired, while thinking his answer would be fascinating.

"A much greater sensitivity and awareness," he said, "and the realization that spirituality and godliness is the most important thing of all—that everything else doesn't really count that much."

"What conclusion does one have about the nature of God?" I continued quietly.

The rabbi seemed absorbed in reflection. "That God manifests himself in everything in the world. You see that the world, in essence, extends from godliness and spirituality. That the world in itself is not a true existence because it's really dependent totally on God and God constantly interacts with the world physically. God *makes* the world exist. There is this link between the physical world and spirit."

"What does one conclude about the point of life, or the meaning of life?" I pressed.

"The purpose of man's existence in the world is to serve God," he spoke slowly, emphasizing each word.

"And, what is the nature of one's service? For example, how does one characterize oneself as a result of this experience?"

"Well, first is the question of how you know what to do. I mean, some guy can come around and say, 'Hey! I'm serving God,' when he is, in fact, being very destructive and definitely not serving God at all. We tell a story about a man who's about to rob a house. He's sitting outside the house and says, 'God, please help me pull off this robbery!'" The Rabbi laughed. My assistant and I joined him.

"Is that serving God?" Rabbi Eliezrie asked. "So, the first question is how do we know what is service of God? We must have a certain level of intellectual and spiritual humility because to find the answer to that question we look into the Torah. When we believe that God gave the Torah to the Jewish people on Mount Sinai and that the Torah gives a direction, a mission, to the Jews to fulfill the six hundred thirteen mitzvahs, we seek to do the will of the Lord as expressed to us through the Torah." His penetrating eyes met mine. "By the way, God gave a mission to the non-Jews to fulfill seven commandments which are really inclusive of many more of the six hundred and thirteen commandments."

"Would you be willing to say what those seven commandments are?" I asked.

"We call these the seven commandments of Noah—meaning

commandments for the whole of society. Some religions believe that the only way you're going to be saved is to believe what they believe. We don't. Judaism believes in different religions. In other words, we have different approaches to God throughout the world, and the fact that Judaism is valid does not invalidate somebody else's approach. However, we believe the non-Jew has an obligation to keep these seven different mitzvahs and that he, the non-Jew, will have a portion of the world to come if he does these things."*

"You speak of the world to come. Please tell me what are the qualities, or characteristics, of the world to come?" I asked.

"I haven't been there yet!" he laughed.

I leaned forward, "Perhaps I should say that yogis, mystics, and most religious people speak of experiences of a higher world or a superconscious state. I'm particularly interested in knowing what are these levels or planes of consciousness that the Hasidic Jew experiences from his contemplation and prayer? For example, in the yogi's state of *samadhi*, the meditator suddenly catches a glimpse of a transcendent reality and beholds what he is meditating upon in its full light. Other meditators are, through God's grace, able to adore God so much that they become absorbed in that divine reality, forgetting ego, forgetting their personal past experience. Suddenly they experience this transformed state due to their absorption."

He nodded. "There are certain stages you can rise to. However, there's another important thing: your feet have to be on the floor. There is a critical place where you have to bring spirituality and godliness into the physical world," the Rabbi replied. "So, there are certain states that a person can rise to, states of closer bonding with God. We don't so much give these states titles. There's a status of bonding and cleaving, each person according to their level, according to their experience," he said.

"You use the word 'levels.' Are you willing to tell me the characteristics of these levels?"

He nodded. "I think *levels* is a critical word because we find the term throughout Jewish mysticism. The word in Hebrew is called *madrigot* which in English is levels, and the person rises from level to level."

---

* According to the *Torah*, Chapter 2, verse 16, the Rabbis established six basic laws: Man may not worship idols; he may not blaspheme God; he must establish courts of justice; he may not kill; he may not commit adultery; he may not rob. And the seventh law was added after the flood—that man may not eat the flesh cut from living animals.

"Could you tell me what they are?"

"Well, there happen to be four different spiritual worlds. We view our world as the lowest level, or the fourth world. This is called the world of *Asiyah*, the world of action. The highest world is the world of *Atzilut*, where there is no sense of self-identity, where everything is 'bonded to God spiritually,'" he said.

"Can one be in God while on this planet earth?" I asked.

"Yes, by observing his commandments as articulated in the Torah. The Baal Shem Tov, founder of Hasidism (also, Chassidism or Hassidism), writes that he rose to the spiritual worlds. He had an out-of-the-body experience and he writes about the levels, how he went up to the palace of the Messiah and asked the Messiah when he's going to come to the earth. Baal Shem Tov wrote these letters to his brother-in-law and we have the original manuscripts—they've been published," he said.

"Well, please tell me, when did Baal Shem Tov say the Messiah is going to come?" I asked.

"We hope soon," he said. "Jews believe the Messiah is to come by the year 6000. We're at the year 5749, according to the Jewish calendar. One of the critical components of Jewish theology is the belief that the Messiah will come anytime. He could come today."

Then he added, "There was a great Rabbi in the last generation called Chofetz Chaim. He used to pack his bags every Saturday night and wait for the Messiah.

"The idea is that God created us," Rabbi Eliezrie continued. "We are, in a sense, like children of the Lord, but there's a tremendous bonding between God and mankind because each person possesses a certain element of God, a soul. A human being basically has two components—the physical and the spiritual. Death is the separation of body and soul. After death, even if you repair the body, it will not come to life, because it lacks the soul. The *soul* is the essence of the individual."

"Is that soul the presence of God in the person?" I asked.

"Yes," the Rabbi responded.

"It is God's presence in us?" I asked.

"It's called *neshama*—a piece of God which actually exists within man," he explained.

"Will you tell me something more about the soul?" I requested. "What are the attributes of the individual soul—as different from the infinite Lord?"

"There are ten basic attributes of the soul—three intellectual ones and seven emotional ones.* God, as an essence, is not limited at all. We can't say God is finite or infinite because then we are trying to limit him.

"The only way we can talk about God accurately is to say he's not just finite, he's not just infinite, and he's not just this or that because the minute we label him into something, we're limiting him," Rabbi Eliezrie explained.

Fascinated by the classification of different worlds and the ten basic attributes of a human soul, I asked, "How does a Hasid become fulfilled?"

"The question is how does a *Jew* become fulfilled. Hasidism is only a tool. A Jew becomes fulfilled by observing God's commandments," he underscored.

"So, in fulfilling God's commandments, what happens?" I asked.

"Then you raise your spiritual state and, more importantly, the spiritual state of the world," he said quietly.

"How does that work? When your spiritual state goes up, how does the spiritual state of the world also go up?"

"When you do a mitzvah, when you do God's command, you bring holiness into the world. For example, if you take food and eat it, the strength and energy you get from eating a piece of meat, for instance, gives you energy for a higher purpose. You have elevated that meat to a higher level of existence. There are four levels of existence—there are dormant things, growing things, living things, and human beings. So, each level is dependent on the level below it for its existence. The fourth level is mankind. We call mankind the communicator," he added.

I felt my mind reaching, "Would you tell me more about how the world is changed by doing acts of . . . ."

"You're bringing spirituality into the world," the Rabbi explained. "There's holiness in everything, and the question is how do you bring it to revelation. By doing a mitzvah, you reveal the holiness in each thing."

---

* The three intellectual attributes are: a) divine willingness—*Keter*; b) wisdom—*Chochmah*; and c) understanding—*Binah*. The emotional aspects are: a) benevolence and kindness—*Chesed*; b) might and power—*Gevurah*; c) beauty—*Tiferet*; d) endurance and victory—*Netzach*; e) splendor and majesty—*Hod*; f) foundation —*Yesod* and; g) sovereignty—*Malchut*. These ten attributes are called the *sefirot*, or ten *spheres* according to *Tanya*, by Rabbi Schneur Zalman, published by Kehot Publication Society, Brooklyn, New York, Chapter 3, pages 896-911.

"So, you're saying there is great hope for the world," I suggested.

"There's definitely hope for the world. The essence of the world is good and holy. The problem is it's all covered up," he said.

"How does a Hasidic Jew view this regular world of activity?"

"A world that you have to live in," Rabbi Eliezrie responded. "This is the world of purpose and creation. At the same time, you have to be like oil in water. You have to be in the world but you have to retain your specialness."

"And the obligation is to follow the commandments, the six hundred and thirteen commandments?" I asked.

"The six hundred and thirteen commandments. Again, it's not specifically a responsibility of the Hasidic Jew, it's for every Jew."

"And a Hasidic Jew has, perhaps, the emotional approach, or perhaps the intellectual approach, through his or her particular Rebbe?" I continued.

"Through a particular Rebbe, or an approach within a particular Hasidic movement," he explained. "You see, these different names for the different movements were usually names of towns where the different Hasidic Rebbes lived in Europe."

"Now that we've covered the goal of Hasidic Judaism, how do you live in permanent spiritual realization? Since your path and the path of Chabad is that of intellectual realization, how do you do it successfully? Do you simply strive to be mindful of God at all times, or . . . ?" I struggled to formulate my question.

"That's critical," he responded. "In all your ways you should know God. In everything you do, you should come to a recognition of spirituality. Everything you do has a purpose and we have to bring out that purpose constantly."

"When you encourage people to do this, how do you tell them to do it? Don't they say, 'Rabbi, I try, but I fail?'"

"You're supposed to try and fail. That's the essence of what being a human being is all about—it's trying and failing, as well as succeeding," he answered.

"What if someone comes to you and says, 'Rabbi, I'm discouraged. I don't know what to do next. I don't seem to be able to progress.'"

"That's why we have a Rebbe," Rabbi Eliezrie seemed to sympathize. "Our Rebbe gives us a little bit of warmth and vitality and energy and he helps us go forward. People right this minute, in Israel, in Australia, can listen to him. He is speaking right now in New York to about three to five thousand Jewish children. He speaks in Yiddish usually. People can listen to him on the radio, on cable television, and even phone and listen to his discourses. The Rebbe speaks and teaches and gives the Hasid guidance, strength and support. Right now, for the holidays, I know that there will be seven to eight thousand people traveling from all over the world to New York to be near the Rebbe. While he speaks in Yiddish, it's translated into English and many other languages and broadcast over the whole world."

"You raise a very interesting point. This Rebbe who is being listened to throughout the world is obviously not considered an ordinary man or merely a teacher. There must be some kind of spiritual grace or blessing upon him and upon his sharing, must there not?" I asked.

"Judaism believes, from the very dawn of Jewish history, that there are in every generation certain individuals who are called *tzadikim*, which means people with unusual spiritual qualities. All throughout history every generation has such people and these tzadikim are of special spiritual caliber and have unusual qualities of leadership. Hasidism only reemphasizes the idea to a certain degree but you will see this throughout Jewish history. Nowadays you hear a Rebbe on cable TV. Two thousand years ago, you had to travel to the great centers of Jewish learning in Babylonia; but it's basically the same thing."

"Would the Rebbe be called a saint?" I asked.

"We don't use that word. It's a Christian concept. Rather than saint, I would use the term *tzadik*, a person who uses all his potential and all his abilities for spirituality and godliness," he concluded.

"Does God's love and grace pour out through the Rebbe? There is a concept in yoga of *darshan*, which is that God's love and grace shines out through such a person and that God uses that person to bless others," I offered.

"Every person can give another a blessing," he smiled. "Tzadik is on a high spiritual level and therefore his blessing has the potential for greater impact."

"How does one who goes before the Rebbe humble himself appropriately? What does one do to be in that state of humility and service?" I asked.

"A Hasid who goes to the Rebbe prepares himself spiritually for that meeting. I travel to New York often. I know myself that the Rebbe gives one that extra motivation," Rabbi Eliezrie spoke happily. "In Chabad philosophy, the bond which is important is the intellectual bond between the Hasid and his or her Rebbe through the Rebbe's teaching of Torah."

"It would seem, then, from what you've said, that *intellectual* also means something like revelation."

"Yes, one hundred percent," he exclaimed. "A lot of what the Rebbe teaches is knowledge of great, spiritual, mystical character."

"Then I'd better clarify. We've talked about this intellectual path of Hasidism. I've been assuming that this intellectual path, or direction, is one of the mind, but I believe now that you're not saying that at all. You're saying that your intellectual path is of the mental faculty in addition to an intuitive or revelatory faculty. Please help us understand: what do you mean by intellectual?" I asked.

"The key to developing spirituality is by understanding as much as we can. The word 'Chabad' means wisdom, understanding and knowledge—which is the intellectual process."

"Understanding as much as you can seems to be some kind of superconscious activity rather than the employment of regular consciousness," I thought aloud. "Correct?"

"No, superconsciousness is at a later stage," he explained. "Every one of us can understand according to our ability."

"Are you saying it's your first duty, in a way, to *understand* according to your abilities?" I asked.

"Yes, that's true. We can't expect the same from a simple, non-intellectual person which we can expect from a great intellect, but each can use the same basic process to elevate himself."

"That's wonderful," I felt moved to comment. "So, everyone has a duty to understand according to his or her abilities. Then, obviously something happens. What happens?"

"What happens is you reach a state of awe, of spirituality and godliness. That's what it comes to," he said.

"Rabbi Stern, who suggested I interview an Hasidic Rabbi, thought I might like to ask you about the theological concept of *Shekinah*."

"Yes?" Rabbi Eliezrie waited for my question.

"My dictionary says Shekinah is: 'the manifestation of the presence of God; or Divine Presence.'* Would you agree with this definition?"

"Yes," he agreed, "basically, Shekinah is the manifestation in the physical world of the Divine Presence."

* From *Webster's New World Dictionary*, Second College Edition, page 1311.

"If I were to come into your place of worship, would I see a physical object? Is Shekinah a physical object?"

"There were times when Shekinah was physically present in the world," the Rabbi spoke thoughtfully. "When the temple was in existence. And, today, when people get together and study the Torah, Shekinah is present. Shekinah can be brought about when the temple is here or when ten or more Jews get together and study the Torah. Or, when people are together in a holy act. When people fulfill a mitzvah, Shekinah can be present."

"What I'm trying to understand," I explained, "is does Shekinah have any *form* whatever?"

"No form. It's a holy, spiritual force."

I was striving to understand man's relationship to the Shekinah and how it is experienced and what it does, as Rabbi Stern had suggested to me during our interview.

"When ten people are together studying the Torah, do they ask Shekinah to come?"

"It's automatically there," Rabbi Eliezrie responded.

"What is that like," I asked, "when you study the Torah and Shekinah comes?"

"There are times when people feel in themselves a spiritual sensitivity and holiness—Shekinah is the Presence of God," he answered.

"Are we looking forward to a time when all will be living in the Presence of God?" This thought seemed only logical to me.

"That will happen when the Messiah comes. When the Messiah comes, the spiritual becomes revealed in the physical. Then we will see the Presence of God within every physical object," the Rabbi spoke with conviction.

"And, what does the word 'Shekinah' derive from?" I asked him.

"Residing, to reside. Shekinah is God residing together with his people."

"This Presence, when people are sitting together reading the Torah or doing a holy act, does the Presence occur *within* them, or does everyone in the room feel it?"

"That depends," he said. "It depends on their sensitivity. For instance, you can be willing to give somebody something but they may not be able to accept it. God is present but not all may be sensitive enough to feel the Divine Presence."

"How, then, can one become sensitive to Shekinah?"

"You become sensitive through learning, praying, and going

through a period of spiritual development. Spiritual development in our religion primarily relates to prayer," he said.

The thought of all men consciously coming into the Presence of God thrilled me. Why can't all of us pray together one day or do a mitzvah and see what happens, I thought silently.

"Before I reluctantly conclude this fascinating interview, can you tell me what you mean when you say 'give a blessing'? I often hear Jewish people speak of giving a blessing and it would be wonderful to conclude this chapter with a blessing. How do you give a blessing, please?"

"You say, 'I bless you.'"

I waited for the Rabbi to say more. He merely smiled back at me.

"Well," I urged him, "what are the dynamics? How does this work?"

"I say, 'I'm giving you a blessing.' This is an action and it represents a flow of spirituality and energy into the world."

"So a blessing is a flow of spirituality into the world?" I tried to get him to explain more.

"Yes."

"So, you just say, 'I bless you,' and energy is generated because of the power of God and because of your intellectual and emotional attunement with God?"

"We believe that, in general, every individual can give another individual a blessing." Rabbi Eliezrie gave us his hand in farewell.

Oh, I thought, when will the great day dawn when people throughout the world attune with God and continually, appreciatively, give one another blessings?

50

RELIGIOUS SCIENCE—
A METAPHYSICAL CHURCH

Metaphysicians are particularly interested in higher consciousness. They attune with it every day. Many metaphysicians have devotedly abided in higher consciousness for years and decades. Religious Science, Unity, and Christian Science are the leading metaphysical churches in the world, but there are a number of smaller groups also. While there are several differences of attitude or philosophy, all such groups of believers focus on the nature of being and essential reality.

Metaphysics is defined by *Webster's New World Dictionary* as: "The branch of philosophy that deals with first principles and seeks to explain the nature of being or reality (ontology) and of the origin and structure of the world (cosmology); it is closely associated with the study of the nature of knowledge (epistemology)."

One of the world's leading teachers and ministers of metaphysics is Reverend William H. D. Hornaday of Founder's Church of Religious Science in Los Angeles, California. Affectionately known as "Dr. Bill" to his congregation of over 7,000, Reverend Hornaday recently celebrated his thirty-ninth year as a minister of Religious

Science. In fact, both the City of Los Angeles and the State of California proclaimed a "Dr. Bill Hornaday Day" in honor of his thirty-fifth anniversary.

A former business executive, Dr. Hornaday earned his Doctor of Divinity in 1952 and studied under such prominent people as Carl Jung, Albert Schweitzer, Karl Barth, and Rheinhold Neibuhr.

He has been active in numerous humanitarian projects, from drug and alcohol rehabilitation programs to world seminars on healing. He has served on Presidential Commissions under Presidents Eisenhower, Kennedy, and Johnson. He is the recipient of numerous awards and honors, including an honorary doctorate from his alma mater, Whittier College. Additionally, he holds memberships in many charitable and philanthropic organizations.

Dr. Hornaday has made numerous television appearances, and his daily inspirational radio program, "This Thing Called Life," has aired for over thirty years in Southern California, as well as around the world via the Armed Forces Radio Service.

A teacher and author, his books include *My Prayer For You, Today*; *Life Everlasting*; *Success Unlimited*; *Help For Today*; and *Your Aladdin's Lamp* (with Harlan Ware).

Reverend Hornaday, and his assistant minister, Reverend George Marks, first greeted my assistant and me in his office at Founder's Church of Religious Science on a sunny, smog-free day in Los Angeles.

"Dr. Bill" is a kindly man with bright blue eyes that look deep into people yet do not burn. He is soft-spoken and has a very rich, beautiful voice. Of medium height, he wore a gray suit with a striped tie. His hair is silver and wavy.

Reverend Marks, a young man, sat with Chris and me as he and Reverend Hornaday turned their attention to my questions. I asked about Reverend Hornaday's background and how he found himself in Religious Science.

"My background is varied," he answered. "I come from five generations of Methodist ministers, and for a while I served as a lay minister for my father. I was interested in children while I was in college. I was fascinated by nature as well, and so I created the first ant villages for the children to study.

"I often wondered where the great studies went wrong, how children suffered, even then, from a lack of communication with their parents. So I created various educational toys and marketed them along with the ant villages throughout the United States, from Macy's in New York to Bullock's here in Los Angeles. These toys were very successful, but still I felt that something was missing in my life. I picked up my search for something more."

"What a fascinating beginning," I said.

"I'm a musician, too, and I paid my way through college by playing the marimba. I played with some of the famous bands of the time."

Reverend Hornaday left a successful business career to express his creativeness and sensitivity by writing for the motion picture industry. His script writing led him to meet his future wife, Louise Wright, a journalism graduate from Scripps College.

"Louise has a wonderful mother who has lived with us most of our married life. She's in a convalescent home now. She is over ninety years of age."

That's a unique mother-in-law story, I thought.

"She's a wonderful woman, and I've always enjoyed her. She was one of the early students of Dr. Ernest Holmes, the founder of the movement of Religious Science and author of *The Science of Mind*. It was through my mother-in-law that I found my way into metaphysics and Religious Science.

"She kept saying, 'You must hear this man, Ernest Holmes. You must!' Finally, I said, 'If I go once, will you lay off?'" Reverend Hornaday laughed.

"Of course, I did go to hear Ernest Holmes. He was small in stature, but large in understanding and wisdom. Speaking of the higher consciousness, Ernest said, 'There's a power greater than you, and you can use it.' Because of my childhood indoctrination in the belief of an anthropomorphic God, I reacted strongly against certain things he said, such as 'All of us are of God, we are within God. Therefore, today we are speaking about the God in you.'

"He said other things that troubled me. He said within this higher consciousness, I could find supply and help. He said that these things have already been given to us because of the higher consciousness, but we must learn to accept them.

"Yet, with all my intellectual arguing, something in me was touched by what he said, and I wanted to know more. My mother-in-law arranged an appointment for me, and I remember that one of the first questions Ernest asked me was, 'Are you a happy person?'

"I said yes. Dr. Holmes replied, 'Your face doesn't show it; I don't have that feeling about you.'

"I took that the wrong way, and began defending myself: 'I'm secure. I have a three-story English home. My wife has a Buick convertible and I have a Cadillac. Of course I am happy.'

"Dr. Holmes finally showed me that in many ways I wasn't happy, and I certainly wasn't free. I was making large payments for material things I thought I enjoyed, but I lacked spiritual understanding which brings peace of mind. As I left his office, he presented me with *The Science of Mind* textbook and said, 'I know this will help you.'

"It was then I enrolled in the courses of the Science of Mind and continued to read everything that was suggested by Ernest Holmes, or by the teachers of the various classes. By the time I completed the basic courses, I knew I had found that for which I had been searching and I enrolled in the advanced courses which would lead to the ministry.

"During this period, Ernest called me to his office and said, 'I need you. I've been looking for someone to take over my radio program, *This Thing Called Life*. You have the enthusiasm, and a wonderful voice. Will you do it?'

"This was to have been my project for the duration of my studies, but it became an integral part of our outreach program. When the broadcasts began in 1927, Dr. Holmes insisted that no requests for contributions be made over the air. To this day, that request has been upheld and all funding has come from grateful listeners and members of Religious Science."

"What is Religious Science?" I asked Reverend Hornaday.

"I feel it is a correlation of philosophy, religion, and science. Religious Science is based upon the reality that each of us is a divine idea in the mind of God. There has never been a duplication of fingerprints, footprints, lip prints, nor of voice prints. This tells me that I must be unique, special. We feel that each of us has a divine compass, a divine perfection within us. We can seek to uncover that divine perfection by understanding and by using that infinite wisdom which is available to each of us. But love is essential as well. It is often said in Religious Science that Love points the way, and the Law makes the way possible.

"Religious Science is Christian, and more, because we study and revere the teachings of the masters of all ages, the truths of all religions.

"In Religious Science we say that the Spirit is that aspect of God which is the knower; that is, which contemplates. The Soul is the aspect of God which is the doer, or the law by which God's contemplation becomes form. Since each one of us is an individualization of these two aspects of God, we have the ability to create our own world by our own thinking. Unfortunately, this power goes unrecognized by most people."

"So the Religious Science member strives to be conscious of that which goes unrecognized by most people, the soul and the spirit?" I asked him.

"Yes, not only to recognize it, but to learn how to use the power of our mind to bring into our environment that which is the highest good for all. For example, our whole membership believes that we could, through a higher consciousness, bring peace not only to ourselves but to the world. Our work is in self-awareness—how to be truly honest, how to know the truth that sets you free, and how to enter into an awareness of a power working through you.

"And, as you know, we do not believe in a duality."

"Could you explain that, please?"

"In Religious Science we believe there is one God, one Reality. There is one law of life. We either abuse that law or we use it.

"Many people focus their attention on people, making personal gods of some and hating others; some focus their attention on material things, directing their energies to the possession of these things; some focus upon the accumulation of wealth and power to maintain a sense of security. In essence, they are making false gods of these, and by doing so, they have lost the true values of living."

"So, while you do not believe in duality, you recognize that some people do," I observed.

"Of course we do. All of us, at one time or another, unknowingly or knowingly, have had devilish ideas, but we believe this is the abuse of the one law."

"I see."

Dr. Hornaday went on, "In our work with people, and especially those in this church, we remind them of Jesus' words: 'Choose ye therefore, God or mammon.' Or the words of Moses: 'Choose ye therefore blessing or cursing,' and tell them they don't have to remain in any set of undesirable or uncomfortable circumstances. You can really be who and what you want to be if you recognize that God has given you the power of choice. But it is your responsibility to choose wisely."

"And this telling people who they can really be, this is your approach to dealing with duality?" I suggested.

"That's right," he agreed.

"You tell people who they really are, the eventuality of what is really their nature?"

"Yes, but it is more than telling them. We help them to recognize their oneness with God."

"How do you do that, for example? How is that done?" I asked.

"Our teaching is based on what we call *treatment*, or *affirmative prayer*. A treatment consists of five steps which clears the thought of negation, of doubt and fear, and causes it to perceive the ever-presence of God. These five steps are called *recognition, unification, realization, thanksgiving,* and *release*.

"First, we recognize the Infinite Spirit—God—as Goodness, a loving presence, a divine power, always available.

"The next step is unification. What are you unified with? This is a real study. It may take weeks, months. Dr. Holmes has stated that unification is based upon the principle as Jesus taught, 'that they may all be one, even as thou, Father, art in me and I in thee and they also in us.' This is the consciousness of God in man. There is no record of any great thinker who has ever taught duality. The teaching of unity, 'The Lord our God is one God,' is the chief cornerstone of the sacred scriptures of the East, as well as our own sacred writings. The word 'unity' signifies the union of parts drawn together into one perfect whole: one Life, of which we are a part; one Intelligence, of which we are a part; one Substance, which is brought into manifold manifestation."

Reverend George Marks opened a pamphlet called *Guide to Creative Thinking* by S. Howell Creed, which had been taken from the August, 1965 edition of the "Science of Mind Magazine." Reverend Marks said, "To quote from the Creed pamphlet, the third step, realization, 'is the step in which you realize how you feel and how things are as you receive that for which you are treating. In other words, you visualize and feel the experiences as though they were actually happening right now. This is the goal of the Realization step in treatment: To build the strongest possible feeling of already having what you want.'"

He continued to quote from the article. "The fourth step is thanksgiving. 'You know that the omnipotent Spirit is already creating what you have treated for. You are happy and excited and grateful. You say, "Thank you, God." You have a *thankful* heart and you show it.'"

Reverend Hornaday interjected joyously, "It was my privilege to meet Mahatma Gandhi, in India. When he was asked to define his philosophy, he used one word, 'Gratitude.'"

"Gratitude," I repeated, surprised, wondering why Gandhi had not said *ahimsa* (harmlessness) or *Satyagraha* (grasping for truth). Then I realized he had used a simple English word which conveys much.

Reverend Hornaday went on, "The fifth step of a Religious Science treatment, or meditative prayer, is the release. You release (the treatment) to the infinite power and intelligence of God's Law for demonstration. The law of mind is automatic in its action and will produce precisely what has been accepted in the treatment.

"When I first went to Ernest Holmes, I expected a prayer or treatment before I left his office, but he was silent for about five minutes. Afterward, he shook my hand, and I left.

"I told his secretary, 'Dr. Holmes was going to have a treatment with me, but he didn't say a word.' She smiled and said, 'That's right.' I discovered that Ernest Holmes rarely gave an audible treatment directly for another person. We are lucky to have a few treatments on cassettes which were given during lectures.

"But I did feel something."

"And what did you feel?" I asked curiously. "The spirit of God move, or . . . ?"

"I came back later and asked Ernest what I'd felt," Reverend Hornaday chuckled. "Ernest told me, 'You've had certain negative experiences which are in your subconscious mind. The conscious mind may change these thought patterns and thereby cause a different flow of energy and intelligence toward the object of its desire. In mental treatment we should feel as though the whole power of the universe were running through the words we speak, whether we speak them for ourselves or for another. By your acceptance, you have a feeling of renewal—a renewal that changes you.'"

"What is the goal of Religious Science?" I continued.

"Peace," Dr. Bill kindly responded.

"And by peace you mean . . . ."

"Peace of mind within the individual. Unless I have peace within myself, how can I share it, how can I promote it worldwide? How can I express my peace with others unless I have experienced love within myself and love of God? It must come from within before it can be shared with others."

I thought about what he said and then asked, "How does a Religious Scientist become—whatever the right word would be—realized, fulfilled, or awakened? What is the process?"

"People of all faiths believe in a power greater than we are, but they do not understand the power. Our hope, then, is to bring *understanding*," he smiled. "Call it awakening, if you wish."

"You wish, then, to bring greater understanding and awakening to people of all faiths? Greater understanding regarding . . . the oneness?"

"First of all, through our example, through our teaching, we are resolvers of hate. We are not disturbers. Love is something wonderful. The love of a person reaches out, little by little. Years ago, I spoke at many universities in Central America. My wife, who speaks fluent Spanish, acted as interpreter.

"Through love, these students were reached. They would keep us for hours afterwards, asking questions, being close to us. Here in Southern California," he further illustrated, "ministers and priests of other denominations have studied with us, and have recommended our classwork to others. Love reaches out."

"How wonderful." I was moved by his intensity and sincerity. "Now, let me rephrase this to see if I understand clearly. The goal of Religious Science is peace—within and without."

"That is right," Reverend Hornaday nodded.

"And a Religious Scientist becomes fulfilled by finding within himself or herself this love, this understanding, and is not fulfilled until the love and understanding are shared with humanity," I summarized.

"We call that 'the Presence.' We feel the Presence," he explained.

"So," I clarified, "you become awakened by feeling the Presence, which is one of love, and this love is to be fulfilled through each Religious Scientist by sharing and helping other people? Is this right?"

"Yes, and we feel, as I said, everyone is unique. There is a reason for each person's being. I tell those who come to me, 'Go ye and find it. There is a reason for you, a reason for your being.'"

"So the reason for one person's being would also be found in that person's career and in that person's activities?" I asked.

"Yes. That inner calling to become a musician, a nurse."

"And each person is working through love and understanding, universal love and understanding," I said.

"Universal love."

"So this is how one becomes awakened. Please tell me, what is the process by which this awakening happens?"

"Again, we use treatment, or affirmative prayer. We seek to know that our lives are being divinely guided toward our highest and best good. When we have an inner feeling that this is happening, it is reflected on the outside by our actions toward others. This starts a chain reaction. If I share my joy with someone, they too are uplifted. I can treat for others, too, so that they will come to recognize God." His smile shone on us.

"And by 'treat' you mean going through a process of identifying with the truth . . . ."

"Yes, truth and love," he replied. "Also, we know that as long as we keep our eyes focused upon a problem, it compounds itself. I, or the one treating, must see the answer, not the problem. We must see peace. We must see hands outstretched to nations across the seas. I must come like Thoreau into Walden Pond. People call us idealists."

"They certainly would, and without question," I heartily agreed.

"But idealists build the lighthouses, don't they? In other words, idealists are the visionaries who provide the light for others to follow. I feel that we, as Religious Scientists, as metaphysicians, combine idealism and realism to become a beacon individually. For instance, as an example, a couple who were members of Founder's were having some problems with their children. They lived in a lower-income neighborhood so we went there with gifts. I said to the family, 'Let's think of something you can do together.' I asked the children, 'What would make you happy?' There were all kinds of suggestions. One wanted to go to the beach, another wanted more time with Daddy. The wife said, 'If only we could find a nicer home, ours is shabby. The landlord won't paint this one and it needs painting badly.'

"Suddenly an idea came from out of nowhere, and I said, 'Wouldn't it be wonderful if you painted the house yourself, as a family project?'

"The wife said with resentment, 'The landlord should do it, and fix the fence, too.' I said, 'Let's bless the landlord, and not be resentful.' I asked the children, 'Wouldn't you like to help paint the house, and fix the fence?'

"'Oh, yes,' they said. They were very happy with the idea.

"So, they painted the house, fixed the fence, and their little home looked beautiful. The landlord was so pleased he lowered the rent for them. The little house stood out, and the others on the block suffered by comparison. The children helped the other neighbors paint their houses too and soon the entire neighborhood was pretty and neat as a pin. The children were no longer in trouble, for they had found a loving outlet for their energy. This simple story shows how idealism is coupled with the realism of action."

"Beautiful," I whispered.

At this point, Reverend Marks gave me a small book. "This book gives a background of Ernest Holmes, who founded Religious

Science. Our teaching came from Dr. Holmes' search to know what prayer is, how it works, and why it works for some and not others. He said there is *Something* greater that responds to the followers of many different paths."

"Based on his wanting to know what prayer is, that's how Religious Science began?" I was fascinated.

Reverend Marks explained, "Dr. Holmes boiled his findings down simply to say that the universe is a spiritual system of good only. Where the duality of good and evil comes into the situation is through man. The evil is created by man and when man doesn't perpetuate evil, *then it's not there.*"

I couldn't resist asking the age-old question, "Why does man perpetuate evil?"

Reverend Marks' eyes twinkled, "From ignorance and from misunderstanding about man's own true nature, man's misunderstanding about God, misunderstanding about the nature of the universe. Also, it is perpetuated from mankind not having the proper relationship with God, with self, and with others. This poor relationship results out of man's fear, ignorance, lack of love, and lack of understanding. So, as man comes to understand and becomes genuinely loving, then he won't do anything to harm another. To understand, we have to become god-like. And assuming that God is love, then all of our actions, our thoughts, our deeds, have to be loving and god-like, too. Therefore, if I'm loving, then I can't kill another. If I'm loving, then I can't hate, criticize, or condemn. We seek perfection in trying to measure up to our goals," he said.

"So, are you saying that as a Religious Scientist one first *conceives* of sin and then one *feels* this sin, or . . . ?" I sought to understand how sin came into the picture.

Dr. Hornaday, at this point, added: "Dr. Holmes always believed that a sin was a missing of the mark, which was the actual Anglo-Saxon meaning, used in archery when an arrow missed its target. Dr. Holmes stated, 'There is no sin, but there is a mistake; and there is no punishment, but a consequence.'"

"And these consequences are given from out of this one universal love, which guides and teaches us through our mistakes?" I questioned.

"Dr. Holmes said, 'God neither punishes nor rewards. Life is a blessing or a curse according to the use we make of it. We believe in a law that governs all things and all people. If we make mistakes, we suffer.'"

I nodded, then went on, "As one grows as a Religious Scientist and communes more deeply in the Presence, are there states, or levels of consciousness, that one ascends as one experiences God and loves more deeply?"

Reverend Hornaday replied, "We believe that each of us is ever evolving into newer and better states of consciousness. Ernest Holmes often used the chambered nautilus shell as an analogy of our spiritual evolution in ever-widening spirals."

"What is your view of people practicing other faiths?" I asked.

"We bless them. We believe there is only one God, but each person must follow his or her own pathway in their search for Truth. Dr. Holmes stated often that Religious Science was not the only way, but it was a good way."

I admired what he had said so simply and I realized, a little sadly, that our interview was coming to an end.

"Dr. Hornaday, you offered many wonderful aids to achieve greater world peace, but I'd like to ask you directly, how may we have a more peaceful world?"

He smiled. "We endeavor to follow the teachings of Jesus. We call him the 'Wayshower.' His whole message was one of love and respect. We believe that through our faith and by our actions others will join us as peacemakers. As we recognize the Christ-spirit within each person, on a one-to-one basis, our unconditional love is the spark that lights the pathway for peace.

"So, my vision is to go forth like this on a one-to-one basis. You're not going to do it through a television program or a radio program. I put my hand out, I put my arms around you. My world vision is that it is going to take all of us to do it. We can't just get into our little chapels and churches and say, 'All right, come. Take this course, or that course.' It's much greater than that. We've got to come out of our churches and find those who have that spark which will turn into a flame. It won't work for us only to say, 'We want peace if you want peace.' God doesn't like that. *On a one-to-one basis, going out to one another, we've got to find those with the spark that will turn into a flame.*"

I understood. What he had just said had been my chief motivation for writing this book.

51

VEDANTA

The Vedanta religion focuses on ultimate reality. Not only does it lead aspirants to transcendental consciousness—beyond normal sense and mental awareness—it leads beyond the transcendental into pure spirit—or absolute knowledge.

Many people think of the Vedanta religion as a form of Hinduism. Others consider Vedanta an intellectual kind of yoga.

I visited Swami Swahananda, the Director of the Vedanta Society of Southern California in Hollywood, who greeted us serenely in full-length orange robes and shawl. As he welcomed me and my assistant, spiritual light shone from his eyes and face. In fact, he literally glowed. In his sixties, he was a vigorous man with very short gray hair. Like many religious leaders, he spoke softly. "Come in, please."

Swami Swahananda came from East Bengal, which is now Bangladesh. He joined the Ramakrishna Order of the Vedanta Society in Calcutta in 1947. Swamiji, as he is called, was a lecturer at Belur Math on the Ganges River in Bengal. He wrote and edited an English magazine in South India, did further spiritual studies in Mysore, and then went to the Himalayas to practice spiritual austerities. After his austerities, he was made the head of the New Delhi Vedanta Center.

After six years serving at the major New Delhi center, he was transferred to San Francisco in 1968. After two years in San Francisco, and then six years in Berkeley, he came to Southern California when the eminent spiritual leader and author, Swami Prabhavananda, passed away. Swami Swahananda became the head of the Vedanta Society of Southern California in 1976.

"Swamiji, what is Vedanta, please?" I began.

He answered in his soft, firm voice, "Vedanta is the essential philosophy original to the Hindus, but we claim it is the essential philosophy of all religions. The major ideas of Vedanta are, first, the ultimate existence. We hold that all the things we see around us are ultimately reducible to one substance. Normally, in every philosophical system, there will be three main questions: What is the nature of man? What is the nature of God as the ultimate reality? What is the nature of nature?

"Different religious systems and different philosophical systems have different answers. Vedanta, especially the non-dualistic Vedanta—*Advaita*, as it is called—says that all three are one. Man in his ultimate nature, nature in its ultimate nature, and God in His ultimate nature are the same. This is the basic position of Vedanta.

"Sri Ramakrishna, in recent days, added one little extra diamond from Vedanta which was there before but not so much stressed: God can be personal as well as impersonal. That is a special stress given by Ramakrishna in this present age. Thereby, he harmonized the three different major systems obtained in Vedanta—the dualistic system, the qualified monistic system, and the monistic system.* Ramakrishna harmonized these different viewpoints by telling us it is the same actuality which becomes the personalized God.

"Vivekananda, a disciple of Sri Ramakrishna, gave the definition of what God is in a very scientific way: 'God is the highest reading of the Absolute,' he said. So, Vedanta, and all religions, have this major idea called ultimate existence, or oneness."

Swami Swahananda looked at me, wondering whether he should continue. I nodded that he go on.

"What is the nature of man, then?" he asked. "Man is of the same nature. But you can approach man's nature from another angle. You can start a search to find out what is the permanent thing

---

* Dualism holds that God, the universe, and individuals are separate, eternal entities. Qualified monism maintains God alone exists and individual souls exists as "cells" in God's universal body. Monism views God, individual souls, and the universe as one Reality.

that exists in this universe. You begin the search from those things regarding which you have no doubt. Since you exist—you have no doubt that you exist—start from there. Philosophers may come, scientists may come and try to argue, still you know that you exist. So, all right, start your search from this position—who are you?

"First comes the body, of course. You ask yourself, 'Am I the body? Is the body real?' After one hundred years it won't be here. Scientifically, after seven years all the cells have changed. But anyhow, after one hundred years the body won't be here. So the body cannot be said to be the real reality, the lasting reality, the ongoing existence.

"So you consider the mind. Is the mind the ultimate existence? But the mind is constantly changing. Even some religions, including Hinduism, which believe in the continuance of mind from rebirth to rebirth, even they believe at some time the mind will come to a stop.

"So, from our method of inquiry, Vedanta says man's ultimate nature is not the body, not the mind, but the spirit. So here you have the idea of the divinity of man. Spirit is man's essential nature—not in his manifestation, where there are defects—but in his essential nature. It's like putting an Indian dress on an American girl. She wears it today; tomorrow it won't be there. She will change it. A loving mother dresses her child. Today she puts a Japanese dress on her child; tomorrow an African dress; then a Chinese dress. But the child is the same. Similarly the soul is the same, the spirit is the same. The garments—the mind and the body—are all changing.

"So you have the idea of the divinity of the soul. We call the divinity of existence *Brahman*. Brahman is the word for the unity of existence. *Atman* is the word we use for the divinity of the soul, the essential nature of man.

"The third important idea of Vedanta is the unity, the oneness, of God. Now, how do I define God? As previously explained, God is the highest reading of the Absolute—as the Absolute appears to the limited mind.

"So, the unity of God is another idea. Different religious leaders say, 'My God is like this, my God is like that.' Hindus say, 'God is like this.' Muslims say, 'God is like that.' Christians say, 'God is like this.' Can all the people be right at the same time? The normal idea is that either you are right or I am right and, of course, I am always right!" He threw back his head, laughing heartily, and we joined him.

"So, Vedanta says no to this. All the people at the same time *can* be right," he emphasized. "How can they be right? We give the example of woman. What is woman? She is mother to somebody, wife to somebody, boss to somebody. She can become even the Prime Minister of a huge country like India, eh? Or a fighting country like Israel.

"But when a child says, 'My mommy comes,' is it the mommy portion of the woman who comes or does the entire woman come—the wife, boss, and so on?

"Similarly, Christians say, 'My God is like this,' Hindus say, 'No, God is like that,' Muslims say, 'No, like this.' *All are right.* All are calling their mommy." Again he burst into infectious laughter and we did too, but we also appreciated what a deep point he was making in such a simple and straightforward manner.

"The child doesn't know the wife aspect, or the boss aspect. He knows the Mommy. But she exists in all aspects. So, real God is not known to anybody completely, exhaustively. He cannot be.

"So we have the third idea, the unity of God.

"The fourth idea of Vedanta is the harmony of religions. Ramakrishna said that people speaking different languages came to a pond to take water. Though they used different names—'jal, pani, water' —the meaning is the same. Similarly, God has different names, but they all point to the same ultimate reality.

"These are the four major ideas of Vedanta."

"Good," I said. "Now, what is the goal of the Vedantist?"

"The Vedantist's ideal is to realize his or her spiritual nature. The ultimate position, as Shankara says: To know that you are not the body, not the mind, but the spirit.

"But there are intermediate stages," he added. "In devotional language we call this quest the realization of God. In Vedantic language we call it the realization of one's spiritual nature.

"In our ordinary lives we human beings don't represent the full spirit because it is mixed with the body and other mental/emotional aspects—with defects.

"But, realization of one's spiritual nature is the ultimate goal of life," he underscored.

"In the process, of course," he went on, "*samadhi* (superconscious awareness) is the method. Through samadhi only can you have these experiences. To gain samadhi you practice the four major yogas, which are means of connecting the individual soul with the Supreme Soul. The four yoga paths are: the path of devotion, the path of knowledge, the path of action, and the path of meditation. These are the four major ways to gain samadhi and experience the ultimate goal of life.

"Why four yogas?" he asked rhetorically, and I encouraged him to continue. "A man has three faculties, according to psychology. We think, we feel, and we have a volitional (will) aspect. Now, when these three are very calm you enter the yogic, or mystic, condition.

"Let's say you come back home after a whole day's work and lie down on your easy chair. You have no strong emotion in your mind —no love or hatred—no activity is going on, no serious thinking is going on. You are in sort of a neutral condition. This is comparable to a yogic condition.

"So these are the four possible states of mind—thinking, feeling, willing, and the mystic, or yogic, condition. This is why Swami Vivekananda scientifically said there are four yogas."

Swami Swahananda looked over at me to clarify his point, "Although, any *part* of yoga is often called yoga, too. The *Bhagavad Gita* has eighteen chapters and each one is a yoga. Whatever pushes a man to realization is yoga. But, technically, there are four major yogas. Kundalini yoga, Japa yoga, Laya yoga—these are all offshoots—mostly offshoots of Raja yoga.* But the major approaches are the yoga of devotion, of knowledge, of action, and of meditation."

"Using these yogas, then, how does a Vedantist become fulfilled, and what is the process?" I was looking forward to learning his views on yoga.

"Now, the Vedantist recognizes that man has two aspects—the essential spiritual aspect and the manifested aspect. When man is in the manifested aspect, that is (mainly conscious) in the body and the mind, he must try to bring perfection of the body and mind as far as possible. So, bodily virtues are to be cultivated. Mental virtues also are to be cultivated. And gradually, transcending the worst aspects of his mind and body, he gradually cultivates the higher aspects.

"When man is in these lower stages, he visualizes that he will be going beyond both good and bad into the higher stage. But, in the normal stage, or the struggling stage, he is to replace the bad tendencies he has with good tendencies, bad habits with good habits, bad ideas with good ideas.

---

* In brief, Raja yoga is union with God through attuned will and activity. Kundalini yoga is spiritual realization through gathering and focusing the life force. Japa yoga is meditation through chanting spiritual phrases, or syllables, called mantrams. Laya yoga is spiritual enlightenment through development of the seven spiritual centers in the spine and brain.

"Now, bad and good are all relative ideas, but in social norms there is a standard, and eventually higher and higher ideas will gradually come. But the major idea is that through love of God, through devotion to God, a man will try to feel the disembodied condition—the ultimate stage, the ultimate existence.

"Now, as to fulfillment for a Vedantist, there are different levels he'll have to take. On the human level, a man knows that he is the body. He knows that he is the mind. So long as he feels that, he has got to do something for the body and something for the mind. Philosophically, he knows he's not the body and not the mind, but Vedanta is not a religion of doctrines. Unless and until he feels it, it has not yet become his full religion.

"So, his God is changing all the time!" Swamiji raised his voice. "As his conception of God changes, his God is actually changing (in his awareness). This developing Vedantist may hear people say that God is impersonal and Absolute, but to him, knowing God as personalized is much easier. That personal God may bless him or help him directly, or in the form of a saint, an avatar, a great teacher, or a deity.

"The Vedantist's conception of God changes as he realizes he's neither body nor mind but spirit. So, along the way, when he is mainly aware of his physical body, some physical satisfactions are necessary; when he is aware mentally, some mental satisfactions are necessary; and then both physical and mental aspects should push him toward what will become spiritual realization.

"So, Vedanta is serious, spiritual, and practical. The enjoyments of the body and the mind are continued for the time being. But the Vedantist feels the body and mind are not eternal conditions for him. He knows he is in a temporary position and must gradually transcend the body idea—and, in time, the mind idea."

Swami Swahananda looked at me for the next question. I simply nodded, feeling he was beautifully explaining Vedanta.

"And then again, there is another idea: What is *pulling* man? Our theory is that *oneness* is there all the time *pulling* man. A double pull is going on all the time. On one side the body pulls, but on the other side spirit pulls. A constant struggle is going on, even in the very ordinary man, not to speak about spiritual seekers.

"So, in answer to your question, I would say that spiritual fulfillment comes on three levels—physical level, the mental level (including intellectual, aesthetic, and moral), and then the spiritual level. On all three levels this fulfillment must come; then only will you be fully satisfied.

"Some monks will say, 'We don't want other fulfillments.' Some others will be saying, 'I want only physical enjoyments.' Someone else will say, 'I want only intellectual enjoyment.' Go ahead and have it! But then a time will come when you will find this is not enough. You want something more."

"Are there levels or states of spiritual fulfillment?" I was eager to hear Swami Swahananda's explanation.

"Yes. Vedantists, or any spiritual seekers, work it out, stage by stage. There are several stages."

"Wonderful. Can you tell us the main stages, or perhaps tell us all the stages?" I urged.

"At first comes *questioning*. A person searches in his young days for higher ideals. Sometimes people come in direct contact with some overwhelming experience, especially the death of a near and dear one. Sometimes a very good experience, like being saved from an accident, may also make him more reflective. Questioning arises when things become different. The inquiry for a purpose of life and the meaningfulness of things brings some answers. Then he is inspired to practice spiritual disciplines. Some type of uplifting experience comes to confirm the intellectual formation.

"In the beginning comes *faith*, general faith. The search brings *company of the holy*—books, as well as persons. That in turn brings the *desire for spiritual practice*. As a result, obstacles are removed, body and mind cooperate better; then comes steadiness in practice and also in attitude. Spiritual life is basically a change of attitude based on spiritual reality or philosophy of life."

"What attitudes?" I asked.

"Various attitudes are practiced: self-surrender, detachment, discrimination, love of God. And self-purification is based on the chosen attitudes.

"Then a *change of valuation in life* takes place. Many people give up at this stage but those who persevere acquire peace and tranquility and steadfastness. Sattvic (balanced, wise) qualities develop. He becomes more compassionate and less judgmental because of the awareness of the inadequacies of his life.

"Then comes a *plateau*, as if nothing new is happening. And there may be many ups and downs. If these seekers stay on the path, they develop a special taste and natural intensity of inclination for higher realities. When this intensity of taste has come, the development becomes more automatic, though God's grace plays a part. Final illumination is in the hands of the Divine, and so the last word in the devotional path is *surrender to the Lord*."

I enjoyed the clarity of his words.

"According to Advaita Vedanta,* Brahman is realized, through meditation, *as* the Self within. To practice meditation on the Atman (the Divine Soul) as identical with Brahman, it is necessary to have the preceptor. Then an aspirant forms a clear idea of the nature of both Atman and Brahman by contemplation. He becomes convinced of the truth of their identity through reasoning. When he forms a definite idea in his mind of quality-less Brahman, he makes the mental mode conform with Reality.

"Ultimately comes *realization*—removing primal ignorance. Hearing, contemplation, and persistent practice of meditation ultimately gives the final realization."

"But what happens to the seeker who is not focused on realization?"

Swamiji calmly answered, "For a normal man who is not yet fully caught up by the idea of realization, but who has a desire for bodily enjoyment and mental achievement, as well as realization, for him the spiritual achievement will be like this: At times he does some meditation with devotion to the Lord, or he does some other type of meditation. Some calmness comes, some measure of calmness comes into his mind. He has serenity of mind once in a while, losing himself in the spiritual thought which is the immediate product of his meditation. His spiritual attitude brings him some calmness, and then through practice of meditation his mind becomes gradually quiet a little. Once in a while his mind becomes absorbed in Spirit.

"Then, other devotees often try to cultivate devotion and love for God. For them, sometimes—because of their singing, spiritual talking, or spiritual thinking—a sort of *Godfulness* idea comes. They feel God's presence, or feel ecstasy.

"Now, for many people these early stages are enough. They enjoy the attitude, or the occasional serenity, or the idea of God's presence.

"But those who go forward suddenly find their mind becomes completely absorbed. In meditation they completely forget their body and mind. They become aware of Spirit.

"So, in all these different kinds of people, if they persist, their minds become completely absorbed. Those who have practiced emotionally in their meditation begin to have visions of God. They may first have dreams about God and these dreams and visions in meditation become a little encouraging. In Vedanta we don't stress too much

* Non-duality, monism.

about these things, but if experiences give us true encouragement, a little boosting in our energy, then they are good.

"But, all the different kinds of meditators come to a stage where form melts away. They experience a formless aspect of God.

"Swami Brahmananda, the first President of our Order, said that both forms of meditation are real—those in which God is seen in vision and those in which God is experienced in formless aspect, pure Spirit. But Brahmananda said that in the higher stages of meditation the forms melt away into formless experience of Spirit.

"Swami Vijnananda, another disciple of Sri Ramakrishna, explained this in yogic language. Vijnananda said that the forms of the chosen deities are seen in vision as long as the mind is at the plane of consciousness relating to the throat level or lower. But when the mind goes above that, all forms melt away. All forms melt away, and with this a feeling of the presence of the Divine comes.

"As for the pure meditators, their mind gets fully absorbed, and the theory is that when the mind is fully free from all waves—modifications of the mind, they're called—then the natural bliss of the Atman will come for awhile. This is the reason why we feel happy at times in meditation.

"There is a physiological reason also for this happiness in meditation: blood pressure is improved and other body functionings are improved. There are true physiological benefits to meditation.

"But, why does it come? Why do I feel a welling up of joy? The Vedantic explanation is that *man's ultimate nature* is the Spirit: eternal existence, eternal knowledge, and eternal bliss. So when all the obstacles within me are removed by raja yoga meditation,* there is no thought remaining in the mind. Then the nature and bliss of the Atman, the true self, manifests itself. This is the theory, the Vedantic explanation.

"Another idea is the jnana yogi's idea. Jnana yogis† analyze themselves and their experiences. Their method is to lessen their attachment, lessen their consciousness of the physical and other realms—especially the body.

"So, they stress non-attachment and they become more and more free. Their idea is, as they analyze, 'This is not worthwhile, that is not worthwhile, this is temporary, this is immaterial.'

---

* Raja yoga meditation is usually based on concentrating on the play of life force within the body and the mind's energy centers until, free of mental modifications, the true nature is apprehended and experienced.

† Jnana yoga is union through wisdom and spiritual discernment.

"Then a stage comes when these yogis of the intellect feel that there is something that must be in existence which is real. Sri Ramakrishna explains this higher reality in giving the analogy of an onion. You go on peeling the onion and then what remains, remains."

For those who prefer to connect with their spiritual nature through the yoga of action, Swami Swahananda explained karma yoga in a nutshell as having two methods.

"Either be detached in work, saying, 'I shall keep my mind in a calm and serene mood, whatever the provocation,' or the other way is the way that devotees do it: 'I offer all my actions to the Lord. My beloved Lord sees my heart and does everything through me, so who am I to take the credit? Or, more importantly, who am I to be discredited, to feel guilty?'

"So, by practicing in this way, those who practice the yoga of action give up the body and the mind by surrendering to the Divine and they experience the Divine.

"Through the right attitude, through devotion, meditation, or action, samadhi (superconsciousness) will take place. Then through samadhi, experience of *oneness* and the *ultimate existence* will come.

"At the superconscious stage a joy feeling comes. At the next stage of superconsciousness, the joy feeling will go away, but the feeling of oneness will be there.

"Also, in samadhi, there are two types of experiences. One samadhi is of the personal God. You feel that you exist and that God exists and a little separation is there between you. The second type of samadhi, the final one, is called *nirvikalpa samadhi*. In this superconscious state there is no other thought. What remains, remains. This is experience of the Absolute. It cannot be described because it is beyond the mind.

"So, that is the goal of Vedanta," he finished.

Swami Swahananda urged us to stay for tea. Since we could not join him but had to rush to future appointments, he urged us to accept some chocolates. A friend of all mankind, he bid us farewell.

Swami Swahananda inspired me to study the words of Swami Prabhavananda, the saintly man and author who formerly directed the Vedanta Society in Southern California. Swami Prabhavananda and Christopher Isherwood collaborated on a number of spiritual classics, including *Shankara's Crest Jewel of Discrimination* and *How To Know God*.

In the magazine *Vedanta And The West*, published in May, 1954, Swami Prabhavananda sums up Vedanta in this way:

The fundamental truth as taught by all religions is that man has to transform his base human nature into the divine that is within him. In other words, he must reach the deeper strata of his being, wherein lies his unity with all mankind. And Vedanta can help us to contact and live that truth which unfolds our real nature—the divinity lying hidden in man.

Vedanta is not a particular religion but a philosophy which includes the basic truths of all religions. It teaches that man's real nature is divine; that it is the aim of man's life on earth to unfold and manifest the hidden Godhead within him; and that truth is universal . . . .

Thus Vedanta preaches a universal message, the message of harmony. In its insistence on personal experience of the truth of God, on the divinity of man, and the universality of truth it has kept the spirit of religion alive since the age of the Vedas (ancient scriptures). Even in our time there have been Ramakrishna, Vivekananda, and men like Gandhi. The modern apostle of Vedanta, Vivekananda, describes the ideal religion of tomorrow as follows:

If there is ever to be a universal religion, it must be one which will have no location in place or time; which will be infinite, like the God it will preach, and whose sun will shine upon the followers of Krishna and of Christ, on saints and sinners alike; which will not be Brahmanic or Buddhistic, Christian, or Mohammedan, but the sum total of all these, and still have infinite space for development; which in its catholicity will embrace in its infinite arms, and find a place for, every human being, from the lowest grovelling savage not far removed from the brute, to the highest man, towering by the virtues of his head and heart almost above humanity, making society stand in awe of him and doubt his human nature. It will be a religion which will have no place for persecution or intolerance in its polity, which will recognize divinity in every man and woman, and whose whole scope, whose whole force, will be centered in aiding humanity to realize its own true, divine nature.

This "sum total" of all religions does not mean that all people on earth have to come under the banner of one prophet or worship one aspect of God. If Christ is true, Krishna and Buddha are also true. Let there be many teachers, many scriptures; let there be churches, temples, and synagogues. Every religion is a path to reach the same goal. When the goal is reached the Christian, the Jew, the Sufi, the Hindu, and the Buddhist realize that each has worshiped the same Reality. One who has attained this knowledge is no longer a follower of a particular path or a particular religion. He has become a man of God and a blessing to mankind.*

*   *Vedanta And The West* Magazine, May, 1954. Used with the permission of the Vedanta Society of Southern California.

52

YOGA AS A SPIRITUAL PATH

Millions of people throughout the world today practice yoga for spiritual reasons. Through yoga they contact their higher consciousness and the Lord of their hearts.

Yoga means "joined together." The word comes from the ancient Sanskrit root word *yug*, which means "to unify." A *yogi* is one who consciously unifies body, mind, emotions, and spirit so that they work together very well.*

The yogi strives to open the gift of life and discover his fullest possibilities. A yogi endeavors to discover the higher consciousness and how the body, mind, and emotional nature can be truly *fulfilled* through *unifying their purposes*—rather than living in constant interior civil war.

Yoga is not a religion. People of many different faiths—Christians, Muslims, Hindus, Jews—as well as agnostics and atheists, practice yoga because of its numerous benefits and life-enrichment. Many millions practice yoga for its *asanas*, its physical exercises, which are regularly acclaimed to be extraordinarily health-giving by

* The author of this chapter and *Keys To Higher Consciousness* is a Guru and teacher of yoga, metaphysics, and mysticism.

419

many doctors around the world. And, too, many millions practice some form of yoga meditation in order to contact their higher consciousness, or commune deeply with the Lord. Many who practice yoga meditation are deeply religious, while many others who practice these meditations are agnostics seeking verifiable experience and personal transformation.

A yoga devotee strives to live in an ongoing and progressively more joyous state of harmony. Body, mind, and emotions are brought into attunement with one another and with one's soul, or spiritual self. The devotee finds this ongoing state of harmony not only to be a wonderful way to live but an essential factor in becoming enlightened—living in higher consciousness.

BUT HOW DO MOST PEOPLE LIVE?

The average person lives in a mental hurricane, with a mind so turbulent that the usual concentration span is only six seconds! Most people live in a storm of ideas: constructive thoughts war against biases, superstitions, fantasies, unremitting memories, dreads, doubts, and occasional frustrating blankness. People become so accustomed to the hurricane they think it's normal!

And, the emotions are storming within almost everyone, too. Anger, jealousy, grief, fear, and guilt create anxieties which often drown peace, joy, and love.

THE YOGA SOLUTION

Yogis discover and affirm life's great possibilities by freeing the body of tension and the ravages of stress, and progressively releasing mental and emotional turbulence. The resulting well being is often considered miraculous; and the new unity which occurs between the individual and others is like the dawn of a new life.

If yoga appeals to you, you will need to find a good teacher who can help you practice correctly and thrive. No chapter or book on yoga can replace personal coaching, but hopefully your study of this chapter will give you a basic understanding of the great enrichment yoga studies will offer you when the opportunity arises.

There are eight main kinds of yoga, each having its own distinct form of meditation. Generally you practice yoga based on your distinct nature. If you seek to be a yoga meditator and use yoga as a means for the discovery of the higher consciousness, you must first examine your own qualities.

ARE YOU MAINLY EMOTIONAL, MENTAL, OR WILL-CENTERED?

In order to ultimately select the form of yoga which you will find easiest and most beneficial, you should first determine whether you are mainly:

a) an emotional person seeking above all an emotional fulfillment,
b) a thinking person seeking deep, satisfying and provable experiences to solve your deep questions about life,
c) a volitional person seeking the attunement of your will with God's will, or the *higher will* of your spiritual self.

EIGHT KINDS OF YOGA

Yoga is designed to enable people to begin from their immediate, present state of consciousness and move forward, day by day, into a state of wholeness, well being, and enlightenment. Even the beginning student is able to shed much physical tension, mental/emotional turbulence, and prepare the way for a life of higher consciousness.

As you ponder the possibilities and methods of the eight types of yoga, bear your own nature in mind. Consider which form most appeals to you. In this way you may find some suggestions which will richly benefit you right now.

Bear in mind also that these brief comments on each of the main yoga paths are meant to give you insights into yoga and yourself. These short discussions are not thorough courses on any of the yogas. They are written for introductory or rudimentary understanding of your magnificent possibilities.

BHAKTI YOGA

Bhakti yoga, or devotional yoga, is the most natural path for those who are dominantly seeking emotional fulfillment and well being. The "bhakta" usually practices meditation by visualizing, thinking and feeling that the Lord is sitting or standing before him. The bhakta pours out his heart's love, adoration, and shares his deepest thoughts and concerns with the Lord until a continual flow of awareness moves between devotee and his or her beloved Lord.

This continuous flow of love and life force brings about a

superconscious state of awareness which is generally called a mood, or bhava. The moods are discussed in detail in Chapters 21 through 27.

Generally, in this form of meditation—bhakti meditation—there is awareness of relationship, or *twoness*. The devotee is aware of the Lord and of his own being, and of the relationship between the Lord and the devotee. Sometimes, however, the devotee loses self-consciousness and is aware only of the Lord. Also, at times the bhakta experiences that the Lord's spirit, or consciousness, moves into the devotee, infilling and indwelling him.

Both in the mood of twoness and in the experience of oneness you are *transformed:* your character is improved. And, periods of higher consciousness come more frequently. With even greater development, the aspirant who does bhakti meditation lives in a sense of *permanent relationship* with his divine Beloved! This permanent relationship is not a static thing. It develops into one exciting dimension of love after another. These relationships are ever-new and ever-refreshing and continue to delight the bhakti yogi throughout life.

The bhakta, also, because of the ease of the mood relationship, is given special ability to experience the deep *samadhis* and other high states of awareness which other yogis focus upon.

KARMA YOGA

Karma means *to do.* Karma refers to the universal principle of cause and effect. For every effect there's a cause, and the devotee realizes that he, in his present life situation, is experiencing the effects of a number of causes which he has entertained and enacted. He recognizes that for a finer, more fulfilling life he has to change his thoughts and feelings and so express himself through his actions that new causes supplant old habits and attitudes. Through establishing new causes, he is confident of more beneficial and successful effects occurring to him and his loved ones in life.

Karma yoga meditation is:

1) Consciously *surrendering* to the Lord the *selfish motives* that tend to abound within one's psyche. One seeks to stop working, speaking, acting, or even meditating in a way that is to reward one's personal desires. A karma yogi wishes to live for God, or for the higher self— the soul—and not for the ego anymore.

2) A dedication of *oneself:* one's actions, thoughts, words, and feelings are offered to God. The karma yogi has faith that *God is the doer,* ideally, and that the lower self—the mind, the heart, the hands—are dedicated to God for his purposes. The individual devotee wishes nothing more than to be an instrument, a servant of the Lord's love, light, and will.

JNANA YOGA

Jnana means *wisdom* or *discernment.* Jnana yoga is the path of wisdom and jnana meditation is many-faceted. The main purpose of jnana meditation is to withdraw the mind and emotions from perceiving life and oneself in a deluded way so that one may behold and live in attunement with Reality, or Spirit.

One principal way that the "jnani," the yogi of discernment, meditates is to patiently release or put aside all thoughts and feelings until the luminous glow of the soul dawns in the mind and heart and is allowed to do a work of transformation and enlightenment within the rapt meditator. One way this is accomplished is through the technique called *neti-neti.*

Neti-neti means "not this, not this." Whenever a thought or feeling which is not the goal of the meditation—that is, which is not the soul, the inner self—occurs to the mind, the meditator simply says, "Not this, not this," and dismisses the thought, image, concept, sound, or sense distraction. Any thought, any feeling, is discarded—patiently discarded—again and again if necessary, until the mind is clear and the soul is revealed. Remember never to meditate in a passive way. This state of consciousness is one of alertness, an amazing application of awareness.

When you get into the habit of "neti-neti," you can also discard worry, doubt, or fear, and become established in the light of your inner self. You can then look back at worries and fears with deep insight and handle them well.

RAJA YOGA

Raja means *royal* or *kingly.* Raja yoga meditation is generally based on directing one's life force to bring the mind and emotions so into balance that the attention may be easily focused on the object of meditation, or the Lord directly.

Generally, life force is directed to move up and down the spine until it is balanced and the mind and emotions are serenely content.

Then awareness is generally directed to move forward into a point in the center of the lower forehead. This meditation point, which is about half an inch above where the eyebrows meet, is called *ajna*, or the third eye.

When the energy is balanced throughout the brain and body and easily moving forward in the area of the third eye, your mind becomes very calm. While your mind is not passive, it is free of meaningless thoughts, worries, and the bric-a-brac of the subconscious mind. This state usually gives you a very pleasant sense of well being and your mind seems filled with a velvety darkness.

As your consciousness continues to move in your third eye, pastel colors begin to appear in your forehead. Sumptuous, glorious pinks, yellows, whites, blues, indigos, greens, and purples take their turn or play in combination in your forehead. Then, you may think you are seeing fireflies, lightning, or moonlight as your life force becomes more concentrated and more actively prepares you to behold higher consciousness. This process is readying you to experience your true nature as pure consciousness, pure spirit, pure awareness.

And then the light in your forehead blazes brighter than the sun! But, you find it is soothing to look into the awesome light, soothing to behold it. This is the brilliance of your inner light, your essence, revealing itself to you.

Raja yoga, particularly, requires a teacher because it is easy to strain yourself, and it's also easy to delude yourself into high level hallucinations rather than actual experiences of your higher consciousness.

However, the genuine raja yogi lives in bliss, with his, or her, will surrendered to God. A raja yogi realizes the profound truth of the Biblical passage: If therefore thine eye be single, thy whole body shall be filled with light.*

MANTRA YOGA

Mantras (or mantrams) are words, phrases, or syllables which are chanted thoughtfully and with growing attention. Mantra yoga meditation involves chanting a word or phrase until the mind and emotions are transcended and the superconscious is clearly revealed and experienced.

Since the mind wanders so much, the music of a mantra easily

---

* Matthew 6:22 of the King James version of *The Holy Bible*.

rescues the mind and brings it back to the object of one's meditation. Both the rhythm of it and the meaning of it combine to guide the mind safely back to the point of meditation—the higher consciousness or the specific spiritual focus.

Typical mantrams are: *Aum*, meaning Spirit, the Word of God, which creates, preserves, and transforms; or the Tibetan Buddhist mantram *Aum Mani Padme Hum* which usually is translated as "Om the jewel is in the Lotus Hum;"* or the Hindu mantram *Asato Ma Sat Gamayo* which means "Lead me from the unreal to the Real."†

There are thousands of mantrams which are mainly from the ancient Sanskrit language. Possibly, in time, mantrams will be in English as well as Sanskrit. What such a development would require is a number of great meditators of modern day to be so attuned to the Lord and so at ease within the realms of higher consciousness that these new mantrams can easily be revealed to them. All mantrams are the result of a revelation, usually to some deeply meditating adept.

Generally mantram meditation involves chanting out loud at first until the body is calm and the atmosphere around oneself is serene and pleasant for meditation. Then whisper meditation almost automatically occurs and the life force begins to withdraw inward from "out-loud" chanting to whisper chanting. In whisper chanting the *prana*, the life force in the body, is balanced and harmonized, preparing the way for a deeper state of serenity—and of the balance of mind and emotions.

Whisper chanting easily dissolves and the life force moves even deeper within as you enter mental chanting. Mental chanting is practiced as long as thoughts are occurring to the mind. Whenever the mind is distracted, the mantram is simply chanted in the same area of the mind that the distraction is occurring. The mantram always wins if given a chance.

As the mantram frees you from one thought, then another, and also helps to dissolve distractions, the mantram then begins to reach the border of superconsciousness. Chanting becomes effortless. No

---

* According to W. Y. Evans-Wentz, in *Tibetan Yoga and Secret Doctrines*, Oxford University Press, London, 1958, page 125: "*Aum* is the symbol for the spiritual power of the Buddha;" and *Hum* is "the symbol of the embodiment of the life-force of Divine Beings . . ." and "is to be visualized as being the life-force of the Buddha Gautama."

† Or, more fully, "Lead me from *attachment* to the unreal into the Real."

effort, nor warding off distractions, is needed. Chanting becomes a pleasure. Peace and gentle joy fill your mind.

At this point of effortless mental chanting the mantram can do two things: a) it may dissolve into superconsciousness, or b) it may first help ventilate the subconscious mind, the storage house of your old thoughts, feelings, and memories which have been sadly neglected or not successfully dealt with. The mantram may create an opportunity for old thoughts and feelings, old fears and guilts, to be released, or healed, or let go.

What happens next? If your mental chanting first becomes effortless and ventilates the subconscious pressures, it then moves into your superconscious self. Or, the effortless chanting bypasses the subconscious basement of your mind, going directly into sublime superconsciousness. Either way, you arrive in your ecstatic, heavenly nature. The words of the mantram fall apart and fall away. Only the *energy surge* of the mantram remains as your awareness becomes blissful and full of light.

In this ecstatic stage of continuous rapture, you feel that you have arrived home. You sense that this is your true nature—and your true estate, which has been ignored due to the dominance of the mind, the emotions, and the outer world.

You will likely have a very pleasant fifteen to twenty minutes in the delight and comfort of your superconscious self; and then the mantram will begin to come out. You will find your higher consciousness *wants* to come back to the outer world. It wants to express, to touch your life and loved ones. The words of the mantram re-emerge in the mind and you reverse the whole process, going gradually into whisper—and then out loud—chanting.

Ultimately a mantram meditator lives in the ecstasy of the mantram, always aglow with the meaning and spiritual insight of the special syllables.

In order to be sure a mantram is right for you, seek a mantram only from a Guru or Master who is qualified to teach and initiate you.

LAYA YOGA

While you need a teacher to help you learn any form of meditation well, you particularly need the aid of a teacher to learn laya yoga meditation. There are five main energy centers in your spine and two in your head. The laya yoga meditator knows exactly how to locate these centers through the kind training of a teacher. When these centers are found, they function very much like *doorways to different realms of higher consciousness.*

Through laya yoga meditation, for example, you sense the heart center which is located inside the spine, directly back of the heart. From this point you can expand your awareness and enter into a realm of great, sky blue light (sometimes other colors as well) and discover how easily and readily you can love. Through laya yoga meditation in the heart center you overcome selfishness and self-centeredness. You become able to deal with your fears and worries because of the tremendous strength and insight you gain from the "heart expansion."

The five centers correspond roughly to the main areas of the spine. One is located in the area of the tailbone. The second center is in the area of the sacrum. The third is located in the spinal cord, back of the navel. Then the heart center, which we have mentioned. The throat center is found inside the spine at the base of the neck, directly back of your collar button.

The first head center is the point half an inch above where your eyebrows meet in your forehead—it's called the third eye. The second head center is at the crown of your head. Technically, this area is not a center at all, but is considered the main source of spiritual light and energy which is expressed throughout the body.

While it is beneficial to sense where your centers are, it is not wise to concentrate on these centers or meditate on any of them without the help of a teacher. Over-stimulation of a center could cause pain, confusion, or intense desires.

On the other hand, most people live on only three levels of consciousness—the material, sensual, and egoic—without ever opening the seven centers which bring higher consciousness. Laya yoga, with a qualified teacher, is an extremely worthwhile endeavor.

TANTRA YOGA

The word *tantra* literally means "expansion." A tantra yogi concentrates on expanding all levels of his or her consciousness to unveil and realize the Supreme Reality. Tantra focuses on the dynamic aspect of divinity called *Shakti*, or "the Cosmic Mother."

The tantric devotee strives to attune with the spiritual dynamic energy in order to transform personal limitations and release subconscious blockages.

True tantra yoga is a pure path, but it has been abused by some self-proclaimed adherents. Tantra yoga is not concerned with sexuality, but with the creative force and transmuting this energy into higher channels. Sometimes self-styled teachers have misconstrued the symbolism of tantra yoga into sex practices for men and women.

Rather, the goal of tantra yoga is to awaken and harmonize the male and female aspects *within* each person in order to spiritually awaken and realize the whole universe as an expression of the Cosmic Mother, the divine life force, or Spirit.

Tantra yoga meditation is often practiced this way: A tantra devotee sits calmly and purifies mind and heart of wayward thoughts and desires. The devotee then senses the life force within his or her being and gradually, through imagination and feeling, directs the life force to rise up the spine, from the tailbone into the neck and then into the forehead.

When considerable life force is gathered in the forehead, the tantra yogi, through practice, directs that the life force move out from the forehead and form a body of light and energy three to six feet before him or her.

The body of light in front of the devotee is encouraged to become dense and expand until it is as large as a human form.

The tantric yogi then directs love and devotion toward the dynamic body of light which is a profound representation of his or her soul and essence.

Usually, after fifteen to thirty minutes of this meditation, the yogi invites the light and energy to slowly return into his forehead and down through the body to the base of the spine.

Through practice, amazing renewal is felt through tantric meditation and spiritual awakening is accelerated. The tantric becomes aware that the life force and essence within each person is truly divine; it is from the Lord. The spirit in each one is from God.

Another interesting aspect of tantra yoga is its dedication to transmutation of negative habits or obsessions—smoking, drinking, and overeating, for example. Of course, the tantric would urge you give up any bad habits you can by simply dropping them. However, if you *can't* give up a self-destructive behavior, no matter how hard you've tried, why not use a tantric approach to it?

The beginning tantric realizes he has failed in giving up his self-destructive habits because they were so strongly established over long periods of time. Often, before taking up tantra yoga, he tried to stop hurting himself through smoking, drinking, and overeating, but failed miserably after many struggles. Now, through tantra he tries to expand his consciousness as he transforms old habits.

If drinking is his problem, for example, he thinks of God as he drinks! Rather than ignoring God or feeling rebellious, he strives to sense God's love, joy, and blessings. The tantric strives to feel God's joy or love filling him, as well as the intoxication of the alcohol. In a short time, the tantric beginner does not need to drink. The thought of God fills him with joy instead.

Similarly, the smoker strives to sense God's presence in the satisfaction of smoking. In time, provided deep love of God is cultivated, the cigarette or pipe is not needed in order to feel pleasure and contentment.

Overeaters use similar principles. Gradually, their satisfaction is in God—not food. Overeaters also do these tantric practices:

1) As they eat, they strive to realize the food is an expression of the infinite spirit; that they are spiritual beings partaking of spirit. This awareness of the food liberates them from a desperate animal approach to mealtimes and snacks.

2) Sometimes they mix all the foods on their plate into one homogeneous mass which doesn't look so appealing to the eyes and the mind. Freed of visual allure, the food is simply conceived as energy, a few hours fuel.

True tantric yogis think of God all their waking hours. In this devotion they are freed from destructive habits and enter enlightenment.

HATHA YOGA

Hatha yoga, in the twentieth century, is mainly practiced for health and vitality. It's a marvelous means of exercising, stretching, and freeing the body so it can be a healthy, long-lived, and vital instrument of the mind and soul. In addition, hatha yogis can become extremely clear-minded and can concentrate well. However, a few yogis do practice hatha yoga as their main method for spiritual realization. Their clear minds and pure, healthy bodies enable them to meditate easily.

In Sanskrit, *ha* means sun, *tha* means moon. Hatha yoga is the practice of harmonizing the body's inner currents (principally the currents of Feeling, Thinking, Willing, and Acting) until they are in perfect balance. Normally the hatha yogi with the calm mind focuses awareness at the ajna center half an inch above where the eyebrows join and directs awareness to move through that center into a super-conscious state. The individual life, the finite life, meets and fuses temporarily, at first, with the infinite life.

Hatha yoga meditation is not well-known today and the purity of life required in order to do hatha yoga meditation well requires more time and application than most people are willing to give. However, those few dedicated men and women who are true hatha yogis live in abundant well being and universal harmony.

These are the eight main yogas: Bhakti, Karma, Jnana, Raja, Mantra, Laya, Tantra, and Hatha. In the event you have heard of Kundalini and Kriya yogas, we'll explore them briefly, too.

KUNDALINI YOGA

Kundalini yoga is sometimes considered a distinct yoga although it generally involves a combination of raja, hatha, tantra, laya, and mantra yogas. Its principal goal is the stimulation of the spiritual life force at the base of the spine (called Kundalini) so that it will rise easily from the lower centers of your being into the spiritual centers in your head where higher consciousness is perceived, experienced and, ultimately, lived in.

KRIYA YOGA

Classically, kriya yoga is a blend of raja, jnana, and bhakti practices. The word *kriya* means "to do, to make an effort," or "to transform."

One of the main ways that kriya is practiced is a daily program of self-discipline of mind and body, introspection, and devotion to God.

Another way that kriya yoga is practiced in the world today is in directing life force to move up and down the spine, transforming the meditator's state of being until spiritual realization occurs. This technique is usually conveyed privately through initiation from a Guru or longtime practitioner of this method.

Both forms of kriya are deeply related and very ancient—well over five thousand years old and probably much older. Several million people practice both forms of kriya yoga throughout the world today.

THE SPIRITUAL PATH AND ITS STAGES

How do most yoga devotees begin their Paths? What unfoldments do they share in common with one another—and with seekers on other Paths throughout the world?

THE CRISIS OR INSPIRATION

A few yoga devotees trace the beginning of their spiritual quest to inspiration. Often these souls meet an inspired yogi and the main goal in life becomes very clear. Haunted by new possibilities which they sense within themselves, they eagerly and faithfully move through the experiences which lead to enlightenment and well being.

Most yogis, however, find their way onto the spiritual path because of a personal crisis. A painful, disappointing, or grief-causing shock forces a reevaluation and a redirection of life. These devotees realize they have been relying on the wrong people or unfulfilling goals. Such seekers find they have no choice but to turn the thrust of their lives and their hopes in another direction.

THE RESTLESSNESS — THE CALL

Whether inspired or recoiling from a personal crisis, the devotee becomes restless for God—restless to know the truth, to find meaning. Night and day mind and heart reach toward the unknown and into the deepest recesses of the soul.

THE PATH IS CHOSEN

Out of the yearning and restlessness, the seeker searches the world for a way to proceed, a way to satisfy the heart's deepest hope. A way of spiritual practice and development is found. Sometimes it seems that the Path chooses the devotee because of its availability and wonderful satisfaction.

At the point when the Path is chosen, effort and dedication truly begin. The propelled devotee realizes which form of yoga is most appropriate and helpful. He dedicates himself to it—usually practicing an hour a day. He, or she, chooses that combination of yoga techniques and meditations which most rapidly enable contact with the Lord of one's true self.

Those who are dominantly emotional choose bhakti yoga; those who are dominantly intellectual choose jnana yoga; those who seek to attune their will with the higher self, with their Creator, choose raja and karma yoga, for example.

INTRINSIC VALUES

At first the devotees practice the different yogas *in order to gain* specific benefits they hope for. Then, as they develop in yoga, they begin to *give* more and more of themselves toward their ideals. They begin to do yoga not just because of what it will give them, but out of love. They begin to practice, whatever their Path, *self-giving*. This self-giving is transformational. No longer living with selfish motive or self-obsession, they are ready to dedicate themselves to their values. Most commonly, they begin to live lives dedicated to Truth and/or Beauty and/or Goodness.

EQUILIBRIUM

The devotee who gives himself or herself to Truth, Beauty, or Goodness finds great peace and wholeness. Body, mind, and spirit enter a deep, abiding state of harmony and well being. This state of equilibrium not only enables a sense of integrity and freedom but also opens the floodgates for a spiritual experience.

BHAVAS AND SAMADHIS

The dominantly emotional seekers enter into deep spiritual moods and become conscious of the presence and the glory of their divine Beloved, the Lord of their hearts and minds. They rejoice in an unfolding series of relationships with God. Awe unfolds into loving service. Loving service unfolds into deep friendship. Friendship moves forward into greater intimacy. The devotee one day recognizes himself or herself to be a son or daughter of the Lord, who is the spiritual source of everything. These moods of love—bhavas—go on and on and are infinitely satisfying and intriguing.

The devotees who have dominantly intellectual and will-centered natures experience amazing and transforming samadhis, spiritually exalted states in which they realize their true nature and behold the presence and spirit of God. As distinct from the devotional devotees in bhavas, these seekers are mainly *inclined* to live in ecstasy and wisdom rather than a mood of love and spiritual relatedness to God. These seekers experience the expansion of their soul, discover profound union with spirit, and realize freedom from all their past habits and tendencies.

SAHAJ

As a result of many bhavas and samadhis, devotees who persist and grow into a moment-by-moment, continuous superconscious state *live* as enlightened beings. Rather than *visit* the higher consciousness regularly, they *come home* and live their lives while *abiding* in higher consciousness. This state is called sahaj yoga, sahaj samadhi, or simply sahaj.

HIGHER STATES

There is no limit! All devotees who live in higher consciousness move forward into never-ending, ever-new, wondrously satisfying spiritual lives. Almost all of them engage themselves in loving service of God and humanity. A once-forlorn seeker returns to mankind and shares what he has been given.

In this chapter we have considered a number of ways that the yoga aspirant takes the help of meditation and other techniques to come home to his true nature and reside in higher consciousness. In meditation you learn, through practice, to overcome the tendency to be self-deluded, or to live a self-destructive life. Freeing your body of tension and your mind and emotions of turbulence, you discover your true self and dwell in it. You make contact with the Lord of your heart and enter an ecstatic, eternal relationship. You find more from life than you ever dared dream. These are the possibilities of your life through yoga.

VIII

YOU ARE ENTERING A LIFE OF HIGHER CONSCIOUSNESS

53

THE MYSTICAL WEDDING

Higher consciousness is real—it is not a fantasy. If you come out of a supposed deep meditation without improved character, greater wisdom, and greater love for all mankind, you can be certain you did not experience higher consciousness while you were in your meditative state. *Higher consciousness changes you for the better whenever you come into contact with it.* It not only enriches you personally but in making you a finer human being, it enriches humanity. Only, perhaps, in taverns and in gambling casinos will you find as many pretenders as you will likely find along the path to higher consciousness. So many would-be aspirants would rather talk, dream, and indulge their opinions than get on with the marvelous prospect of really becoming enlightened.

As you proceed toward higher consciousness, be careful not to be taken in by dreamers who show no signs of character, courage, kindness, or clear-mindedness. At the same time, avoid as you would an epidemic the temptation to pretend you are experiencing higher consciousness when you have no clear signs of self-improvement to indicate you have ventured anywhere at all in your quest.

Specific events must occur in your life if you truly discover your higher consciousness. By now you have studied and hopefully practiced character development, faith, love, and the levels of transcendental consciousness. You have developed the habit of patient practice and the Good Will Witness state.

As you develop day by day, you will proceed through the various planes of consciousness. At the same time you also move through the stages of the heart. Accepting yourself as you are and going forward steadfastly, you will experience most all the exalted states of consciousness mentioned in this book. Great adventures await you.

Different devotees have different experiences and it's wonderful to observe that each person's path is individual and distinct to him or her. Each enlightened person contributes something unique to the overall experience of humanity. Nevertheless, nearly all aspirants on most of the paths to higher consciousness participate in a sublime experience called the mystical marriage. This great wedding is an activity of your higher consciousness which occurs when—and only when—you are appropriately prepared physically (in the conduct of your daily life), mentally, emotionally, and egoically.

THE MYSTICAL MARRIAGE

As you strive to live an honorable life and be a good person, you find you need to make many sacrifices. Many opportunities to get ahead in your personal life or career often require some sort of compromise or dishonesty on your part but you discover you're *unable* to make personal advancements which require a compromise of your ideals and growing sense of what is right. At times you very likely will have to fight, take risks, and stand up for your ideals. These crises or turning points often become times of loss or sorrow in that you will lose friends, opportunities, or be thought ill of by those who have a casual attitude about morality, ethics, or the value of the lives of others. You, however, feel you have no choice but to be true to yourself and that you must necessarily take the consequences of your heartfelt commitments.

Proceeding in this way, you grow a great deal in your character and become a fitting person to experience higher consciousness. You become a person who will not try to dominate others or take advantage of people when you have greater power and insight through your enlightenment.

You may also, during this formative time, feel periods of loneliness. You feel out of touch with former friends who have fewer values and sensitivities than you do. You also feel deeply lonely because you have not yet experienced your higher consciousness. You are caught between two worlds; yet you have the courage and conviction to go on into the unknown, whatever the consequences. You have faith in the reality and the supreme value of what you are endeavoring to do.

After many trials and deeply important learning experiences, you begin to form a humble but gratifying self-esteem. You feel at home in your quest and realize you are more committed to it now than you were even at the excited, enthusiastic beginning. Indeed, your determination and delight in the path are consolidated and strong. Perhaps at this time you've experienced some higher moods or tasted of samadhi. Perhaps not.

Suddenly—by a timing you cannot perceive or understand— you find yourself thoroughly committed and dedicated to your higher self, even though you have not experienced it in many—or any—direct ways. Somehow your life has been coordinated by subtle means so that your most special day of "the wedding" may come. Generally, this wedding experience does not occur deliberately and no preparation other than your good conduct of life is involved. Because you are living dedicated to and committed to your higher consciousness and your Creator, a change must necessarily occur in you. It's only a matter of time, and somehow today is the day.

Determined to be true to your path, no matter what, you suddenly feel yourself called to sit down, to pause in your activities, and enter a meditation or reverie. Perhaps you feel like praising the Lord or are unable to speak the deep gratitude and love you feel in your heart. Suddenly this major event in your life, which once you never dreamed could happen to you, begins to thrill you. Deeply calm but sweetly surrendered, you feel an inner upheaval. A delightful, ecstatic movement of energy begins to rumble or shoot up your body. From your lower back and legs, powerful, ecstatically thrilling energy warmly (on rare occasions it may feel cool) pushes with great strength all the way up your body past your heart and throat, face, and into your head. This rush of ecstasy pushes on beyond your head and out into infinite space! All you are aware of is infinite, super-vivid light, love, and power.

You might later reflect that you felt, in this state, like a bird finally let out of its tiny cage to experience universal freedom. You might also reflect that you were not aware of your inert body sitting there motionless. However, while in this state you are only aware of the infinite nature. While in the experience, you do not reflect on your body, mind, or concoct some inappropriate metaphors. Rather, you experience your lofty and grand higher consciousness. You now know your essence, your source, and that it is ever so real and profoundly worth any sacrifice. However, even these mental thoughts and this verbiage are too slow for the state you're in. These reflections occur only afterward.

This ineffable rush of consciousness is called the wedding, or the mystical marriage. In this indescribable event your finite, limited consciousness, your distinct individuality, has embraced your infinite self, your spiritual or divine self, and it's love at first sight. This rush of your finite being into your infinite being is an embrace you will never forget and never want to leave. Your feeling nature has become one with your knowing nature. Your small will has met and abides for a time in the greater will.

However, fortunately, or unfortunately, depending on your view, your body can only stand so much ecstasy and bliss. Also, the higher consciousness does not want to crisp you into a cinder, to wipe out your individual life. So, you return blissfully and ever so sweetly to regular consciousness, usually twenty minutes to half an hour after the experience begins. You come out feeling not only that you have been in heaven, but everything you behold around you in your room, or in the park, seems to have that hue, that tincture, of blessedness. You feel astonished and amazed that such an experience happened to you, that it was so much grander, vaster, and more powerful than you could have ever conceived it to be.

With profound memory of the experience and a yearning it happen again soon, you resume your normal activities and find yourself keenly motivated to meditate again whenever the opportunity presents itself. No longer is meditation a chore or a difficulty. You now know what meditation can provide and what a life lived for higher values can mean to you.

Other people may mention that they see light around you. Dogs, cats, butterflies may love to be close to you, to enjoy the free flow of higher consciousness as its momentum continues to a beautiful extent, *resonating* in your individual life. Little girls and boys might think of you as their dear friend and feel perfectly at home with you on first meeting. Financial and other opportunities may also gravitate toward you as if moved by an invisible hand.

You see the world in a new perspective. You are now feeling your completeness. The finite wave of the infinite ocean has sensed its true source and how great that source really is. In this mystical marriage your finite and infinite nature have embraced in love. From now on they will work together, the finite and the infinite, each serving and helping one another as mates, as partners in love.

Likely you do not understand after this first experience what the wedding really means to you and your life. You may have many questions but this new sweetness in your life tends to give you faith and patient confidence that you will know everything that you need to know. After all, that great consciousness has embraced you as its own.

From this point on, you conduct your life like a wave on an ocean of joy. You see people and things as part of this oceanic consciousness. You recognize how few people sense or are in any way aware of their true nature and birthright, so you strive to be helpful and inspiring, but never dominating or proselytizing. Each individual must proceed at his own rate—which is based on the development of character and a willingness to surrender egocentricity for a state of humble self-surrender.

Your greatly stretched and transparent ego now seeks to re-experience the celestial wedding, to experience the divine lover. The ego seeks to arrange time and appropriate circumstances so that the finite individual consciousness may rush into the arms of the infinite consciousness often and without interruption.

You begin to realize that these ecstatic meditations and towering exaltations are not an end in themselves but something more is about to happen.

THE BIRTH

As your finite and infinite nature play together and ecstatic rapture fills your being, you begin to discover that from the very first embrace, the very first wondrous experience of the rapture and unification of your being, something new has been planted within you, much like a seed. During the colossal periods of unification with the higher consciousness your mind and ego are completely absorbed in the universal awareness. However, you then find yourself coming down out of that state to function in your daily life, conducting regular activities against the background of immense joy and a sense of fulfillment.

Still, you begin to realize that the goal is not yet reached. The wedding, no matter how beautiful, has not had its true fruition. Somehow *you yourself are being changed*. While the wedding was very transforming in the new perspective and in the new powerful comfort that you realized, you now understand that there is a good part of your daily life and consciousness which remains separate from the higher self, separate from the higher consciousness, except when in deep embrace in meditation. You begin to recognize that you are now as if "with child." Somehow a new being is stirring within you. This new being, this seedling, is of the quality of the higher consciousness; yet it is growing within you in your regular daily consciousness. This inner life continues to develop as the days and often months go by.

And now, on another great and special day—perhaps even a few days in a row which have been suddenly made available to you, a vacation or special time off from work—you find yourself extremely quiet and ever so full of the ecstasy of higher consciousness. You become very still and, like a woman in labor, totally concentrated on the birth that is about to occur. This birth begins to have the feeling of inevitability. This birth challenges your mind with this mystery— a birth which, in its coming forth, pushes your mind and emotions back into a reliance and trust on a great life process which is in the hands of a master midwife.

Gradually, birth occurs. Then, you suddenly realize the cry of your new being! *You know in your totality that you are reborn.* Your birth is a transformation of your finite consciousness. You now understand. You have become, truly, *a new creature.* You are a new person, free of old tendencies, habits, and attitudes which have bothered you throughout your life and caused harm and misery to yourself and others. You are new. You are filled with the infinite consciousness and yet you are able to maintain that realization of the infinite consciousness here in your sweet finitude. You, the individual, are a conscious part of the infinite ocean of awareness; yet you are human, finite, and distinct also.

You wonder at the birth. You wonder at your Creator. You realize that you now are the finite beloved of the infinite. It is no longer a matter of "something within" your consciousness being married to the infinite consciousness. That was during the period of the wedding. Now, your entire being—inside and out—is reborn. You are aware of the infinite consciousness moving in every cell and tissue of your being, from your toes to your hair. You recognize yourself *completely renewed,* and the *beloved* of your Creator! Your life takes on immortal and eternal dimensions. Your wonder and your joy, along with your gratitude, are never-ending.

Most all aspirants for higher consciousness experience this wedding and great rebirth. May you in your quest one day know yourself and the higher consciousness in this new incomparable way.

REFLECTION

To understand the mystery,
You must love.

54

TWO VITAL CONCERNS

While higher consciousness will prove itself to you as your greatest asset and your true resource for a finer life, there is a misconception about higher consciousness that can prove very dangerous. Understand higher consciousness for what it *is* or you might pay a very big price.

Consider the patient who watched with apprehension as the doctor sawed the casts off his two broken arms. "Doctor, Doctor, will I be able to play the piano?"

The doctor examined the arms minutely, tested the fingers: "Yes," the doctor replied, "you will be able to play the piano."

"That's strange," replied the patient, "I couldn't play it before I broke my arms."

Remember, in finding your higher consciousness, you are not entering into the realm of miracles or dreamland. You are rapidly accelerating your consciousness. You're discovering a vast amount of talent and awareness that goes unused and undiscovered in the life of the average person. Through your higher consciousness you are realizing "Who am I?"—solving the riddle of your existence, satisfying the yearning of your heart. But becoming awakened to your higher consciousness does not mean you will, necessarily, pole vault the world record or "knock 'em dead" on your concert tour of Europe.

What the awakening of higher consciousness represents to you is remarkable improvements in many areas of life, of course. There are higher states of consciousness which are sublime and which will magnificently enrich you. Also, through discovering your higher consciousness you will find that most everything works better. Your mind becomes more and more capable of thinking clearly and penetrating deeply into whatever you want to think about. Your emotions become free of chaos; you develop a continual sense of well being. Then, too, your empathy increases and you become an extremely thoughtful person in your sensitivity to the lives of others. Your physical body inevitably gains more vitality, and greater health usually occurs, provided you have not strained in order to achieve higher consciousness.

Also, with body, mind, and emotions working together, you will find yourself much more coordinated. You will also sleep better and face obstacles and stress with much increased confidence, having discovered marvelous inner resources with which to face life's challenges.

Living in inspiration and progressively higher levels of love and joy, you now have faith and confidence. You will be extremely intuitive, often being amazed at the insights which flood your mind with new opportunities and precious solutions to daily problems.

YOUR TRUE POTENTIAL

The attributes of higher consciousness become yours. Insight, security, peace, and joy, along with an inner power to change circumstances, will come within your easy, immediate access. You will be awakened in your true nature and begin to live a new life at last. You find yourself participating in the creation of a new and happier world.

Now, as to pole vaulting higher than anyone has ever vaulted, or becoming a sudden genius in piano playing, higher consciousness will definitely help you a great deal toward these goals; but the physical skills, which are complex and intricate, still need to be developed. The coordination of the body with the mind and the backlog of experience required in the mind would have to be instilled through much training. The emotions have to be attuned, and to develop that coordination between the mind and emotions takes great courage and sensitivity. So, while higher consciousness will accelerate you in developing abilities and talents in such desires as pole vaulting or virtuosity at the keyboard, higher consciousness in no way guarantees fulfillment of your ego's fantasies.

Higher consciousness is really concerned with your soul's deepest expression. *It enables realization of your true potential.* This realization of potential is far more valuable than the accomplishment of fantasies—higher consciousness being a very thorough expression of *your reality.* The potential of your being in harmony with the creative consciousness can bring about, in most instances, a life and world *beyond* fantasies and dreams.

In awakening to your higher consciousness, you truly give yourself a chance at a finer life. You enable yourself to find the greatest satisfaction you can ever know: you discover the other nine-tenths of yourself. Because higher consciousness is an aspect of reality and your very own nature, you establish, at every level of your being, lasting and ongoing fulfillment. You experience the true zest of life and see in many ways the wonder of your individual nature. Daily you can see the great possibilities of life. Your life, even in the midst of bustle, is ever blissful.

Many of the main relationships that you can experience with higher consciousness have already been discussed. These moods of relationship—*bhavas*—progressively take you from the state of awe into greater and greater intimacy with your higher consciousness and potential. An extremely happy life could be spent developing and becoming consolidated in *one* of these relationships. Of course, once one relationship, or bhava, has been matured, it will develop into a more intimate and even higher level. Those who consolidate a mood live in constant attunement and overcome unhappiness.

Any one of these bhavas—awe, servant, friend, child, beloved—with the Source of your consciousness is so deeply satisfying that life becomes a much grander and nobler project. The beauty within you and the beauty of your world becomes progressively harmonized. There develops an exciting interplay between your life and your world. A cause and effect relationship is clearly established which brings continuously more satisfying experiences throughout your life, not that there aren't challenges and obstacles with which you and your higher consciousness must contend from time to time.

Considering also how profound and lofty the higher bhavas (relationships) are, you can conceive that there is no end to the possibilities of deeply satisfying relationships with the higher consciousness. Imagine one day entering the wonder of Nitya Lila, the eternal play of love.

But bhavas, as we have indicated in many ways, are not the only ways higher consciousness is experienced. The states of transcendental consciousness, as mentioned in Chapter 39, grow into astonishing states of well being. Consider with joy also the subtleties of superconscious awareness as shared with the kindly and dedicated spiritual leaders mentioned in the previous chapters. They share the life of higher consciousness, among other things, with their spiritual fellowships in churches, synagogues, mosques, and temples.

But, please, however you conceive of higher consciousness and whatever your approach toward its development, do not misconceive that higher awareness is the world of "wishes." Higher consciousness is not a plane of fantasy but the reality of your true potential which is ready and eager to come forth and move in your life right here and now. It lifts you up to a realization and expression of all the good, the beauty, and the power that abides within your universal self.

AVOID SELF-DECEPTION

In your awakening to your true stature as a being of higher consciousness, as one who no longer ignores inner capacities, you must be abidingly aware of another great caution. Early in your quest for higher consciousness, while your mind and emotions are not yet subtle enough to easily and clearly relate to the awakening process—or to distinguish it from fantasies and psychic experiences—you may find it extremely tempting to deceive yourself. Through vivid imagination, coupled with strong desires, you'll be able to "hear" whatever you want to hear and "see" whatever you want to see.

You will find you can infuse your subconscious mind with strong opinions and egocentric yearnings for a few days or weeks and then you will be able to behold some great astral personage speaking to you from a cloud of light, or you will hear a "heavenly voice" revealing into your quiet reflections what you secretly designed. In other words, you can have visions which appear to be from on high but which are self-aggrandizing fantasies. Because you are not yet developed or clear in mind and heart, you may be inclined to presume your "new views" to be true, perhaps even direct information from God.

The caution, then, is be kind to yourself. Avoid the embarrassment and heartbreak of seeing your words and actions smash against reality. Remember, the test of all genuine experience of higher consciousness is that each and every insight from the inner self, or wherever it may come from, must be tried in the light of day—practically expressed and shaped. If your new realization works well in the long and short run, fine. If, on the other hand, the insight doesn't bring excellent results, then a more intense search for wisdom and a new way must be sought.

As with humble amazement you go forward to your new home in higher consciousness, keep these two great, all-important cautions in mind:

1) Higher consciousness does not fulfill fantasies but unfolds your wondrous potential.
2) Since it's possible—even easy—to be deceived, test all your insights and inspirations in the light of day.

CONSIDER THIS

Your discovery of your own higher consciousness is one of the greatest contributions you can make to your fellow man and especially your loved ones. The human world is the way it is right now because of the way people think about themselves and one another. People act and react based on their concepts of what life is about and where happiness or success lie. We wake up and go to bed in a world that could be annihilated in a few minutes. This perilous existence is an indication of our overall human consciousness. Certainly our ability to destroy the world reflects our considerable skills in using matter—electrons, in particular—but, while we are trying, we seem unable to walk away from the edge of oblivion.

Great wise men and women, saints, sages, and above all, the Incarnations who have come to earth from time to time, show us the way to a new awareness—a new way of thinking, a satisfying way of living. A new, more universal way of consciousness is required and they show us, each in his or her own distinctive method, ways for attaining a universal and constructive state of mind. One saint after another demonstrates the healing and joy of a higher consciousness. Consider your own higher consciousness as important, not only to yourself and your career or your family's esteem, but a priceless contribution to people you don't know in far-off countries—a great gift not only to them but to their children and their children's children.

Without more people discovering and abiding in higher consciousness, humanity could lose its future. Caught in ignorance and imprisoning biases, we have lost access to our creative intelligence—and one another. Due to our ignorance and inability to meet human needs—East and West—we may behold the terror-fire of potent, unthinking technology. In split seconds we could become vapor as adeptly-conceived bombs deny life globally. Not only will our future on this planet be over, but our children's futures will be ended, too. And those of any human being again, ever. Finished.

You, in your kindly quest of a higher consciousness—a healing consciousness—are needed. Your love, your insights, your creative intelligence, and your inner power to change circumstances are required.

Do the work. Make the effort. Balance your mind and your life. Awaken in your higher consciousness.

REFLECTION

What is my gift to the world?
What do I leave the children?

55

POSSIBILITIES

What are the possibilities of higher consciousness? Who can truly say how great the possibilities are?

After all, we have only begun to learn our address in a vast universe—a universe which we presume to be the only one. Thinking, struggling, man has worked through many conceptions and misconceptions over the past fifteen thousand years of history and has, with brave science, astonishing mathematics, and pieces of glass in long tubes, finally been able to figure out where he lives in the physical universe. According to Timothy Ferris, in his book, *Galaxies,* your correct address (after you write down your street number, your city or town, your state or province, and country) is: "The Earth, The Solar System, The Sun's Neighborhood, Vicinity of the Orion Arm, The Milky Way Galaxy, The Local Group of Galaxies, The Local Supercluster, The Universe, Circa 18 Billion Years After the Beginning of Its Expansion."

So, at least we can be comforted in knowing where we live in the physical universe.

While we know extremely little about our physical universe and are still wondering whether there is life on other planets within the inconceivable vastness, we know even less about the universe be-

450

hind closed eyes. What is this stuff of life? Where does it come from? How does it work? It is conscious, we know, but how conscious is this life and what is the point of it? Where is life coming from? Where is it going? And why?

"Who am I?" is a most fundamental question regularly occurring in the hearts of people around the world. Even after living seventy or eighty years, people confide that they wonder what their life was about and whether they lived it appropriately. They confess they still don't quite know who they are and very often yield up their lives in the same manner that they lived them—perplexed.

Ramana Maharshi was one of the great masters of our twentieth century, recognized in the East and West as an enlightened man. He commonly responded to the questions of existence and the yearning of human hearts in saying that the main problem of people is *we don't know who we are!* If we could figure out who we are, we would live our lives entirely differently—more harmoniously and constructively, he taught. People would recognize easily and naturally how to attain true peace and well being. Maharshi advised that while there are many beautiful techniques and practices to help a person solve the riddle and mystery of his or her existence and aching heart, there is a much more simple and direct procedure: ask yourself, "Who am I?"

Maharshi advised some people to ask this question several times a day but there were others, he knew, who were ready for the intensity of inquiry which would bring a quicker realization and a profound experience of the answer; and he counseled them to chant the question, "Who am I?" ten thousand times each day!

In this beautiful practice the ego, or false sense of self, gradually turns from its delusions and pretensions toward the higher consciousness and ultimately the soul, the spirit of the Divine within each of us. In time the ego is transformed and the soul stands resplendent.

The question is only resolved for periods of time at first, as the ego now and then—due to old momentums and habit patterns—reclaims dominance. But eventually the false sense of self is seen as a delusion and is happily discarded. The great "Who am I?" riddle is solved in bliss and wisdom.

By considering the inner universe and life itself more important than mankind's discoveries in the physical universe, no disparagement is intended. Courageous, brilliant men and women guided people away from terrifying superstitions about the world. These honest scientists bravely led us from ages of human sacrifice—which were supposed to influence capricious gods—into the age of heart transplants, global communications, and manned space flight. Great men and women have shone their insights outward on the universe and we have marvelled. We have been *set free* of much ignorance by the Galileos, Newtons, Einsteins, and Curies. We have been *enabled* by them to improve and lengthen our lives in innumerable ways. Too, great explorers of our physical universe have often made extreme sacrifices in serving truth as best they could. They were very often ridiculed, persecuted, imprisoned, and tortured by benumbed people. And, often these heroes and heroines did work which itself was dangerous—Madame Curie, for example, died of leukemia caused by the effects of radiation.

However, a study of the lives of our great discoverers in the sciences reveals that almost always the seeker of truth needed moments of reflection, had to go within, in order to know the physical world better. Moments of inner communion inspired the humble seeker with new insights that resulted in almost every important discovery of chemistry, physics, medicine, mathematics, optics, calculus. All of their inventions and all their ways of knowing the physical world, it seems, came from the higher consciousness, from revelations within.

The physical world would hardly be known at all were it not for these seekers of truth finding within themselves the clues, or the procedures, or the insights, which have brought about every advancement in science and knowledge of the physical world.

But no one has claimed bringing rocks back from the moon can show people who we are or how to live together harmoniously. Brain surgery can preserve a life but it can't reveal what life—or a person—*is*. Nor do the leaders in the social sciences, with their considerable light, say they can solve our deep yearnings or give us lasting peace.

In finding our higher consciousness, remote possibilities come near. As you find your superconscious awareness dawning, many hopes become possible. As groups of people become more conscious, the world changes.

THE POSSIBILITIES OF HIGHER CONSCIOUSNESS

What are the possibilities of higher consciousness? Let's speculate together about some wonderful improvements in life and our world which will likely become commonplace as people solve the mystery of "Who am I?" and discover they can use their higher consciousness as easily as their eyes, ears, mind, and feelings.

The woes of the world so far are mainly the effects of what we have caused in the past. Old, burdensome, and oppressive effects will yield to new, thoughtful causes engendered by inspired people. And these new possibilities may at some date in the future be looked upon as a very rudimentary and extremely partial glimpse of the wonderful life that humanity has long since found for itself.

On the other hand, a hundred years of hindsight may look upon these ideas as insubstantial as wishes and fantasies. However, people who experience higher consciousness generally find their lives benefited in every area. It is not absurd, then, to speculate that with more people becoming awakened to their inner faculties society will gradually enjoy its great undiscovered legacies. The dream of our American forefathers—Franklin, Washington, Jefferson, and all—will be real and blissfully commonplace to our whole world; a world which chose fulfillment instead of worry and emptiness.

Here is a small list of new possibilities which are becoming available to the world:

ECSTASY

Lasting, ever-new joy frees people from addiction to drugs, alcohol, and much neurotic behavior. In the profound ecstasy of their true natures, people are free to love and understand one another. The burdens of deep, personal confusion no longer pour outward, inflicting pain on society.

LESS FRUSTRATION IN A SANER WORLD

Higher consciousness will immeasurably increase our ability to evaluate personal and national goals. We will also have a clear understanding of our internal and outer resources for achieving our objectives. People will begin to clearly see and thoroughly achieve their life-enriching quests. There will be less frustration from failure. Fewer people will be floundering about wondering what to do.

With more success in seeing and achieving goals, people will feel less guilt. There will be less outer-directed hostility as people focus instead on satisfying, meaningful endeavors and enjoy the well being which results from purposeful accomplishments. Through goal satisfaction, people will likely seek more positive goals. There will be a progression of accomplishments at more and more subtle levels.

Having solved one's creature needs and goals, a person will move on to even greater satisfaction in fulfilling mental, emotional, social, and spiritual aims.

A more successful and fulfilled populace will be less frustrated and angry. As a result, there will be less crime. There will be fewer expressions of violence, fewer cruel expressions of inner exasperation. Also, successful people will feel no need to steal or block others from fulfilling their goals. There will be less depression and mental illness as the newfound capacities for fulfillment and creativity become the norm.

PLENTY — PROSPERITY

As people waken to their missing components for success, they will gain a greater capacity to understand the world and to act within the framework of reality. They will become much more able to manifest the newfound inner well being outward into the external world. People will find that their inner resources will attune them to opportunities for financial and material abundance. A person attuning with the inner self and functioning through the higher consciousness has difficulty *avoiding* prosperity and material well being. Having enough money, people won't be thinking about it all the time. They will begin to discover, through their material comfort, the other aspects of life that are infinitely more important and satisfying.

By prosperity, a person of higher consciousness does not think —necessarily—of vast amounts of money in the bank. Rather, by prosperity is meant having all one's needs met—not only materially, but on other levels of life as well. "Enough and to spare" is the key. Not only having enough to meet one's daily needs, but living day by day in the knowledge that there is always enough—that whatever one truly needs in order to be a constructive person, or to be of benefit to another in any positive way is always at hand. Financial security, food, shelter, every need is met.

A WAY OUT OF THE SUBCONSCIOUS

Today most people behave mechanically—unthinkingly. They do today each and every task as they did it yesterday and the years before. People usually have the same attitudes, the same prejudices, as they did in years past—prejudices often passed down from generation to generation.

The modern field of psychology emphasizes how much your

personality—the way you're going to be all your life—is influenced by your first three years. "Everything's pretty much set before you're five years old," they often say. Psychotherapists, almost inevitably, take a person who has problems back to the time when he or she was an infant, back to the time when life's patterns and attitudes were established in the tender young child.

When you find your higher consciousness, you will realize how profoundly true it is that people are so often near-automatons, acting out their early formative training from childhood. People go through their lives generally stuck in the behavior patterns of yesteryear. They are slaves of their subconscious mind, that part of the mind which holds the patterns—however crude and inapplicable.

Still, the person of higher consciousness laments that people who begin to become free of the subconscious do not go farther and discover how to make their subconscious a friend. With wisdom, you can enable your subconscious mind to become a very constructive force in your life, a force of good habits, good mental attitude, from which to declare your freedom for a better life and from which to instantaneously make changes for the better. The subconscious can become an ally and inspire you to flourish.

Until you step free of your subconscious and its domination, you live in a chaos of past thoughts and feelings which so dominate your mind that you find it next to impossible to think clearly or to know love in a constructive way. It's also impossible, when dominated by the subconscious, to look at another person or anything in the outer world without misperceiving it greatly.

Higher consciousness liberates you and all who are stuck in the hindering mire of the past to step into a life of your choosing, a life that moves in the light rather than the shadows of old impressions.

SOLVE SELF-ESTEEM PROBLEMS

Through higher consciousness people will discover who they really are. They will no longer have to pretend to be significant personalities or patch together egos which tend to fall apart each day. As you discover your true nature and the ineffable love showered on you through your higher consciousness, your self-esteem problems will vanish. You will become fully aware that you are an accepted being. You will end your orphan years. You will come home through higher consciousness and feel no need to bluff or be arrogant, no need to fear or go through days and months of self-doubt. Your higher consciousness will reveal to you, as you progressively develop, your true nature and you will have an abiding self-esteem which becomes a strength and a joy. Your new self-esteem will enable you to enter enchanting dimensions of satisfying relationships and, also, comfort you when you're alone.

NEW OPPORTUNITIES

Today people tend to spend most of their life dealing with their problems, endeavoring to solve them or somehow avoid them. For most people today, problem-solving is a full-time occupation. However, so many people are focused on problem-solving that they miss most of the *opportunities* that come their way. People in higher consciousness clearly behold thousands or millions of new opportunities that were never conceived of while life was a wrestling match. Often the new opportunities are much more important than solving the old problems.

So, a person of higher consciousness with far vaster perspectives on life becomes mindful and alert to the opportunities that abound in all directions—left, right, in front, behind, above, below, and beyond.

PROBLEM-SOLVING

While it's important to look at life anew and see its fresh opportunities, a major aspect of higher consciousness is that it unleashes creative intelligence which enables you to solve old problems. Your creative intelligence and inner power will solve with ease problems which once were so difficult to solve despite the application of all your personal might. Higher consciousness unleashes energies and abilities which most people do not know they have. It makes problems into opportunities. It makes problems, and even the failures of life, steppingstones toward success. A problem with shyness becomes self-assurance, deep compassion, and love for all.

As one multimillionaire said recently on television, he was once a busboy hopeful of "moving up" in the restaurant business. He greatly wanted to be promoted to a waiter's position. However, he was passed up several times and his failure in becoming a waiter forced him to study how money is made. He went to school and learned how a person becomes successful in this great country. His problem in becoming a waiter pushed him into an opportunity. As a result of his studies, he can now hire a thousand waiters. His higher consciousness helped him to see his problem in a new way and to so phenomenally solve his problem that he now travels the country showing other people how they can become wealthy.

You will generally find that your higher consciousness looks upon your problems differently from the way you normally think about them. Your higher consciousness is undaunted and very able at dealing with problems, and it awaits your attention.

MEANINGFUL LIVES

Is your life meaningful? Do you feel your activities and time spent on this earth are deeply satisfying? Do your activities seem extremely worthwhile?

Parades of people go to counselors every day because their lives have no meaning. They can't figure out why they work, eat, sleep, and go on with what life demands of them.

Through your growing superconsciousness, your higher insight will begin to abide with you and regularly share or shine into your mind and heart. It will reveal the underlying meaning and purpose of everything you do. What you see, what you hear, will become filled with a deeper understanding which gives great satisfaction and joy. Thinking becomes a pleasure because it ends with understanding and insight rather than even more questions. And questions themselves abide gracefully in the mind, not creating anxiety, but excitement and inspiration. Meaning and purpose unfold as you build up days and then years of what you know to be —before your heart, mind, conscience, and Creator—a meaningful life.

SYMPATHY

Other parades of people, in addition to those who are seeking more meaning in their lives, or any meaning at all, proceed to their counselors' waiting rooms because they feel so lonely. They feel that no one loves them, or perhaps they've discovered that they're incapable of giving love, neither able to give nor receive love.

Plowing deeper within yourself, you will find that contrary to the blockages on the surface of your consciousness, there is an ease in sensing the life and concerns of another person. You will sense a oneness that is easily shared between two people, two dozen, or two million. You will find that in your higher consciousness abides a *universal sympathy*. This special feeling is much like a mother's: because she has helped her children through their awkward and helpless years, she can feel a sense of motherhood for all little ones, from any country, even a country that hates her country. Similarly, you'll find you can care about people so naturally and in such a universal manner that your heart and mind become big enough to hold everyone.

This condition of universal sympathy frees you to love with ease and greatness. This state of universal sympathy develops into higher states of consciousness as well. It not only frees you to love and to feel for others, it enables you to enter into a state called cosmic consciousness, a level of awareness which is characteristic of most saints and sages throughout history. All of them, too, cared as much as you in your higher consciousness are learning to do.

MORE MIGHT

Why must the cancer win? Why must the bully prevail? Why must evil terrorize us and demand so much of our thought and our compensating effort?

Your higher consciousness has, as one of its chief attributes, a higher power, a mighty power, which will help you with your life. This higher power can vitalize your physical body, clear your mind, and make your heart readily able to give and receive great love. This mighty power can enable you to be victorious over your ignorance and egoism.

Devotees who have experienced their higher consciousness over a period of years learn never to underestimate the power of the higher consciousness within themselves and within each person. This universal power which can make the sun shine and the earth revolve and rotate, and which can sustain the life in your whole body—in each and every tissue—is assuredly capable of helping you mentally, emotionally, and spiritually, too.

INVENTIVENESS

Studying the lives of inventors, artists, and other creative people, there appears to be a very common factor. Their creative genius occurs during a moment of reflection, of inward turning, or of quiet —during sleep, while taking a walk, or enjoying an absent-minded shower, for example. Possibly, it could be argued that all creativity and all inventiveness occurs when our world's great creative people have been able—consciously or unknowingly—to enter the portals of their higher consciousness. From the invention of the wheel to the jumbo jet, the novelty and inventiveness of the human spirit seems to come from a supernormal level of awareness found deep within people who are able to attune themselves, individually or in groups, to the higher consciousness.

In being more attuned, we can use technology constructively; not as a means of ruining lands, oceans, habitats, the atmosphere, the earth's vegetation, and the health of mankind and all creatures. We will reverse the present trends. We will think long-term, with more common sense and compassion.

When you find your way into your own higher consciousness, you will find yourself becoming much more creative and inventive. The challenges of your life will find fresh answers and new, creative possibilities—possibilities you had not dreamed of prior to entering your higher creativity.

LESS AGGRESSION

As people become more conscious and are able to clearly conceive of their goals, they will be able to bring forth their inner resources for success. Because of their practice and their training and working with their own higher consciousness, they will more easily and reliably achieve the important goals in their life. *They will not need to maintain a fighting stance as a way of life.* They will be able to succeed in achieving their important objectives without feeling the need to beat out someone else or to live in a mad scramble as if life is a deadly game of "King of the Mountain."

Instead of lashing out from states of gloom and frustration, men and women will be able to evaluate their capacities for success and choose pathways which highlight their particular talents. People discovering reliable principles for success will not need to generate enemies, heart attacks, ulcers, orphans, and widows or widowers as they endeavor to thrive.

Aggression is a problem which is mainly peculiar to the male of the human species. Men are trained and encouraged to be aggressive from infancy. Societies generally accept that aggressive males are needed to provide for families or fight wars to protect their states. The down side of this philosophy is that male aggressiveness is destructive in so many ways.

In our country multitudes of men feel free to reach out and take a woman of their choice—often someone they don't know—and rape her while holding a knife to her throat or by some other means forcing a degrading compliance. In our nation, a woman is forcibly raped every six minutes.* And, appallingly, many are gang raped. Some experts estimate one out of every ten women in our nation will be raped during her lifetime.† And, according to *Time* Magazine, "about two million women in the U.S. are battered by their husbands or lovers each year."‡ *Two million*. Male aggression, how much longer can we afford to ignore this problem and its cost?

A terrible reflection of male aggression is that most recent statistics about crime show that males—mainly young males—commit 78.4 percent of the crime (of any sort) in our country. Women commit "only" 21.6 percent. That is to say, women who comprise nearly 53 percent of the population commit 21.6 percent of the crime. The male minority commit 78.4 percent.§

By aggression we do not only mean physical aggression but also attitudes of superiority, attitudes by which people feel licensed to take what is not theirs, or to hurt people because of a personal opinion, or even a whim.

Awakening one's higher consciousness would, of course, be of inestimable help in converting one's destructive, aggressive tendencies into constructive and harmonious self-mastery. Ultimately, what was once aggression becomes dedicated service to others and to one's own ideals.

PEOPLE WHO LIVE IN SAFETY

So often a boy who is battered by his father or mother grows up to mutilate or cripple others, or commit murder, which astonishes him and all of society. It has become commonplace to hear on the news that some lady, or perhaps a man, jogging through the park was stabbed fifty-one times and left bleeding—to die without reason.

The violence *in* people comes *out* of them, and it is a very profuse killer. Most every human being has some resentment, anger, or

---

* *Crime in the U.S.*, The F.B.I. Uniform Crime Report, 1987, page 6.

† According to *CBS News Nightwatch,* May 18, 1989.

‡ *Time* Magazine, March 27, 1989, Law Section.

§ *Crime in the U.S.*, U.S. Department of Justice, F.B.I., release date July 10, 1988 (based on 1987 data), page 181. (In the category of arrests for violent crimes—murder, forcible rape, robbery, and aggravated assault—88.9% were male; 11.1% were female. In arrests for property crime—burglary, larceny-theft, motor vehicle theft, arson—75.6% were male; 21.6% were female.) Figures on the convictions based on these arrests were not available at the time of this book's publication.

possibility of violence *inside*. This is where the insecurity of the human race begins, and this is the principal place where safety can start.

Through raising your consciousness, and through the power of your higher awareness, you will find that you can overcome—transform—your inclination to violence. You can turn your inclinations for violence into a power for good, into a willingness to understand and be of service to others. You, and others like you, who have found personal safety in being free of inner violence, can then endeavor to live lives that do not hurt or cripple others—lives which, rather, inspire and nurture, lives which encourage others to also take up lives of self-mastery and maturity. In any case, the violence which comes out of people can be changed, can be soothed and healed, when we raise our consciousness and learn what it feels like to live in trust and security with society as a whole.

Only a few decades ago people built houses with decorative, thin windows reaching from floor to ceiling right beside their front doors. At that time it was impossible to conceive that anyone would even have the inclination to put a fist through those windows and easily open the door in order to step inside and do some horrible crime. Now, we live in the era of fortresses. People form communities behind guarded walls where entrance is possible only by passing a guard at a small gate.

Many people can remember when they lived year in, year out, without ever locking their doors. There was trust and confidence. There was joy in the certainty that no one would be so mad or so unkind as to break the sanctity of another's home or car. Policemen were greeted with respect and treated as friends.

Hopefully society has many options that it can try until the right combination is found and people are safe—safe to walk in the streets that they have paid for with their taxes, safe to enjoy the parks they have created for pleasant rather than criminal events.

Higher consciousness, too, can prove a beginning point of change in transforming personal violence into a constructive love and service, along with the dignity of self-mastery. A change in understanding will create the joy of daily life in each neighborhood, in each home throughout this country, and through every country that is suffering the malady of senseless violence and insecurity.

Higher consciousness is also available to help each person deal in strength and confidence with his or her bullies. Ultimately, each of us can find that abiding good will and strength prevails over a diminishing evil. We can have a saner world!

MORE RESPONSIBLE PEOPLE

As people become more conscious, and especially when they become awakened, they will be able to perceive clearly the consequences of their actions. They will be able to know, through their experience and through the beautiful insights of higher consciousness, what are the likely consequences of particular actions, words, thoughts, feelings, or attitudes. People will become able to choose the consequences which they most prefer simply by contributing to better and better effects—*causing* them. Through appropriate and attuned thoughts, feelings, and actions, they will realize a beautiful way of experiencing life.

But, in addition, as people begin to recognize that their lives are basically the results of previous actions, of previous ways of treating other people, for example, they will begin to realize that in most ways each person is responsible for the consequences of life which he or she is experiencing.

While some events in life are enigmatic—a cause and effect relationship is not discernible—the person of higher consciousness faces them with a willingness to learn and eagerness to be changed. A person in higher consciousness strives to transform all the causes which he finds to be clearly harmful to himself or others. He takes responsibility for what is happening in his life.

When people become more conscious, they will begin not only to sense why the bad or painful things happen in life but how to make the good and wonderful aspects of life come about—how to make their hopes and dreams realities. To be on this planet is to be educated about the consequences of one's actions. We're all here, growing in our understanding of causes and effects. A person who seeks the higher consciousness finds tremendous release in comprehending how to meet a problem more successfully at the next opportunity due to a deeper grasp of the relationship between cause and effect.

Throughout the world, people who become more conscious will not blame others for what happens to them in life but will start a wave of improvement occurring from pole to pole. This is happening at this time. More people are accepting responsibility for what happens to them in life. They are often aware of the consequences of what they have done in the past—good and bad—and they realize it's not only their actions but their *attitudes*—the ways they think and feel—which directly contribute to making life fulfilling or sad.

People will get up each morning and address the problems of life, focus their higher awareness, and mindless chaos will cease.

UNIVERSAL LIFE

As the seeker of higher consciousness becomes aware of the great and wondrous life within, he or she is changed. Simply looking at another person becomes a delightful experience. One recognizes that beautiful life, that inestimably precious and rare gift of life which is expressing in a unique and special way in each person one sees—in everyone who walks the earth. This recognition of the beauty of life within oneself, and within others, leads to a geometrically increasing rate of understanding and appreciation of other people.

Sensing this preciousness of life, one begins to lead a universal life—a life based on the golden rule: doing unto others as you would have them do unto you. From this comes a life of love—a universal life. Love becomes easier and more natural. Love is less and less of an effort because love springs forward powerfully when there is the insight of the shared experience of life: between oneself and every person now living, or who has lived, or who is about to live.

These are some of the major possibilities for our world, and our loved ones, when we contact higher consciousness. Most amazingly, the talent and the power are already available. They rest within us, awaiting our notice.

REFLECTION

Claim your inheritance now!

56

EXCITING SPIRITUAL DIMENSIONS

Consider another possibility of contact with higher consciousness: more than ever, religion will assist men and women Godward. Oftentimes man's ignorance and the power trips of tyrants have intruded on religion. (Religion is the linking of man with God, or the returning of mankind to his true spiritual state.) Yet, despite these negative influences, churches, synagogues, and temples are becoming filled with inspired and spiritually-awakened men and women who are eager to assist their fellow worshippers into a deeper *experience* and communion with the Lord of all.

Sri Ramakrishna, a monk with little formal education, lived in superconsciousness and changed the world of spiritual thought.*

He was considered, as mentioned earlier (Chapter 25), an avatar, or an Incarnation, by millions of people. A number of his central points are found, fully or partly, in religious and philosophical thought throughout the world; but some of his ideas are new to mankind. His views are particularly interesting to seekers of higher

---

* Sri Ramakrishna is not to be historically confused with Sri Krishna, the avatar and king who lived in India many centuries before Christ, and who is the spiritual focus of the modern Hare Krishna movement.

consciousness. Leaders—and followers—of many religious paths study his words and the way he lived in God-consciousness.

Since Sri Ramakrishna dedicated his life to replacing the bloodshed and hatred between people of different religions with love and appreciation, his uplifting precepts have become very popular throughout the world. Politicians, as well as priests, take hope in his teachings about true brotherhood and world peace.

To simply ponder one of the following spiritual concepts which Sri Ramakrishna shared with humanity in the last century will likely fill you with amazement and hope at the spiritual potential hiding within you and all others who seek a better life and a more spiritual world.

You may wish to consider each of these ideas as possibilities for you. They are grand possibilities, indeed.* Even better, meditate on these great truths so that you can experience them.

1   All people are spiritual beings, individual expressions of the Divine.

2   This is a spiritual world, comprised of Spirit (conscious energy).

3   Each person is called in his or her own way to make mind and body subtle enough to attune with the soul† and with the Lord.

4   Man's yearning for God, love, and wisdom is natural, valid, and divine.

5   All the main religions are from God, provided by His infinite love and wisdom.

6   Religion must be dynamic.

7   When devotees of different paths embrace their own path fully and experience the Lord's nature, they will become tolerant and appreciative of the other God-given religions.

8   Religious differences are as important as their similarities. In *appreciating* the views of others, one will often be enriched and inspired on one's own path.

---

*   These possibilities are among the ideals of the Spiritual World Society founded by the author in Costa Mesa, California.

†   The spiritual essence within each person.

9 Spiritual pride, bigotry, and exclusivity limit the seeker from spiritual experience.

10 The living soul in each person actively yearns for a spiritual relationship.

11 The living soul in each person actively strives for a dynamic, creative expression of Truth, Beauty, and Goodness.

12 Suffering and confusion is a result of man trying to halt his soul's creative, loving expression of spiritual values.

13 The aspirant is precious in the eyes of the Lord. One's individuality is God-given and the ego is not to be hated but appreciated and developed into a spiritual relationship.

14 God can be experienced in both form and formlessness.

15 Meditation and prayer are among the most direct ways to experience God, one's soul, and divine realities.

16 Through devoted meditation and prayer, the cells of the physical body become divinized, spiritually transformed, to enter a new dimension of interplay with one's Creator.

17 A new species of man is thus emerging. The divinized body is developed through receiving spiritual radiance into every thought, breath, and cell.

18 Through the divinized body, a new relationship is established between God and man. It is an eternal play of love between the devotee and his or her dear Lord God.

19 The purpose of spiritual practice is to become attuned enough to realize that the Kingdom of God is at hand, that God is here—now.

20 Enlightenment is often gradual, a continuous, ever-new process, always developing. Spontaneous awakening is rare, but also occurs.

21 Repressed, ignored desires always cause sorrow. Desires, when faced with clarity and meditation, are transformed by God's power and one's character becomes stronger.

22 God is Divine Mother as well as Father and Son, available to all seeking comfort, delight, and refuge.

23 One ideally lives from Spirit first. If you allow, the higher plane always controls the lower.

24   There is no end to God-realization. No matter what you have realized, there is something more.

25   Individual spiritual experiences, thoughts, and actions help all of humanity because they radiate love and energy to the whole planet. One's individual experiences and realizations benefit all other lives on this good earth.

Sri Ramakrishna often said the easiest way for you—for most people—to know God is real, and to experience God as your dear Lord, is to focus your mind on thought of the Divine Beloved while chanting His (Her) name, repetitiously and with love. Don't chant vain, mindless repetitions; but chant with attention, even adoration, as best you can. You could also chant some attribute of the Lord, like *love* or *peace,* and experience God through that quality. "Chant the name and glories of God" was Sri Ramakrishna's most frequent advice to people seeking spiritual experience, human happiness, or both.

Hopefully you'll find these possibilities breathtakingly exciting and you'll wish to explore them with your heart and mind. Often the spiritual possibilities made known to man are so far ahead of the general consciousness of people that it takes a lot of living and a great deal of trial and error before one begins to sense that spiritual potentialities are perfectly real.

If you're already a person of deep faith, what joy must be yours in personally *experiencing* each of the dimensions made clearly known to you through your dear scriptures.

However you proceed toward the fascinating capacities available to you as part of your inheritance, as part of the very gift of life which you possess, you can know for a certainty that your life will be richer. Likely, you'll have, through awakening into your true nature, more material success and physical well being. You'll know greater emotional wholeness and the beauty of being able to give and receive true, lasting love. You will know the other aspects of happy thought—peace, contentment, ecstasy, and ever-new joy. You will know mental clarity and have the ability to use your mind as a dear friend rather than as most people have to live: their mind is their worst enemy, a most destructive, worrying, turbulent, self-destructive entity.

You'll know who you really are, instead of having to put up with a thrown-together, makeshift ego. You will discover your true self through your higher consciousness and be able to make a genuine contribution in the lives of your loved ones. You'll become enabled to express your nature for the benefit of humanity as well.

Of course, you will know the indescribable joy of living in attunement with your higher consciousness. Merely to be in a state of attunement with it is to know that you have been welcomed home. You are finally living in your true state. Your life gives up its boredom because so many wonderful talents within you interplay with one another and with the world. Your life becomes what is called a *lila*, a play or dance of awareness, an interplay between human being and creation, a conscious relationship and dance between your life and your world.

What are your personal possibilities in discovering the dimensions and richness of your higher consciousness? Only you—deep within your being—can say.

REFLECTION

For so many, life is a battle.
For so few, life is a dance.

57

YOU CAN CHOOSE YOUR FUTURE!

Your future is your choice! Hopefully, by now you are open to the idea that higher consciousness is available to *you*. It already exists within you. All you need do is make the effort to discover it and unleash it into your life. Without knowing your faculty of higher consciousness, you are missing out on at least nine-tenths of your potential for happiness and fulfillment. While this quest takes work and sincerity, no pursuit is more worthwhile or so rewarding in every way.

Not only do each of us deeply need to awaken and become aware of our own faculties of higher consciousness, but it seems our world will be in deep trouble until more and more people go beyond the limitations of their present awareness and stand in the glorious presence of their true nature. Our world is so full of misunderstanding, there are so many wants and unfulfilled needs. Because of ignorance of our inner abilities, there is much suffering almost everywhere on our planet.

In your quest for higher consciousness, don't be put off by old tendencies and conceptions. Be new, fresh, when you approach higher consciousness. Be willing to explore it. Be honest with yourself. Don't pretend results that aren't really there. Higher consciousness is not a fantasy realm. Higher consciousness has to be discovered as a *reality* and it must have **distinct** and **definite impacts on your life before you can say you have even begun to know it.** Of course your old tendencies and limited thoughts will try to stand in the way whenever you're dealing with something new, something relatively unknown. Don't worry. Push forward. You will succeed.

Of course, it's very helpful if you can find the companionship of some fellow seekers and enlightened people nearby. They will be good friends and very helpful to you. Hopefully one day you will find a special teacher who will be qualified to help you in the development of your life in higher consciousness.

START NOW!

But, above all, if you have determined to seek your higher consciousness, **start now!** *Then all you have to do is continue and you will make it.* A journey of a thousand miles, it is often said, begins with one step. Enthusiastically and joyfully take that step now. But if circumstances, people, or events seem to prevent you, know that higher consciousness is waiting within you and is your very own essential nature. One day you can seek to realize it—hopefully soon. Most likely, however, you took that big step toward higher consciousness when you began studying this book. Likely you have come a long way already in getting to know your superconscious nature.

Remember what the ancient lovers of truth said: *An unexamined life is not worth living.* Can you imagine living in poverty when there is great wealth in a nearby room? And the room happens to be a part of your own home? How absurd! Yet people, all of whom are filled with higher consciousness, too often live in complete ignorance of its nearness and its benefits.

"Know thyself!" wise men said. How can you walk the earth without seeking to know your true nature? How much longer can you live without opening the gift of life? How often people accept the gift of life as a fact, a reality, but never think of opening the gift and discovering what it is! You already have your greatest wealth. Open it! Let it out of the box of self-limitation.

Study. Be sincere. Make the effort. Be a scientist. Practice observation and experiment. Be definite and sure in your development of higher consciousness.

Your search will reveal many wonderful faiths and disciplines which can help lead you to higher consciousness and inspire you along the way. Find the path best suited to your individuality and be true to it. You will succeed. Stay on the road and you will arrive ⟨ your destination. At the same time, value and appreciate those who travel other roads toward higher consciousness. Whatever terms they use, whatever different concepts may be involved, *appreciate* the reality of the higher consciousness in each true seeker and his path.

At the same time, as you make your journey, avoid being a fool. There are marvelous nuances of differences in each path. Do not stupidly disregard the nuances as unimportant. Each subtlety is valuable and contributes something. The differences of paths and seekers must be appreciated and valued. More than one seeker has tried to practice two or more great, true paths at the same time. Such enthusiasts not only became greatly confused, they failed miserably in realizing success in *any* of their quests.

Remember, the quest for higher consciousness is not the same in the different paths. Some teachings focus on vigorous acts of charity and service as the way to enlightenment. Some other schools of thought recommend withdrawal from society for continual periods of contemplation. Some paths focus on austerities. Some develop the mental nature, while others emphasize the will, obedience, or cultivation of the heart's love. And different *attributes* of higher consciousness are yearned for, or cultivated, in the various excellent roads toward enlightenment. Some masters emphasize absolute, infinite awareness as the goal; other adepts focus on the personal *relationship* between the seeker and the Creator. Surely, enjoy the similarities and great harmony of constructive action expressed by seekers around the world. But, very importantly, also realize that many paths and goals are definitely not "all the same."

As you progress in your development of higher consciousness, a special day will come when, through your experience and realization, your state of higher consciousness will become continuous. Higher consciousness will not be a place that you *go to* for encouragement, wisdom, or inner power. Instead, you will be so intimate with the higher consciousness that you will *live in it*. You will be aware of it night and day.

Your doubt and disbelief that your higher consciousness exists, or that it is good, will be suspended. Higher consciousness will prove itself so thoroughly beneficial and helpful that you will enter a delightful state of being. You will feel that you were *as if dead* in those days prior to your life in higher consciousness. The numbness, the stupidity, the frustrations and agonies of unattuned life will fall away gradually as you discover your new life and serve to create a better world.

You will live in a natural, ongoing state of higher consciousness filled with ever-new joy and continually refreshing, helpful insights. You will sense, with great humility, that you consciously live in the presence of your Creator. You will no longer block or sabotage your own prospects for fulfillment.

Keep in mind that higher consciousness generally does not require a great outward change in your career or relationships—unless they are destructive. Basically, higher consciousness makes a huge change *in you*. It starts with you and your life as it is, here and now, radiating benefits into your entire life situation. You will discover life itself has been fulfilled within you—the primary goal of your life has been accomplished and the adventure of enlightenment begins.

THE GLIMPSE

Your higher consciousness is so great that one glimpse, one brief experience of it, will change your life forever. In contacting your higher consciousness you will know that you are richer than any king who ever lived. In one sure glimpse of higher consciousness you will be struck with the insight that most of the suffering and want in the world is not necessary, *it does not need to be*. Suffering and deprivation are but the consequences of ignorance of our true natures. We have the consciousness, ability, and energy to establish the world we deeply pine for, the place where well being and good will between people is the way of life. After one glimpse of your higher consciousness you'll wonder how long people will live like sleepy, lost vagabonds, struggling against others for brief moments of satisfaction. How absurd this confused life seems in the light of higher consciousness when true wealth, aptitude, and strength are so near at hand.

After one glimpse of your higher consciousness you become easily dedicated and ready to put forth any effort toward its fuller realization. In one glimpse the revelation of life's potential will motivate you to make every constructive effort toward the day that you will reside in your true nature. In time you will truly *awaken* in your higher consciousness. The glimpse, the vision, becomes constant.

May you have that glimpse which makes everything clear and your quest easy. May you discover your true self, and that you shall never be impoverished again.

What Do You Want From Life?
What Do You Really Want?

INDEX

INDEX

AN INVITATION

You are invited to mentally join with the members of the Spiritual World Society and pray for world peace every day at 12 Noon (your time).

Simply pray in your own way, or pray this prayer:

"Beloved Lord, bless all of us throughout mankind to love one another person to person, nation to nation, race to race, religion to religion, and sect to sect. Bless us to receive and abide in world peace, universal love and compassionate understanding. Amen."

And then enjoy five minutes of loving meditation and contemplation.

FOR QUANTITY PURCHASES

For information about our rates for quantity purchases of eight or more copies of *Keys to Higher Consciousness*: contact your local bookstore or write us at Everest Publishing Company.

OTHER PUBLICATIONS

Write us if you wish information about our:
- Classes, retreats and seminars
- New books as they become available
- Newsletter when it becomes available
- Tape Cassettes

Please write: Everest Publishing Company
                   445 East 17th Street (#I)
                   Costa Mesa, California 92627
                   U.S.A.